Hugh Johnson's Pocket Encyclopedia of Wine 1990

Hugh Johnson, author of

Vintage: The Story of Wine and host of

"Vintage: A History of Wine"

A Fireside Book
Published by Simon & Schuster Inc.
New York London
Toronto Sydney Tokyo

© 1977 Mitchell Beazley Publishers
Text © Hugh Johnson 1977, 1978, 1979, 1980, 1981, 1982, 1983, 1984, 1985, 1986, 1987, 1988, 1989
First edition published 1977
Revised editions published 1978, 1979, 1980, 1981, 1982, 1983, 1984, 1985, 1986, 1987, 1988, 1989
© 1989 Mitchell Beazley Publishers

Fireside
Simon & Schuster Building
Rockefeller Center
1230 Avenue of the Americas
New York, New York 10020

ISSN 0893-259X

FIRESIDE and colophon are registered trademarks of Simon & Schuster Inc.

ISBN 0-671-68701-8

Managing Editor   Chris Foulkes
Assistant Editors   Alison Melvin, Alessandra Perotto, Cathy Rigby, Doris Wood
Production   Stewart Bowling
Filmsetting by Litho Link Ltd, Welshpool, Powys, Wales
Produced by Mandarin Offset
Printed in Malaysia

How to read an entry

The top line of most entries consists of the following information.

1. Which part of the country in question the wine comes from. (References to the maps in this book.)

2. Whether it is red, rosé or white (or brown/amber), dry, sweet or sparkling, or several of these.

3. Its general standing as to quality: a necessarily rough and ready guide based principally on an ascending scale:

    * plain, everyday quality

  ** above average

*** well known, highly reputed

**** grand, prestigious, expensive

So much is more or less objective. Additionally there is a subjective rating: shading around the stars of any wine which in my experience is usually particularly good (which means good value) within its price range. There are good everyday wines as well as good luxury wines. The box system helps you find them.

4. Vintage information: which were the more successful of the recent vintages which *may* still be available. And of these which are ready to drink this year, and which will probably improve with keeping. Your first choice for current drinking should be one of the vintage years printed in **bold** type. Buy light-type years for further maturing.

The German vintage information works on a different principle: see the Introduction to Germany, page 105.

Acknowledgements

This store of detailed recommendations comes partly from my own notes and partly from those of a great number of kind friends. Without the generous help and co-operation of every single member of the wine trade I have approached, I could not attempt it. I particularly want to thank the following for help with research or in the areas of their special knowledge.

Rodrigo Alvarado	Tony Laithwaite
Gerry Amdor	John Lipitch
Burton Anderson	Miles Lambert-Gócs
Anthony Barton	Tim Marshall
Jean-Claude Berrouet	Patrick Matthews
Tim Bleach	Lindsay Messenger
Bernhard Breuer	Christian Moueix
Michael Broadbent M.W.	David Peppercorn M.W.
Pierre Coste	István Pusztai
Terry Dunleavy	Jan, Maite & Carlos Read
Len Evans	Belle Rhodes
Dereck Foster	Dr. Bernard Rhodes
Chris Foulkes	Bertrand de Rivoyre
Rosemary George M.W.	Dr. Bruno Roncarati
James Halliday	Peter M.F. Sichel
Phyllis Hands	Patrick Skinner
Peter Hasslacher	Serena Sutcliffe M.W.
Ian Jamieson M.W.	Bob Thompson
Nathaniel Johnston	Peter Vinding-Diers
Graham Knox	Manfred Völpel
Matt Kramer	David Wolfe

Grape varieties

The most basic of all differences between wines is the flavour (or lack of it) of the grapes they are made of. Centuries of selection have resulted in each of the long-established wine areas having its favourite single variety, or a group of varieties whose juice or wine is blended together. Red burgundy is made of one grape, the Pinot Noir; red Bordeaux of three or four: two kinds of Cabernet, Merlot, Malbec and sometimes others (the proportions at the discretion of the grower). The laws say which grapes must be used, so the labels do not mention them.

So in newer regions the choice of a grape is the grower's single most crucial decision. Where he is proud of it, and intends his wine to have the character of a particular grape, the variety is the first thing he puts on the label. Hence the originally Californian term "varietal wine" – meaning, in principle, *one* variety.

Familiarity with at least a few grape varieties, then, is the single most helpful piece of knowledge in finding wines you will like wherever they are grown. Learn to recognize the characters of the most important. At least seven – Cabernet, Pinot Noir, Riesling, Sauvignon Blanc, Chardonnay, Gewürztraminer and Muscat – have memorable tastes and smells distinct enough to form international categories of wine. To these you might add Merlot, Syrah, Sémillon . . .

Further notes on grapes will be found in the sections on Germany, Italy, central and south-east Europe, South Africa, etc. The following are the best and/or commonest wine grapes.

Grapes for white wine

Aligoté Burgundy's second-rank white grape. Crisp (often sharp) wine, needs drinking young. Perfect for mixing with cassis (blackcurrant liqueur) to make a "Kir".

Arneis Traditional Piemontese grape being revived for high-quality, rich-textured whites.

Blanc Fumé
Another name for SAUVIGNON BLANC, referring to the reputedly "smoky" smell of the wine, particularly on the upper Loire (Sancerre and Pouilly). Makes some of California's best whites.

Bual Makes top-quality sweet Madeira wines.

Chardonnay *The* white burgundy grape, one of the grapes of Champagne, and considered the best white grape of California and more recently Australia. Gives dry wine of rich complexity, especially when aged some months in new barrels. Italy, Spain, New Zealand, Bulgaria, Oregon, Washington, New York all also now make good Chardonnays. One wishes they would try something else for a change.

Chasselas A prolific and widely grown early-ripening grape with little flavour, also grown for eating. Best known as Fendant in Switzerland (where it is supreme), Gutedel in Germany. Perhaps the same as Hungary's Leanyka and Romania's Feteasca.

Chenin Blanc
The leading white grape of the middle Loire (Vouvray, Layon, etc.). Wine can be dry or sweet (or very sweet), but always retains plenty of acidity – hence its popularity in California, where it can make fine wine, but is rarely so used. See also Steen.

Clairette A dull neutral grape formerly widely used in the s. of France.

Fendant See Chasselas.

Folle Blanche
High acid and little flavour makes it ideal for brandy. Known as Gros Plant in Brittany, Picpoul in Armagnac. Perhaps at its best in California.

Furmint A grape of great character: the trade mark of Hungary both as the principal grape in Tokay and as vivid vigorous table wine with an appley flavour. Called Sipon in Yugoslavia.

Grecheto or Greco
Ancient grape of central and s. Italy with vitality and style.

Gewürztraminer (or Traminer)
The most pungent wine grape, distinctively spicy to smell and taste, with flavours often identified as being like rose petals or grapefruit. Wines are often rich and soft, even when fully dry. Best in Alsace; also good in Germany, e. Europe, Australia, California, New Zealand.

Grüner Veltliner
An Austrian speciality. Round Vienna and in the Wachau and Weinviertel can be delicious: light but dry and lively. Drink young.

Italian Riesling
Grown in n. Italy and all over central eastern Europe. Much inferior to Rhine Riesling with lower acidity. Alias Wälschriesling, Olaszrizling (but no longer legally labelled "Riesling").

Kerner The most successful of a wide range of recent German varieties, largely made by crossing Riesling and Sylvaner (but in this case Riesling and [red] Trollinger). Early-ripening, flowery wine with good acidity. Popular in Rheinpfalz, Rheinhessen, etc.

Malvasia Known as Malmsey in Madeira, Malvasia in Italy, Malvoisie in France. Alias Vermentino. Also grown in Greece, Spain, W. Australia, eastern Europe. Makes rich brown wines or soft whites with superb potential, ageing magnificently, not often realized.

Müller-Thurgau
Dominant variety in Germany's Rheinhessen and Rheinpfalz; a cross between Riesling and Sylvaner. Ripens early to make soft flowery wines to drink young. Makes good sweet wines but dull dry ones.

Muscadet (alias Melon de Bourgogne)
Makes light, very dry wines round Nantes in Brittany. They should not be sharp, but faintly salty, savoury and v. refreshing.

Muscat (Many varieties; the best is Muscat blanc à petits grains.)
Universally grown easily recognized pungent grapes, mostly made into perfumed sweet wines, often fortified (as in France's VIN DOUX NATURELS). Muscat d'Alsace is unusual in being dry.

Palomino Alias Listan. Makes all the best sherry but v. wishy-washy table wine.

Pedro Ximénez
Said to have come to s. Spain from Germany. Makes very strong wine in Montilla and Malaga. Used in blending sherry. Also grown in Australia, California, South Africa.

Pinot Blanc
A close relation of CHARDONNAY without its strength of character. Grown in Champagne, Alsace (increasingly), n. Italy (good sparkling wine), s. Germany, eastern Europe. Called Weissburgunder in Germany. California's "Pinot Blanc" is apparently actually Muscadet.

Pinot Gris
Makes rather heavy, even "thick", full-bodied whites with a certain spicy style. Known as Tokay in Alsace, Tocai in n.e. Italy and Yugoslavia, Ruländer in Germany. Almost extinct (but traditional) in Burgundy.

Pinot Noir
Superlative black grape (see under Grapes for red wine) used in Champagne and occasionally elsewhere (e.g. California) for making white wine, or a very pale pink "vin gris".

Riesling Germany's finest grape, and the world's most underrated. Wine of brilliant sweet/acid balance, flowery in youth but maturing to subtle oily scents and flavours. Successful in Alsace (for dry wine), Austria, parts of eastern Europe, Australia (where it is widely grown), California, South Africa. Often called White, Johannisberg or Rhine Riesling. Subject to "noble rot". Due for a major revival, since it does not need high alcohol for character.

Sauvignon Blanc
Very distinctive aromatic, herby and sometimes smoky scented wine, can be austere (on the upper Loire) or buxom (in Sauternes, where it is combined with SEMILLON, and parts of California). Also called Fumé Blanc or vice versa. Recently brilliant in New Zealand.

Scheurebe Spicy-flavoured German Riesling x Silvaner cross, very successful in Rheinpfalz, esp. for Ausleses.

Sémillon The grape contributing the lusciousness to great Sauternes; subject to "noble rot" in the right conditions but increasingly important for Graves and dry white Bordeaux too. Makes soft dry wine of great potential. Traditionally called "Riesling" in parts of Australia. Old Hunter Valley Sémillon can be great wine.

Sercial Makes the driest Madeira; where they claim it is really Riesling.

Seyval Blanc
French-made hybrid between French and American vines. Very hardy and attractively fruity. Popular and successful in the eastern States and England.

Steen South Africa's most popular white grape: good, lively, fruity wine. Said to be the Chenin Blanc of the Loire.

Sylvaner (Silvaner)
Germany's workhorse grape: wine rarely better than pleasant except in Franconia where it is savoury, and ages admirably in the Rheinhessen, where it is enjoying a renascence. Good in the Italian Tyrol and useful in Alsace. V.g. as "Johannisberg" in Switzerland.

Tokay See Pinot Gris. Also a table grape in California and a supposedly Hungarian grape in Australia. The wine Tokay is made of FURMINT.

Traminer See Gewürztraminer.

Trebbiano Important grape of central Italy, used in Orvieto, Chianti, Soave, etc. Also grown in s. France as Ugni Blanc, and Cognac as "St-Emilion". Thin, neutral wine, really needs blending.

Ugni Blanc See Trebbiano.

Verdejo The grape of Rueda in Castile, potentially fine and long-lived.

Verdelho Madeira grape making excellent medium-sweet wine.

Verdicchio Gives its name to good dry wine in central Italy.

Vermentino See Malvasia.

Vernaccia Grape grown in central and s. Italy and Sardinia for strong, smooth, lively wine inclining towards sherry.

Viognier Rare but remarkable grape of the Rhône valley, grown at Condrieu to make very fine fragrant wine. A little in California.

Welschriesling (or Wälschriesling) See Italian Riesling.

Weissburgunder See Pinot Blanc.

Grapes for red wine

Barbera One of several productive grapes of n. Italy, esp. Piemonte, giving dark, fruity, often sharp wine. Useful in blends in California.

Brunello S. Tuscan form of SANGIOVESE, splendid at Montalcino.

Cabernet Franc
The lesser of two sorts of Cabernet grown in Bordeaux; the Cabernet of the Loire making Chinon, etc., and rosé.

Cabernet Sauvignon
Grape of great character; spicy, herby and tannic. The first grape of the Médoc, also makes the best Californian, Australian, South

Contents

Introduction

The world of wine has had some (metaphorically) showery weather recently. It has been pestered by hypochondriacs disguised as health-lobbyists. Their natural home is the USA, but their joyless viewpoint, once unexportable, is showing signs of catching on elsewhere. Unfortunately pleasure in life, interest, friendship and joy – all attributes of intelligent wine drinking – are not susceptible to measurement. Sheer length of years seems to be the goal of too many people today. God give me a timely and a merry end!

That is the first sermon in 13 editions of this little annual, and I hope it will be the last. There are better uses for our confined space. 1988/9 has been eventful all round the wine world, and such of its events as touch the wine-lover are recorded here as faithfully as I and my growing crowd of helpers can manage. Much of the work on this edition, which has no extra pages but about 200 new entries, every old one x-rayed for structural faults (or superfluous syllables), concerns the ever-growing "new" world of wine. But revolutions are brewing in the old world, too (especially Germany and Italy) and these have needed considerable investigation. As for France, keeping abreast of its riches is an endlessly rewarding task. I believe there are six or seven truly enthusiastic entries in this edition for every one in the first, way back in 1977.

To new readers I should explain that this book is a continuing attempt to squeeze in as much up-to-date information about the wines of the world as possible. The information is gleaned from many sources through innumerable visits and tastings and via a perpetual spate of correspondence. The process of revision never stops, whether it involves a change of emphasis or fact or vintage or a new entry. There is a constant pressure by new producers for inclusion; newness itself, however, is not a qualification for entry ... old producers also do newsworthy things.

The arrangement of the book is intended to be as helpful as possible when you are buying a bottle, whether you are on the nursery slopes or an old hand with a bad memory. You are faced with a list of wines or an array of bottles in a restaurant, wine merchant's or bottle store. Your mind goes blank. You fumble for your little book. All you need to establish is what country a wine comes from. Look up the principal words on the label in the appropriate country's section. You will find enough potted information to let you judge whether this is the wine you want.

Specifically, you will find information on the colour and type of wine, its status or prestige, whether it is usually particularly good value, which vintages are good and which are ready to drink – and often considerably more ... about the quantity made, the grapes used, ownership and the rest. Hundreds of cross-references help you delve further.

American and eastern European reds. Its red wine always needs ageing and usually blending. Makes v. aromatic rosé.

Carignan By far the commonest grape of France, covering hundreds of thousands of acres. Prolific with dull but harmless wine. Also common in North Africa, Spain and California.

Cinsaut Common bulk-producing grape of s. France; in S. Africa crossed with PINOT NOIR to make Pinotage.

Dolcetto Source of soft, seductive dry red in Piemonte.

Gamay The Beaujolais grape: light very fragrant wines at their best young. Makes even lighter wine on the Loire and in Switzerland and Savoie. Known as Napa Gamay in California.

Gamay Beaujolais
Not Gamay but a variety of PINOT NOIR grown in California.

Grenache (alias Garnacha)
Useful grape for strong and fruity but pale wine: good rosé. Grown in s. France, Spain, California. Usually blended.

Grignolino Makes one of the good cheap table wines of Piemonte.

Malbec (also called Cot)
Minor in Bordeaux, major in Cahors and Argentina.

Merlot Adaptable grape making the great fragrant and rich wines of Pomerol and St-Emilion, an important element in Médoc reds, soft and strong in California, lighter but good in n. Italy, Italian Switzerland, Yugoslavia, Argentina, etc.

Mourvèdre (alias Mataro)
Excellent, dark, aromatic, tannic grape used for blending in Provence (esp. in Bandol).

Nebbiolo (also called Spanna and Chiavennasca)
Italy's best red grape, the grape of Barolo, Barbaresco, Gattinara and Valtellina. Intense, nobly fruity and perfumed wine but very tannic, taking years to mature.

Pinot Noir
The glory of Burgundy's Côte d'Or, with scent, flavour, texture and body unmatched anywhere. Less happy elsewhere; makes light wines of no great distinction in Germany, Switzerland, Austria, Hungary. The great challenge to the winemakers of California and Australia. Shows great promise in Oregon.

Sangiovese The main red grape of Chianti and much of central Italy. See also Brunello.

Spätburgunder
German for PINOT NOIR, but a v. pale shadow of burgundy.

Syrah (alias Shiraz)
The best Rhône red grape, with tannic purple wine, which can mature superbly. Very important as "Shiraz" in Australia.

Tempranillo
The characteristic fine Rioja grape, called Ull de Lebre in Catalonia, Cencibel in La Mancha. Early ripening.

Zinfandel Fruity adaptable grape peculiar to California. Also makes "blush" white wine.

Wine & Food

There are no statutes or laws about what wine goes with what food, but there is a vast body of accumulated experience which it is absurd to ignore, even while trying out new ideas.

This list of dishes and appropriate wines records many of the conventional combinations and suggests others that I personally have found good. But it is only a list of ideas intended to help you make quick decisions. Any of the groups of recommended wines could have been extended almost indefinitely, drawing on the whole world's wine list. In general I have stuck to the wines that are widely available, at the same time trying to ring the changes so that the same wines don't come up time and time again – as they tend to do in real life.

The stars refer to the rating system used throughout the book.

Before the meal – apéritifs

The traditional apéritif wines are either sparkling (epitomized by champagne) or fortified (epitomized by sherry). They are still the best, but *avoid peanuts* with them, they destroy wine flavours. Eat almonds or walnuts instead. The current fashion for a glass of white wine before eating calls for something light and stimulating, dry but not acid, with a degree of character, such as:

France:

   Alsace Pinot Blanc, Riesling or Sylvaner; Chablis; Muscadet; Sauvignon de Touraine; Graves Blanc; Mâcon Blanc; Crépy; Bugey, Haut-Poitou, Côtes de Gascogne.

Germany:

   Any Kabinett wine or QbA. Choose a "halbtrocken" – nearly dry.

Italy:

   Soave; Orvieto Secco; Frascati; Gavi; Pinot Bianco; Montecarlo; Vernaccia; Tocai; Lugano; Albana di Romagna.

Spain:

   Rioja Blanco Marqués de Caceres or Faustino V, or Albariño. But fino sherry, Manzanilla or Montilla is even better.

Portugal:

   Any vinho verde; Bucelas.

Eastern Europe:

   Leanyka, Welschriesling, Riesling, Chardonnay, Tokay Szamarodni.

USA:

   California "Chablis"; Chenin Blanc; Riesling; French Colombard; Fumé Blanc; Gewürztraminer, or a good "house blend"; Riesling from New York or Oregon, Sémillon from Washington.

Australia:

   Barossa or Coonawarra Riesling. Houghton's "White Burgundy".

South Africa:

   Steen is ideal. (The K.W.V. labels it Chenin Blanc).

England:

   Almost any English wine is ideal before a meal.

References to these wines will be found in national A-Z sections.

First courses

Aïoli A thirst-quencher is needed with so much garlic. ★→★★ white Rhône, or Frascati, or Verdicchio, and lots of mineral water.

Antipasto (See also Hors d'oeuvre)
 ★★ dry or medium white, preferably Italian (e.g. Soave) or light red, e.g. Valpolicella, Bardolino or young ★ Bordeaux. Or fino sherry.

Artichoke
 ★ red or rosé.
 vinaigrette ★ young red, e.g. Bordeaux, Côtes-du-Rhône.
 hollandaise ★ or ★★ full-bodied dry or medium white, e.g. Mâcon Blanc, Rheinpfalz, or a California "house blend".

Asparagus
 A difficult flavour for wine, so the wine needs plenty of its own. ★★→★★★ white burgundy or Chardonnay, or Corsican rosé.

Assiette anglaise (assorted cold meats)
 ★★ dry white, e.g. Chablis, Muscadet, Silvaner, Riesling; esp. Trocken wines from the Mosel-Saar-Ruwer.

Avocado
 with prawns, crab, etc. ★★→★★★ dry to medium white, e.g. Rheingau or Rheinpfalz Kabinett, Graves, California or Australian Chardonnay or Sauvignon, Cape Steen, or dry rosé.
 vinaigrette ★ light red, or manzanilla sherry.

Bisques ★★ dry white with plenty of body: Pinot Gris, Chardonnay. Fino or amontillado sherry, or Montilla.

Bouillabaisse
 ★→★★ very dry white: Muscadet, Alsace Silvaner, Entre-Deux-Mers, Pouilly-Fumé, Cassis, Tuscan Trebbiano, Grechetto.

Carpaccio
 Seems to work well with the flavour of most wines, including ★★★ reds. Top Tuscan vino da tavola is appropriate.

Caviar ★★★ champagne or iced vodka (or both).

Cheese fondue
 ★★ dry white: Fendant or Johannisberg du Valais, Grüner Veltliner, Alsace Riesling, NZ Sauvignon Blanc.

Chicken liver pâté
 Appetizing dry white, e.g. ★★ white Bordeaux, Pouilly-Fumé or Rheingau Spätlese Trocken, or light fruity red; Beaujolais, Gamay de Touraine, young Chianti or Valpolicella.

Clams and Chowders
 ★★ big-scale white, not necessarily bone dry: e.g. Rhône, Pinot Gris, Dry Sauternes, Napa Chardonnay. Or fino sherry.

Consommé ★★→★★★ medium-dry sherry, dry Madeira, Marsala, Montilla.

Crudités ★→★★ light red or rosé, e.g. Côtes-du-Rhône, Beaujolais, Minervois, Chianti, Zinfandel, fino sherry.

Eggs (See also Soufflés)
 These present difficulties: they clash with most wines and spoil good ones. So ★→★★ of whatever is going. I can bear champagne with scrambled eggs at any time.

Empanadas
 ★→★★ Chilean or Argentine Cabernet, Zinfandel.

Escargots
 ★★ red or white of some substance: e.g. Burgundy, Côtes-du-Rhône, Chardonnay, Shiraz, etc.

Fish terrine
 Rheingau Riesling, Trocken, Chablis, Washington Riesling, Rioja Blanco.

Foie gras
 ★★★→★★★★ white. In Bordeaux they drink Sauternes. Others prefer vintage champagne or a late-harvest Gewürztraminer.

Gazpacho Sangria (See Spain) is refreshing, but to avoid too much liquid intake dry Manzanilla or Montilla is better.

Grapefruit

If you must start a meal with grapefruit try Port, Madeira or sweet sherry with (or in) it.

Gravlax Akvavit, or Grand Cru Chablis, or ✳✳✳ Californian or Australian Chardonnay. Or vintage champagne.

Haddock, smoked mousse of

A wonderful dish for showing off any stylish full-bodied white.

Ham, raw

See Prosciutto.

Herrings, raw or pickled

Dutch gin (young, not aged) or Scandinavian akvavit, and cold beer.

Hors d'oeuvres (See also Antipasto)

✳→✳✳ clean fruity sharp white: Sancerre or any Sauvignon, Alsace Silvaner, Muscadet, Cape Steen – or young light red Bordeaux, Rhône or equivalent. Or fino sherry.

Mackerel, smoked

✳✳→✳✳✳ full-bodied tasty white: e.g. Gewürztraminer, Tokay d'Alsace or Chablis Premier Cru. Or Manzanilla sherry.

Mayonnaise

Adds richness that calls for a contrasting bite in the wine. Côte Chalonnaise whites (e.g. Rully) are good. Try NZ Sauvignon Blanc.

Melon Needs a strong sweet wine (if any) ✳✳ Port, Bual Madeira, Muscat, Oloroso sherry or Vin doux naturel.

Minestrone

✳ red: Grignolino, Chianti, Zinfandel, Shiraz, etc.

Mushrooms à la Grecque

Robola from Cephalonia or any hefty dry white, or fresh young red.

Omelettes See under Eggs.

Onion/leek tart

✳→✳✳✳ fruity, concentrated dry white, e.g. Alsace Pinot Gris or Riesling. Mâcon-Villages of a good vintage, Jurançon, California or Australian Riesling.

Pasta ✳→✳✳ red or white according to the sauce or trimmings, e.g.

with seafood sauce (vongole, etc.) Verdicchio, Soave, Pomino, Sauvignon.

meat sauce Chianti, Montepulciano d'Abruzzo, Montefalco d'Arquata.

tomato sauce Barbera or Sicilian or Yugoslav red or Zinfandel.

cream sauce Orvieto, Frascati or Italian Chardonnay.

Pâté According to constituents and quality e.g. chicken livers call for a pungent white, a smooth red like a light Pomerol, or even amontillado sherry for simple pâté – ✳✳ dry white: e.g. Mâcon-Villages, Graves, Fumé Blanc.

Peppers or aubergines (eggplant), stuffed

✳✳ vigorous red: e.g. Chianti, Dolcetto, Zinfandel.

Pizza Any ✳✳ dry Italian red or a ✳✳ Rioja, Australian Shiraz or California Zinfandel. Or Corbières or Roussillon.

Prawns or shrimps

✳✳→✳✳✳ dry white: burgundy or Bordeaux, Chardonnay or Riesling. ("Cocktail sauce" kills any wine, or indeed, in time, human beings.)

Prosciutto with melon

✳✳→✳✳✳ full-bodied dry or medium white: e.g. Orvieto or Frascati, Pomino, Fendant, Grüner Veltliner, Alsace or California Gewürztraminer, Australian Riesling.

Quenelles de brochet

✳✳✳ White Hermitage or white Châteauneuf-du-Pape, Grand Cru Chablis, Alsace Pinot Gris, Hunter Valley Sémillon.

Quiches ★—→★★ dry white with body (Alsace, Graves, Sauvignon, Rheingau dry) or young red (e.g. Beaujolais-Villages), according to the ingredients. Never a fine wine dish.

Ratatouille
★★ vigorous young red, e.g. Chianti, Zinfandel, Bulgarian or young red Bordeaux.

Salade niçoise
★★ very dry not too light or flowery white, e.g. white (or rosé) Rhône or Corsican, Catalan white, Dão, California Sauvignon.

Salads As a first course, especially with blue cheese dressing, any dry and appetizing white wine. After a main course: no wine.
N.B. Vinegar in salad dressings destroys the flavour of wine. If you want salad at a meal with fine wine, dress the salad with wine or a little lemon juice instead of vinegar.

Salami ★—→★★ powerfully tasty red or rosé: e.g. Barbera, young Zinfandel, Tavel or Ajaccio rosé, young Bordeaux.

Salmon, smoked
A dry but pungent white, e.g. fino sherry, Alsace Gewürztraminer. Chablis Grand Cru, Rheinpfalz Riesling Spätlese, vintage champagne.

Soufflés As show dishes these deserve ★★—→★★★ wines.
Fish Dry white, e.g. burgundy, Bordeaux, Alsace, Chard, etc.
Cheese Red burgundy or Bordeaux, Cabernet Sauvignon, etc.

Taramasalata
Calls for a rustic southern white of strong personality; not necessarily the Greek Retsina. Fino sherry works well.

Terrine As for pâté, or the equivalent red; e.g. Beaune, Mercurey, Beaujolais-Villages, fairly young ★★ St-Emilion, California Cabernet or Zinfandel, Bulgarian or Chilean Cabernet, etc.

Tomato sauce (on anything)
The acidity of tomato sauce is no friend to fine wines. ★★ red will do. Try Chianti or a German wine with good acidity.

Trout, smoked
Sancerre, Pouilly-Fumé, or California or NZ Fumé Blanc. Or Rully.

Vegetable terrine
Not a great help to fine wine, but Californian and Australian Chardonnays make a fashionable marriage.

Fish

Abalone ★★—→★★★ dry or medium white: e.g. Sauvignon Blanc, Chardonnay, Pinot Grigio, Muscadet sur Lie.

Bass, striped
Same wine as for sole.

Cod A good neutral background for fine dry or medium whites, e.g. ★★—→★★★ Chablis, Meursault, cru classé Graves, German Kabinett or dry Spätleses and their equivalents.

Coquilles St Jacques
An inherently slightly sweet dish, best with medium-dry whites.
in cream sauces ★★★ German Spätlese or a –Montrachet.
grilled or fried Hermitage Blanc, Gewürztraminer, California Chenin Blanc, Riesling or champagne.

Crab, cold, with salad
★★★ California or Rheinpfalz Riesling Kabinett or Spätlese, or Condrieu.

Crab, softshell
★★★ Chardonnay or top-quality German Riesling.

Eel, jellied
NV champagne or a nice cup of tea.
smoked Either strong or sharp wine, e.g. fino sherry or Bourgogne Aligoté. Or schnapps.

Fish and chips, fritto misto (or tempura)

    ★ white Bordeaux, Orvieto Secco, Koshu, tea . . .

Haddock ★★→★★★ dry white with a certain richness: e.g. Meursault, California or Australian Chardonnay.

Herrings Need a white with some acidity to cut their richness. Burgundy Aligoté or Gros Plant from Brittany or dry Sauvignon Blanc.

Kippers A good cup of tea, preferably Ceylon (milk, no sugar).

Lamproie à la Bordelaise

    ★★ young red Bordeaux, St-Emilion, Pomerol or Fronsac.

Lobster or Crab

    salad ★★→★★★★ white. Non-vintage champagne, Alsace Riesling, Chablis Premier Cru, Condrieu, Mosel Spätlese.

    richly sauced Vintage champagne, fine white burgundy, cru classé Graves, California or Australian Chardonnay, Rheinpfalz Spätlese, Hermitage Blanc.

Mackerel ★★ hard or sharp white: Sauvignon Blanc from Bergerac or Touraine, Gros Plant, vinho verde, white Rioja. Or Guinness.

Mullet, red

    ★★ Mediterranean white, even Retsina, for the atmosphere. Reds go well, too.

Mussels ★→★★ Gros Plant, Muscadet, California "Chablis".

Oysters ★★→★★★ white. Champagne (non-vintage), Chablis or (better) Chablis Premier Cru, or Muscadet or white Graves.

Salmon, fresh

    ★★★ fine white burgundy: Puligny- or Chassagne-Montrachet, Meursault, Corton-Charlemagne, Chablis Grand Cru, California, Idaho or Australian Chardonnay, or Rheingau Kabinett or Spätlese, California Riesling or equivalent. Some (not me) like Beaujolais or a young ★★ red Bordeaux.

Sardines, fresh grilled

    ★→★★ very dry white: e.g. vinho verde, Dão, Muscadet.

Scallops See Coquilles St Jacques.

Shad ★★→★★★ white Graves or Meursault or Hunter Semillon.

Shellfish (general)

    Dry white with plain boiled shellfish, richer wines with richer sauces.

Shrimps, potted

    Fino sherry, Chablis, Gavi or New York Chardonnay.

Skate with black butter

    ★★ white with some pungency (e.g. Alsace Pinot Gris) or a clean straightforward one like Muscadet or Entre-Deux-Mers.

Sole, plaice, etc.

    plain, grilled or fried An ideal accompaniment for fine wines: ★ up to ★★★★ white burgundy, or its equivalent.

    with sauce Depending on the ingredients: sharp dry wine for tomato sauce, fairly rich for sole véronique, etc.

Sushi (and sashimi)

    Sparkling wines, incl. Californian, or California or Australian Chardonnay or Sauvignon. Chablis Grand Cru. Rheingau Riesling Halbtrocken.

Swordfish

    ★★ dry white of whatever country you are in.

Tuna, grilled

    ★★ white or red (or rosé) of fairly fruity character. NZ Sauvignon Blanc or a top Côtes-du-Rhône would be fine.

Trout Delicate white wine, e.g. ★★★ Mosel.

    smoked A full-flavoured ★★→★★★ white: Gewürztraminer, Pinot Gris, Rhine Spätlese or Australian Hunter white.

Turbot Fine rich dry white, e.g. ★★★ Meursault or its California, Australian or New Zealand equivalent. Viognier from Condrieu. Mature Rheingau, Mosel or Nahe Spätlese or Auslese.

Meat, poultry, etc.

Barbecues

** red with a slight rasp, therefore young, Shiraz, Chianti, Zinfandel, Turkish Buzbag.

Beef, boiled

** red: e.g. Bordeaux (Bourg or Fronsac), Côtes-du-Rhône-Villages, Australian Shiraz. Or good Mâcon-Villages white.

Beef, roast

An ideal partner for fine red wine. **→**** red of any kind.

Beef stew

→* sturdy red, e.g. Pomerol or St-Emilion, Hermitage, Shiraz, California or Oregon Pinot Noir, Torres Sangre de Toro.

Beef Stroganoff

→* suitably dramatic red: e.g. Barolo, Brunello, Valpolicella, Amarone, Hermitage, late-harvest Zinfandel − or even Georgian.

Cassoulet

** red from s.w. France, e.g. Madiran, Cahors or Corbières, or Barbera or Zinfandel or Shiraz.

Chicken or turkey, roast (or guinea fowl)

Virtually any wine, including your very best bottles of dry or medium white and finest old reds. The meat of fowl can be adapted with sauces to match almost any fine wine (e.g. coq au vin with red burgundy). Avoid tomato sauces for any good bottles.

Chili con carne

*→** young red: e.g. Bull's Blood, Chianti, Mountain Red.

Chinese food

Canton or Peking style **→**** dry to medium-dry white: e.g. Yugoslav "Riesling", Mâcon-Villages, Premier Cru Chablis, California Chardonnay. Or NV champagne.

Szechuan style Very cold beer.

Choucroute

Alsace Pinot Gris or Sylvaner.

Cold meats

Generally taste better with full-flavoured white wine than red. Mosel Spätleses, Hochheimer are v.g.

Confit d'oie

→* rather young and tannic red Bordeaux helps to cut the richness. Alsace Tokay or Gewürztraminer matches it.

Coq au vin

→** red burgundy. In an ideal world one bottle of Chambertin in the dish, two on the table.

Corned beef hash

** Zinfandel, Chianti, Côtes-du-Rhône red.

Curry *→** medium-sweet white, very cold: e.g. Orvieto abboccato, California Chenin Blanc, Yugoslav Traminer, Indian "Champagne".

Duck or goose

*** rather rich white, e.g. Rheinpfalz Spätlese or Alsace Réserve Exceptionelle, or *** Bordeaux or burgundy.

With oranges or peaches, the Sauternais propose Sauternes.

Wild duck *** big-scale red: e.g. Hermitage, Châteauneuf-du-Pape, Bandol, California. or S. African Cabernet, Australian Shiraz, Torres Gran Coronas.

Frankfurters

*→** German or Australian white, or Beaujolais. Or beer.

Game birds

Young birds plain roasted and not too well hung deserve the best red wine you can afford. With older birds in casseroles **→*** red, e.g. Gevrey-Chambertin, Pommard, Grand Cru St-Emilion, Napa Cab. With very high game, Hermitage, Châteauneuf-du-Pape, Vega Sicilia.

Game pie
(Hot) ★★★ red wine. (Cold) Equivalent white.

Goulash ★★ strong young red: e.g. Zinfandel, Bulgarian Cabernet, Kadarka.

Grouse See Game birds – but push the boat out.

Ham ★★→★★★ fairly young red burgundy, e.g. Volnay, Savigny, Beaune, Corton, or a slightly sweet German white, e.g. a Rhine Spätlese, or a Tuscan red, or a lightish Cabernet (e.g. Chilean).

Hamburger
★→★★ young red: e.g. Beaujolais, Corbières or Minervois, Chianti, Zinfandel, Kadarka from Hungary.

Hare Jugged hare calls for ★★→★★★ red with plenty of flavour: not-too-old burgundy or Bordeaux, or Rhône; Cornas e.g. The same for saddle. Grange Hermitage would be an experience.

Kebabs ★★ vigorous red: e.g. Greek Demestica, Turkish Buzbag, Bulgarian or Chilean Cabernet, Zinfandel.

Kidneys ★★→★★★ red: Pomerol or St-Emilion, Rhône, Barbaresco, Rioja, California, Spanish or Australian Cabernet, Bairrada from Portugal.

Lamb cutlets or chops
As for roast lamb, but less grand.

Lamb, roast
One of the traditional and best partners for very good red Bordeaux – or its Cabernet equivalents from the New World.

Liver ★★→★★★ young red: Beaujolais-Villages, St-Joseph, Médoc, Italian Merlot, Zinfandel, Oregon Pinot Noir.

Meatballs
★★→★★★ red: e.g. Mercurey, Crozes-Hermitage, Madiran, Rubesco, Dão Bairrada, Zinfandel or Cabernet.

Mixed grill
A fairly light easily swallowable red; ★★ red Bordeaux from Bourg, Fronsac or Premières Côtes; Chianti; Bourgogne Passe-tout-grains, Chilean Cabernet.

Moussaka ★→★★ red or rosé: e.g. Naoussa, Chianti, Corbières, Côtes de Provence, Ajaccio or Patrimonio, California Burgundy.

Oxtail ★★→★★★ rather rich red: e.g. St-Emilion or Pomerol, Burgundy, Barolo or Chianti Classico, Rioja Reserva, California or Coonawarra Cabernet or a dry Riesling Spätlese.

Paella ★★ Young Spanish r., dry w. or rosé, e.g. Penedès or Rioja.

Partridge, pheasant See under Game birds.

Pigeons or squabs
★★→★★★★ red Bordeaux, Chianti Classico, California or Australian Cabernet. Silvaner Spätlese from Franconia.

Pork, roast
Pork is a good, rich, neutral background to very good white or red.

Rabbit ★→★★★ young red: Italian for preference.

Ris de veau See Sweetbreads.

Risotto Pinot Grigio from Friuli, Gavi, youngish Sémillon.

Sauerkraut
Lager.

Sausages The British banger requires a 3-year-old n. Italian Merlot. (A red wine, anyway.) See also salami.

Shepherd's Pie
★→★★ rough and ready red seems most appropriate, but no harm would come to a good one.

Steak and kidney pie or pudding
Red Rioja Reserva or mature ★★→★★★ Bordeaux.

Steaks
Alligator Watch this space.
Au poivre A fairly young ★★★ Rhône red or Cabernet.

Tartare ★★ light young red: Beaujolais, Bergerac, Valpolicella.

Filet or Tournedos ★★★ red of any kind (but not old wines with Béarnaise sauce).

T-bone ★★→★★★ reds of similar bone-structure: e.g. Barolo, Hermitage, Australian Cabernet or Shiraz.

Fiorentina (bistecca) Chianti Classico Riserva or Brunello.

Ostrich South African Pinotage.

Stews and casseroles

A lusty full-flavoured red, e.g. young Côtes-du-Rhône, Corbières, Barbera, Shiraz, Zinfandel, etc.

Sweetbreads

These tend to be a grand dish, suggesting a grand wine, e.g. ★★★ Rhine Riesling or Franken Silvaner Spätlese, or well-matured Bordeaux or burgundy, depending on the sauce.

Tongue Ideal for favourite bottles of any red or white of abundant character, esp. Italian.

Tripe ★→★★ red: Corbières, Mâcon Rouge, etc., or rather sweet white, e.g. Liebfraumilch. Better: W. Australian "white burgundy".

Veal, roast

A good neutral background dish for any fine old red which may have faded with age (e.g. a Rioja Reserva) or a ★★★ German white.

Venison ★★★ big-scale red (Rhône, Bordeaux of a grand vintage) or rather rich white (Rheinpfalz Spätlese or Tokay d'Alsace).

Vitello tonnato

Light red (Valpolicella, Beaujolais) served cool.

Wiener Schnitzel

★★→★★★ light red from the Italian Tyrol (Alto Adige) or the Médoc: or Austrian Riesling, Grüner Veltliner or Gumpolds-kirchener.

Cheese

Very strong cheese completely masks the flavour of wine. Only serve fine wine with mild cheeses in peak condition.

Bleu de Bresse, Dolcelatte, Gorgonzola, Stilton

Need emphatic accompaniment: young ★★ red wine (Barbera, Dolcetto, Moulin-â-Vent, etc.) or sweet white – or port.

Cream cheeses: Brie, Camembert, Bel Paese, Edam, etc.

In their mild state marry with any good wine, red or white.

English cheeses

Can be either mild or strong and acidic. The latter need sweet or strong wine.

Cheddar, Cheshire, Wensleydale, Gloucester, etc. If mild, claret. If strong, ruby, tawny or vintage-character (not vintage) port, old dry oloroso sherry, or a very big red: Hermitage, Châteauneuf-du-Pape, Barolo, Barbaresco etc.

Goat cheeses

★★→★★★ white wine of marked character, either dry (e.g. Sancerre) or sweet (e.g. Monbazillac, Sauternes).

Hard Cheese, Parmesan, Gruyère, Emmenthal, old Gouda, Jarlsberg

Full-bodied dry whites, e.g. Tokay d'Alsace or Vernaccia, or fino or amontillado sherry. But it's worth experimenting with anything good: old Gouda and Jarlsberg have a sweetness that encourages fine old reds.

Roquefort, Danish Blue

Are so strong-flavoured that only the youngest, biggest or sweetest wines stand a chance. Old dry amontillado or oloroso sherries have the necessary horse-power.

Desserts

Apple pie, apple strudel

  ★★→★★★ sweet German, Austrian or Hungarian white.

Apples, Cox's Orange Pippins

  Vintage port (55, 60, 63, 66, 70, 75).

Bread and butter pudding

  10-year-old Barsac from a good château.

Cakes Bual or Malmsey Madeira, Oloroso or cream sherry.

Cheesecake

  ★★→★★★ sweet white from Vouvray or Coteaux du Layon.

Chocolate cake, mousse, soufflés

  Huxelrebe Auslese or California orange muscat.

Christmas pudding, mince pies

  Sweet champagne or Asti Spumante, or cream sherry.

Creams and custards

  ★★→★★★ Sauternes, Monbazillac or similar golden white.

Crème brûlée

  The most luxurious dish, demanding ★★★→★★★★ Sauternes or
  Rhine Beerenauslese, or the best Madeira or Tokay.

Crêpes Suzette

  Sweet champagne or Asti Spumante.

Fruit, fresh

  Sweet Coteaux du Layon white, light sweet muscat (e.g. California).

  Pears in red wine A pause before the port.

  Raspberries (no cream, little sugar) Excellent with fine reds.

  Rhubarb Rhubarb wine, I suppose.

Fruit flans (i.e. peach, raspberry)

  ★★★ Sauternes, Monbazillac or sweet Vouvray or Anjou.

Fruit salads, orange salad

  No wine.

Nuts Oloroso sherry, Bual, Madeira, vintage or tawny port, Vinsanto.

Sorbets, ice-creams

  No wine.

Stewed fruits, i.e. apricots, pears, etc.

  Sweet Muscatel: e.g. Muscat de Beaumes de Venise, Moscato di
  Pantelleria or from Tarragona.

Strawberries and cream

  ★★★ Sauternes or Vouvray Moelleux.

Wild strawberries

  Serve with ★★★ red Bordeaux poured over them and in your glass
  (no cream).

Summer pudding

  Fairly young Sauternes of a good vintage (e.g. 79, 80, 82, 83).

Treacle tart

  Too sweet for any wine but a treacly Malmsey Madeira.

Trifle No wine: should be sufficiently vibrant with sherry.

Sweet soufflés

  Sweet Vouvray or Coteaux du Layon. Sweet Champagne.

Zabaglione

  Light gold Marsala.

Savouries

Generally highly seasoned, these are not ideal partners for the
last glass of a fine wine. A Bual or Verdelho Madeira would come
to no harm. But **cheese straws** make an admirable meal-ending
with a final glass (or bottle) of any particularly good red wine.

A little learning . . .

The last fifteen years have seen a revolution in wine technology. They have also heard a revolution in wine-talk – and a timely reaction to it. Attempts to express the characters of wine used to get no further than such vague terms as "fruity" and "full-bodied". Then came the demand for sterner, more scientific, stuff: the jargon of laboratory analysis. This hard-edge wine-talk is very briefly explained below.

The most frequent references are to the ripeness of grapes at picking; the resultant alcohol and sugar content of the wine; various measures of its acidity; the amount of sulphur dioxide used as a preservative, and the amount of "dry extract" – the sum of all the things that give wine its characteristic flavours.

The fashion today (French in origin) is for analogues with a quasi-poetic effect: "Scents of apricots, raspberries, leather; flavours of plum and truffle, shading to farmyard with a hint of fish-glue". Anybody can play. Few can play well.

The **sugar** in wine is mainly glucose and fructose, with traces of arabinose, xylose and other sugars that are not fermentable by yeast, but can be attacked by bacteria. Each country has its own system for measuring the sugar content or ripeness of grapes, known as the **"must-weight"**. The chart below relates the three principal ones (German, French and American) to each other, to specific gravity, and to the potential alcohol of the wine if all the sugar is fermented.

Specific Gravity	°O °Oechsle	Baumé	Brix	% Potential Alcohol v/v
1.065	65	8.8	15.8	8.1
1.070	70	9.4	17.0	8.8
1.075	75	10.1	18.1	9.4
1.080	80	10.7	19.3	10.0
1.085	85	11.3	20.4	10.6
1.090	90	11.9	21.5	11.3
1.095	95	12.5	22.5	11.9
1.100	100	13.1	23.7	12.5
1.105	105	13.7	24.8	13.1
1.110	110	14.3	25.8	13.8
1.115	115	14.9	26.9	14.4
1.120	120	15.5	28.0	15.0

Residual sugar is the sugar left after fermentation has finished or been artificially stopped, measured in grammes per litre.

Alcohol content (mainly ethyl alcohol) is expressed as a percentage by volume of the total liquid. (Also known as "degrees").

Acidity is both fixed and volatile. **Fixed acidity** consists principally of tartaric, malic and citric acids which are all found in the grape, and lactic and succinic acids, which are produced during fermentation. **Volatile acidity** consists mainly of acetic acid, which is rapidly formed by bacteria in the presence of oxygen. A small amount of volatile acidity is inevitable and attractive. With a larger amount the wine becomes "pricked" – i.e. starts to turn to vinegar.

Total acidity is fixed and volatile acidity combined. As a rule of thumb for a well-balanced wine it should be in the region of 1 gramme/thousand for each 10° Oechsle (see over).

pH is a measure of the strength of the acidity, rather than its volume. The lower the figure the more acid. Wine normally ranges in pH from 2.8 to 3.8. Winemakers in hot climates can have problems getting the pH low enough. Lower pH gives better colour, helps prevent bacterial spoilage, allows more of the SO_2 to be free and active as a preservative.

Sulphur dioxide (SO_2) is added to prevent oxidation and other accidents in wine-making. Some of it combines with sugars, etc., and is known as "bound". Only the "free SO_2" that remains in the wine is effective as a preservative. Total SO_2 is controlled by law according to the level of residual sugar: the more sugar the more SO_2 needed.

Temperature

No single aspect of serving wine makes or mars it so easily as getting the temperature right. White wines almost invariably taste dull and insipid served warm and red wines have disappointingly little scent or flavour served cold. The chart below gives an indication of what is generally found to be the most satisfactory temperature for serving each class of wine.

Left	°F • °C	Right
	68 • 20	
Room	66 • 19	
temperature	64 • 18	
	63 • 17	Best red wines especially Bordeaux
Red Burgundy	61 • 16	
	59 • 15	Chianti, Zinfandel Côtes-du-Rhône
Best white Burgundy	57 • 14	
Port, Madeira		
	55 • 13	Ordinaires
	54 • 12	Lighter red wines e.g. Beaujolais
Ideal	52 • 11	
cellar Sherry		
Fino sherry	50 • 10	Rosés
Most dry white wines	48 • 9	Lambrusco
Champagne	46 • 8	
Domestic	45 • 7	
fridge	43 • 6	Most sweet white wines
	41 • 5	Sparkling wines
	39 • 4	
	37 • 3	
	35 • 2	
	33 • 1	
	32 • 0	

Is there an ideal wine glass?

Many of the traditional wine-growing regions of Europe have a design of glass considered ideal for enjoying their products. Some are based more on folklore than practicality. All good wine glasses are clear, thin, without cutting on the bowl, have a stem of moderate length and a relatively large bowl curving inwards towards the rim. The author is responsible for the design of the glasses illustrated. They constitute a matching set to do justice to all the main styles of wine.

Red Bordeaux Champagne Red burgundy

White wines Sherry Port

The 1988 vintage

Good summer weather across much of Europe led to a vintage which, with some important exceptions, will become known as one to rely on. There are well-founded hopes of some great wines from Bordeaux and Burgundy. On the other hand, June downpours ruined any hopes of a vintage in the Port country and much of Spain and Italy suffered from a wet spring.

For the first time for some years, quantity and quality failed to go hand in hand in Bordeaux. 1988 is a vintage of moderate size but potentially excellent quality. There were sighs of relief from château proprietors and négociants who found the large and excellent 85 and 86 vintages too much to handle. St-Emilion and Pomerol are particularly well-structured wines for a long life.

In Burgundy a dry summer meant an early harvest of an average-sized crop. Deep, full red wines promise very well. The Côte d'Or whites will also be fine but Chablis may lack concentration. Beaujolais is good. Fine sweet wines were made in the Loire and in Alsace. The Rhône made some great wines for keeping and Champagne's crop was smaller than hoped.

In Germany, rain dulled hopes of an Auslese vintage, but Kabinett and Spätlese wines will be of high quality. Italy was patchy, with good news from Tuscany. Spain also had weather problems, but Rioja escaped the worst.

In Australia the crop was generally smaller than expected but quality was good. California produced some fine white wines and early-maturing Cabernets that promise pleasure.

Despite the moderate Bordeaux crop the world's cellars are full of quality wine, and there is no need to be apprehensive about stocks. It has been – so far – a wonderful wine decade.

France

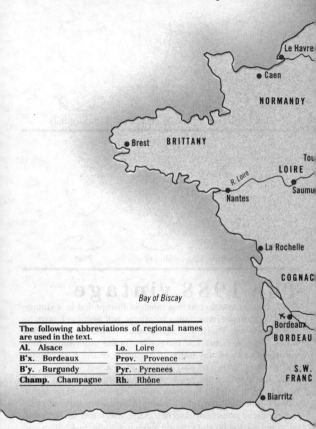

Cal.

English Channel

Le Havre

Caen

NORMANDY

Brest   BRITTANY

R. Loire   Tou

LOIRE

Saumu

Nantes

La Rochelle

COGNAC

Bay of Biscay

Bordeaux

BORDEAU

S.W.
FRANC

Biarritz

The following abbreviations of regional names are used in the text.	
Al. Alsace	**Lo.** Loire
B'x. Bordeaux	**Prov.** Provence
B'y. Burgundy	**Pyr.** Pyrenees
Champ. Champagne	**Rh.** Rhône

France has not even a remote challenger as the motherland of wine. Tens of thousands of properties make wine of all complexions over a large part of her surface. This is a guide to their names, types and producers: the essential information in identifying what is authentic and good of its kind.

All France's best wine regions (producing about 30% of all her wine) have Appellations Contrôlées, which may apply to a single small vineyard or a whole large district. The system varies from region to region, with Burgundy on the whole having the smallest and most precise appellations, grouped into larger units by complicated formulae, and Bordeaux having the widest and most general appellations, in which it is the particular property (or "château") that matters. In between lie an infinity of variations.

An Appellation Contrôlée is a guarantee of origin and of

production method, of grape varieties and quantities produced, but only partially one of quality. All "AC" wines are officially tasted, but many of shoddy quality get through the net.

Appellations therefore help to identify a wine and indicate that it comes from a major area. They are the first thing to look for on a label. But the next is the name of the maker.

Wine regions without the overall quality and traditions required for an appellation can be ranked as Vins Délimités de Qualité Supérieure (VDQS), or (a third rank, created largely to encourage the improvement of mediocre wines in the south of France) Vins de Pays. VDQS wines (a shrinking category) are almost always good value. Vins de Pays are increasingly worth trying. They include some brilliant originals and often offer France's best value for money.

Recent vintages
of the French classics

Red Burgundy

Côte d'Or Côte de Beaune reds generally mature sooner than the bigger wines of the Côte de Nuits. Earliest drinking dates are for lighter commune wines: Volnay, Beaune, etc. latest for the biggest wines of Chambertin, Romanée, etc. Different growers make wines of different styles, for longer or shorter maturing, but even the best burgundies are much more attractive young than the equivalent red Bordeaux.

1988 Exceptional quality; a great vintage.

1987 Small crop with promising ripe fruit flavours. Will need time.

1986 A very mixed bag – generally lacks flesh; but wait and see.

1985 A great vintage. Concentrated wines will be splendid. Now-2000.

1984 Lacks natural ripeness; tends to be dry and/or watery. Now-'96.

1983 Powerful, vigorous, tannic and attractive vintage, compromised by rot. The best are splendid, but be careful. Now-2000.

1982 Big vintage, pale but round. Best in Côte de Beaune. Drink soon.

1981 A small crop, ripe but picked in rain. Some pleasant wines: Now.

1980 A late, wet year, but attractive wines from the best growers who avoided rot. Better in the Côte de Nuits. Keep (only) the best another year or two.

1979 Big generally good ripe vintage with weak spots. Drink up.

1978 A small vintage of outstanding quality. The best will live to 2000.

1977 Very wet summer. Better wine than expected, but drink up.

1976 Hot summer, excellent vintage. As usual great variations, but the best (esp. Côte de Beaune) rich and long-lived – to 1995.

1973 Light wines, but many fruity and delicate. Most are already too old.

1972 Firm and full of character, ageing well. Few need keeping longer now.

1971 Very powerful and impressive wines, not as long-lasting as they first appeared. Most now ready. The best have 3 or 4 years ahead.

Older fine vintages: '69, '66, '64, '62, '61, '59 (all mature).

Beaujolais 1988 was attractive with Crus to keep. 1987 was highly satisfactory, but not great. 86s should be drunk. 1985 was a wonderful vintage, with Crus to keep still. Generally avoid older vintages except possibly some Moulin à Vent.

White Burgundy

Côte de Beaune Well-made wines of good vintages with plenty of acidity as well as fruit will improve and gain depth and richness for some years – anything up to ten. Lesser wines from lighter years are ready for drinking after two or three years.

1988 Extremely good; some great wines.

1987 Mainly disappointing, though a few exceptions are emerging.

1986 Powerful wines with better acidity and balance than '85. Now-2000.

1985 Very ripe; many wines are too soft; be careful. Now-'95.

1984 Some well-balanced wines; most rather lean or hollow. Drink soon.

1983 Potent wines; some exaggerated, some faulty but the best splendid. -'95.

1982 Fat, tasty but delicate whites of low acidity, not for keeping.

1981 A sadly depleted crop with great promise. The best are excellent now.

1980 A weak, but not bad, vintage. Drink up.

1979 Big vintage. Overall good and useful, not great. Drink soon.

1978 Very good wines, firm and well-balanced. Keep only the best.

1977 Rather light; some well-balanced and good. Drink up.

1976 Hot summer, rather heavy wines; good but mostly passed it now.

1973 Very attractive, fruity, typical and plentiful. Drink up.

1972 High acidity, but plenty of character. All are now ready to drink.

1971 Great power and style. Top wines are now wonderful.

The white wines of the Mâconnais (Pouilly-Fuissé, St-Véran, Mâcon-Villages) follow a similar pattern, but do not last as long. They are more appreciated for their freshness than their richness.

Chablis Grand Cru Chablis of vintages with both strength and acidity can age superbly for up to ten years. Premiers Crus proportionally less, but too many growers are stressing quantity, which results in wines that fade away without ever achieving the classic Chablis flavour. Only buy Petit Chablis of ripe years, and drink it young.

1988	Almost a model: great pleasure in store.
1987	Rain at harvest but balanced wines for the short term. Drink soon.
1986	A splendid, big vintage. Now-1995.
1985	Good but often low-acid wines. The best Grands Crus will age 6 years.
1984	A small vintage. Most too feeble to last long. Drink up.
1983	Superb vintage if not over-strong. The best will improve until '93.
1982	Charming soft wines. Good value. Not to keep.
1981	Small, concentrated and fine harvest. Keeping well. Drink soon.
1980	More successful than the rest of burgundy. Drink up.
1979	Very big crop. Good easy wines, not for storing.
1978	Excellent wines now passing their peak.

F

Red Bordeaux

Médoc/red Graves For some wines bottle-age is optional: for these it is indispensable. Minor châteaux from light vintages need only two or three years, but even modest wines of great years can improve for 15 years or so, and the great châteaux of these years need double that time.

1988	Generally excellent; ripe, balanced, for long keeping.
1987	Difficult; at best sound. Strict selection necessary. Not for long keeping.
1986	Another splendid (and huge) heatwave harvest. Most will probably be superior to '85.
1985	Very good vintage, in a heatwave. Some great wines. Now-2010.
1984	Only fair. Little Merlot but good ripe Cabernet. Originally overpriced. -'95?
1983	A classic vintage: abundant tannin with fruit to balance it. -2010.
1982	Made in a heatwave. Huge rich strong wines which promise a long life. Many Pomerols and St-Emilions and most petits châteaux are now rich and delicious. Keep the best.
1981	Admirable despite rain. Not rich, but balanced and fine. Now-'98.
1980	Small, late harvest, ripe but rained-on. Many delicious light wines. Drink soon.
1979	Abundant harvest of above average quality. Now-'95.
1978	A miracle vintage: magnificent long warm autumn saved the day. Some superb wines. Now-2000.
1977	Pleasant light wine, many better than 1974. Now.
1976	Excessively hot, dry summer; rain just before vintage. Generally very good, maturing rather quickly. Generally ready.
1975	A very fine vintage, with deep colour, high sugar content and (sometimes excessive) tannin. For long keeping but begin to drink: some may improve.
1974	Oceans of disappointing light wines. Be very careful.
1973	A huge vintage, attractive young and still give pleasure. Now or very soon.
1972	High acidity from unripe grapes. Now.
1971	Small crop. Less fruity than '70 and less consistent. All are ready to drink.
1970	Big excellent vintage with scarcely a failure. Now-'95.
1969/68	Avoid them both.
1967	Never seductive, but characterful in its maturity. Drink soon.
1966	A very fine vintage with depth, fruit and tannin. Now.
Older fine vintages: '62, '61, '59, '55, '53, '52, '50, '49, '48, '47, '45, '29, '28.	

St-Emilion/Pomerol

1988	Generally excellent; ideal conditions.
1987	Some very adequate wines but for drinking soon.
1986	A prolific vintage; quality depends on the grower's restraint.
1985	One of the great years, with a long future. -2010.
1984	A sad story. Most of the crop wiped out in spring. Not for laying down.
1983	Conditions were ideal. Some growers prefer this vintage to 1982.
1982	Enormously rich and concentrated wines, most excellent. Now-2000+.
1981	A very good vintage, if not as great as it first seemed. Now-'95+.
1980	A poor Merlot year; very variable quality. Choose carefully. Soon.
1979	A rival to '78, but not developing as well as hoped. Now-'95.
1978	Fine wines, but some lack flesh. Now-'92.
1977	Very wet summer. Mediocre with few exceptions. Drink up.
1976	Very hot, dry summer, but vintage rain. Some excellent. Drink fairly soon.
1975	Most St-Emilions good, the best superb. Frost in Pomerol cut crops and made splendid concentrated wine. Now-2000.
1974/73/72	All need drinking soon, if at all.
1971	On the whole better than Médocs but generally now ready.
1970	Beautiful wines with great fruit and strength. Very big crop. Now.
Older fine vintages: '67, '66, '64, '61, '59, '53, '52, '49, '47, '45.	

Abel-Lepitre Brut NV, Cuvée 134 Blanc de Blanc 83, Rèserve Crèmant 83, Rosé 83 Champagne house, founder of Les Grands Champagnes de Reims, also owning GOULET and St-Marceaux.

Abymes Savoie w. dr. ★ D.Y.A.
Hilly little area nr. Chambéry known for light mild wine from the Jacquère grape.

Ackerman-Laurance Champagne-method house of the Loire, at SAUMUR, said to be the first of the region. Fine CREMANT de Loire.

Ajaccio Corsica r. p. or w. dr. |★→★★★| 85′ 86 87
The capital of Corsica. AC for some v. good SCIACARELLO reds.

Aligoté Second-rank burgundy white grape and its wine, often agreeably sharp and fruity and with considerable local character when young. BOUZERON (AC) makes the best but don't hesitate to try others. Value.

Aloxe-Corton B'y. r. or w. ★★★ 69 71 76 78 79 80 82 83 84 85 86 87
Northernmost village of COTE DE BEAUNE famous for its Grands Crus: CORTON (red) and CORTON-CHARLEMAGNE (white). Village wines (called Aloxe-Corton) are lighter but can be good value.

Alsace Al. w. or (r.) |★★| 76 81 83′ 85′ 86 87
Aromatic, fruity, often strong dry white of rather Germanic character from eastern foothills of Vosges Mtns, bordering on the R. Rhine. Normally sold by grape variety (RIESLING, GEWÜRZTRAMINER, etc.). Matures well up to 5, even 10, years; the next entry even longer.

Alsace Grand Cru |★★★| 71 76 79 81 82 83′ 84 85 86 87
Appellation restricted to about 45 of the best named v'yds.

Alsace Grand Vin or Réserve Wine with minimum 11° natural alcohol.

Amance, Marcel See Maufoux, Prosper.

Ampeau, Robert Dependable grower and specialist in MEURSAULT, POMMARD, etc.

Anjou Lo. (r.) p. or w. (sw. dr. or sp.) |★→★★★| 76 78 82 83 85′ 86
Very various Loire wines, incl. good CABERNET rosé, luscious COTEAUX DU LAYON white. Maturity depends on style.

Anjou-Côteaux de la Loire AC for CHENIN BLANC whites, incl. the notable dry SAVENNIERES.

Appellation Contrôlée ("AC" or "AOC") Government control of origin and production of all the best French wines (see France Introduction).

Apremont Savoie w. dr. |★★| D.Y.A.
One of the best villages of SAVOIE for pale delicate whites, recently including CHARDONNAY.

Arbin Savoie r. ★★ Drink at 1-2 years
Deep-coloured lively red of Mondeuse grapes, rather like a good LOIRE Cabernet. Ideal après-ski wine.

Arbois Jura r. p. or w. (dr. sp.) ★★ On the whole, D.Y.A.
Various good and original light wines; speciality VIN JAUNE.

l'Ardèche, Coteaux de Central France r. (w. dr.) |★→★★| D.Y.A.
Light country reds, the best made of SYRAH. A useful change from BEAUJOLAIS. Also remarkable burgundy-like CHARDONNAY from e.g. Louis LATOUR – a bargain.

Armagnac Region of s.w. France famous for its sometimes excellent brandy, a fiery spirit of rustic character. The red wine of the area is MADIRAN.

Auxey-Duresses B'y. r. or w. |★★→★★★| 76 78 79 82 83 85 86 87 88
Officially second-rank (but v. pretty) COTE DE BEAUNE village: has affinities with VOLNAY and MEURSAULT. Best estates: Duc de Magenta, Prunier, Leroy, Diconne. HOSPICES DE BEAUNE Cuvée Boillot. Often a best buy.

Avize Champ. ★★★★
One of the best CHARDONNAY villages of CHAMPAGNE.

Ay Champ. ★★★★
One of the best black-grape villages of CHAMPAGNE.

Ayala NV "Château d'Ay" **75 76** 79 **82** and Blanc de Blancs **79** 82
   Once-famous Ay-based old-style champagne concern. To watch.

Bandol Prov. r. p. or (w.) **★★★** 76 **78 80 81 82 83 84** 85′ 86 87′
   Little coastal region near Toulon with vigorous reds from the
   Mourvèdre grape; esp. Ch Vannières, Domaine Tempier, Domaine
   Ott, Mas de la Rouvière, Domaine de Pibarnon, Ch Pradeaux.

Banyuls Pyr. br. sw. **★★** normally NV
   One of the best VIN DOUX NATURELS (fortified sweet red wines) of the s.
   of France. Technically a distant relation of port.

Bar-sur-Aube Champ w. (p.) sp. **★★★**
   Secondary champagne to the s. Some good lighter wines and excellent
   Rosé des RICEYS.

Barancourt Cramant NV, Cramant Grand Cru 76 78 79 80 81, Bouzy
   Brut, Bouzy 81, Rosé NV Grower at Bouzy making full-bodied
   champagnes. Pricey.

Barsac B'x. w. sw. **★★→ ★★★★** 70 71 75 76′ 78 79′ 80 81 82 83′
   84 85 86′ Neighbour of SAUTERNES with similar superb golden wines,
   generally less rich and more racy. Top ch'x: CLIMENS and COUTET.

Barton & Guestier Bordeaux shipper since 18th century, now owned by
   Seagram's.

Bâtard-Montrachet B'y. w. dr. **★★★★** 71 78 79 81 82 83 84 85 86 87 88
   Larger neighbour of MONTRACHET, the top white burgundy. Should be
   v. long-lived and intense in flavour. Top growers incl. LEFLAIVE,
   BOUCHARD PERE, Gagnard, Morey, Niellon.

Baumard, Domaine des Leading grower of Anjou wine, especially
   SAVENNIERES and COTEAUX DU LAYON (Clos Ste Catherine).

Béarn s.w. France r. p. or w. dr. **★** D.Y.A.
   Minor appellation of growing local (Basque country) interest, esp.
   wines from the coop of Sallies de Béarn-Bellocq.

Beaujolais B'y. r. (p. w.) **★** D.Y.A.
   The simple appellation of the very big Beaujolais region: light short-
   lived fruity red of GAMAY grapes.

---

*Confusingly, the best wines of the Beaujolais region are not identified as
such on their labels by their appellations. They are known simply by the
names of their "crus": Brouilly, Côte de Brouilly, Chénas, Chiroubles,
Fleurie, Juliénas, Morgon, Moulin-à-Vent, Regnié, St-Amour. See entries
for each of these. Since 1984 the Confrérie des Compagnes du Beaujolais
have offered a "Beaujolais Grumé" label to selected wines from the
region.*

Beaujolais de l'année The Beaujolais of the latest vintage, until the next.

Beaujolais Primeur (or Nouveau) The same made in a hurry (often only
   4-5 days fermenting) for release at midnight on the third Wednesday
   in November. Ideally soft, fruity and tempting but often crude, sharp
   and too alcoholic. BEAUJOLAIS-VILLAGES *should* be a better bet.

Beaujolais Supérieur B'y. r. (w.) **★** D.Y.A.
   Beaujolais 1° of natural alcohol stronger than the 9° minimum. Since
   sugar is almost always added this means little or nothing.

Beaujolais-Villages B'y. r. **★★** 88
   Wines from the better (northern) half of Beaujolais, should be tastier
   than plain Beaujolais. The 10 (easily) best "villages" are the "crus":
   FLEURIE, BROUILLY, etc. (see note above). Of the 30 others the best lie
   around Beaujeu. The crus cannot be released "en primeur" before
   December 15th. They are best kept till spring (or longer).

Beaumes de Venise Rh. (r. p.) br. sw. **★★★** NV
   Generally France's best dessert MUSCAT, from the s. COTES-DU-RHONE;
   can be high-flavoured, subtle, lingering (e.g. Domaine de Coyeux,
   Domaine Durban). The red and rosé from Ch Redortier and the
   cooperative are also good.

Beaune B'y. r. or (w. dr.) ★★★ 76 78' 82 83' 84 85 86 87 88
Middle-rank classic burgundy. Négociants' "CLOS" wines (usually "Premier Cru") are often best e.g. DROUHIN's superb "Clos des Mouches". "Beaune du Château" is a (good) brand of BOUCHARD PÈRE. Best V'yds incl: Grèves, Bressandes, Teurons, Marconnets, Fèves.

Becker, Caves J. Proud old family firm at Zellenberg, ALSACE.

Bégadan Leading village of the n. MÉDOC (apellation Médoc), with commendable coop (Cave St Jean), and ch'x incl: LA TOUR DE BY, VIEUX-CH-LANDON, GREYSAC, LAUJAC, PATACHE D'AUX. Often v.g. value.

Bellet Prov. p. r. w. dr. ★★★
Fashionable, much above average, local wine from near Nice. Ch'x de Bellet and Crémat are serious producers. Costs what the market will bear.

Bergerac Dordogne r. or w. sw. or dr. ★★ 82 83 85 86 88
Lightweight, often tasty, Bordeaux-style. Drink young, the white very young. See also Pécharmant, Montravel, Monbazillac. Growers incl. CH DE PANISSEAU, JAUBERTIE, Courts-les-Muts, Tiregand.

Besserat de Bellefon Cuvée Blanc de Blancs, NV, 75 79 82, Rosé 79, Brut Intégral 79 Rising champagne house for fine light wines, esp. CREMANT.

Beyer, Leon Ancient ALSACE family firm at Eguisheim making forceful dry wines that need ageing at least 2-3 yrs, esp. Comtes d'Eguisheim.

Bichot, Maison Albert One of BEAUNE's biggest grower and merchants. V'yds (Domaine du Clos Frantin is very good) in CHAMBERTIN, CLOS DE VOUGEOT, RICHEBOURG, etc. and Domaine Long-Depaquit in CHABLIS, plus many other brand-names.

Billecart-Salmon NV, 75 76 78 79 82, Rosé NV, Bl. de Blancs 79 82 83 Good small champagne house. Fresh-flavoured wines incl. a very tasty rosé.

Bize, Simon Admirable grower with 35 acres at SAVIGNY-LES-BEAUNE. Model wines; fair prices.

Blagny B'y. r. or w. dr. ★★→★★★ 76 78 82 83 85 86 87 88
Hamlet between MEURSAULT and PULIGNY-MONTRACHET; affinities with both and VOLNAY for reds. Ages well. Growers incl. LATOUR, AMPEAU, Matrot.

Blanc de Blancs Any white wine made from (only) white grapes, esp. CHAMPAGNE, which is usually made of both black and white. *Not* an indication of quality.

Blanc de Noirs White (or slightly pink or "blush") wine from black grapes.

Blanck, Marcel High-quality Alsace grower at Kientzheim.

Blanquette de Limoux Midi w. dr. sp. ★★ normally NV
Good bargain sparkler from near Carcassonne made by a version of the METHODE CHAMPENOISE. Very dry and clean and increasingly tasty.

Blaye B'x. r. or w. dr. ★ 85 86 88
Your daily Bordeaux from e. of the Gironde. PREMIERES COTES DE BLAYE are better.

Boisset, Jean Claude Dynamic Burgundy merchant/grower at NUITS-ST-GEORGES, owns the houses of VIENOT, Bassot, Lionel Bruck and Pierre Ponnelle. High commercial standards.

Bollinger NV "Special Cuvée", Grande Année 69 70 73 75 76 79 82 83 Année Rare 73 75, Rosé 81 82 Top champagne house, at AŸ. Dry full-flavoured style. Luxury wines "RD" 73 75 76 79 and "Vieilles Vignes Françaises" 69 70 75 79 80 81 from ungrafted vines.

Bommes Village of SAUTERNES. Best ch'x: LATOUR-BLANCHE, LAFAURIE-PEYRAGUEY, etc.

Bonneau du Martray, Domaine Major producer (with 22 acres) of CORTON-CHARLEMAGNE of the highest quality; also admirable red Grand Cru CORTON.

Bonnes Mares B'y. r. ★★★★ 66 69 71 76 78′ 79 80 82 83 84 85′ 86 87 88 37-acre Grand Cru between CHAMBOLLE-MUSIGNY and MOREY-SAINT-DENIS. Sometimes (not often) better than CHAMBERTIN. Top growers: DE VOGUE, Dom des VAROILLES, DUJAC, Groffier, Roumier.

Bonnezeaux Lo. w. sw. ★★★ 76 78 81 82 84 85 86 Unusual fruity/acidic wine from CHENIN BLANC grapes, the best of COTEAUX DU LAYON. Esp. Ch de Fesles.

Bordeaux B'x. r. or (p.) or w. ★ 85 86 88 (for ch'x see p. 56) Basic catch-all appellation for low-strength Bordeaux wine not to be despised.

Bordeaux Supérieur ★→★★★ Ditto, with slightly more alcohol.

Bordeaux Côtes-de-Francs B'x. r. or w. dr. ★ 82 83 85 86 88 Fringe Bordeaux from east of ST-EMILION. Increasingly attractive and tasty wines, esp. from Ch'x PUYGUERAUD, de Belcier, Puyfromage.

Borie-Manoux Admirable Bordeaux shippers and château-owners, owned by the Castéja family. Ch'x incl. BATAILLEY, HAUT-BAGES MONPELOU, DOMAINE DE L'EGLISE, TROTTEVIEILLE, BEAU-SITE.

Bouchard Aîné Long-established burgundy shipper and grower with 62 acres in BEAUNE, MERCUREY, etc. Good, not top, quality.

Bouchard Père et Fils Important burgundy shipper (est. 1731) and grower with 209 acres of excellent v'yds, mainly in the COTE DE BEAUNE, and cellars at the Château de Beaune. Reliable quality.

Bourg B'x. r. or (w. dr.) ★★ 82 83 85 86 87 88 Meaty, un-fancy claret from e. of the Gironde. For ch'x see COTES DE BOURG.

Bourgogne B'y. r. (p.) or w. dr. ★★ 85 86 87 88 Catch-all appellation for Burgundy, but with theoretically higher standards than basic BORDEAUX. Light but often good flavour, best at 2-3 yrs. BEAUJOLAIS crus can also be labelled Bourgogne.

Bourgogne Grand Ordinaire B'y. r. (w.) ★ D.Y.A. The lowest burgundy appellation for GAMAY wines. Rare.

Bourgogne Passe-tout-grains B'y. r. or (p.) ★ Age 1-2 years Often enjoyable junior burgundy. ⅓ PINOT NOIR and ⅔ GAMAY grapes mixed in the vat. Not as "heady" as BEAUJOLAIS.

Bourgueil Lo. r. ★★★ 76′ 81 82 83′ 85 86 Normally delicate fruity CABERNET red from Touraine, the best from St Nicolas de Bourgueil. Deep-flavoured and long-lasting in exceptional years. Growers incl. Caslot-Galbrun, Lame-Delille-Boncard, Audebert, Cognard, Jamet.

Bouvet-Ladubay Major producer of sparkling SAUMUR, controlled by TAITTINGER. Excellent CREMANT de Loire. "Saphir" is vintage wine, "Trésor" the top grade.

Bouzeron Village of the COTE CHALONNAISE distinguished for the only single-village appellation ALIGOTE.

Bouzy Rouge Champ. r. ★★★ 82 83 85 86 Still red wine from famous black-grape CHAMPAGNE village. Like light burgundy, ageing early but sometimes lasting well.

Brédif, Marc One of the most important growers and traders of VOUVRAY.

Bricout Minor champagne house at AVIZE with good cuvée Charles Koch.

Brouilly B'y. r. ★★★ 85 86 87 One of the 10 best CRUS of BEAUJOLAIS: fruity, round, refreshing. One year in bottle is usually enough. Ch de la Chaize is top estate.

Brut Term for the driest wines of CHAMPAGNE until recently, when some completely unsweetened wines have become available as "Brut Intégrale", "Brut non-dosé", "Brut zéro" etc.

Bugey Savoie w. dr. or sp. ★→ ★★ D.Y.A. District with a variety of light sparkling, still or half-sparkling wines. Grapes incl. Roussette (or Roussanne) and good CHARD.

Buxy B'y. (r.) w. dr. ★★
Village in the AC Montagny with a good coop.

Buzet s.w. France, r. or w. dr. ★★ 82 83 85 86 88
Good Bordeaux-style wines from just s.e. of Bordeaux. Good-value area with well-run cooperative. Best wine: Cuvée Napoleon.

Cabernet See Grapes for red wine.

Cabernet d'Anjou Lo. p. ★→★★ D.Y.A.
Delicate, grapey, often rather sweet rosé.

Cahors s.w. France r. ★→ ★★ 75 78 79 80 81 82 83 85' 86 88
Historically a hard "black" wine of Malbec grapes, now made more like Bordeaux, but can be full-bodied and increasingly distinct. Top growers: Baldès (esp. for "Prince Probus"), Jouffreau, Vigouroux (esp. Ch de Haute-Serre), Ch de Caix, Ch de Chambert, Ch Lagrezette, Ch St Didier, Clos la Coutale, Dom Euganie.

Cairanne Rh. r. p. or w. dr. ★★ 83 84 85 86
Village of CÔTES-DU-RHÔNE-VILLAGES. Good solid wines, esp. from Domaine Rabasse-Charavin.

Calvet Famous old shippers of Bordeaux and Burgundy, now owned by Whitbread. Some reliable standard wines, especially from Bordeaux.

Canard-Duchêne NV Brut, rosé and Charles VII NV, Vintage Charles VII and (sometimes) Coteaux Champenois. Medium-quality champagne house owned by VEUVE CLICQUOT, hence Moët.

Canon-Fronsac B'x. r. ★★ 70 75 78 79 81 82 83' 85 86 88
Tannic, often full-flavoured reds of increasing quality and style from small area w. of POMEROL. Bottle age is essential. Ch'x include Canon, Canon-Moueix, Canon de Brem, Coustolle, Junayme, Mazeris-Bellevue, Moulin-Pey-Labrie, Toumalin, Vraye-Canon-Boyer. See also Fronsac.

Cantenac B'x. r. ★★★
Village of the HAUT-MÉDOC entitled to the appellation MARGAUX. Top ch'x include PALMER, BRANE-CANTENAC, etc.

Cap Corse Corsica w. dr. br. ★★→★★★
The wild north cape of the island. Splendid muscat and rare dry VERMENTINO white. *Vaut le détour*, if not *le voyage*.

Caramany Pyr. r. (w. dr.) ▩ 85 86 87 88
New appellation for part of CÔTES DE ROUSSILLON-VILLAGES.

Cassis Prov. (r. p.) w. dr. ★★ D.Y.A.
Seaside village e. of Marseille known for its lively dry white, exceptional for Provence (e.g. Domaine du Paternel). Not to be confused with cassis, a blackcurrant liqueur made in Dijon.

Castellane, de Long-established ÉPERNAY champagne house. Good wines incl. Maxim's house champagne.

Cave Cellar, or any wine establishment.

Cave coopérative Wine-growers' cooperative winery. Coops now account for 55% of all French production. 4 out of 10 of all French growers are coop members. Almost all coops are now well run, well equipped and making some of the best-value wine of their areas.

Cépage Variety of vine, e.g. CHARDONNAY, MERLOT.

Cérons B'x. w. dr. or sw. ★★ 79 80 81 83 84 85 86
Neighbour of SAUTERNES with some good sweet-wine ch'x, e.g. Ch de Cérons et de Calvimont.

Chablis B'y. w. dr. ★★ 85 86 87
Distinctive full-flavoured greeny-gold wine. Made only of CHARDONNAY in n. Burgundy. Top growers incl. Raveneau, Dauvissat, LAROCHE, Long-Depaquit, Michel, Droin, Pic, Fèvre, etc. Simple unqualified "Chablis" may be thin: all the best Chablis is either Premier Cru or Grand Cru (see over). The modern growers coop, "La Chablisienne", has v.g. standards.

Chablis Grand Cru B'y. w. dr. ■■■■ 78 81 82 83 84 85 86 87 88
Strong, subtle and altogether splendid. Some of the great white
burgundies, though less succulent than the top COTE DE BEAUNE. There
are seven v'yds: Blanchots, Bougros, Clos, Grenouilles, Preuses,
Valmur, Vaudésir. See also Moutonne.

Chablis Premier Cru B'y. w. dr. ■■■ 81 83 85 86 87 88
Second-rank but often excellent and more typical of Chablis than
Grands Crus. Best v'yds incl: Côte de Lechet, Fourchaume, Mont de
Milieu, Montée de Tonnerre, Montmains, Vaillons.

Chai Building for storing and maturing wine, esp. in Bordeaux.

Chambertin B'y. r. ■■■■ 69 71 76 78 79 80 82 83 84 85 86 87 88
32-acre Grand Cru giving the meatiest, most enduring and often the
best red burgundy, 15 growers, incl. ROUSSEAU, BOUCHARD PERE, Camus,
Damoy, Tortochot, Rebourseau, Trapet, Ponsot.

Chambertin-Clos-de-Bèze B'y. r. ■■■■ 76 78 79 80 81 82 83 84 85
86 87 88   37-acre neighbour of CHAMBERTIN. Similarly splendid wine.
10 growers incl. CLAIR-DAU, DROUHIN, DROUHIN-LAROSE, Damoy,
ROUSSEAU.

Chambolle-Musigny B'y. r. (w.) ■■■ 76 78 80 82 83 84 85 86 87
420-acre COTE DE NUITS village with fabulously fragrant, complex,
never heavy wine. Best v'yds: MUSIGNY, part of BONNES-MARES, Les
Amoureuses, Les Charmes. Growers incl: DE VOGUE, DROUHIN, FAIVELEY,
Roumier, Moine-Hudelot, Mugnier, Hudelot-Noëllat.

Champagne Sparkling wine of Pinots Noir and Meunier and/or
Chardonnay from 60,000 acres 90 miles e. of Paris, made by the
METHODE CHAMPENOISE. Wines from elsewhere, however good, cannot
be Champagne. (See also names of brands.)

Champagne, Grande The appellation of the best area of COGNAC.

Champigny See Saumur.

Chandon de Briailles, Domaine Small burgundy estate at SAVIGNY. Makes
v.g. CORTON.

Chanson Père et Fils Growers (with 110 acres) and négociants at BEAUNE.

Chantovent Major brand of VIN DE TABLE, largely from MINERVOIS.

Chapelle-Chambertin B'y. r. ■■■ 76 78 80 82 83' 85 86 87 88
13-acre neighbour of CHAMBERTIN. Wine more "nervous", not so
meaty. Top producers: CLAIR-DAU, Drouhin-Larose, LEROY, Trapet.

Chapoutier Long-established growers and traders of fine Rhône wines.

Charbaut, A. et Fils NV, Blanc de Blancs, Rosé NV, 73 76 79
EPERNAY champagne house. Clean light wines. Good Rosé.

Chardonnay See Grapes for white wine.

Charmes-Chambertin B'y. r. ■■■ 71 76 78 79 80 82 83' 85 86 87 88
76-acre neighbour of CHAMBERTIN. Wine more `"supple", rounder.
Growers incl. Bachelet, Castagnier, Roty, ROUSSEAU.

Chartron & Trebuchet Young company with delicate and harmonious
white burgundies, esp. Domaine CHARTRON's PULIGNY-MONTRACHET, Clos
de la Pucelle.

Chassagne-Montrachet B'y. r. or w. dr. ■■■-■■■■ (reds ■■■)
76 78 80 (r.) 82 (r.) 83 84 85 86 87 88   750-acre COTE DE BEAUNE
village with excellent rich dry whites and sterling hefty reds. The
whites rarely have the exceptional finesse of PULIGNY-MONTRACHET next
door. Best v'yds: MONTRACHET, BATARD-MONTRACHET, CRIOTS-BATARD-
MONTRACHET, Ruchottes, Caillerets, Boudriottes (r. w.), Morgeot (r. w.),
CLOS-ST-JEAN (r.) Growers incl. RAMONET-PRUDHON, Morey, MAGENTA,
DELAGRANGE-BACHELET, Gagnard-Delagrange, Niellon, M. Colin-
Deleger, J-N. Gagnard, Lamy-Pillot, Bachelet-Ramonet.

Chasseloir, Domaine du The HQ of the firm of Chéreau-Carré, makers of
several excellent domaine MUSCADETS, esp. Ch de Chasseloir, which
are among the appellation's leaders.

Château An estate, big or small, good or indifferent, particularly in Bordeaux. In Burgundy the term "domaine" is used. For all Bordeaux châteaux see pp. 57-76.

Château-Chalon Jura w. dr. ★★★
Unique strong dry yellow wine, rather like a modest FINO sherry. Usually ready to drink when bottled (at about 6 years). A curiosity.

Château Corton-Grancey B'y. r. ★★★ 76 78 79 81 82 83 85 86 88
Famous estate at ALOXE-CORTON, the property of Louis LATOUR. The white wines are generally his best.

Château d'Arlay Major JURA estate; 160 acres in skilful hands.

Château de Beaucastel Rh. r. w. dr. ★★★ 79 80 81 83 84 85 86 87 88
One of the biggest (173 acres) and best-run estates of CHATEAUNEUF-DU-PAPE. Deep-hued wines intended for at least 10 yrs ageing. A small amount of wonderful white. See Côtes du Ventoux, La Vieille Ferme.

Château de la Chaize B'y. r. ★★★ 88
The best known estate of BROUILLY, with 200 acres.

Château de la Maltroye B'y. r. w. dr. ★★★
Very good 32-acre estate in CHASSAGNE-MONTRACHET and SANTENAY. Unpredictable wines.

Château de Meursault B'y. r. w. ★★★
100-acre estate owned by PATRIARCHE with good v'yds and v.g. wines in MEURSAULT, VOLNAY, POMMARD, BEAUNE. Splendid cellars open to the public for tasting. *Vaut le détour, mais? le prix.*

Château de Panisseau Dordogne r. p. w. dr. ★★ D.Y.A.
Leading estate of BERGERAC: good dry SAUV BLANC and Sémillon.

Château de Selle Prov. r. p. or w. dr. ★★
Estate of the OTT family near Cotignac, Var. Well-known and typical wines.

Château des Fines Roches Rh. r. ★★★ 78 79 80 81 83 84 85 86
Large (112 acres) and distinguished estate in CHATEAUNEUF-DU-PAPE wines maturing relatively quickly.

Château du Nozet Lo. w. dr. ★★★ 85 86 87
Biggest and best-known estate of Pouilly (FUME) sur Loire. Top wine, Baron de L, can be wonderful (at a price).

Château Fortia Rh. r. (w. dr.) ★★★ 79 80 81 83 84 85 86
First-class property in CHATEAUNEUF-DU-PAPE. Traditional methods. The owner's father, Baron Le Roy, also fathered the APPELLATION CONTROLEE system in the 1920s.

Château-Grillet Rh. w. dr. ★★★★ 83 84 85 86 87 88
3½-acre v'yd with one of France's smallest appellations. Intense, fragrant, over-expensive. Drink fairly young.

Château-Gris B'y. r. ★★★ 78 82 83 85 86 88
Well-known estate at NUITS-ST-GEORGES. Linked with BICHOT.

Châteaumeillant Lo. r. p. or w. dr. ★ D.Y.A.
Small VDQS area near SANCERRE. Light GAMAY and P NOIR.

Châteauneuf-du-Pape Rh. r. (w. dr.) ★★★ 78 79 80 81 82 83 84 85 86
7,400 acres near Avignon with standards steadily rising. Best estate ("domaine") wines are dark, strong, exceptionally long-lived. Others may be light and/or disappointing. The white can be heavy: most now made to D.Y.A. Top growers incl. Ch'x FORTIA, RAYAS, Doms de BEAUCASTEL, VIEUX TELEGRAPH, Clos des Papes, Dom les Cailloux, etc.

Château Rayas Rh. r. (w. dr.) ★★★ 78 80 81 83 84 85 86
Famous old-style property of only 38 acres in CHATEAUNEUF-DU-PAPE. Concentrated wines are entirely GRENACHE, yet can age superbly. "Pignan" is 2nd label.

Château Simone Prov. r. p. or w. dr. ★★ Age 2-6 yrs.
Well-known property in Palette; the only one with a name in this appellation near Aix-en-Provence. The red is best: herby and peppery. Since '85 the white has been catching up.

Château Vignelaure Prov. r. ⁕⁕ 82 83' 84 85 86 87 88
135-acre Provençal estate near Aix making good Bordeaux-style wine
with CABERNET, Syrah and Grenache grapes.

Chatillon-en-Diois Rh. r. p. or w. dr. ★ D.Y.A.
Small appellation e. of the Rhône near Die. Adequate GAMAY reds;
white (some ALIGOTE) mostly made into CLAIRETTE DE DIE.

Chauvenet, F. Large commercial Burgundy firm linked with MARGNAT.
Sound wines, esp. COTE DE BEAUNE whites.

Chave, Gérard To many the top grower of HERMITAGE, red, and white.

Chavignol Village of SANCERRE with famous v'yd, Les Monts Damnés.
Chalky soil gives vivid wines that age 4-5 years.

Chénas B'y. r. ⁕⁕⁕ 85 86 87
Good BEAUJOLAIS CRU, neighbour to MOULIN-A-VENT and JULIENAS. One of
the weightier Beaujolais.

Chenin Blanc See Grapes for white wine.

Chevalier-Montrachet B'y. w. dr. ⁕⁕⁕⁕ 78 81 83 84 85 86 87
17-acre neighbour of MONTRACHET with similar luxurious wine,
perhaps a little less powerful. Includes Les Demoiselles (LATOUR,
JADOT). Other growers incl. BOUCHARD PERE, LEFLAIVE, Niellon, Prieur.

Cheverny Lo. r. p. or w. dr. (sp.) ★→⁕⁕⁕ D.Y.A.
Loire VDQS from near Chambord. CHENIN BL or SAUV BL whites, GAMAY,
P NOIR or CAB reds; generally light but fresh and tasty.

Chevillon, R. Little 21-acre estate at NUITS; outstanding wine-making
since 1980.

Chignin Savoie w. dr. ★ D.Y.A.
Light soft white of Jacquère grapes for Alpine summers. Chignin-
Bergeron should be slightly better.

Chinon Lo. r. ⁕⁕⁕ 82 83' 85 86 88
Delicate fruity CABERNET FRANC from TOURAINE. Drink cool when young.
Exceptional vintages age like Bordeaux. Top growers: Couly-Dutheil,
Joguet, Raffault, Plouzeau.

Chiroubles B'y. r. ⁕⁕⁕ 88
Good but tiny Beaujolais cru next to FLEURIE; freshly fruity silky wine
for early drinking (at 1-2 years).

Chorey-lès-Beaune B'y. r. ⁕⁕ 83 85 86 87 88
Minor appellation on flat land n. of BEAUNE notable for one fine
grower: TOLLOT-BEAUT.

Chusclan Rh. r. p. or w. dr. ★ 86 88
Village of COTE-DU-RHONE-VILLAGES. Good middle-weight wines (rosé
best) from the cooperative.

Cissac HAUT-MEDOC village just w. of PAUILLAC.

Clair, Bruno Recent little domaine at MARSANNAY. V.g. wines from FIXIN,
MOREY-ST-DENIS, SAVIGNY.

Clair-Daü First-class 100-acre burgundy estate of the northern COTE DE
NUITS, with cellars at MARSANNAY. Bought in 1986 by (and now sold as)
JADOT.

Clairet Very light red wine, almost rosé.

Clairette Mediocre white grape of the s. of France. Gives neutral wine.

Clairette de Bellegarde Midi w. dr. ★ D.Y.A.
Plain neutral white from near Nîmes.

Clairette de Die Rh. w. dr. or s./sw. sp. ⁕⁕ NV
Popular dry or (better) semi-sweet rather MUSCAT-flavoured sparkling
wine from the e. Rhône, or straight dry CLAIRETTE white, surprisingly
ageing well 3-4 years.

Clairette du Languedoc Midi w. dr. ★ D.Y.A.
Plain neutral white from near Montpellier.

La Clape Midi r. p. or w. dr. ★→⁕⁕⁕
Full-bodied VDQS wines from limestone hills between Narbonne and
the sea. The red gains character after 2-3 years, the Malvasia white
even longer. V.g. rosé. Some experiments with CHARDONNAY.

Claret Traditional English term for red BORDEAUX.

Climat Burgundian word for individual named v'yd, e.g. Beaune Grèves, Chambolle-Musigny les Amoureuses.

Clos A term carrying some prestige, reserved for distinct, usually walled, v'yds, often in one ownership. Frequent in Burgundy and Alsace. Les Clos is Chablis's Grandest Cru.

Clos-de-Bèze See Chambertin-Clos-de-Bèze.

Clos de la Roche B'y. r. ★★★ 71 76 78 79 80 82 83 84 85′ 86 87
38-acre Grand Cru at MOREY-ST-DENIS. Powerful complex wine like CHAMBERTIN. Producers incl. BOUCHARD PERE, Ponsot, DUJAC, ROUSSEAU Rémy, Castagnier, Lignier.

The Confrèrie des Chevaliers du Tastevin is Burgundy's wine fraternity and the most famous of its kind in the world. It was founded in 1933 by a group of Burgundian patriots, headed by Camille Rodier and Georges Faiveley, to rescue their beloved Burgundy from a period of slump and despair by promoting its inimitable products. Today it regularly holds banquets with elaborate and sprightly ceremonial for 600 guests at its headquarters, the Cistercian château in the Clos de Vougeot. The Confrèrie has branches in many countries and members among lovers of wines all over the world. See also under Tastevin, p. 54.

Clos des Lambrays B'y. r. ★★★ 78 83 84 85 86 87 88
15-acre Grand Cru v'yd at MOREY-ST-DENIS. Changed hands in 1979 after a shaky period. Now looking good.

Clos des Mouches B'y. r. or w. dr. ★★★
Splendid Premier Cru v'yd of BEAUNE owned by DROUHIN. The unusual white made with Pinot Gris is particularly well-made and rewarding.

Clos de Tart B'y. r. ★★★ 71 76 78 79 80 82 83′ 84 85 86 87
18-acre Grand Cru at MOREY-ST-DENIS owned by MOMMESSIN. At best wonderfully fragrant, whether young or old.

Clos de Vougeot B'y. r. ★★★ 71 76 78 80 82 83 85 86 87 88
124-acre COTE-DE-NUITS Grand Cru with many owners. Bewilderingly variable, occasionally sublime. Maturity depends on the grower's technique and position on the hills. Top growers incl: DROUHIN, CLAIR-DAU, DROUHIN-LAROSE, FAIVELEY, Gros, JADOT, Mugneret, Roumier, Grivot.

Clos du Roi B'y. r. ★★★
Part of the Grand Cru CORTON. Also a Premier Cru of BEAUNE.

Clos St Denis B'y. r. ★★★ 76 78 79 80 82 83′ 84 85 86 87 88
16-acre Grand Cru at MOREY-ST-DENIS. Splendid sturdy wine. Growers incl. DUJAC, Lignier, Ponsot.

Clos St Jacques B'y. r. ★★★ 71 76 78 79 80 82 83 84 85 86 87 88
17-acre Premier Cru of GEVREY-CHAMBERTIN. Excellent powerful velvety wine, often better (and dearer) than some of the CHAMBERTIN Grands Crus. Main grower: ROUSSEAU.

Clos St Jean B'y. r. ★★★ 78 79 80 82 83′ 84 85 86 87
36-acre Premier Cru of CHASSAGNE-MONTRACHET. Very good red, more solid than subtle from e.g. CH DE LA MALTROYE.

Coche-Dury 16-acre MEURSAULT domaine (+1 acre CORTON-CHARLEMAGNE) with sky-high reputation.

Cognac Town and region of western France and its brandy.

Collioure Pyr. r. ★ 80 81 82 83 84 85 86
Strong dry RANCIO red from BANYULS area. Small production.

Condrieu Rh. w. dr.★★★★ D.Y.A.
Outstanding soft fragrant white of great character (and price) from the Viognier grape. Only 35 acres of vines. The leading growers are Vernay, Ch du Rozay, Guigal, Pinchon and DELAS. CHATEAU-GRILLET is similar.

Corbières Midi r. or (p.) or (w.) ★—→★★★ 85 86 87 88
Good vigorous bargain reds, steadily improving and now rewarded with AC Rarely disappointing at their price. Best growers incl. Ch'x des Ollieux, Aiguilloux, de Quéribus, Dom de Villemajou, Coops de Paziols, St Laurent-Cabrerisse, etc.

Cordier, Ets D. Important Bordeaux shipper and château-owner, including Ch'x GRUAUD-LAROSE, TALBOT, CANTEMERLE, MEYNEY, LAFAURIE-PEYRAGUEY and also SANCERRE, Clos de la Poussie.

Cornas Rh. r. ★★—→★★★ 78′ 79 80 82 83′ 84 85′ 86 88
Expanding 400-acre district s. of HERMITAGE. Typical sturdy Rhône wine of v.g. quality from the SYRAH grape. Needs 3-6 years ageing. Growers incl. Clape, JABOULET.

Corse The island of Corsica. Strong wines of all colours. Better appellations incl. PATRIMONIO, SARTENE, AJACCIO, CAP CORSE.

Corton B'y. r. ★★★★ 71 76′ 78′ 80 82 83 84 85′ 86 87 88
The only Grand Cru red of the COTE DE BEAUNE. 200 acres in ALOXE-CORTON incl. les Bressandes and CLOS DU ROI. Rich powerful wines should be long-lived. Many good growers.

Corton-Charlemagne B'y. w. dr. ★★★★ 78′ 79 81 82 83 84 85 86 87
The white section (one-third) of CORTON. Rich, spicy, lingering wine. Behaves like a red wine and ages magnificently. Top growers: BONNEAU DU MARTRAY, LATOUR, JADOT.

Costières du Gard Midi r. p. or w. dr. ★—→★★ D.Y.A.
VDQS of moderate (improving) quality from the Rhône delta.

Coteaux Champenois Champ r. (p.) or w. dr. ★★★
The appellation for non-sparkling champagne. Vintages (if mentioned) follow those for Champagne. Do not pay inflated prices.

Coteaux d'Aix-en-Provence Prov r. p. or w. dr. ★—→★★★
An appellation on the move. The established CH VIGNELAURE is challenged by Ch'x Fonscolombe, de Beaulieu, Commanderie de la Bargemone.

Coteaux d'Ancenis Lo. r. p. w. dr. ★ D.Y.A.
Light CABERNET and GAMAY reds and pinks; sharpish whites from MUSCADET country.

Coteaux de la Loire Lo. w. dr. sw. ★★—→★★★ 79 82 83 84 85 86 88
Forceful and fragrant CHENIN BLANC whites from Anjou. The best are in SAVENNIERES. Excellent as an apéritif.

Coteaux de l'Ardéche Central France r. (p. w. dr.) ★ D.Y.A
Flourishing vin de pays: bargain GAMAY, etc.

Coteaux de l'Aubance Lo. p. or w. dr./sw. ★★ D.Y.A.
Light and typical minor ANJOU wines. The best are MOELLEUX.

Coteaux de Peyriac Midi r.p. ★ D.Y.A.
Much the most-used vin de pays name of the Aude département. Huge quantities.

Coteaux de Pierrevert Rh. r. p. or w. dr. or sp. ★ D.Y.A.
Minor southern VDQS from nr. Manosque. Well-made coop wine mostly rosé, with fresh whites.

Coteaux de Saumur Lo. w. dr./sw. ★★ D.Y.A.
Pleasant dry or sweetish fruity CHENIN BLANC.

Coteaux des Baux-en-Provence Prov. r. p. or w. dr. ★—→ ★★
Neighbour of COTEAUX D'AIX, also gathering speed. N.B. Domaine de Trévallon (CABERNET and SYRAH).

Coteaux du Giennois Lo. r. w. dr. ★ D.Y.A.
Minor Loire area n. of SANCERRE. Light GAMAY and PINOT NOIR, SAUVIGNON and CHENIN BLANC.

Coteaux du Languedoc Midi r. p. or w. dr. ★—→★★
Scattered better-than-ordinary Midi areas with AC status. The best reds, (e.g. FAUGERES, St Saturnin, LA CLAPE, ST CHINIAN, Quatourze, St-Georges-d'Orques, Cabrières) age for 2-3 years.

Coteaux du Layon Lo. w. s./sw. or sw. **★★** 78 81 82 83 85 86 88
District centred on Rochefort, s. of Angers, making sweet CHENIN BLANC wines above the general Anjou standard. "C. du L-Chaume" is a slightly higher appellation.

Coteaux du Loir Lo. r. p. or w. dr./sw. **★★** 78 82 83 85 86 88
Small region n. of Tours. Occasionally excellent wines. Best v'yd: JASNIERES. The Loir is a tributary of the Loire.

Coteaux du Lyonnais Rh. r. p. (w. dr.) **★** D.Y.A.
Junior Beaujolais, and whites in keeping, Best EN PRIMEUR.

Coteaux du Tricastin Rh. r. p. or w. dr. **★** 85 86 88
Fringe CÔTES-DU-RHÔNE of increasing quality from s. of Valence. Pierre Labeye is the chief producer. Attractive PRIMEUR red.

Coteaux du Vendomois Lo. r. p. or w. dr. **★** D.Y.A.
Fringe Loire from n. of Blois. Mainly GAMAY.

Coteaux Varoís Prov. r. p. w. dr. **★→★★**
Substantial new VDQS zone with one California-style property, Domaine de St Jean de Villecroze.

Côte(s) Means hillside; generally a superior vineyard to those on the plain. Many appellations start with either Côtes or Coteaux, which means the same thing. In ST-EMILION it distinguishes the valley slopes from the higher plateau.

Côte Chalonnaise B'y. r. w. dr. sp. **★★→★★★**
Lesser-known v'yd area between BEAUNE and MACON. See Mercurey, Givry, Rully, Montagny. Alias "Région de Mercurey".

Côte de Beaune B'y. r. or w. dr. **★★→★★★★**
Used geographically: the southern half of the CÔTE D'OR. Applies as an appellation only to parts of BEAUNE.

Côte de Beaune-Villages B'y. r. or w. dr. **★★** 78 80 83 85 86 87
Regional appellation for secondary wines of the classic area. They cannot be labelled "Côte de Beaune" without either "Villages" or the village name.

Côte de Brouilly B'y. r. **★★★** 86 88
Fruity, rich, vigorous Beaujolais cru. One of the best. Leading estates: Ch Thivin, Domaine de Chavanne.

Côte de Nuits B'y. r. or (w. dr.) **★★→★★★★**
The northern half of the CÔTE D'OR. Nearly all red wine.

Côte de Nuits-Villages B'y. r. (w.) **★★** 78 83 85 86 87
A junior appellation, rarely seen but worth investigating.

Côte d'Or Département name applied to the central and principal Burgundy v'yd slopes, consisting of the CÔTE DE BEAUNE and CÔTE DE NUITS. The name is not used on labels.

Côte Rôtie Rh. r. **★★★** 78 79 80 82 83' 84 85' 86 88
Potentially the finest Rhône red, from just s. of Vienne; achieves complex, almost Bordeaux-like, delicacy with age. Top growers include JABOULET, CHAPOUTIER, VIDAL-FLEURY, Barge, Dervieux, Jasmin, Guigal, Jamet, Rostaing.

Côtes d'Auvergne Central France r. p. or (w. dr.) **★** D.Y.A.
Flourishing small VDQS area near Clermont-Ferrand. Red (at best) like light BEAUJOLAIS. Chanturgues is the best known.

Côtes de Blaye B'x. w. dr. **★** D.Y.A.
Run-of-the-mill Bordeaux white from BLAYE. (Reds are called Premières Côtes de Blaye.)

Côtes de Bordeaux Saint-Macaire B'x. w. dr./sw. **★** D.Y.A.
Run-of-the-mill Bordeaux white from east of SAUTERNES.

Côtes de Bourg B'x. r. **★→★★★** 78 79 81 82 83 85 86 88
Appellation used for many of the better reds of BOURG. Ch'x incl. de Barbe, La Barde, du Bousquet, La Croix de Millorit, de la Grave, Grand-Jour, Font Guilhem, Guerry, Rousset, Lalibarde, La Grolet, Tayac, Lamothe, Mendoce, Falfas, Peychaud, de Thau.

Côtes de Castillon B'x. r. [icon] ★←→★★ 78 82 83 85 86 87 88
Flourishing region just e. of St-Emilion. Similar wines, though a touch lighter. Ch'x incl. Fonds-Rondes, Haut-Tuquet, Lardit, PITRAY, Ste Colombe, Moulin-Rouge, Rocher-Bellevue.

Côtes de Duras Dordogne r. or w. dr. [icon] ★ 85 86 88
Neighbour to BERGERAC, dominated by its v. competent coop. Similar light wines.

Côtes de Francs See Bordeaux – Côtes de Francs.

Côtes de Fronsac See Fronsac.

Côtes de Gascogne s.w. France (r.) w. dr. [icon] ★ D.Y.A.
Vin de pays gaining a name for deliciously floral SAUVIGNON whites in bountiful supply.

Côtes de Montravel Dordogne w. dr./sw. [icon] ★ NV
Part of BERGERAC; traditional medium-sw. wine, now often dry.

Côtes de Provence Prov. r. p. or w. dr. ★→★★
The wine of Provence; still often with more alcohol than character, though standards are rapidly improving as new investors move in. 60% is rosé, 30% red. See under Coteaux d'Aix, Bandol, etc.

Côtes de Saint-Mont s.w. France r. w. dr. p. [icon] ★
Promising VDQS from the Gers, not unlike MADIRAN. The same coop AS COTES DE GASCOGNE.

Côtes de Thongue Midi r. w. dr. [icon] ★ D.Y.A.
Above-average Vins de Pays from the HERAULT.

Côtes de Toul e. France r. p. or w. dr. ★ D.Y.A.
Very light wines from Lorraine; mainly VIN GRIS (rosé).

Côtes du Forez Central France r. or p. [icon] ★ D.Y.A.
Light Beaujolais-style red, can be good in warm years.

Côtes du Frontonnais s.w. France r. or p. [icon] ★→★★ D.Y.A.
The local wine of Toulouse, gaining admirers elsewhere. Ch Bellevue-la-Forêt (250 acres) makes outstanding silky red.

Côtes du Haut-Roussillon s.w. France br. sw. ★→★★ NV
Area for VINS DOUX NATURELS n. of Perpignan.

Côtes du Jura Jura r. p. or w. dr. (sp.) ★ D.Y.A.
Various light tints and tastes. ARBOIS is theoretically better.

Côtes du Luberon Rh. r. p. or w. dr. sp. [icon] ★←→★★
Improving country wines from northern Provence. The star is Ch Val-Joannis, with good largely SYRAH red, and whites as well. Others incl. a good coop and Ch de Sannes.

Côtes du Marmandais Dordogne r. p. or w. dr. ★ D.Y.A.
Light wines from s.e. of Bordeaux. The coop at Cocumont makes most of the best.

Côtes-du-Rhône Rh. r. p. or w. dr. ★→★★ 88
The basic appellation of the Rhône valley. Best drunk young – even as PRIMEUR. Wide variations of quality due to grape ripeness, therefore tending to rise with alcohol %. See Côtes-du-Rhône-Villages.

Côtes-du-Rhône-Villages Rh. r. p. or w. dr. ★→ ★★ 85 86 88
The wine of the 17 best villages of the southern Rhône. Substantial and on the whole reliable. Sometimes delicious.

Côtes du Roussillon Pyr. r. p. or w. dr. [icon] ★←→★★ 85 86 87 88
Country wine of e. Pyrenees. The hefty reds are best and can be very tasty. Some whites are sharp VINS VERTS.

Côtes du Roussillon-Villages Pyr. r. ★★ 83 84 85 86 87 88
The best reds of the region, incl. CARAMANY and LATOUR DE FRANCE.

Côtes du Ventoux Prov. r. (w. dr.) ★★ 83 85 86
Booming appellation for tasty reds between the Rhône and Provence. La Vieille Ferme, owned by CH DE BEAUCASTEL, is top producer.

Côtes du Vivarais Prov. r. p. or w. dr. ★
Pleasant country wines from s. Massif Centrale. Like light COTES-DU-RHONE.

38

Côtes Roannaises Central France r. ✷ D.Y.A.
Minor GAMAY region high up the LOIRE.

Coulée de Serrant Lo. w. dr./sw. ✭✭✭ 76 78 79 81 82 83 84 85 86
10-acre v'yd on n. bank of LOIRE at SAVENNIERES, Anjou. Intense strong fruity/sharp wine, good as an apéritif. Ages well.

Crémant In Champagne means "Creaming" – i.e. half-sparkling. Since 1975 an appellation for high-quality champagne-method sparkling wines from Alsace, the Loire and Bourgogne – often a notable bargain. e.g. . . .

Crémant de Loire w. dr. sp. ✭✭ NV
High-quality sparkling wine from ANJOU and TOURAINE.

Crépy Savoie w. dr. ✭✭ D.Y.A.
Light, soft, Swiss-style white from s. shore of Lake Geneva. "Crépitant" has been coined for its faint fizz.

Criots-Bâtard-Montrachet B'y. w. ✭✭✭ 78 79 81 82 83 84 85 86 88
4-acre neighbour to BATARD-MONTRACHET. Similar wine.

Burgundy boasts one of the world's most famous and certainly its most beautiful hospital, the Hospices de Beaune, founded in 1443 by Nicolas Rolin, Chancellor to the Duke of Burgundy, and his wife Guigone de Salins. The hospital he built and endowed with vineyards for its income still operates in the same building and still thrives, tending the sick of Beaune without charge, on the sale of its wine. Many growers since have bequeathed their land to the Hospices. Today it owns 125 acres of prime land in Beaune, Pommard, Volnay, Meursault, Corton and Mazis-Chambertin. The wine is sold by public auction every year on the third Sunday in November.

Crozes-Hermitage Rh. r. or (w. dr.) ✭✭ 78 80 82 83 84 85 86
Larger and less distinguished neighbour to HERMITAGE. Robust and often excellent reds, but choose carefully: e.g. Domaine de Thalabert of JABOULET.

Cru "Growth", as in "first-growth" – meaning vineyard. Also, in BEAUJOLAIS, one of the top nine villages.

Cru Bourgeois General term for MEDOC châteaux below CRU CLASSE.

Cru Bourgeois Supérieur (Cru Grand Bourgeois) Official rank one better than the last. Must be aged in barrels.

Cru Classé Classed growth. One of the first five official quality classes of the Médoc, classified in 1855. Also any classed growth of another district (e.g. GRAVES, ST-EMILION, SAUTERNES).

Cru Grand Bourgeois Exceptionnel Official rank above CRU BOURGEOIS SUPERIEUR, immediately below CRU CLASSE. Several fine châteaux are unofficially acknowledged (and labelled) as Exceptionnel, which makes them on a par with many CRUS CLASSES.

Cruse et Fils Frères Long-established Bordeaux shipper. Owned by the Société des Vins de France. Members of the Cruse family own Ch D'ISSAN.

Cubzac, St.-André-de B'x. r. or w. dr. ✭ 82 83 85 86 88
Town 15 miles n.e. of Bordeaux, centre of the minor Cubzaguais region. Sound reds have the appellation Bordeaux. Estates include: Ch du Bouilh, Ch de TERREFORT-QUANCARD, Ch TIMBERLAY, Domaine de Beychevelle.

Cussac Village just s. of ST JULIEN. Appellation Haut-Médoc.

Cuve Close Short-cut method of making sparkling wine in a tank. The sparkle dies away in the glass much quicker than with METHODE CHAMPENOISE wine.

Cuvée de la Commanderie Pleasant blend made for the Commanderie du Bontemps, the ceremonial/promotional body of the Médoc and Graves.

Cuvée The quality of wine produced in a "cuve" or vat. Also a word of many uses, incl. "blend". In Burgundy interchangeable with "Cru". Often just refers to a "lot" of wine.

d'Angerville, Marquis Famous burgundy grower with immaculate estate in VOLNAY.

Degré alcoolique Degrees of alcohol, i.e. percent by volume.

De Ladoucette Leading producer of POUILLY-FUME, based at CH DE NOZET. Luxury brand "Baron de L". Also SANCERRE Comte Lafond.

Delagrange-Bachelet Leading proprietors in CHASSAGNE-MONTRACHET with many family ramifications.

Delas Frères Long-established and excellent firm of Rhône-wine specialists at Tournon, v'yds at COTE ROTIE, HERMITAGE, esp. Cuvée de la Tourette CORNAS, CONDRIEU, etc. Owned by DEUTZ.

Delorme, André Leading merchants and growers of the COTE CHALONNAISE. Specialists in sparkling wine and excellent RULLY.

De Luze, A. et Fils Bordeaux shipper owned by Rémy-Martin of Cognac. Members of the De Luze family own Ch PAVEIL DE LUZE.

Demi-Sec "Half-dry": in practice more than half sweet.

Depagneux, Jacques de Cie Well-regarded merchants of BEAUJOLAIS.

Deutz Brut NV and 75 76 79 81 82, Rosé 82, Blanc de Blancs 78 79 81 82 One of the best of the smaller champagne houses. Full-flavoured wines. Luxury brand: Cuvée William Deutz (75 79 82).

Domaine Property, particularly in Burgundy.

Domaine de l'Eglantière Important CHABLIS estate. See Durup.

Domaine du Vieux Télégraphe Rh. r. (w. dr.) ★★★ 76 78 79 81 83 84 85 86 A leader in fine modern CHATEAUNEUF-DU-PAPE.

Dom Pérignon 70 71 73 75 76 78 80 82 and Rosé 75 78 Luxury brand of MOET & CHANDON, named after the legendary Abbey cellarmaster who "invented" champagne. The '82 is exceptionally good.

Dopff "au Moulin" Ancient and top-class family wine-house at Riquewihr, Alsace. Best wines: Riesling Schoenenbourg, Gewürztraminer Eichberg. Pioneers of sparkling wine in Alsace.

Dopff & Irion Another excellent Riquewihr (ALSACE) business. Best wines include Muscat les Amandiers, Riesling de Riquewihr.

Doudet-Naudin Burgundy merchant and grower at Savigny-lès-Beaune. V'yds incl. BEAUNE CLOS DU ROI. Dark long-lived wines supplied to Berry Bros & Rudd of London.

Dourthe Frères Well-reputed Bordeaux merchant representing a wide range of ch'x, mainly good Crus Bourgeois, incl. Ch'x MAUCAILLOU, TRONQUOY-LALANDE, BELGRAVE. "Beau-Mayne" is their reliable branded Bordeaux.

Doux Sweet.

Drouhin, J. & Cie Deservedly prestigious Burgundy grower (130 acres) and merchant. Offices in BEAUNE, v'yds in BEAUNE, MUSIGNY, CLOS DE VOUGEOT, CHABLIS, etc. Drouhin also owns Jaffelin et Cie and a v'yd in Oregon. Top wines incl. Beaune Clos de Mouches and Puligny-Montrachet Les Folatières.

Drouhin-Larose Prosperous little domaine in GEVREY-CHAMBERTIN, CLOS DE VOUGEOT, etc.

Duboeuf, Georges Top-class BEAUJOLAIS merchant at Romanèche-Thorin. The leader of the region in every sense, with a huge range of admirable wines.

Dufouleur Frères Large scale growers and merchants of burgundy at NUIT-ST-GEORGES and MERCUREY.

Dujac, Domaine Fashionable burgundy grower at MOREY-ST-DENIS with v'yds in that village, ECHEZEAUX, BONNES-MARES, GEVREY-CHAMBERTIN, etc. His best wines are splendidly vivid and long-lived.

Durup, Jean One of the biggest Chablis growers with 140 acres, including the DOMAINE DE L'EGLANTIERE and admirable Ch de Maligny.

Echézeaux B'y. r. ■ *** 76 78' 79 80 82 83' 84 85 86 87 88
74-acre Grand Cru between vosne-romanee and clos de vougeot. Can be superlative fragrant burgundy without great weight e.g. from Mugneret, Gouroux, dom de la romanee-conti, Jacqueline Jayer.

Edelzwicker Alsace w. ■ * D.Y.A.
Light white from mixture of grapes, often fruity and good.

Engel, R. Well-known grower of vosne-romanee and neighbourhood.

Entre-Deux-Mers B'x. w. dr. ■ * D.Y.A.
Standard dry white Bordeaux from between the Garonne and Dordogne rivers. Often a good buy, esp. "La Gamage", Ch'x st bonnet, Gournin, Latour-Laguens, Launay, Thieuley.

Eschenauer, Louis Famous Bordeaux merchants, owners of Ch'x rausan-segla and smith-haut-lafitte, de lamouroux and la garde in graves. Controlled by John Holt, part of the Lonrho group.

L'Estaudon The vin ordinaire of Nice (AC Côtes de Provence).

l'Etoile Jura w. dr./sw./sp. **
Sub-region of the Jura known for stylish whites, incl. vin jaune like chateau-chalon and good sparkling.

Faiveley, J. Family-owned growers (with 182 acres) and merchants at nuits-st-georges, with v'yds in chambertin-clos-de-beze, chambolle-musigny, corton, nuits, mercurey (150 acres). Consistent high quality recently. Wines for serious ageing.

Faller, Théo Top alsace grower at the Domaine Weinbach, Kaysersberg. Concentrated firm wines need ageing.

Faugères Midi r. (p. or w. dr.) ■→*** 86 87 88
Isolated village of the coteaux du languedoc making above-average wine. Became Appellation Contrôlée in 1982.

Fessy, Sylvain Dynamic beaujolais merchant with wide range.

Feuillatte, Nicolas NV Brut, Rosé
Champagne marque popular in restaurants. Rosé esp. good.

Fèvre, William Conservative Chablis grower with the biggest Grand Cru holding (40 acres). His label is Domaine de la Maladière.

Fitou Midi r. ** 84 85 86 88
Superior corbieres red; powerful and ages well. Mostly from coop at Tuchan. Recent popularity has not improved standards.

Fixin B'y. r. ■ ** 78 80 83 84 85 86 87 88
A worthy and under-valued neighbour to gevrey-chambertin. Often splendid reds. Best v'yds: Clos du Chapitre, Les Hervelets, Clos Napoléon. Top growers: Clair, Bertheau, Gelin.

Fleurie B'y. r. *** 85 86 87 88
The epitome of a beaujolais cru: fruity, scented, silky, racy.

Frais Fresh or cool.

Frappé Ice-cold.

Froid Cold.

Fronsac B'x. r. ■→** 75 78 79 81 82 83 85 86
Pretty hilly area of good reds just w. of St-Emilion. Ch'x incl. Dalem, La Dauphine, Mayne-Vieil, la Rivière, de Carles, La Valade, Villars, La Vieille Cure. See also Canon-Fronsac.

Frontignan Midi br. sw. ■ * NV
Strong sweet and liquorous muscat wine.

Gagnard-Delagrange, Jacques Estimable small (13-acre) grower of chassagne-montrachet, including some le montrachet.

Gaillac s.w. France r. p. or w. dr./sw. or sp. ■ *
Ancient area showing signs of new life after generations of dullness. Slightly fizzy "Perlé" is good value. Reds can age well. Ch Larroze is the quality leader. The major coop at Labastide de Lévis has recently produced some lovely fruity wines.

Gallairé Bordeaux merchant house of Peter A. Sichel, much-respected owner of Ch d'angludet.

Gamay See Grapes for red wine.

Geisweiler et Fils One of the bigger merchant-houses of Burgundy: cellars and 50 acres of v'yds at NUITS-ST-GEORGES. Also 150 acres at Bevy in the HAUTES COTES DE NUITS and 30 in the COTE CHALONNAISE.

Gevrey-Chambertin B'y. r. ★★★ 76 78 79 80 82 83 85 86 87 88
The village containing the great CHAMBERTIN and many other noble v'yds, as well as a considerable number more commonplace. Top growers incl. Leclerc, ROTY, ROUSSEAU, DROUHIN-LAROSE, FAIVELEY.

Gewürztraminer The speciality grape of ALSACE: perfumed and spicy, whether dry or sweet.

Gigondas Rh. r. or p. ★★ 78 80 81 83 84 85 86 88
Worthy neighbour to CHATEAUNEUF-DU-PAPE. Strong, full-bodied, sometimes peppery wine, e.g. Dom du Pesquier, Dom du Cayron, Dom les Pallières, Dom Raspail-Ay, and wines from MEFFRE.

Gilbey, S.A. British firm long-established as Bordeaux merchants at Ch LOUDENNE in the MEDOC. Now owned by Grand Met.

Gisselbrecht, Louis High-quality Alsace shippers at Dambach-la-Ville.

Givry B'y. r. or w. dr. ★★ 83 84 85 86 87 88
Underrated village of the COTE CHALONNAISE: light but tasty and typical burgundy from e.g. Baron Thénard, Clos Salomon.

Gosset NV, 73 75 76 78 79 80 81 82 83 85 "Grande Réserve" and Rosé NV Small, very old champagne house at Ay. Fine full wines (esp. Grande Réserve). Now linked with Philipponnat.

Gouges, Henri Worthy burgundy grower of NUITS-ST-GEORGES. Good reds and very rare white "La Perrière".

Goulaine, Château de The ceremonial showplace of MUSCADET; a noble family estate and its appropriate wine.

Goulet, Georges NV, rosé 76 79, Crémant Blanc de Blancs 79 and 71 73 75 76 79 81 High-quality Reims champagne house linked with Abel Lepitre. Luxury brand: Cuvée du Centenaire 74 76 79.

Goût Taste, e.g. "goût anglais" – as the English like it (i.e. dry).

Grand Cru One of the top Burgundy v'yds with its own appellation contrôlée. Similar in Alsace but more vague elsewhere. In ST-EMILION the third rank of château, numbering about 200.

Grand Roussillon Midi br. sw. ★★ NV
Broad appellation for muscat and other sweet fortified wines ("Vins Doux Naturels") of eastern Pyrenees.

Grands-Echézeaux B'y. r. ★★★★ 69 71 76 78 79 80 82 83 84 85 86 87 88 Superlative 22-acre Grand Cru next to CLOS DE VOUGEOT. Top grower: Dom de la ROMANEE-CONTI.

Gratien, Alfred and Gratien & Meyer Excellent smaller champagne house (fine, very dry, long-lasting wines 73 76 79 82 83) and its counterpart at SAUMUR on the Loire.

Graves B'x. r. or w. ★→★★★★
Large region s. of Bordeaux city. Most of its best wines are red, but the name is used chiefly for its dry whites.

Graves-Pessac-Léognan New AOC for part of n. Graves, incl. the area of most of the Grands Crus. Since 1987 Pessac-Léognan alone has been allowed.

Graves de Vayres B'x. r. or w. ★
Part of ENTRE-DEUX-MERS; of no special character.

Les Gravières B'y. r. ███
Famous Premier Cru v'yd of SANTENAY. Incl. Clos des Tavannes.

Grivot, Jean 25-acre COTE DE NUITS domaine, in VOSNE-ROMANEE, CLOS DE VOUGEOT, etc. Top quality.

Griotte-Chambertin B'y. r. ★★★ 69 71 76 78' 79 80 83 84 85' 86 87 14-acre Grand Cru adjoining CHAMBERTIN. Similar wine, but less masculine and more "tender". Growers incl. DROUHIN.

Gros Plant du Pays Nantais Lo. w. ███ D.Y.A.
Junior cousin of MUSCADET, sharper and lighter; made of the COGNAC grape also known as Folle Blanche, Ugni Blanc, etc.

Haut-Benauge B'x. w. dr. ★ D.Y.A.

    Appellation for a limited area within ENTRE-DEUX-MERS.

Hautes-Côtes de Beaune B'y. r. or w. dr. ★★ 85 86 87 88

    Appellation for a dozen villages in the hills behind the COTE DE BEAUNE. Light wines worth investigating.

Hautes-Côtes de Nuits B'y. r. or w. dr. ★★ 78 83 85 86 87 88

    The same for the COTE DE NUITS. An area on the way up. Has a large coop in BEAUNE. Also good wines from GEISWEILER.

Haut-Médoc B'x. r. ★★→★★★ 70 75 76 78 79 80 81 82 83 84 85 86 88

    Big appellation including all the best areas of the Médoc. Most of the zone has communal appellations (e.g. MARGAUX, PAUILLAC). Some fine ch'x (e.g. LA LAGUNE) are simply AC Haut-Médoc.

Haut-Montravel Dordogne w. sw. ★ 82 83 85 86 88

    Medium-sweet BERGERAC.

Haut Poitou Lo. (r.) w. d.r. ★★→★★★ D.Y.A.

    Up-and-coming VDQS area south of ANJOU. Cooperative makes v. good whites, incl. CHARDONNAY and SAUVIGNON BLANC.

Heidsieck, Charles NV, rosé 81 and 73 75 76 79 81

    Major champagne house of Reims, now controlled by Rémy Martin; also includes Trouillard and de Venoge. Luxury brands: Cuvée Champagne Charlie 79 81. Fine quality recently.

Heidsieck, Monopole NV, rosé and 73 75 76 79 82

    Important champagne merchant and grower of Reims now owned by MUMM. V.g luxury brand: Diamant Bleu (76 79) and Diamant rosé 82.

Henriot NV, Blanc de Blancs Crémant Brut Souverain NV; Brut Rosé 81 83; Cuvée Baccarat 79; and 79 Old family champagne house now owned by VEUVE CLICQUOT. Very big dry style. Luxury brand: Réserve Baron Philippe de Rothschild.

Hérault Midi

    The biggest v'yd département in France with 400,000 hectares of vines. Chiefly vin ordinaire but some good COTEAUX DU LANGUEDOC.

Hermitage Rh. r. or w. dr. ★★★ 71 76 79 80 82 83' 84 85 86 88

    The "manliest" wine of France. Dark, powerful and profound. Needs long ageing. The white is heady and golden; now usually made for early drinking, though the best wines mature for many years. Top makers: CHAVE, JABOULET, CHAPOUTIER, Guigal, Grippat.

Hospices de Beaune Historic hospital in BEAUNE, with excellent v'yds in MEURSAULT, POMMARD, VOLNAY, BEAUNE, CORTON, etc. See panel on p. 38.

Hugel Père et Fils The best-known ALSACE growers and merchants. Founded at Riquewihr in 1639 and still in the family. Best wines are sweet: Cuvées Exceptionnelles, Selections de Grains Nobles.

I'Ile de Beauté Name given to VIN DU PAYS from CORSICA. Two-thirds of it is red.

Imperiale Bordeaux bottle holding 8½ normal bottles (5 litres).

Irancy B'y. r. (or p.) ★★ 83 85 86 88

    Good light red made near CHABLIS of PINOT NOIR and "César". The best vintages are long-lived and mature well. To watch.

Irouléguy s.w. France r. p. (or w. dr.) ★★ D.Y.A.

    Agreeable local wines of the Basque country.

Jaboulet, Paul Old family firm at Tain, leading growers of HERMITAGE (esp. "La Chapelle" ★★★★) and merchants in other RHONE wines.

Jaboulet-Vercherre et Cie Well-known Burgundy merchant-house with v'yds (34 acres) in POMMARD, etc, and cellars in Beaune. Middling wines.

Jadot, Louis Much-respected top-quality Burgundy merchant-house with v'yds (50 acres) in BEAUNE, CORTON, etc. Includes former estate of CLAIR-DAU (e.g. Bonnes Mares, etc).

Jaffelin Independently-run high-quality négociant, owned by DROUHIN.

Jardin de la France Name given to VINS DU PAYS of the LOIRE valley. The great majority is dry white.

Jasnières Lo. (r.) (p.) or w. dr. ★★★ 71 76 78 79 80 82 83 84 85 86
Rare dry, rather vouvray-like wine of n. Touraine.

Jaubertie, Domaine de la Top bergerac estate of 114 acres, English-owned. Cuvée Mirabelle is a sumptuous luxury Sauvignon Blanc. The reserve red is equally fine.

Jayer, Henri Tiny vosne-romanee domaine acknowledged even by rivals as superlative. (Monsieur J. retired in '88).

Jeroboam In Bordeaux a 6-bottle bottle (holding 5 litres), or triple magnum; in Champagne a double magnum.

Josmeyer Family house at Wintzenheim, alsace. V.g. long-ageing wines, esp. gewürz and pinot blanc.

Juliénas B'y. r. ★★★ 88
Leading cru of Beaujolais: vigorous fruity wine.

Jura See Côtes de Jura.

Jurançon s.w. France w. sw. or dr. ★★ 78 79 81 82 83 84 85 86
Unusual high-flavoured and long-lived speciality of Pau in the Pyrenean foothills. Both sweet and dry should age well for several years. Top growers: Barrère, Chigné, Guirouilh, Lamouroux, Ramonteu. Also the coop's "Grain Sauvage".

Kressman, E.S. & Cie Bordeaux merchants and owners of Ch latour-martillac in graves. "Monopole Rouge" is a standard blend. The Kressman family owns Ch Latour Martillac.

Kriter Popular low-price sparkling wine processed in Burgundy by patriarche.

Krug "Grande Cuvée" (NV), 64 66 69 71 73 75 76 79 81, Rosé and Clos du Mesnil Blanc de Blancs 79 80 Small but very prestigious champagne house known for full-bodied very dry wines of the highest quality.

Kuentz-Bas Top-quality alsace grower and merchant at Husseren-les-Châteaux, esp. for gewürztraminer.

Labarde Village just s. of margaux and included in that appellation. Best ch: giscours.

Labouré-Gontard Makes high-quality cremant de Bourgogne at nuits.

Labouré-Roi V. good merchant at nuits-st-georges. Many domaine wines, esp. Remé Manuel's meursault.

Lafarge, Michel 23-acre cote de beaune estate, mainly in volnay and Meursault. Fine quality.

Lafon, Domaine des Comtes 31-acre top-quality Burgundy estate in volnay, meursault and le montrachet.

Laguiche, Marquis de Largest owner of le montrachet. Wines made by drouhin.

Lalande de Pomerol B'x. r. ▬▬ ★★ 75 78 81 82 83 85 86 88
Neighbour to pomerol. Wines similar but considerably less fine. Top ch'x, Les Annereaux, Les Hauts-Conseillants, Les Hauts-Tuileries, Moncets, Tournefeuille, Belair, Siaurac.

Langlois-Château Producer of sparkling saumur, controlled by bollinger.

Langon The principal town of the s. graves/sauternes district.

Lanson Père et Fils Black Label NV, rosé NV, Red Label 75 76 79 81 82 Important Champagne house, cellars at Reims. Luxury brand: Noble Cuvée 81. Black Label is a reliable fresh NV.

Laroche Important (238 acres) grower and merchant of chablis, incl. Domaines Laroche, La Jouchère. Labels incl. Bacheroy-Josselin. Also runs the Château de puligny-montrachet.

Latour, Louis Top Burgundy merchant and grower with v'yds. (120 acres) in corton, beaune, etc. Among the best, esp. for white wines.

Latour de France r. (w. dr.) ★→★★ 83 85 86 87 88
New appellation in cotes de roussillon-villages.

Latricières-Chambertin B'y. r. ★★★ 76 78 79 80 82 83 84 85' 86 87 88
17-acre Grand Cru neighbour of chambertin. Similar wine, but lighter and "prettier" e.g. from faiveley, Ponsot, Trapet.

44

Laudun Rh. r. p. or w. dr. ★
Village of COTES-DU-RHONE-VILLAGES. Attractive wines from the cooperative incl. fresh whites.

Laugel, Michel One of the biggest ALSACE merchant-houses, at Marlenheim.

Laurent-Perrier NV, rosé brut and 71 73 75 76 78 79 81 82
Excellent and highly successful young champagne house at Tourssur-Marne. Luxury brand: Cuvée Grande Siècle. Ultra Brut is the best buy.

Leflaive, Domaine Perhaps the best of all white burgundy growers, at PULIGNY-MONTRACHET. Best v'yds: Clavoillons, Pucelles, Bienvenue-, Chevalier-Montrachet.

Leflaive, Olivier Négociant at Puligny-Montrachet since '84, nephew of the above. Excellent whites and reds, incl. less famous appellations.

Léognan B'x.
Leading village of the GRAVES. Best ch'x: DOMAINE DE CHEVALIER, MALARTIC-LAGRAVIERE and HAUT-BAILLY.

Leroy Important négociant-élèveur at AUXEY-DURESSES with a small domaine and the finest stocks of old wines in Burgundy. Part-owners and distributors of the DOMAINE DE LA ROMANEE-CONTI.

Burgundy: a grower's own label

MISE EN BOUTEILLES
AU DOMAINE
VOLNAY
LES CAILLERETS
APPELLATION CONTROLEE
DOMAINE DE LA POUSSE D'OR
A VOLNAY, COTE D'OR

Domaine is the burgundy equivalent of château.
The Appellation Contrôlée is Volnay.
The individual v'yd in Volnay is called Les Caillerets.
The name and address of the grower/producer.
(The word propriétaire is often also used.)

A merchant's label

GEVREY-CHAMBERTIN
CLOS ST JACQUES
APPELLATION CONTROLEE
REMOISSENET PERE ET FILS
NEGOCIANTS A BEAUNE

The village.
The vineyard.
The wine qualifies for the Appellation Gevrey-Chambertin Premier Cru.
Remoissenet Père et Fils is a négociant, or merchant, who bought the wine from the grower to mature, bottle and sell.

Lichine, Alexis et Cie Post-war Bordeaux merchants, proprietors of Ch LASCOMBES. No longer connected with the author Alexis Lichine (see Château Prieuré Lichine, Bordeaux).

Lie, sur "On the lees." Muscadet is often bottled straight from the vat, without "racking" or filtering (or so its makers say), for maximum freshness.

Limoux Pyr. r. or w. dr. ★★ NV
The austerely dry non-sparkling version of BLANQUETTE DE LIMOUX (sometimes labelled Limoux Nature) and a good fresh claret-like red from the cooperative: Anne des Joyeuses.

Lirac Rh. r. p. or (w. dr.) ★★ 81 83 84 85 86
Neighbouring village to TAVEL. Similar wine; the red becoming more important than the rosé, esp. Ch de Segriés, Dom St-Roch.

Listel Midi r. p. w. dr. ✱—➤✱✱✱ D.Y.A.

Vast historic estate on the sandy beaches of the Golfe du Lion. Owned by the giant Salins du Midi, making very pleasant light "vins des sables" incl. sparkling. Domaine du Bosquet is a light fruity red. Domaine de Villeroy is a fresh blanc de blancs "SUR LIE". Also a fruity, almost non-alcoholic "Pétillant".

Listrac B'x. r. ✱✱➤ ✱✱✱

Village of HAUT-MEDOC next to MOULIS. Best ch'x: FOURCAS-HOSTEN, FOURCAS-DUPRE, CLARKE, Fonreaud.

Long-Depaquit V.g. CHABLIS domaine (esp. MOUTONNE), owned by BICHOT.

Lorentz Two small high-quality Alsace houses at Bergheim, Gustave L. and Jerome L, have the same management.

Loron et Fils Big-scale burgundy grower and merchant, specialist in BEAUJOLAIS and sound VINS DE TABLE.

Loupiac B'x. w. sw. ✱✱ 76 79 80 81 83 85 86 88

Across the R. Garonne from SAUTERNES Top ch'x: Loupiac-Gaudiet, de Ricaud, Haut-Loupiac, Clos-Jean, Rondillon.

Ludon HAUT-MEDOC village s. of MARGAUX. Best ch: LA LAGUNE.

Lugny ("Macon-Lugny") B'y. r. w. dr. sp. ✱✱ 86 87 88

Village next to VIRE with active and good cooperative. Wine of Les Genevrières v'yd is sold by Louis LATOUR.

Lupé-Cholet et Cie Merchants and growers at NUITS-ST-GEORGES controlled by BICHOT. Best estate wines: Château Gris and Clos de Lupé.

Lussac-Saint-Emilion B'x. r. ✱✱ 78 79 81 82 83 85 86 88

N.e. neighbour to ST-EMILION. Top ch'x incl. Lyonnat, Tour de Grenat, Bel Air, Villadière. Coop (at PUISSEGUIN) makes "Roc de Lussac".

Macau HAUT-MEDOC village s. of MARGAUX. Best ch: CANTEMERLE.

macération carbonique Traditional technique of fermentation with whole bunches of unbroken grapes in a vat full of carbon dioxide. Fermentation inside each grape eventually bursts it, giving vivid and very fruity mild wine for quick consumption. Esp. in BEAUJOLAIS; now much used in the MIDI and elsewhere.

Machard de Gramont Burgundy family estate: cellars in NUITS and v'yds in NUITS, SAVIGNY, BEAUNE, POMMARD. Extremely well-made reds.

Mâcon B'y. r. (p.) or w. dr. ✱✱ 86 87 88

Southern district of sound, usually unremarkable, reds and tasty dry (CHARDONNAY) whites. Wine with a village name (e.g. Mâcon-Prissé) is better. POUILLY-FUISSE is best appellation of the region. See also Mâcon-Villages.

Mâcon-Lugny See Lugny.

Mâcon Supérieur The same but slightly better, from riper grapes.

Mâcon-Villages B'y. w. dr. ✱✱—➤✱✱✱ 86 87 88

Increasingly well-made and typical white burgundies. Mâcon-Prissé, MACON-VIRE, MACON-LUGNY, Mâcon-Clessé are examples.

Mâcon-Viré See Mâcon-Villages and Viré.

Madiran s.w. France r. ✱✱ 75 78 79 81 82 83 84 85 86 88

Dark vigorous fragrant red from ARMAGNAC. Well worth ageing. Top growers: Dom de Bouscassé, Peyros, Laplace, Barréjat. Value.

Magenta, Duc de Burgundy estate (30 acres) based at CHASSAGNE-MONTRACHET, managed by JADOT.

Magnum A double bottle (1.5 litres).

Mähler-Besse First-class Dutch wine-merchants in Bordeaux, with a share in Ch PALMER. Brands incl. Cheval Noir.

Maire, Henri The biggest grower and merchant of JURA wines. Not the best.

Marc Grape skins after pressing; also the strong-smelling brandy made from them (cf. Italian "Grappa").

Marcillac s.w. France r. p. ✱ D.Y.A.

Good rustic VDQS from the coop.

46

Margaux B'x. r. ★★→★★★★ 66 70 75 76 78 79 80 81 82 83' 84 85 86
Village of the HAUT-MEDOC making the most "elegant" red Bordeaux. The appellation includes CANTENAC and several other villages as well. Top ch'x include MARGAUX, LASCOMBES, etc.

Margnat Major producer of everyday VIN DE TABLE.

Marque déposée Trade mark.

Marsannay B'y. (r.) p. or w. dr. ███ ★★★ 78 80 83 85 86 87 (rosé D.Y.A.)
Village near Dijon with excellent light red and delicate PINOT NOIR rosé, perhaps the best rosé in France. Growers incl. CLAIR, Quillardet, Trapet.

Mas de Daumas Gassac Midi r. (w. dr) ███ ★★★ 80 81 82 83 84 85 86
The outstanding estate of the MIDI, producing huge Bordeaux-like, largely CABERNET wines on apparently unique soil. Also "Rosé Frisant" and now a sumptuous white of CHARDONNAY and VIOGNIER. Alarming quality.

Maufoux, Prosper Family firm of burgundy merchants at SANTENAY. Reliable wines esp. whites, with good keeping qualities. Alias Marcel Amance.

Maury Pyr. r. sw. ★→★★ NV
Red VIN DOUX NATUREL from ROUSSILLON.

Mazis (or Mazy) Chambertin B'y. r. ★★★ 76 78 80 82 83 85 86 87 88
30-acre Grand Cru neighbour of CHAMBERTIN. Lighter wine. Best from LEROY.

Médoc B'x. r. ★★ 78 79 81 82 83 84 85 86 88
Appellation for reds of the less good (n.) part of Bordeaux's biggest and best district. Flavours tend to slight earthiness. HAUT-MEDOC is better.

Meffre, Gabriel The biggest southern Rhône estate, based at GIGONDAS. Includes Ch de Vaudieu, CHATEAUNEUF-DU-PAPE. Variable quality.

Ménétou-Salon Lo. r. p. or w. dr. ★★ D.Y.A.
Attractive light wines from w. of SANCERRE. SAUVIGNON white; PINOT NOIR red.

Mercier et Cie NV, Extra Rich and Rosé 80 81 82 and 73 75 76 78 80 81 82 One of the biggest champagne houses, at Epernay. Controlled by MOET & CHANDON. Commercial quality. Belle d'Or is new (1988) NV.

Mercurey B'y. r. or w. dr ███ ★★ 78 83 84 85 86 87
Leading red-wine village of the COTE CHALONNAISE. Good middle-rank burgundy. Growers incl. Ch de Chamirey, FAIVELEY, Chanzy.

Mercurey, Région de The up-to-date way of referring to the COTE CHALONNAISE.

Métaireau, Louis The ring-leader of a group of top Muscadet growers. Expensive well-finished wines.

méthode champenoise The traditional laborious method of putting the bubbles in champagne by refermenting the wine in its bottle.

Meursault B'y. (r.) w. dr. ★★★ 78 81 82 83 85 86 87 88
COTE DE BEAUNE village with some of the world's greatest whites: rich, savoury, dry but mellow. Best v'yds: Perrières, Genevrières, Charmes. Others v.g. incl. Goutte d'Or, Meursault-Blagny, Poruzots, Tillets. Top growers incl: AMPEAU, COCHE-DURY, Delagrange, LAFON, LATOUR, MAGENTA, Matrot, Michelot-Buisson, CH DE MEURSAULT, P. Morey, G. ROULOT, Manuel, Jobard. See also Blagny.

Meursault-Blagny See Blagny.

Midi General term for the south of France, where standards have risen consistently in recent years.

Minervois Midi r. or (p.) (w.) or br. sw. ███ ★→★★ 85 86 88
Hilly VDQS area with some of the best wines of the Midi: lively and full of flavour esp. from Ch de Gourgazaud and la Livinère. Also sweet MUSCAT de St Jean de M.

mise en bouteilles au château, au domaine Bottled at the château, at the property or estate. N.B. dans nos caves (in our cellars) or dans la région de production (in the area of production) are often used although they mean little.

Moelleux Mellow. Used of the sweet wines of VOUVRAY, etc.

Moët & Chandon NV, rosé 81, Dry Imperial 71 73 75 76 78 80 81 82
The biggest champagne merchant and grower, with cellars in Epernay and sparkling wine branches in Argentina, Brazil, Spain, Australia and California. Consistent quality. Luxury brand: DOM PERIGNON.

Moillard Big family firm of growers and merchants in NUITS-ST-GEORGES, making dark and tasty COTE DE NUITS wines.

Mommessin, J. Major BEAUJOLAIS merchant. Owner of CLOS DE TART.

Monbazillac Dordogne w. sw. ✶✶ 71 75 76 78 79 80 81 83 85 86 88
Golden SAUTERNES-style wine from BERGERAC. Ages well. Ch Monbazillac is best known.

Mondeuse Savoie r. ✶✶ D.Y.A.
Red grape of SAVOIE. Good, vigorous, deep-coloured wine.

Mongeard-Mugneret 40-acre VOSNE-ROMANEE estate. Fine ECHEZEAUX, VOUGEOT, etc.

Monopole Vineyard in single ownership.

Montagne-Saint-Emilion B'x. r. ✶✶ 75 78 79 81 82 83 85 86 88
North-east neighbour of ST-EMILION with similar wines, becoming more important with each year. Top ch'x: Calon, St-André-Corbin, Vieux-Ch-St-André, Roudier, Teyssier, des Tours.

Montagny B'y. (r.) w. dr. ✶✶→✶✶✶ 86 87 88
COTE CHALONNAISE village between MACON and MEURSAULT, both geographically and gastronomically. A little red, too.

Montée de Tonnerre B'y. w. dr. ✶✶✶ 85 86 87 88
Famous and excellent PREMIER CRU of CHABLIS.

Monthelie B'y. r. ✶✶✶ 78 80 82 83 85 86 87
Little-known neighbour and almost equal of VOLNAY. Excellent fragrant reds. Best estate: Château de Monthélie.

Montlouis Lo. w. sw./dr. ✶✶ 75 76 78 81 82 83' 84 85 86 88
Neighbour of VOUVRAY. Similar sweet or dry long-lived wine.

Montrachet B'y. w. dr. ✶✶✶✶ 69 71 78 79 80 81 82 83 84 85 86 87 88
19-acre Grand Cru v'yd in both PULIGNY and CHASSAGNE-MONTRACHET. Potentially the greatest white burgundy: strong, perfumed, intense, dry yet luscious. (Both "t"s are silent.)

Montravel See Côtes de Montravel.

Mont-Redon, Domaine de Rh. r. (w. dr.) ✶✶✶ 79 80 81 83 84 85 86 88
Outstanding 235-acre estate in CHATEAUNEUF-DU-PAPE. Reliable, fairly early-maturing wines.

Moreau et Fils CHABLIS merchant and grower with 175 acres. Also major table-wine producer. Best wine: Clos des Hospices (Grand Cru). Owned by Hiram Walker.

Morey, Domaines 50 acres in CHASSAGNE-MONTRACHET. V.g. wines made by family members.

Morey-Saint-Denis B'y. r. ✶✶✶ 71 76 78 79 80 82 83 84 85 86 87 88
Small village with four Grands Crus between GEVREY-CHAMBERTIN and CHAMBOLLE-MUSIGNY. Glorious wine, often overlooked. Growers incl. Amiot, DUJAC, Lignier, Ponsot, Serveau.

Morgon B'y. r. ✶✶✶ 85 86 87 88
The "firmest" cru of BEAUJOLAIS, needing time to develop its rich and savoury flavour.

Moueix, J-P et Cie The leading proprietor and merchant of St-Emilion, Pomerol and FRONSAC. Ch'x incl. MAGDELAINE, LAFLEUR-PETRUS, and part of PETRUS. Now also has a venture in California: see Dominus.

Moulin-à–Vent B'y. r. **★★★** 83 85 86 87 88
The "biggest" and best wine of Beaujolais; powerful and long-lived, eventually tasting more like COTE D'OR wine.

Moulis B'x. r. **★★→★★★**
Village of the HAUT-MEDOC with its own appellation and several Crus Exceptionnels: CHASSE-SPLEEN, POUJEAUX-THEIL, MAUCAILLOU, etc. Wines are growing steadily finer.

Mousseux Sparkling.

Mouton Cadet Best-selling brand of blended red and white Bordeaux.

Moutonne CHABLIS GRAND CRU *honoris causa*, owned by BICHOT.

Mumm, G. H. & Cie NV "Cordon Rouge", rosé 79 82, Crémant de Cramant (NV) and 69 71 73 75 76 79 82 Major champagne grower and merchant owned by Seagram's. Luxury brand: René Lalou (79, 82). The Cramant is superb. Cordon Rouge can be pretty tasteless.

Muscadet Lo. w. dr. **★★** D.Y.A.
Popular, good-value, often delicious dry wine from round Nantes in s. Brittany. Should never be sharp. Perfect with fish. The best wines are bottled "sur lie" – on their lees.

Muscadet de Sèvre-et-Maine Wine from the central and usually best part of the area.

Muscat Distinctively perfumed grape and its (usually sweet) wine, often fortified as VDN. Made dry in ALSACE.

Muscat de Beaumes de Venise One of the best French muscats (see Beaumes de Venise).

Muscat de Frontignan Midi br. sw. **★★** D.Y.A.
Sweet Midi muscat. Quality improving.

Muscat de Lunel Midi br. sw. **★★** NV
Ditto. A small area but good.

Muscat de Mireval Midi br. sw. **★★** NV
Ditto, from near Montpellier.

Muscat de Rivesaltes Midi br. sw. **★** NV
Sweet muscat from a big zone near Perpignan.

Musigny B'y. r. (w. dr.) **★★★★** 69 71 76 78 79 80 82 83 84 85 86 87 88
25-acre Grand Cru in CHAMBOLLE-MUSIGNY. Often the best, if not the most powerful, of all red burgundies (and a little white). Best growers: DE VOGUE, DROUHIN, LEROY, Roumier, Mugnier.

Nature Natural or unprocessed, esp. of still champagne.

Néac B'x. r. **★★**
Village n. of POMEROL. Wines sold as LALANDE-DE-POMEROL.

Négociant-élèveur Merchant who "brings up" (i.e. matures) the wine.

Nicolas, Ets. Paris-based wholesale and retail wine merchants controlled by Rémy-Martin. One of the biggest in France and one of the best.

Nuits-St-Georges r. **★★→★★★** 69 71 76 78' 80 82 83 84 85' 86 87 88
Important wine-town: wines of all qualities, typically sturdy and full-flavoured. Name can be shortened to "Nuits". Best v'yds incl. Les St-Georges, Vaucrains, Les Pruliers, Clos de Corvées, Les Cailles, etc. Many growers and merchants esp. FAIVELEY, Chevillon, MACHARD DE GRAMONT, JAYER, RION.

Oisly & Thesée, Vignerons de Go-ahead cooperative in e. TOURAINE (Loire), experimenting successfully with superior grapes, esp. SAUV BL, CAB, and (since '85) CHARD. Blended wines labelled Baronnie d'Aignan. Good value.

Orléanais, Vin d' Lo. r. p. w. dr. **★** D.Y.A.
Once a great supplier of Paris, now a small AC area with light but fruity wines.

Ott, Domaine The most important producer of high-quality PROVENCE wines, incl. Ch de Selle and Clos Mireille. V.g. rosés.

Pacherenc-du-Vic-Bilh s.w. France w. sw. **★** NV
Rare minor speciality of the ARMAGNAC region.

FRANCE/Mou-Phi **49**

Paillard, Bruno NV, Crémant Blanc de Blancs, Rosé, **75 76 79 81**
    Small but prestigious young champagne house with excellent silky vintage and NV wines at fair prices.

Palette Prov. r. p. or w. dr. **★★**
    Near Aix-en-Provence. Aromatic reds and good rosés from CH SIMONE.

Parallèle 45 Excellent brand of COTES DU RHONE from JABOULET.

Parigot-Richard Producer of high-quality CREMANT de Bourgogne at SAVIGNY.

Pasquier-Desvignes Very old firm of Beaujolais merchants at St Lager, BROUILLY.

Patriarche One of the bigger firms of burgundy merchants. Cellars in Beaune; also owns CH DE MEURSAULT (100 acres), KRITER, etc.

Patrimonio Corsica r. w. dr. p **★★→★★★**
    Wide range from dramatic chalk hills in n. Corsica. Fragrant reds, crisp whites, fine VDN. Top grower: Gentile.

Pauillac B'x. r. **★★→★★★★** 66 70 75 76 78 79 81 82 83 84 85 86 87 88
    The only village in Bordeaux (HAUT-MEDOC) with three first-growths (Ch'x LAFITE, LATOUR, MOUTON) and many other fine ones, famous for high flavour; very various in style.

Pécharmant Dordogne r. **★★** 85 86 88
    Usually better-than-typical light BERGERAC red, with more "meat". Top estate: Ch de Tiregand.

Pelure d'oignon "Onion skin" – tawny tint of certain rosés.

Perlant or Perlé Very slightly sparkling.

Pernard-Vergelesses B'y. r. or (w. dr.) **★★★** 78 80 82 83 85 86 87 88 Village next to ALOXE-CORTON containing part of the great CORTON and CORTON-CHARLEMAGNE v'yds and one other top v'yd: Ile des Vergelesses. Growers incl. BONNEAU DE MARTRAY, Dubreuil-Fontaine, Rapet, Chandon, Delarche.

Perrier, Joseph NV, rosé and 71 73 75 76 79 82
    Family-run champagne house with considerable v'yds at Chalon-sur-Marne. Consistent light and fruity style.

Perrier-Jouet NV, Blason de France NV, 71 73 75 76 79 82
    Excellent champagne-growers and makers at Epernay now linked with MUMM. Luxury brands: Belle Epoque 79 (in a painted bottle), Blason de France (NV). Also Belle Epoque Rosé 79 82.

"Noble rot" (in French pourriture noble, *in German* Edelfäule, *in Latin* Botrytis cinerea) *is a form of mould that attacks the skins of ripe grapes in certain vineyards in warm and misty autumn weather.*

    Its effect, instead of rotting the grapes, is to wither them. The skin grows soft and flaccid, the juice evaporates through it, and what is left is a super-sweet concentration of everything in the grape except its water content.

    The world's best sweet table wines are all made of nobly rotten grapes. They occur in good vintages in Sauternes, the Rhine, the Mosel (where wine made from them is called Trockenbeerenauslese), in Tokaji in Hungary, in Burgenland in Austria, and occasionally elsewhere – California included. The danger is rain on pulpy grapes already far gone in noble rot. All too often, particularly in Sauternes, the grower's hopes are dashed by a break in the weather.

Pétillant Slightly sparkling.

Petit Chablis B'y. w. dr. **★★** D.Y.A.
    Wine from fourth-rank CHABLIS v'yds Lacks great character.

Philiponnat NV, NV Rosé, Grand Blanc Vintage 76 81 82, Clos des Goisses 70 71 73 75 76 78 79 82 Small champagne house with well-structured wines, esp. the remarkable single v'yd Clos Goisses. Owned by GOSSET.

Piat Père & Fils Important growers and merchants of BEAUJOLAIS and MACON wines at Mâcon, now controlled by Grand Metropolitan Ltd. V'yds in MOULIN-A-VENT, also CLOS DE VOUGEOT. BEAUJOLAIS, MACON-VIRE in special Piat bottles maintain a fair standard.

Pic, Albert Fine CHABLIS producer, controlled by DE LADOUCETTE.

Picpoul-de-Pinet Midi w. dr. ★ NV
Rather dull very dry southern white, best v. cold on the spot.

Pineau de Charente Strong sweet apéritif made of white grape juice and Cognac.

Pinot See Grapes for white and red wine.

Piper-Heidsieck NV, Pink 79, Vintage 71 73 75 76 79 82, Année Rare 76 79, Brut Sauvage 79 82 Champagne-makers of old repute at Reims.

Pol Roger NV, rosé 75 79 82, Blanc de Chardonnay 79 82 and 71 73 75 76 79 82 Excellent champagne house at Epernay. Particularly good non-vintage White Foil, Rosé, Réserve PR and Chardonnay. Luxury cuvée: "Sir Winston Churchill" 75 79 82 85.

Pomerol B'x. r. ★★ →★★★★ 70 71 75 76 78 79 81 82 83 85 86 88
The next village to ST-EMILION: similar but more "fleshy" wines, maturing sooner, reliable and delicious. Top ch PETRUS, TROTANOY, LA FLEUR-PETRUS, VIEUX-CH-CERTAN, LATOUR A POMEROL, etc. . . .

Pommard B'y. r. ★★★ 69 71 76 78 80 82 83 84 85 86 87 88
The biggest and best-known village in Burgundy. No superlative wines, but many warmly appealing ones. Best v'yds: Rugiens, Epenots and HOSPICES DE BEAUNE cuvées. Growers incl: Courcel, Gaunoux, LEROY, Armand, Pothier-Rieusset.

Pommery & Greno NV, NV rosé and 71 73 75 76 78 79 80 81 82
Very big CHAMPAGNE growers and merchants at Reims. Wines are much improved. The luxury brand: Louise Pommery 80, 81 is outstanding.

Pouilly-Fuissé B'y. w. dr. ★★→★★★ 86 87 88
The best white of the MACON area. At its best (e.g. Ch Fuissé Vieilles Vignes) excellent, but almost always over-priced.

Pouilly-Fumé Lo. w. dr. ★★→★★★ 86 87 88
"Gun-flinty", fruity, often sharp pale white from the upper Loire, next to SANCERRE. Grapes must be SAUVIGNON BLANC. Good vintages improve for 2-3 yrs. Top producers incl. LADOUCETTE, Bailly, Dagueneau, Redde, Saget, Renaud, Ch de Tracy.

Pouilly-Loché B'y. w. dr. ★★
Neighbour of POUILLY-FUISSE. Similar wine but little of it.

Pouilly-sur-Loire Lo. w. dr. ★ D.Y.A.
Inferior wine from the same v'yds as POUILLY-FUME, but different grapes (CHASSELAS). Rarely seen today

Pouilly-Vinzelles B'y. w. dr. ★★ 86 87 88
Neighbour of POUILLY-FUISSE. Similar wine, worth looking for.

Pousse d'Or, Domaine de la 32-acre estate in POMMARD, SANTENAY and (esp.) VOLNAY, where its "monopoles", "Bousse d'Or" and "Clos des 60 Ouvrées" are tannic, austere, powerful and justly famous.

Preiss Zimmer, Jean Old-established Alsace wine-merchants at Riquewihr.

Premières Côtes de Blaye B'x. r. w. dr. ★→★★★ 82 83 85 86 88
Restricted appellation for better reds of BLAYE. Ch'x include Barbé, Charron, Bourdieu, Haut-Sociondo, La Tonnelle, l'Escadre, Segonzac, Le Menaudat.

Premier Cru First-growth in Bordeaux (see p. 57), but the second rank of v'yds (after Grand Cru) in Burgundy.

Premières Côtes de Bordeaux B'x. r. (p.) or w. dr. or sw. ★→★★★
Large area east of GRAVES across the R. Garonne: a good bet for quality and value, though never brilliant. Ch'x incl. Laffitte [sic.], Gardera, Fayau, Haut-Brignon, REYNON, Tanesse.

Prieur, Domaine Jacques 35-acre estate all in top Burgundy sites, incl. Premier Cru MEURSAULT, VOLNAY, PULIGNY- and CHEVALIER-MONTRACHET. Recently disappointing.

Primeur "Early" wine for refreshment and uplift; esp. of BEAUJOLAIS.

Prissé See Mâcon-Villages.

Propriétaire-récoltant Owner-manager.

Provence See Côtes de Provence.

Puisseguin-Saint-Emilion B'x. r. ★★ 82 83 85 86 88
Eastern neighbour of ST-EMILION; wines similar – not so fine but often good value. Ch'x incl. Laurets, Guibeau, Puisseguin, Soleil, Teyssier. Also "Roc de Puisseguin" from coop.

Puligny-Montrachet B'y. w. dr. (r.) ★★★ 78 81 82 83 85 86 87 88
Bigger neighbour of CHASSAGNE-MONTRACHET with even more glorious rich dry whites. Best v'yds: MONTRACHET, CHEVALIER-MONTRACHET, BATARD-MONTRACHET, Bienvenue-Bâtard-Montrachet, Les Combettes, Clavoillon, Pucelles, Champ-Canet, etc. Top growers incl: AMPEAU, BOUCHARD PERE, CHARTRON, LEFLAIVE, SAUZET, L. Carillon.

Quarts de Chaume Lo. w. sw. ★★★ 75 76 78 82 84 85 86 88
Famous 120-acre plot in COTEAUX DU LAYON. CHENIN BLANC grapes. Long-lived, intense, rich golden wine, esp. Ch La Suronde, Dom. des Beaumard.

Quatourze Midi r. (p.) or w. dr. ★ 86 87 88
Minor VDQS area near Narbonne.

Quincy Lo. w. dr. ★★ 85 86 87
Small area making v. dry SANCERRE-style wine of SAUV BL.

Ramonet-Prudhon One of the leading proprietors in CHASSAGNE-MONTRACHET with 34 acres. Sometimes excellent whites, and red Clos St-Jean.

Rancio Term for the tang of wood-aged fortified wine, esp. BANYULS and other VINS DOUX NATURELS. A fault in table wines.

Rasteau Rh. r. (p. w. dr.) or br. sw. ★★ 85' 86 88
Village of s. Rhône valley. Very sound reds. Good strong sweet dessert wine is the local speciality.

Ratafia de Champagne Sweet apéritif made in Champagne of ⅔ grape juice and ⅓ brandy.

Récolte Crop or vintage.

Regnié Beaujolais village between MORGON and BROUILLY, promoted to "Cru" status in 1988. About 1,800 acres.

Reine Pédauque, La Burgundy growers and merchants at ALOXE-CORTON.

Remoissenet Père et Fils Fine Burgundy merchants (esp. for white wines) with a tiny estate at BEAUNE.

Rémy Pannier Important Loire-wine merchants at SAUMUR.

Reuilly Lo. (r. p.) w. dr. ★★ 86 87 88
Neighbour of QUINCY with similar wine; also good PINOT GRIS.

Riceys, Rosé des Champ. p. ★★ D.Y.A.
Minute appellation in southern Champagne for a notable PINOT NOIR rosé. Principal producer; A. Bonnet.

Richebourg B'y. r. ★★★★ 69 70 71 76 78 79 80 81 82 83 84 85 86 87 88
19-acre Grand Cru in VOSNE-ROMANEE. Powerful, perfumed, fabulously expensive wine, among Burgundy's best. Top growers: DOM DE LA ROMANEE-CONTI, GRIVOT, Gros, Méo-Camuzet.

Riesling See Grapes for white wine.

Rivesaltes Midi r. w. dr. br. sw. ★★ NV
Fortified sweet wine, some of it muscat-flavoured, from e. Pyrenees. An ancient tradition still very much alive, if struggling these days.

La Roche-aux-Moines Lo. w. dr./sw. ★★★ 75 76 78 79 82 83 85 86 88
60-acre v'yd in Savennières, Anjou. Intense strong, fruity/sharp wine needs long ageing.

Rodet, Antonin Substantial Burgundy merchant and a well-known grower of MERCUREY (Ch de Chamirey).

Roederer, Louis Brut Premier NV, Rosé 75 and **71 73 75 76 78 79 81**
    One of the best champagne-growers and merchants at Reims. V.
    reliable non-vintage wine with plenty of flavour. Luxury brand:
    Cristal Brut 79 (in white glass bottles) is sumptuous.

La Romanée B'y. r. ★★★★ **76 78 80 82 83 84 85 86 87 88**
    2-acre Grand Cru in VOSNE-ROMANEE just uphill from ROMANEE-CONTI,
    distributed by BOUCHARD.

Romanée-Conti B'y. r. ★★★★ **66 71 73 76 78 79 80 81 82 83 84 85 86
87 88** 4⅓-acre Grand Cru in VOSNE-ROMANEE. The most celebrated
    and expensive red wine in the world. Sometimes the best: '85 is
    astonishing.

Romanée-Conti, Domaine de la The grandest estate of Burgundy,
    owning the whole of ROMANEE-CONTI and LA TACHE and major parts of
    RICHEBOURG, GRANDS ECHEZEAUX, ECHEZEAUX and ROMANEE-ST-VIVANT. Also
    a very small part of LE MONTRACHET. Keep D.R.C. wines for decades.

Romanée-St-Vivant B'y. r. ★★★★ **71 76 78 79 80 82 83 84 85 86 87 88**
    23-acre Grand Cru in VOSNE-ROMANEE. Similar to ROMANEE-CONTI but
    lighter and less sumptuous.

Ropiteau Burgundy wine-growers and merchants at MEURSAULT. Special-
    ists in MEURSAULT and COTE DE BEAUNE wines.

Rosé d'Anjou Lo. p. ★ D.Y.A.
    Pale, slightly sweet, rosé. Cabernet d'Anjou *should* be better.

Rosé de Loire Lo. p. dr. ★→★★ D.Y.A.
    Appellation for dry Loire rosé (Anjou is sweet).

Roty, Joseph Small grower of classic GEVREY-CHAMBERTIN.

Rousseau, Domaine A. Major burgundy grower famous for CHAMBERTIN,
    etc. of highest quality.

Rousette de Savoie Savoie w. dr. ■■ D.Y.A.
    The tastiest of the fresh whites from s. of Geneva.

Roussillon See Côtes du Roussillon. "Grands Roussillons" are VINS DOUX
    NATURELS.

Ruchottes-Chambertin B'y. r. ★★★ **71 76 78 79 80 82 83 84 85 86 87 88**
    7½-acre Grand Cru neighbour of CHAMBERTIN. Similar splendid long-
    lasting wine.

Ruinart Père et Fils NV, rosé 79 and Bl. de Blancs **71 73 75 76 78 79 81**
    The oldest champagne house, now belonging to Moët-Hennessy.
    Luxury brand: Dom Ruinart, Blanc de Blancs **79**. N.B. the Rosé.

Rully B'y. r. or w. dr. or (sp). ■■ **85 86 87**
    Village of the COTE CHALONNAISE famous for sparkling burgundy. Still
    white and red light but tasty and good value, esp. the whites. Growers
    incl. DELORME, FAIVELEY, Jacquesson, Dom de la Folie.

Sablet Rh. r. (p.) w. dr. ■■
    Admirable COTE-DU-RHONE village, esp. Ch du Trignon.

Saint-Amour B'y. r. ★★ **85 87**
    Northernmost cru of BEAUJOLAIS: light, fruity, irresistible.

Saint-Aubin B'y. (r.) or w. dr. ■■ **83 85 86 87 88**
    Little-known neighbour of CHASSAGNE-MONTRACHET, up a side-valley.
    Not top-rank, but typical and good value. Also sold as COTE-DE-BEAUNE-
    VILLAGES. Top growers: J. Lamy, JADOT, Thomas, Roux, Clerget.

Saint Bris B'y. (r.) w. dr. ■ D.Y.A.
    Village w. of CHABLIS known for its fruity ALIGOTE, making good
    sparkling burgundy, but chiefly for SAUVIGNON DE ST BRIS.

Saint Chinian Midi r. ★→★★ **87 88**
    Hilly area of growing reputation in the COTEAUX DU LANGUEDOC.
    Appellation Contrôlée since 1982. Tasty reds.

Sainte-Croix-du-Mont B'x. w. sw. ■■ **75 76 79 80 81 82 83 84 86 88**
    Neighbour to SAUTERNES with similar golden wine. No superlatives but
    well worth trying, esp. Ch Loubens, Ch du Mont, Clos des Coulinats.
    Often a bargain.

Sainte-Foy-Bordeaux B'x. w. sw. ★ D.Y.A.
Part of ENTRE-DEUX-MERS, more akin to BERGERAC.

Saint-Emilion B'x. r. ★★→★★★★ 70 71 75 76 78 79 81 82 83 85 86
The biggest (13,000 acres) top-quality Bordeaux district; solid, rich,
tasty wines from hundreds of ch'x, incl. CHEVAL-BLANC, AUSONE, CANON,
MAGDELAINE, FIGEAC, etc. Also a v.g. coop.

Saint-Estèphe B'x. r. ▨▨ →★★★★ 75 78 79 80 81 82 83 84 85 86
88 Northern village of HAUT-MEDOC. Solid, structured, occasionally
superlative wines. Top ch'x: CALON-SEGUR, COS D'ESTOURNEL, MONTROSE,
etc, and many notable CRUS BOURGEOIS.

St-Gall Brand-name used by Union-Champagne the very good
champagne-growers' cooperative at AVIZE.

Saint-Georges-Saint-Emilion B'x. r. ▨▨ 82 83 85 86 88
Part of MONTAGNE-ST-EMILION with high standards. Best ch'x: ST-GEORGES,
Belair-Montaiguillon, Marquis-St-Georges, Tour-du-Pas-St-Georges.

Saint-Joseph Rh. r. (p. or w. dr.) ▨▨ 76 78 79 80 82 83 85 86
Northern Rhône appellation of second rank but reasonable price.
Substantial wine often better than CROZES-HERMITAGE esp. from
JABOULET, Rostaing.

Saint-Julien B'x. r. ▨▨▨ →★★★★ 70 75 76 78 79 80 81 82' 83'
84 85' 86 88 Mid-Médoc village with a dozen of Bordeaux's best
ch'x, incl. three LEOVILLES, BEYCHEVELLE, DUCRU-BEAUCAILLOU, GRUAUD-
LAROSE, etc. The epitome of well-balanced red wine.

Saint-Laurent Village next to ST-JULIEN. Appellation HAUT-MEDOC.

Saint-Nicolas-de-Bourgueil Lo. r. ★★ 82 83 84 85 86 88
The next village to BOURGUEIL: the same light but lively and fruity
CABERNET red. Top growers: Ammeux, Audebert, Cognard, Jamet.

Saint-Péray Rh. w. dr. or sp. ★★ NV
Rather heavy white from the n. Rhône, much of it made sparkling. A
curiosity worth investigating.

Saint Pourçain Central France r. p. or w. dr ▨ D.Y.A.
The venerable local wine of Vichy, rather chic in Paris. Made from
GAMAY and/or PINOT NOIR, the (light) white from Tressalier and/or
CHARDONNAY or SAUVIGNON BLANC.

Saint Romain B'y. r. w. dr. ▨▨ 85 86 87
Overlooked village just behind the COTE DE BEAUNE. Value, esp. for
young whites. Top growers: LEROY, Thévenin, Gros, Fèvre.

Saint-Sauveur HAUT-MEDOC village just w. of PAUILLAC.

Saint-Seurin-de-Cadourne HAUT-MEDOC village just n. of ST-ESTEPHE.

Saint-Véran B'y. w. dr. ▨▨ 85 86 87 88
Next-door appellation to POUILLY-FUISSE. Similar but better value: real
character from the best slopes of MACON-VILLAGES.

Salins du Midi, Domaine Viticole See Listel.

Salon Le Mesnil 61 64 66 69 71 73 76 79
The original Blanc de Blancs champagne, from Le Mesnil. Fine very
dry wine with extraordinary keeping qualities. Bought in 1988 by
LAURENT-PERRIER.

Sancerre Lo. (r. p.) or w. dr. ★★★ 86 87 88
Very fragrant and fresh SAUVIGNON white almost indistinguishable
from POUILLY-FUME, its neighbour over the Loire. Drink young. Also
light P NOIR red (best drunk at 2-3 yrs) and rosé. Top growers incl.
Crochet, Delaporte, CORDIER, Gitton, Reverdy.

Santenay B'y. r. or (w. dr.) ▨▨ 76 78 79 80 82 83 84 85 86 87 88
Very worthy, rarely rapturous, sturdy reds from the s. of the COTE DE
BEAUNE. Best v'yds: Les Gravières, Clos de Tavannes, La Comme. Top
grower: DOM DE LA POUSSE D'OR, Lequin-Roussot.

Saumur Lo. r. p. or w. dr. and sp. ★→ ▨▨
Big versatile district in ANJOU, with fresh fruity whites, v.g. CREMANT,
pale rosés and increasingly good CABERNET reds, the best from
Saumur-Champigny, esp. Ch de Targé, Dom Filliatreau.

Sauternes B'x. w. sw. ▓▓ ★★ →★★★★ 67 71 75 76 78 79 80 81 82 83 84 85 86 88 District of five villages (incl. BARSAC) making France's best sweet wine: strong (14%+ alcohol) luscious and golden, demanding to be aged. Top ch'x: D'YQUEM, SUDUIRAUT, COUTET, CLIMENS, GUIRAUD, etc. Also dry wines which cannot be sold as Sauternes.

Sauvignon Blanc See Grapes for white wine.

Sauvignon-de-St-Bris B'y. w. dr. ★★ D.Y.A. A baby VDQS cousin of SANCERRE from near CHABLIS. To try.

Sauvion et Fils Ambitious and well-run MUSCADET house, based at the Ch de Cléray. Top wine: Cardinal Richard.

Sauzet, Etienne White burgundy estate at PULIGNY-MONTRACHET. Clearly-defined, well-bred wines at best superb.

Savennières Lo. w. dr./sw. ★★★ 75 76 78 81 82 83 84 85 86 88 Small ANJOU district of pungent, long-lived whites, incl. COULÉE DE SERRANT, LA ROCHE AUX MOINES, Clos du Papillon.

Savigny-lès-Beaune B'y. r. or (w. dr.) ★★★ 78 82 83 85 86 87 88 Important village next to BEAUNE, with similar well-balanced middle-weight wines, often deliciously delicate and fruity. Best v'yds: Marconnets, Dominode, Serpentières, Vergelesses, les Guettes. Top growers incl: BIZE, Girard-Vollot, TOLLOT-BEAUT, CLAIR.

Savoie E. France r. or w. dr. or sp. ★★ D.Y.A. Alpine area with light dry wines like some Swiss wine or minor Loires. CREPY, SEYSSEL and APREMONT are best known whites, ROUSSETTE is often more interesting. Also MONDEUSE red.

Schlumberger et Cie ALSACE grower-merchants of luscious wines at Guebwiller.

Schröder & Schyler Old family firm of Bordeaux merchants, owners of Ch KIRWAN.

Sciacarello Red grape of Corsica's best red and rosé, e.g. AJACCIO, Sartène.

Sec Literally means dry, though champagne so-called is medium-sweet (and better at breakfast and tea-time than Brut).

Selection de Grains Nobles Descriptions coined by HUGEL for Alsace equivalent to German BEERENAUSLESE. "Grains nobles" are individual grapes with "noble rot" (see p. 49).

Sèvre-et-Maine The département containing the best v'yds of MUSCADET.

Seyssel Savoie w. dr. or sp. ★★★ NV Delicate pale dry white making admirable sparkling wine.

Sichel & Co. Two famous merchant houses. In Bordeaux owners of Ch D'ANGLUDET and part-owners of Ch PALMER. In Germany, maker of BLUE NUN and respected trader.

Soussans Village just n. of MARGAUX, sharing its appellation.

Sylvaner See Grapes for white wine

Syrah See Grapes for red wine

La Tâche B'y. r. ★★★★ 69 70 71 73 76 78 79 80 81 82 83 84 85 86 87 88 15-acre Grand Cru of VOSNE-ROMANEE and one of the best v'yds on earth: dark, perfumed and luxurious wine. Owned by the DOMAINE DE LA ROMANEE-CONTI.

Taittinger NV, Collection Brut 78 and 71 73 75 76 78 79 80 82 Fashionable champagne growers and merchants of Reims with a light touch. Luxury brand: Comtes de Champagne 76 79 81 (also v.g. rosé 79).

Tastevin, Confrèrie des Chevaliers du Burgundy's colourful and successful promotion society. Wine carrying their Tastevinage label will be approved by them and will usually be of a fair standard. A tastevin is the traditional shallow silver wine-tasting cup of Burgundy. See panel on p. 34.

Tavel Rh. p. ★★★ D.Y.A. France's most famous, though not her best, rosé, strong and dry, starting vivid pink and fading to orange. Avoid orange bottles.

Tempier, Domaine Top grower of BANDOL, with noble reds (incl. single-v'yd wines) and rosé.

Tête de Cuvée Archaic term vaguely used of the best wines of an appellation.

Thénard, Domaine The major grower of GIVRY, but best known for his substantial portion (4½ acres) of LE MONTRACHET.

Thevenet, Jean A master maker of white Mâcon-Clessé (Domaine de la Bon Gran) at Quintaine-Clessé, near LUGNY. Even some Botrytis wines.

Thorin, J. Grower and major merchant of BEAUJOLAIS, at Pontanevaux, owner of the Château des Jacques, MOULIN A VENT. Recently bought by Racke of Germany.

Thouarsais, Vin de Lo. r. 🔲 D.Y.A.
Light GAMAY VDQS area south of SAUMUR.

Tokay d'Alsace See Pinot Gris under Grapes for white wine.

Tollot-Beaut Stylish burgundy grower with some 50 acres in the COTE DE BEAUNE, incl. CORTON, BEAUNE Grèves, SAVIGNY (Les Champs Chevrey) and at Chorey-lès-Beaune where he is based.

Tortochot, Domaine 25-acre estate at GEVREY-CHAMBERTIN. Classic wines.

Touraine Lo. r. p. w. dr./sw./sp. 🔲🔲🔲🔲
Big mid-Loire province with immense range of wines, incl. dry white SAUVIGNON, dry and sweet CHENIN BLANC (e.g. VOUVRAY), red CHINON and BOURGUEIL, light red CABERNETS, GAMAYS and rosés. Cabernets, Sauvignons and Gamays of good years are bargains. Amboise, Azay-le-Rideau and Mesland are sub-sections of the appellation.

Trimbach, F. E. Distinguished ALSACE grower and merchant at Ribeauvillé. Best wines (incl. the austere Riesling Clos Ste Hune) mature magnificently.

Tursan s.w. France r. p. w. dr. ★
Emerging VDQS in the Landes. Sound reds.

Vacqueyras Rh. r. 🔲🔲 78 80 82 83 85 86 88
Prominent village of S. COTES-DU-RHONE, neighbour to GIGONDAS; comparable with CHATEAUNEUF-DU-PAPE but less heavy and more "elegant". Try JABOULET's version.

Valençay Lo. w. dr. ★ D.Y.A.
Neighbour of CHEVERNY: similar pleasant sharpish wine.

Val-Joannis, Ch de Prov. r. p. w. dr. ★★
Impressive new estate making v.g. COTES DU LUBERON wines.

Valréas Rh. r. (p. w. dr.) 🔲🔲
Côtes-du-Rhône-village with big coop "Enclave des Papes" and good red wines.

Varichon & Clerc Principal makers and shippers of SAVOIE sp. wines.

Varoilles, Domaine des Burgundy estate of 30 acres, principally in GEVREY-CHAMBERTIN. Tannic wines with great keeping qualities.

Vaudésir B'y. w. dr. 🔲🔲🔲🔲 78 81 83 84 85 86 87
Arguably the best of 7 CHABLIS Grands Crus (but then so are the others).

VDQS Vin Délimité de Qualité Supérieure (see p. 23).

Vendange Harvest.

Vendange tardive Late vintage. In ALSACE equivalent to German AUSLESE.

Veuve Clicquot NV ("Yellow label"), NV Demi-Sec (White Label) and (Gold Label) 73 75 76 78 79 80 82 and rosé 83 Historic champagne house of the highest standing, now owned by Moët-Hennessy. Full-bodied wines. Cellars at Reims. Luxury brand: La Grande Dame 79 83.

Vidal-Fleury, J. Long-established shippers and growers of top Rhône wines, esp. HERMITAGE and COTE-ROTIE.

Vieilles Vignes "Old vines" – therefore the best wine. Used for such wine by BOLLINGER, DE VOGUE and others.

Viénot, Charles Grower-merchant of good burgundy, owned by BOISSET at NUITS. 70 acres in NUITS, CORTON, RICHEBOURG, etc.

Vignoble Area of vineyards.

Vin de garde Wine that will improve with keeping. The serious stuff.

Vin de l'année This year's wine. See Beaujolais, Beaujolais-Villages.

Vin de paille Wine from grapes dried on straw mats, consequently very sweet, like Italian passito. Especially in the JURA.

Vin de Pays The junior rank of country wines. Well over 100 are now operational, mainly in the Midi. Don't turn up your nose; there are some gems.

Vin de Table Standard everyday table wine, not subject to particular regulations about grapes and origin. Choose the previous entry.

Vin Doux Naturel ("VDN") Sweet wine fortified with wine alcohol, so the sweetness is "natural", not the strength. The most distinguished product of ROUSSILLION. A vin doux liquoreux is several degrees stronger.

Vin Gris "Grey" wine is very pale pink, made of red grapes pressed before fermentation begins, unlike rosé, which ferments briefly before pressing. Oeil de Perdrix means much the same; so (though I blush to say it) does "blush".

Vin Jaune Jura w. dr. ★★★
Speciality of ARBOIS: odd yellow wine like fino sherry. Normally ready when bottled. The best is CHATEAU-CHALON.

Vin nouveau See Beaujolais Nouveau.

Vin vert A very light, acidic, refreshing white wine, a speciality of ROUSSILLON and v. necessary in summer in those torrid parts.

Vinsobres Rh. r. (p. or w. dr.) ★★ 81 83 85 86 88
Contradictory name of good s. Rhône village. Strong substantial reds which mature well.

Viré B'y. w. dr. ★★ 86 87 88
One of the best white-wine villages of MACON. Good wines from coop, Ch de Viré, Clos du Chapitre, JADOT.

Visan Rh. r. p. or w. dr. ★★ 85 86 88
One of the better s. Rhône villages. Reds better than white.

Viticulteur Wine-grower.

Vitteau-Alberti Producer of excellent CREMANT de Bourgogne at RULLY.

Vogüé, Comte Georges de First-class 30-acre burgundy domaine at CHAMBOLLE-MUSIGNY. At best the ultimate MUSIGNY and BONNES MARES. Avoid his '83s.

Volnay B'y. r. ★★★ 76 78 79 80 82 83 84 85' 86 87 88
Village between POMMARD and MEURSAULT: often the best reds of the COTE DE BEAUNE, not strong or heavy but fragrant and silky. Best v'yds: Caillerets, Clos des Ducs, Champans, Clos des Chênes, etc. Best growers: POUSSE D'OR, d'ANGERVILLE, Lafarge.

Volnay-Santenots B'y. r. ★★★
Excellent red wine from MEURSAULT is sold under this name. Indistinguishable from VOLNAY.

Vosne-Romanée B'y. r. ★★★→★★★★ 76 78 79 80 81 82 83 84 85 86 87 88 The village containing Burgundy's grandest Crus (ROMANEE-CONTI, LA TACHE, etc.). There are (or rather should be) no common wines in Vosne. Many good growers incl: Arnoux, JAYER, Gros, Mongeard-Mugneret, Mugneret, ROMANEE-CONTI, Castagnier, Engel.

Vougeot See Clos de Vougeot.

Vouvray Lo. w. dr./sw./sp. ★★→★★★★ 71 76 78 79 82 83 85 86 88
Small district of TOURAINE with very variable wines, at their best intensely sweet and almost immortal. Good dry sparkling. Best producers: Huet, Foreau, Ch Moncontour, Brédif, Poniatowski.

Willm, A Northerly ALSACE grower at Barr, with v.g. GEWÜRZ Clos Gaensbronnel.

"Y". (Pronounced ygrec) 78 79 80 84 85
Dry wine produced occasionally at Ch D'YQUEM.

Ziltener, André Swiss burgundy grower and merchant with cellars in Gevrey-Chambertin. Reds especially good.

Zind-Humbrecht 64-acre Alsace estate in Wintzenheim, Turckheim and Thann. First-rate individual v'yd wines (esp. Clos St Urbain Riesling).

Châteaux of Bordeaux

Some 400 of the best-known Bordeaux châteaux are listed here. Information on the current state of each vintage of each château (whether it is ready for drinking or needs keeping; whether it is a wine of which its maker is particularly proud) is complete up to the 1987 vintage. For red Bordeaux '87 was a very patchy vintage, disappointing for most people, with many thin wines, but as always some exceptional successes (and very good whites). Early tastings in most cases show a smaller wine than the '84, but the '84s have improved, and we can expect many '87s to do the same. It has been followed by the generally excellent '88, which is a vintage everyone will want to buy in due course. And it was preceded by the overall very good vintages of '86 and '85 – not to mention '83 and '82. There is therefore a great deal of desirable Bordeaux at all stages from the grower's chai to the consumer's cellar, and in this current superfluity '87 is a vintage you do not need to buy, even at the fair discount (30%+) on the previous vintage that the châteaux offered and that you should find in the stores. In due course the restaurant trade will absorb most of the '87s, as it does all "off-vintages". That will be the time to drink them, at a fair price for an honourable, not a resplendent, wine. It should always be remembered that in Bordeaux the making of a vintage is only the beginning . . .

Bx

MEDOC

R. Gironde

ST-SEURIN-DE-CADOURNE

ST-ESTEPHE St Est

ST-SAUVEUR St-Sau

PAUILLAC Pau

ST-LAURENT St-Lau

ST-JULIEN St-Jul

CUSSAC

LISTRAC-MEDOC

MOULIS

SOUSSANS-MARGAUX Sou-Mar

MARGAUX Mar

LABARDE-MARGAUX Lab-Mar

CANTENAC-MARGAUX Cant-Mar

ARSAC-MARGAUX Ar-Mar

HAUT MEDOC

FRONSAC

LALANDE
DE POMEROL

Bordeaux

Libourne

POMEROL

ST-GEORGES St-Geo

Castillion

ST-EMILION St-Em

R. Dordogne

GRAVES

R. Garonne

ENTRE-DEUX-MERS

BARSAC

SAUTERNES

Langon

d'Agassac Haut-Médoc r. ⭐⭐ 75' 78 79 80 81 82' 83 84 85 86
14th-century moated fort with 86 acres. Same owners as Ch'x CALON-SEGUR and DU TERTRE. Very tasty wines.

Andron-Blanquet St-Est. r. ⭐⭐ 82 83 84 85' 86
Sister-château to COS LABORY. Rather "open" and easy wine. 40 acres.

L'Angélus St-Em. r. ⭐⭐ 75' 78 79' 80 81' 82 83 85' 86
Well-situated classed-growth of 57 acres on the St-Emilion Côtes w. of the town. More steady than exciting, but looking good recently.

d'Angludet Cant-Mar. r. ⭐⭐⭐ 70' 75 76' 78' 79 80 81' 82 83' 84 85' 86 87 75-acre Cru Exceptionnel of classed-growth quality owned by Peter A. Sichel. Lively fragrant Margaux of great style.

d'Archambeau Graves r. and w. dr. (sw.) ⭐⭐ (r.) 85 86 87 (w.) 84 85 86 87 Up-to-date 54-acre property at Illats. V.g. fruity dry white; since '84 fragrant barrel-aged reds.

d'Arche Sauternes w. sw. ⭐⭐ 78 79 80 81 82 83' 85
Substantial second-rank classed-growth of 88 acres rejuvenated since 1980. Ch d'Arche-Lafaurie was its second label until '81.

d'Arcins Central Médoc r. ⭐⭐
185-acre property of the Castel family (cf. Castelvin); sister-château to neighbouring Barreyres (160 acres).

l'Arrosée St-Em. r. ⭐⭐ 78 79 81 82 83 84 85 86
Substantial 24-acre Côtes property. Seriously fine wine with "stuffing", despite its name (which means watered).

Ausone St-Em. r. ⭐⭐⭐⭐ 70 75 76' 78 79' 80 81 82' 83' 85 86' 87
Celebrated first-growth with 17 acres (about 2,500 cases) in the best position on the Côtes and famous rock-hewn cellars under the vineyard. The firmest, most elegant and subtle St-Emilion. See also Ch Belair.

Bahans-Haut-Brion Graves r. ⭐⭐⭐ NV and 83 87
The second-quality wine of Ch HAUT-BRION.

Balestard-la-Tonnelle St-Em. r. ⭐⭐ 70' 75' 76' 78 79 81 82 83 85 86'
Historic 30-acre classed-growth on the plateau near the town. Mentioned by the 15th-century poet Villon and still in the same family (which also owns Ch CAP-DE-MOURLIN). Big flavour; more finesse since '85.

de Barbe Côtes de Bourg r. (w.) ⭐⭐ 79' 81 82' 83 85 86
The biggest (148 acres) and best-known ch of the right bank of the Gironde. Good tasty, light but fruity, Merlot red.

Bastor-Lamontagne Sauternes w. sw. ⭐⭐ 76 79 80 82 83' 84 85 86'
Large "bourgeois" Preignac property; excellent rich wines. 10,000 cases.

Batailley Pauillac r. ⭐⭐⭐ 70 71 75' 78' 79' 80 81 82' 83 84 85 86
The bigger of the famous pair of fifth-growths (with HAUT-BATAILLEY) on the borders of Pauillac and St-Julien. 110 acres. Fine, firm strong-flavoured wine. Owned by the Castéja family of BORIE-MANOUX.

Beaumont Cussac, Haut-Médoc r. ⭐⭐ 78' 79 81 82 83 84 85 86 87
200-acre+ Cru Bourgeois, well-known in France for rather light but increasingly attractive wines. Second label: Ch Moulin d'Arvigny. 35,000 cases. In same hands as Ch BEYCHEVELLE since '87.

Beauregard Pomerol r. ⭐⭐⭐ 75' 76 79' 81 82' 83 85 86
32-acre v'yd with pretty 17th-century ch near LA CONSEILLANTE. Well-made delicate "round" wines to drink quite young.

Beau Séjour-Bécot St-Em. r. ⭐⭐⭐ 75' 76' 78 79 81 82' 83 85' 86
Half of the old Beau Séjour Premier Grand Cru estate on the w. slope of the Côtes. Easy, tasty wines. 45 acres. Controversially demoted in class in '85. The Bécots also owns Ch GRAND PONTET.

Beauséjour-Duffau-Lagarosse St-Em. r. ⭐⭐⭐ 70 75 76 78 79 80 81 82 83 85 86 The other half of the above, 17 acres in old family hands, making well structured (not heavy) wine for long maturing.

Beau-Site St-Est. r. ★★ 70' 75' 76 78' 79 80 81 82 83 84 85 86'
55-acre Cru Bourgeois Exceptionnel in same hands as Ch'x BATAILLEY, TROTTEVIEILLE, etc. Regular quality and substance typical of St-Estèphe.

Belair St-Em. r. ■■■ 70 71 75' 76' 78 79' 80 82' 83' 85' 86'
Sister-ch and neighbour of AUSONE with 34.5 acres on the Côtes. Wine a shade heartier and less subtle. A very high standard in recent vintages (esp. '85 and '86). Makes an NV, "Roc-Blanquant", in magnums only.

de Bel-Air Lalande de Pomerol r. ■■ 75' 76 79 81 82' 83 85 86
The best-known estate of this village just n. of Pomerol, with very similar wine. 25 acres.

Bel Air-Marquis d'Aligre Sou-Mar. r. ■■ 70' 75' 76 78 79 80 81 82' 83 84 85 Cru Exceptionnel with 42 acres of old vines. The owner likes gutsy wine.

Belgrave St-Lau. r. ★★ 81 82 83 85 86'
Obscure fifth-growth in St-Julien's back-country. 107 acres. Managed by DOURTHE since 1979. '86 shows real promise.

Bel-Orme-Tronquoy-de-Lalande St-Seurin-de-Cadourne (Haut-Médoc) r. ★★ 70' 71 75' 76 78 79' 81 82' 83 84 85 86 Reputable 60-acre Cru Bourgeois n. of St-Estèphe. Old v'yd producing tannic wines. Same owner as Ch RAUZAN-GASSIES.

Berliquet St-Em. r. ★★ 79 81 82 83 85 86
Tiny Grand Cru Classé recently v. well run (by the coop).

Beychevelle St-Jul. r. ★★★ 61 66 70' 75' 78 79 80 81 82' 83 84 85 86 87
170-acre fourth-growth with the Médoc's finest mansion. Wine of more elegance than power, patchy to '82, now steady.

CHATEAU LANGOA-BARTON GRAND CRU CLASSE APPELLATION ST-JULIEN CONTROLEE MIS EN BOUTEILLES AU CHATEAU	**A Bordeaux label** A château is an estate – not necessarily with a mansion or a big expanse of vineyard. Reference to the local classification. It varies from one part of Bordeaux to another. The Appellation Contrôlée: look up St-Julien in the France A-Z. "Bottled at the château" – now the normal practice with classed-growth wines.

Bonnet Entre-Deux-Mers r. and w. dr. ■■ (w.) D.Y.A.
Big-scale producer of some of the best Entre-Deux-Mers.

Bon-Pasteur, le Pom. r. ★★★ 70 75 76 78 79 81 82 83 84 85 86
Excellent very small property on the St-Emilion boundary. Concentrated, sometimes even creamy, wines.

Boscq, Le St-Est. r. ■■ 82 83 84 85 86
Another Cru Bourgeois giving excellent value in tasty St-Estèphe.

Le Bourdieu Haut-Médoc r. ■■ 75' 78' 79 80 81 82 83 85 86
Cru Bourgeois at Vertheuil with sister Ch Victoria (134 acres in all) known for well-made St-Estèphe-style wines.

Bourgneuf Pomerol r. ■■—■■■■ 75' 76 78 79 81 82 83 84 85' 86 87
22-acre v'yd on chalky clay soil making fairly rich wines with good typically plummy Pomerol perfume. 5,000 cases.

Bouscaut Graves r. w. dr. ★★★ 70' 75' 78' 81 82' 83 85 86'
Classed-growth at Cadaujac bought in 1980 by Lucien Lurton, owner of Ch BRANE-CANTENAC, etc. 75 acres red (largely Merlot); 15 acres white. Never yet brilliant, but getting there.

du Bousquet Côtes de Bourg r. ■■ 78 79 81 82 83 85 86
Reliable estate with 148 acres making attractive solid wine.

Boyd-Cantenac Margaux r. ■■■ 75' 76' 78' 79 80 81 82' 83' 84 85 86' 44-acre third-growth regularly producing attractive wine, full of flavour and tending to improve. See also Ch Pouget.

Branaire (Ducru) St-Jul. r. ■■■ 70' 75' 76 78 79' 80 81 82' 83 84 85 86 Fourth-growth of 125 acres producing notably spicy and flavoury wine: attractive and reliable.

Brane-Cantenac Cant-Mar. r. ■■■ 75' 78' 79 80 81 82' 83 84 85 86' Big (211 acres) well-run second-growth. Fragrant, gamey wines of strong character. Same owners as Ch'x DURFORT-VIVENS, VILLEGEORGE, CLIMENS, BOUSCAUT, etc. Second label: Ch Notton.

Brillette Moulis, Haut-Médoc r. ★★ 75 78 79 80 81' 82 83 84 85' 86 70-acre v'yd. Reliable and attractive; fulfilling high promise.

La Cabanne Pomerol r. 71 75' 76 78' 79' 81 82' 83 85 86 Highly regarded 25-acre property near the great Ch TROTANOY. Recently modernized; expect to hear more.

Cadet Piola St-Em. r. ★★ 70' 75' 76 78 79 81 82 83' 84 85' 86 Distinguished little property just n. of the town of St-Emilion. 3,000 cases. Ch Faurie de Souchard has same owner; slightly less fine wine.

Caillou Sauternes w. sw. ★★ 81 82 83 85 86 Well-run second-rank 37-acre Barsac vineyard for firm, fruity wine. "Private Cuvée" is a top selection.

Calon-Ségur St-Est. r. ★★★ 70 75 78' 79' 80 81 82' 83 84 85' 86 Big (123-acre) third-growth of great reputation. A great classic for big hearty wines, but recently suffering in reputation.

Cambon-la-Pelouse Haut-Médoc r. ■■ 82 83 84 85 86 Huge (145-acre) accessible Cru Bourgeois. A sure bet for fresh typical Médoc without wood ageing.

Camensac St-Lau. r. ★★ 75' 78 79 80 81 82' 83 84 85 86' 87 149-acre fifth-growth, replanted in the '60s with new equipment and the same expert direction as LAROSE-TRINTAUDON. Good vigorous but not exactly classic wines.

Canon St-Em. r. ■■■ 70 71 75' 76 78 79' 80 81 82' 83' 85' 86 Famous first-classed-growth with 44+ acres on the plateau w. of the town. Conservative methods; very impressive wine.

Canon Canon-Fronsac r. ■■ 81 82 83 85 86' Tiny property of Christian MOUEIX. Long-ageing wine.

Canon-la-Gaffelière St-Em. r. ★★ 75 79 81 82' 83 85 86' 47-acre classed-growth on the lower slopes of the Côtes with Austrian ownership. Reliable lightish wines.

Canon de Brem Canon-Fronsac r. ■■ 78 80' 81 82' 83 84 85 86 One of the top Fronsac v'yds for dark, tannic and vigorous wine. MOUEIX property.

Canon-Moueix Canon-Fronsac r. ★★ 83 85 86 The latest MOUEIX investment in this rising appellation. V. stylish wine.

Cantemerle Macau r. ■■■ 61 70' 75' 78 79 81 82 83' 84 85 86 Superb estate at the extreme s. of the Médoc, with a romantic ch in a wood and 150 acres of vines. Officially fifth-growth: potentially nearer second. Problems hampered quality in late '70s. A new broom (CORDIER) since 1981 is fulfilling potential.

Cantenac-Brown Cant-Mar. r. ★★★ 70 75 78 79 80 81 82 83 84 85 86 87 Formerly old-fashioned 77-acre third-growth, with very promising '82 and '83. Big wines. New owners since '87 investing heavily. 2nd label: Canuet.

Capbern-Gasqueton St-Est. r. ★★ 75 78 79 81 82 83 84 85 86 Good 85-acre Cru Bourgeois; same owner as CALON-SEGUR.

Cap de Mourlin St-Em. r. ■■ 70' 75' 78 79' 81 82' 83 84 85 86 Well-known 37-acre property of the Cap de Mourlin family, owners of Ch BALESTARD and Ch Roudier, Montagne-St-Em. Classic St-Emilion.

Carbonnieux Graves r. and w. dr. ★★★ (r.) 78′ 79 81 82 83 85 86 87 (w.)
Historic estate at Léognan making good fairly light wines. The whites
of e.g. '83, '86, '87 have the structure to age 10 yrs. Ch'x Le Pape and
Le Sertre are also in the family.

Cardaillan Graves r. ★★
The red wine of the distinguished (Sauternes) Ch de MALLE.

La Cardonne Blaignan (Médoc) r. ★★ 78 79 81′ 82 83 84 85 86
Large (300+ acres) Cru Bourgeois in the n. Médoc bought in 1973 by
the Rothschilds of LAFITE. A safe bet for early drinking.

Les Carmes-Haut-Brion Graves r. ★★ 75 78 79 80 81′ 82′ 83 85 86
Small neighbour (9-acre) of HAUT-BRION with high bourgeois standards. Old vintages show its classic potential.

Caronne-Ste-Gemme St-Lau. (Haut-Médoc) r. ★★→★★★ 75 78 79 80
81 82′ 83 84 85 86 Cru Bourgeois of 100 acres. Steady quality
repays patience. At minor cru classé level. ⟨8x⟩

du Castéra Médoc r. ★★ 75 78 79 81 82 83 84 85 86
Historic property at St-Germain in the n. Médoc. Recent investment;
to watch for tasty but not tannic wine.

Certan de May Pomerol r. ★★★ 70 75 78 79 81 82′ 83 84 85′ 86
Neighbour of VIEUX-CHATEAU-CERTAN. Tiny property (2,000 cases) with
full-bodied rich and tannic wine recently flying very high.

Certan-Giraud Pomerol r. ★★★ 71 75 78 79 81 82 83′ 85 86
Small (17-acre) property next to the great Ch PETRUS.

Chambert-Marbuzet St-Est. r. ★★ 78 79 80 81 82 83 84 85 86
Tiny (20-acre) sister-ch of HAUT-MARBUZET. Very good fruity wine aged
in new oak matures quite fast.

Chantegrive Graves r. w. dr. ★★ 83 84 85 86 87 (w.)
180-acre estate half white, half red; modern Graves of high quality.
Other labels incl. Mayne-Levéque; Bon-Dieu-des-Vignes.

Chasse-Spleen Moulis r. ★★★ 70′ 75′ 76 78′ 79 80 81′ 82′ 83′ 84 85
86 87 180-acre Cru Exceptionnel of classed-growth quality. Consistently good, usually outstanding, long-maturing wine. 2nd label:
Ermitage de C-S. One of the surest things in Bordeaux.

Chéret-Pitres Graves r. w. dr. ★→★★
Substantial estate in the up-and-coming village of Portets.

Cheval Blanc St-Em. r. ★★★★ 66 70 75′ 76 78 79 80 81′ 82′ 83′ 84 85 86
This and AUSONE are the "first-growths" of St-Emilion. Cheval Blanc is
richer, more full-blooded, intensely vigorous and perfumed, from 100
acres on the border of Pomerol.

Chicane Graves r. ★★
Satisfying and reliable product of the Langon merchant Pierre Coste.
Domaine de Gaillat is another. Drink at 2-6 years.

Cissac Cissac r. ★★ 70′ 75′ 76 78′ 79 80 81 82′ 83′ 84 85 86
A pillar of the bourgeoisie. 80-acre Grand Bourgeois Exceptionnel
with a steady record for tasty long-lived wine.

Citran Avensan, Haut-Médoc r. ★★ 70′ 75 78′ 81 82 83 85 86
Grand Bourgeois Exceptionnel of 178 acres bought by Japanese in
'87. Stylish wine.

Clarke Listrac, Haut-Médoc r. (p.) ★★→★★★ 78 79 80 81 82 83 84
85′ 86 Huge (350-acre) Cru Bourgeois Rothschild development, incl.
visitor facilities. 2nd labels: Ch'x Malmaison and Peyrelebade.

Clerc-Milon Pauillac r. ★★★ 75′ 76 78′ 79 80 81 82′ 83′ 84 85 86 87
Once forgotten little fifth-growth bought by the late Baron Philippe de
Rothschild in 1970. Now 73 acres. Not normally thrilling, but a v.g.
'83, '85 and '86.

Climens Sauternes w. sw. ★★★ 71′ 75′ 76′ 78′ 79 80′ 81 82 83′ 85 86′
74-acre classed-growth at Barsac making some of the best and most
stylish sweet wine in the world for a good 10 years' maturing. A
superb '83. (Occasional) 2nd label: Les Cyprès. Same owner as Ch
BRANE-CANTENAC, etc.

Clinet Pomerol r. ★★ 75 76 78 79 81 83 85
15-acre property in central Pomerol making tannic "Pauillac-style" wine. Progress in recent vintages.

Clos l'Eglise Pomerol r. ★★★ 75 78 79′ 81 82′ 83 85 86
14-acre v'yd in one of the best sites in Pomerol. Excellent wine without great muscle or flesh. The same family owns Ch PLINCE.

Clos Floridéne Graves w. dr. ★★
Tour de force by one of the best white winemakers of B'x, Denis Dubourdieu. Drink young or keep 5 years.

Clos Fourtet St-Em. r. ★★★ 78 79 80 81 82′ 83 85 86
Well-known 42-acre first-growth on the plateau with cellars almost in the town. Back on form after a middling patch. Same owners as CLIMENS, BRANE-CANTENAC, etc.

Clos Haut-Peyraguey Sauternes w. sw. ★★ 78 79 80 81 82 83 84 85 86′ Tiny production of good medium-rich wine. The v.g. Cru Bourgeois Ch Haut-Bommes is in the same hands.

Clos des Jacobins St-Em. r. ★★ 75′ 78 79 80 81 82′ 83′ 85 86
Well-known and well-run little (18-acre) classed-growth owned by the shipper CORDIER. Wines of notable depth and style.

Clos du Marquis St-Jul. r. ★★ 75 76 78 79 80 81 82 83 84 85 86 87
The second wine of LEOVILLE-LAS CASES.

Clos l'Oratoire St-Em. r. ★★ 78 79 80 81 82 83 85 86
Richly typical Grand Cru. See also Ch Peyreau.

Clos René Pomerol r. ★★★ 70 71′ 75 78 79 80 81 82′ 83 85 86
Leading ch on the w. of Pomerol. 38 acres making powerful wine; eventually delicate. Also sold as Ch Moulinet-Lasserre.

La Closerie-Grand-Poujeaux Moulis (Haut-Médoc) r. ★★
Small but respected traditional middle-Médoc. To keep.

La Clotte St-Em. r. ★★ 75′ 78 79 81 82 83′ 85 86
Tiny Côtes Grand Cru with marvellously scented "supple" wine .

Colombier-Monpelou Pauillac r. ★★ 82 83 85 86
Reliable small Cru Bourgeois made to a high standard.

La Conseillante Pomerol r. ★★★ 70′ 75′ 76 78 79 80 81′ 82′ 83 84 85 86 87 29-acre historic property on the plateau between PETRUS and CHEVAL BLANC. Some of the noblest and most fragrant Pomerol, worthy of its superb position.

Corbin (Giraud) St-Em. r. ★★ 75 76 78 79 81 82′ 83′ 85 86
28-acre classed-growth in n. St-Emilion where a cluster of Corbins occupy the edge of the plateau. Can be very rich.

Corbin-Michotte St-Em. r. ★★ 75 78 79 81 82 83 85 86
Well-run 19-acre property; "generous" Pomerol-like wine.

Cos-d'Estournel St-Est. r. ★★★★ 61 66 70 71 73 75′ 76′ 78′ 79 80 81′ 82′ 83 84 85 86 87 140-acre second-growth with eccentric chinoiserie building overlooking Ch LAFITE. Always full-flavoured, often magnificent, wine. Now regularly one of the best in the Médoc. Maître d'Estournel is a good blend.

Cos Labory St-Est. r. ★★ 75′ 78′ 79′ 80 81′ 82′ 83 84 85 86
Little-known fifth-growth neighbour of COS D'ESTOURNEL with 37 acres. Blunt fruity wines mature early. To watch.

Coufran St-Seurin-de-Cadourne (Haut-Médoc) r. ★★ 78′ 79 81 82′ 83 85 86 Coufran and Ch VERDIGNAN, on the northern-most hillock of the Haut-Médoc, are under the same ownership. Coufran has mainly Merlot vines; soft lightish wine. 148 acres.

Couhins-Lurton Graves w. dr. ★★ 83 84 85 86′ 87′
Small quantity of very fine Sauvignon wine for maturing.

La Couronne Pauillac r. ★★ 75 76 78 79 81′ 82′ 83
Excellent (very) small Cru Exceptionnel made at Ch HAUT-BATAILLEY, though not since '83.

Coutet Sauternes w. sw. ★★★ 70′ 71′ 73 75′ 76 79 81 82 83′ 84 85 86
Traditional rival to Ch CLIMENS; 91 acres in Barsac. Often slightly less rich; at its best equally fine but recently less reliable. "Cuvée Madame" is a v. rich selection of the best. A dry GRAVES sold under the same name is not v. special.

Couvent des Jacobins St-Em. r. ▮▮ 75 78 79′ 80 81 82′ 83 85 86
Well-known vineyard of 22 acres adjacent to the town of St-Emilion on the east. Among the best of its kind.

Le Crock St-Est. r. ▮▮ 79 80 81 82 83 84 85 86
Well-situated Cru Bourgeois of 74 acres in the same family as Ch LEOVILLE-POYFERRE. Among the many excellent C.B's of the commune.

La Croix Pomerol r. ★★ 70′ 71′ 75′ 78 79′ 81 82′ 83 85 86
Well-reputed property of 32 acres. Appealing plummy Pomerol with a spine; matures well. Also La C.-St-Georges, La C.-Toulifaut and Clos des Litanies.

La Croix de Gay Pomerol r. ★★★ 70′ 75′ 76′ 78 79 81 82′ 83′ 85 86
30 acres in the best part of the commune. Recently on fine form. Has underground cellars, rare in Pomerol. "La Fleur de Gay" is the best selection.

Croizet-Bages Pauillac r. ▮▮ 70′ 75′ 78′ 79 81 82′ 83 84 85 86
52-acre fifth-growth (lacking a ch) with the same owners as Ch RAUZAN-GASSIES. Wines with growing finesse (at last).

Croque-Michotte St-Em. r. ★★ 75 78 79 81 82′ 83 85 86
35-acre Pomerol-style classed-growth on the Pomerol border.

du Cruzeaux Graves r. w. dr. ★★
100-acre GRAVES-LEOGNAN v'yd recently developed by André Lurton of LA LOUVIERE etc. V. high standards; to try.

Curé-Bon-la-Madeleine St-Em. r. ★★★ 71′ 75 76′ 78 81 82′ 83 85 86
Small (12-acre) property among the best of the Côtes; between AUSONE and CANON. Managed by MOUEIX.

Why do the Châteaux of Bordeaux have such a large section of this book devoted to them? The reason is simple: collectively they form by far the largest supply of high-quality wine on earth.

A single typical Médoc château with 150 acres (some have far more) makes approximately 26,000 dozen bottles of identifiable wine a year – the production of two or three California "boutique" wineries. The tendency over the last two decades has been for the better-known châteaux to buy more land. Many classed-growths have expanded very considerably since they were classified in 1855.

Dassault St-Em. r. ▮▮ 78 79 81 82 83 85 86
Consistent early-maturing middle-weight Grand Cru. 58 acres.

Dauzac Lab-Mar. r. ▮▮→▮▮▮ 75 78 79′ 80 81 82′ 83′ 84 85′ 86
Substantial fifth-growth near the river s. of Margaux. Doing well since '79; new owner in '89. 120 acres. 22,000 cases.

Desmirail Mar. r. ★★→★★★ 81 82 83′ 84 85 86
Third-growth, now 45 acres. A long-defunct name recently revived by the owner of BRANE-CANTENAC. Gentle wines for drinking young.

Dillon Haut-Médoc r. (w. dr.) ★★ 75′ 78′ 79′ 81 82 83 84 85 86
Local wine college of Blanquefort, just n. of Bordeaux. 85 acres. Dry white: Ch Linas (D.Y.A.) 15,000 cases.

Doisy-Daëne Barsac w. sw. and dr. ▮▮▮ 75 76′ 78 79 80 81 82 83′ 84 85 86 Forward-looking 34-acre estate making crisp dry white (incl. Riesling grapes) and red Ch Cantegril as well as notably fine sweet Barsac.

Doisy-Dubroca Barsac w. sw. ▮▮ 75′ 76 78 79 80 81 83 84 85 86 87
Tiny (8½-acre) Barsac classed-growth allied to Ch CLIMENS.

Doisy-Védrines Sauternes w. sw. ▮▮▮ 71 75′ 76′ 78 79 80 81 82′ 83′ 85 86   50-acre classed-growth at Barsac, near CLIMENS and COUTET. Deliciously sturdy rich wines designed for a long life.

Bx

Domaine de Chevalier Graves r. and w. dr. ★★★★ (r.) 61 66 70′ 71 75′ 76 78′ 79′ 80 81′ 82′ 83 84 85 86 87′ Superb small estate of 36 acres at Léognan. The red is stern at first, richly subtle with age. The white is delicate but matures to rich flavours. (w. 75 76′ 78 79′ 81 82 83′ 84 85 87′). Changed hands (but not management) in 1983. Up to 9,000 cases red, 1,000 cases white.

Domaine de l'Eglise Pomerol r. ★★ 70 75 76 78 79′ 81 82′ 83 85 86 Small property: solid wine distributed by BORIE-MANOUX.

Domaine la Grave Graves r. w. dr. ★★ 82 83 84 85 86 (w. 87) Innovative little estate with lively medal-winning reds made for a long life. Oak-aged delicious whites. Wines made at Ch de Lauderas by Peter Vinding Diers.

La Dominique St-Em. r. ★★★ 70 71′ 75 76 78 79 80 81 82′ 83 85 86′ 87 Fine 45-acre classed-growth next door to Ch CHEVAL BLANC, making wine almost as arresting.

Ducru-Beaucaillou St-Jul. r. ★★★ 61 66 70′ 71 75′ 76 78′ 79 80 81 82′ 83′ 84 85′ 86′ 87 Outstanding second-growth; 120 acres overlooking the river. The owner, M. Borie, makes classic "oak-scented" claret for v. long ageing. See also Grand-Puy-Lacoste, etc.

Duhart-Milon-Rothschild Pauillac r. ★★★ 75′ 78 79 80 81 82′ 83 85 86 Fourth-growth neighbour of LAFITE under the same management. Maturing vines; increasingly fine quality. 110 acres.

Duplessis-Fabre Moulis r. ★★ 82 83 84 85 86 Small sister-château of FOURCAS-DUPRE, replanted since '74.

Durfort-Vivens Margaux r. ★★★ 78′ 79′ 80 81 82′ 83 85′ 86 Relatively small (49-acre) second-growth owned by M. Lurton of BRANE-CANTENAC. Recent wines (except '84) have real finesse.

Dutruch-Grand-Poujeaux Moulis r. ★★ 70 75 76 78′ 79 80 81 82′ 83 84 85 86 One of the leaders of MOULIS; full-bodied and tannic wines.

L'Eglise-Clinet Pomerol r. ★★★ 70 75 76 78 79 80 81 82′ 83′ 84 85′ 86 11 acres. Highly ranked; full, fleshy wine. Changed hands in '82; '85 is noble. 2,000 cases.

L'Enclos Pomerol r. ★★ 70 75 76 78 79 80 81 82′ 83 85 86 Respected 26-acre property on the w. side of Pomerol, near CLOS-RENE. Big, well-made, long-flavoured wine.

L'Evangile Pomerol r. ★★★ 70′ 71′ 75′ 76 78 79 80 81 82′ 83′ 84 85′ 86 33 acres between PETRUS and CHEVAL BLANC. Impressive wines. In the same area and class as LA CONSEILLANTE.

Fargues Sauternes w. sw. ★★★ 70′ 71′ 75′ 76′ 78 79 80 81 83 85′ 86 87 25-acre v'yd in same ownership as Ch YQUEM. Fruity and extremely elegant wines, maturing earlier than YQUEM.

Ferrande Graves r. (w. dr.) ★★ 82 83 84 85 86 87 Major estate of Castres with 100+ acres. Easy enjoyable red. Early drinking is fun; the proprietor prefers to wait.

Ferrière Margaux r. ★★ 75 78 79 81 82 83 85 86 Phantom third-growth of only 10+ acres. Now in same hands as CHASSE-SPLEEN.

Feytit-Clinet Pomerol r. ★★ 70′ 71′ 75′ 78 79 81 82′ 83 85 86 87 Little property next to LATOUR-POMEROL. Has made some fine big strong wines. Managed by J-P MOUEIX.

Fieuzal Graves r. and (w. dr.) ★★★ 75′ 78′ 79 80 81′ 82′ 83 84 85′ 86′ 87 75-acre classed-growth at Léognan. Finely made memorable wines of both colours esp. since '84. Recent whites are keepers.

Figeac St-Em. r. ★★★ 70′ 71 75 76 78 79 80 81 82′ 83 84 85′ 86 87 Famous first-growth neighbour of CHEVAL BLANC. 98-acre gravelly v'yd gives one of Bordeaux's most attractive rich but elegant wines, maturing relatively quickly, but lasting almost indefinitely.

Filhot Sauternes w. sw. and dr. ★★★ 75 76′ 79′ 80 81 82′ 83′ 85 86′ Second-rank classed-growth with splendid ch, 148-acre v'yd. Lightish sw. wines for fairly early drinking, a little dry, and red.

La Fleur St-Em. r. ★★ 75 78 79 80 81 82' 83 85 86
Very small Côtes estate producing luxuriously fruity wines.

La Fleur-Gazin Pomerol r. ★★ 78 79 80 81 82 83 85' 86
Tiny MOUEIX-run property. Appealing, not over-aweing wines.

La Fleur-Pétrus Pomerol r. ■■■ 70 75' 76' 78 79 80 81' 82 83' 84 85
86 87 18-acre v'yd flanking PETRUS and under the same MOUEIX
management. Exceedingly fine plummy wines; Pomerol at its most
stylish.

Fombrauge St-Em. r. ■■ 75' 78' 79 80 81 82' 83 84 85 86
Major property of St-Christophe-des-Bardes, e. of St-Emilion, with
120 acres. Reliable St-Emilion making great efforts.

Fonbadet Pauillac r. ■■ 70 75 78 79 80 81' 82' 83 84 85 86
Cru Bourgeois of high repute with 38 acres next door to PONTET-CANET.
Old vines and no oak give solid wine needing long bottle-age. Notable
value.

⬛ Bx

Fonplégade St-Em. r. ★★ 75 76 78 79 81 82' 83 85 86
48-acre v'yd on the Côtes w. of St-Emilion in another branch of the
MOUEIX family. Fragrant and appealing.

Fonréaud Listrac r. ★★ 78' 79 80 81 82' 83 84 85' 86'
One of the bigger (96 acres) and better Crus Bourgeois of its area.
New broom (and barrels) since '83. See also Ch Lestage

Fonroque St-Em. r. ■■■ 70 71' 75' 76' 78 79 80 81 82 83' 84 85' 86
87 48 acres on the plateau n. of St-Emilion, MOUEIX property. Big
deep dark wine that needs lots of time.

Les Forts de Latour Pauillac r. ■■■ 70' 75 76 78' 79 80 81 82' 83
The second wine of Ch LATOUR; well worthy of its big brother. Unique
in being bottle-aged at least three years before release.

Fourcas-Dupré Listrac r. ■■ 70' 75 76 78' 79 80 81 82' 83' 84 85'
86 87 A top-class 100-acre Cru Bourgeois Exceptionnel making
consistent and elegant wine. To follow.

Fourcas-Hosten Listrac r. ■■→■■■ 70 75 76 78' 79 80 81 82' 83'
84 85 86' 87 96-acre Cru Bourgeois currently considered the best
of its commune. Firm wine with a long life.

La Gaffelière St-Em. r. ★★★ 70 79 81 82' 83' 85 86
61-acre first-growth at the foot of the Côtes below Ch BEL-AIR.
Justifying its reputation since '82.

La Garde Graves r. (w. dr.) ★★ 75' 78 79 81 82' 83' 84 85 86
Substantial ESCHENAUER property making reliably sound red.

Le Gay Pomerol r. ★★★ 70 71 75' 76' 78 79 81 82' 83' 85 86
Well-known 14-acre v'yd on the northern edge of Pomerol. Same
owner as Ch LAFLEUR, different management since '85. Splendid wine.

Gazin Pomerol r. ★★★ 71' 75' 76 78 81 82 83 85 86
Large property (for Pomerol) with 56 acres. Not quite as splendid as
its position next to PETRUS. 2nd label: Ch l'Hospitalet.

Gilette Sauternes w. sw. ★★★ 37 49 53 55 59 61 62
Extraordinary small Preignac château which stores its sumptuous
wines in cask to a great age. Only about 5,000 bottles of each. Ch Les
Justices is the sister-château.

Giscours Lab-Mar. r. ■■■ 70 71' 75' 76 78' 79' 80 81' 82' 83 84 85
86' 87 Splendid 182-acre third-growth s. of CANTENAC. Dynamically
run and making excellent vigorous wine for long maturing.

du Glana St-Jul. r. ★★ 70' 75' 78 79 81 82' 83 85 86
Big Cru Bourgeois in centre of St-Julien. Undemanding quality.

Gloria St-Jul. r. ■■■ 70' 75' 76 78' 79' 80 81 82' 83 84 85 86 87
Outstanding Cru Bourgeois making wine of vigour and finesse, among
classed-growths in quality. 110 acres. The owner, Henri Martin,
bought Ch ST-PIERRE in 1982.

Grand-Barrail-Lamarzelle-Figeac St-Em. r. ■■ 70 75 78 79 81 82'
83 85 86 48-acre property near FIGEAC, incl. Ch La Marzelle. Well-
reputed and popular, if scarcely exciting.

Grand-Corbin-Despagne St-Em. r. ✶✶ **70 75 78 79 81** 82' 83 85 86
One of the biggest and best Grands Crus on the CORBIN plateau.

Grand-Pontet St-Em. r. ✶✶ **75 78 79 81** 82' 83 85 86'
Widely distributed 35-acre neighbour of Ch BEAU SEJOUR-BECOT, in the same hands since 1980. "Supple", smooth wine.

Grand-Puy-Ducasse Pauillac r. ✶✶✶ **75 76 78 79 80 81** 82' 83 84 85 86 Well-known little fifth-growth bought in '71, renovated and enlarged to 90 acres under expert management. A best buy. 2nd label: Ch Artigues Arnaud.

Grand-Puy-Lacoste Pauillac r. ✶✶✶ **70'** 71 75 76 78' 79' 80 81' 82' 83 84 85 86 87 Leading fifth-growth famous for excellent full-bodied vigorous Pauillac. 110 acres among the "Bages" ch'x s. of the town, owned by the Borie family of DUCRU-BEAUCAILLOU.

Gravas Sauternes w. sw. ✶✶ **83'** 85 86
Small Barsac property; impressive firm wine.

La Grave-Figeac St-Em r. ✶✶
V. small neighbour of CHEVAL BL becoming known for sumptuous wine.

La Grave Trigant de Boisset Pom. r. ✶✶✶ **75' 76'** 78 79 80 81' 82' 83 84 85 86' 87 Verdant ch with small but first-class v'yd owned by Christian MOUEIX. Firm, beautifully structured Pomerol.

Gressier Grand Poujeaux Moulis. r. ✶✶✶ **70 75' 76 78 79'** 80 81 82 83' 84 85 86 Good Cru Bourgeois, neighbour of CHASSE-SPLEEN. Fine firm wine with a good track record.

Greysac Médoc r. ✶✶ **78 79'** 81' 82 83 85 86
Elegant 140-acre property. Easy, early-maturing wines.

Gruaud-Larose St-Jul. r. ✶✶✶ **70'** 73 75' 76 78' 79 80 81 82' 83 84 85 86 One of the biggest and best-known second-growths. 189 acres making smooth rich stylish claret. Owned by CORDIER. The excellent second wine is called Sarget de Gruaud-Larose.

Guadet-St-Julien St-Em. ✶✶ **82 83 85 86**
Extremely well-made wines from v. small Grand Cru Classé.

Guiraud Sauternes (r.) w. sw. (dr.) ✶✶✶ **70'** 76 78' 79' 81 82 83' 84 85 86' Newly restored classed-growth of top quality. 250+ acres. At best excellent sweet wine of great finesse and a small amount of red and dry white. The '83 will be superb in time.

Guiteronde-du-Hayot Sauternes w. sw. ✶✶
One of the larger Barsac ch'x. Good wines well distributed.

La Gurgue Margaux r. ✶✶ **79 81 82 83'** 84 85' 86
Small (30-acre) well-placed property with fine typical Margaux, recently bought by owners of Ch CHASSE-SPLEEN. To watch.

Hanteillan Cissac r. ✶✶ **75 79'** 80 81 82' 83 84 85 86'
Large (200+ acres) v'yd renovated and enlarged since 1973. Admirable bourgeois wine. Ch Larrivaux-Hanteillan is second quality. 50,000 cases.

Haut-Bages-Averous Pauillac r. ✶✶ **81 82 83 84** 85 86 87
The second wine of Ch LYNCH BAGES. Delicious easy drinking.

Haut-Bages-Libéral Pauillac r. ✶✶ **75 76 78 80 81** 82' 83 84 85 86'
Lesser-known fifth-growth of 64 acres in same stable as CHASSE-SPLEEN since '83. The results are excellent.

Haut-Bages-Monpelou Pauillac r. ✶✶ **75'** 78 79 80 81 82' 83 84 85 86
25-acre Cru Bourgeois stable-mate of Ch BATAILLEY on former DUHART-MILON land. Good minor Pauillac.

Haut-Bailly Graves r. ✶✶✶ **70'** 75 78 79' 80 81' 82 83 84 85 86 87
60+ acre estate at Léognan famous for ripe, round, intelligently made, sometimes "feminine" wine since '79. 2nd label: La Parde de H-B.

Haut-Batailley Pauillac r. ✶✶✶ **70'** 75' 78' 79 80 81 82' 83 84 85 86 87 The smaller section of the fifth-growth Batailley estate: 49 acres. Often in a gentler vein than its sister ch, GRAND-PUY-LACOSTE. 2nd label La Tour-d'Aspic.

Haut-Brignon Premières Côtes r. and w. dr. ★
Big producer of standard wines at Cénac, owned by a major
Champagne coop. Do not confuse with the next!

Haut-Brion Pessac, Graves r. (w.) ★★★★ 61 62 64 66 70' 71 75' 76
78' 79 80 81' 82' 83 84 85' 86 87 The oldest great ch of Bordeaux
and the only non-Médoc first-growth of 1855. 108 acres. Reds of
singular balance, particularly good since 1975. A little full dry white
in 78 79 81 83 84 85 86 87. See Bahans-Haut-Brion, la Mission H-B.

Haut-Marbuzet St-Estèphe r. ██ ★★ 75' 76 78' 79 80 81 82' 83 84 85 86
One of the best of many good St-Estèphe Crus Bourgeois. 100 acres.
Ch'x Tour de Marbuzet, CHAMBERT-MARBUZET, MacCarthy-Moula in
same hands. New oak gives them all classic style.

Haut-Pontet St-Em. r. ★★ 70 71 75 78 79 81 82' 83 85 86
12-acre v'yd of the Côtes well deserving its Grand Cru status.

Haut-Quercus St-Em. r. ★★
Oak-aged cooperative wine to a very high standard.

Haut-Sarpe St-Em. r. ██ ★★ 78 79 81 82 83' 85 86
Small Grand Cru Classé with a very fine château. Same owner as Ch
LA CROIX. To follow.

Arguments for and against Decanting

*Fierce arguments take place between wine-lovers over whether it is a good
or a bad thing to decant wine from its bottle into a carafe. The argument
in favour is that it allows the wine to "breathe" and its bouquet to expand;
against, that its precious breath is dissipated – or at the least that it makes
no difference.*

*Two additional practical reasons in favour concern old wine which has
deposited dregs, which can be left in the bottle by careful decanting, and
young wine being consumed before it is fully developed: thorough aeration
helps to create the illusion of maturity. An aesthetic one is that decanters
are handsome on the table.*

*Decanting is done by pouring the wine into another container very
steadily until any sediment reaches the shoulder of the bottle. To see the
sediment clearly hold the bottle's neck over a light bulb or a candle.*

Haut-Ségottes St-Em. r. ★★ 85' 86
22-acre Grand Cru resolutely run. To watch.

Hortevie St-Jul. r. ██ ★★ 81 82 83 84 85' 86
One of the few St Julien Crus Bourgeois. This tiny v'yd and its bigger
sister TERREY-GROS-CAILLOU are shining examples.

Houissant St-Estèphe r. ★★ 78 79 80 81 82 83 84 85 86
Typical, robust, well-balanced St-Estèphe Cru Bourgeois Exceptionnel, also called Ch Leyssac; well known in Denmark.

d'Issan Cant-Mar. r. ███ ★★★ 70 75' 78 79' 80 81 82' 83' 84 85 86' 87
Beautifully restored moated ch with 75-acre third-growth v'yd well
known for fragrant, virile but delicate wine.

Kirwan Cant-Mar. r. ███ ★★★ 75' 78 79' 81 82' 83' 84 85 86 87
Well-run 86-acre third-growth owned by SCHRÖDER & SCHYLER. New
planting of '60s now mature and results tasting v. good.

Labégorce Margaux r. ★★ 75' 76 78 79 80 81' 82' 83' 84 85 86
Substantial 69-acre property north of Margaux with long-lived wines
of true Margaux quality.

Labégorce-Zédé Margaux r. ██ ★★ 75' 78 79 80 81' 82' 83' 84 85 86
Outstanding Cru Bourgeois on the road n. from Margaux. 62 acres.
Typical delicate, fragrant Margaux, truly classic since '81. The same
family as VIEUX-CHATEAU-CERTAN.

Lacoste-Borie The second wine of Ch GRAND-PUY-LACOSTE.

Lafaurie-Peyraguey Sauternes w. sw. ★★★ 75' 76' 78' 80 81 82 83' 85
86 Fine classed-growth of only 49 acres at Bommes, belonging to
CORDIER. After a lean patch, good, rich and racy wines.

Lafite-Rothschild Pauillac r. ★★★★ 70' 75' 78 79 80 81' 82' 83 84 85 86 87 First-growth of fabulous style and perfume in its great vintages, which keep for decades. Off-form for several years but resplendent since '76. Amazing circular cellars opened '87; joint ventures in Chile ('88) and California ('89). 2nd wine: MOULIN DES CARRUADES. 225 acres.

Lafleur Pomerol r. ★★★ 70' 71' 75' 78 79 81 82' 83' 85 86 Property of 12 acres just n. of PETRUS. Excellent wine of the finer, less "fleshy" kind. Same owner as LE GAY. MOUEIX oenology.

Lafleur-Gazin Pomerol r. ★★ 70 71' 75' 76' 78 79 81 82' 83 85 Distinguished small MOUEIX estate on the n.e. border of Pomerol.

Lafon-Rochet St-Est. r. ★★ 70' 75' 78 79 81 82 83' 85 86 87 Fourth-growth neighbour of Ch COS D'ESTOURNEL, restored in the '60s and again recently. 110 acres. Rather hard, dark, full-bodied St-Estèphe. Same owner as Ch PONTET-CANET.

Lagrange Pomerol r. ★★★ 70 71' 75' 76 78 79 80 81 82' 83 85' 86 87 20-acre v'yd in the centre of Pomerol run by the ubiquitous house of MOUEIX. Maturing vines are giving deeper flavour.

Lagrange St-Jul. r. ★★★ 70' 75' 78 79' 81 82 83' 84 85 86' 87 Formerly run-down third-growth inland from St-Julien, bought by Suntory in 1982. 123+ acres, restored to tip-top condition. To watch. Second label: Les Fiefs de Lagrange 83' 85 86

La Lagune Ludon r. ★★★ 70' 75' 76' 78' 79 80 81 82' 83 84 85 86 87 Well-run ultra-modern 160-acre third-growth in the extreme s. of the Médoc. Attractively rich and fleshy wines; usually brilliant quality.

Lalande-Borie St-Jul. r. ★★ 78 79 81 82 83 84 85 86 A baby brother of the great DUCRU-BEAUCAILLOU created from part of the former v'yd of Ch LAGRANGE.

Lamarque Lamarque (Haut-Médoc) r. ★★ 75' 78 79 81' 82 83' 84 85' 86' Splendid medieval fortress of the central Médoc with 113 acres giving admirable and improving wine of high "Bourgeois" standard.

Lanessan Cussac (Haut-Médoc) r. ★★ 75' 78' 79 80 81 82' 83 84 85 86' Distinguished 108-acre Cru Bourgeois Exceptionnel just s. of St-Julien. Lots of flavour.

Langoa-Barton St-Jul. r. ★★★ 70' 75' 76 78' 79 80 81 82' 83 84 85 86 87 49-acre third-growth sister-ch to LEOVILLE-BARTON. V. old family property with impeccable standards, and value.

Larcis-Ducasse St-Em. r. ★★★ 70' 75' 78 79 81 82' 83 84 85' 86 87 The top property of St-Laurent, eastern neighbour of St-Emilion, on the Côtes next to Ch PAVIE. 30 acres. Coasting?

Larmande St-Em. r. ★★ 75' 78 79 80 81 82 83 84 85 86 Substantial 54-acre property related to CAP-DE-MOURLIN. Replanted and now making rich, strikingly scented wine.

Laroque St-Em. r. ★★ 70' 75' 76' 78 79 80 81 82' 83 84 85 86 Important 108-acre v'yd with an impressive mansion on the St-Emilion côtes in St Christophe.

Larose-Trintaudon St-Lau. (Haut-Médoc) r. ★★ 75' 78 79 80 81 82 83 84 85 86' The biggest v'yd in the Médoc: 388 acres. Modern methods make reliable fruity and charming Cru Bourgeois wine.

Laroze St-Em. r. ★★ 75' 78' 79 80 81 82 83 85 86 Big v'yd (74 acres) on the w. Côtes. Relatively light wines from sandy soil; soon enjoyable. Sometimes excellent.

Larrivet-Haut-Brion Graves r. (w.) ★★ 75' 76 79' 80 81 82' 83 84 85 86 87 Little property at Léognan with perfectionist standards. 500 cases of white to age up to 5 years.

Lascombes Margaux r. (p.) ★★★ 61 70' 75' 78 79 81 82 83 84 85 86 240-acre second-growth owned by the British brewers Bass-Charrington and lavishly restored. After a poor patch, new vigour and skill since '82. Second wine: Ch Segonnes.

Latour Pauillac r. ★★★★ 61 62 64 66 67 70' 71 73 75' 76' 78' 79' 80 81' 82' 83 83 84 85 86 87   First-growth. The most consistent great wine in Bordeaux, in France and probably the world: rich, intense and almost immortal in great years, almost always classical and pleasing even in bad ones. British-owned (though different company since '89). 150 acres. Second wine LES FORTS DE LATOUR.

Latour à Pomerol Pomerol r. ★★★★ 70' 71' 75' 76' 78 79' 80' 81 82' 83 84 85 86 87   Top growth of 19 acres under MOUEIX management. Pomerol of great power and perfume, yet also ravishing finesse.

Laujac Médoc r. ★★ 75' 78 81 82 83 85 86   Cru Bourgeois in the n. Médoc owned by the CRUSE family. Well known but scarcely outstanding. 62 acres.

des Laurets St-Em. r. ★★ 75' 78 79 81 82 83 85 86   Major property of Puisseguin and Montagne-St-Emilion (to the e.) with 160 acres on the Côtes. Sterling wine.

Laville-Haut-Brion Graves w. dr. ★★★★ 71 75 78 79 81 82 83' 84 85 86 87   A tiny production of one of the very best white Graves for long maturing, made at Ch LA MISSION-HAUT-BRION.

Léoville-Barton St-Jul. r. ★★★ 61 66 70' 75' 76 78' 79 80 81 82' 83 84 85 86 87   90-acre portion of the great second-growth Léoville v'yd in the Anglo-Irish hands of the Barton family for over 150 years. Powerful and classic claret, made by traditional methods. Always moderately priced.

Léoville-Las Cases St-Jul. r. ★★★★ 61 66 70' 75' 76 78' 79 80 81 82' 83 84 85' 86' 87'   The largest portion of the old Léoville estate, 210 acres, with one of the highest reputations in Bordeaux. Elegant, complex, powerful but never heavy wines. Second label: Clos du Marquis.

Léoville-Poyferré St-Jul. r. ★★★ 70' 75' 78' 79 80 81 82' 83 84 85 86' 87   For years the least outstanding of the Léovilles; since 1980 again living up to the great name. '82 is a triumph and '86 even better. 156 acres. Second label: Ch Moulin-Riche.

Lestage Listrac r. ★★ 75' 78' 81 82' 83 84 85 86'   130-acre Cru Bourgeois in same hands as Ch FONREAUD. Light, quite stylish wine, aged in oak since '85.

Liot Barsac w. sw. ★★ 70' 71 75' 76 78 79' 80 81 83 85 86   Consistent fairly light golden wines from 94 acres.

Liversan St-Sau. (Haut-Médoc) r. ★★ 75' 78 79 81 82' 83 84 85 86'   116-acre Grand Cru Bourgeois inland from Pauillac. Change of regime in 1984 is greatly improving standards. Ch Fonpiqueyre is a second wine in certain markets.

Livran Médoc r. ★★ 75 78' 79 81 82' 83 85   Big Cru Bourgeois at St-Germain in the n. Médoc. Consistent round wines (half Merlot).

Loudenne St-Yzans (Médoc) r. ★★★ (r.) 75' 78' 81 82' 83 84 85 86'   Beautiful riverside ch owned by Gilbeys since 1875. Well-made Cru Bourgeois red and a very agreeable dry white from 120 acres. The white is best at 2-3 years.

Loupiac-Gaudiet Loupiac w. sw. ★★   Reliable source of good-value almost-Sauternes, just across the river Garonne.

La Louvière Graves r. and w. dr. ★★ (r.) 75 78 79 80 81 82' 83 84 85 86 87 (w.)   Noble 135-acre estate at Léognan. Excellent white for drinking or maturing, and red recently of classed-growth standard.

de Lussac St-Em. r. ★★ 75' 78' 81 82 83 85 86   One of the best estates in Lussac-St-Emilion (to the n.e.).

Lynch-Bages Pauillac r. ★★★ 61 66 70' 75' 76 78' 79 80 81 82' 83' 84 85 86 87   Always popular, but now one of Pauillac's regular stars. 200 acres making rich robust wine: deliciously brambly; occasionally great, with recent vintages esp. notable.

Lynch-Moussas Pauillac r. ★★ 75′ 78 79 81 82′ 83 84 85 86
Fifth-growth restored by the director of Ch BATAILLEY since 1969. Now 60+ acres and new equipment are making serious wine, gaining depth as the young vines age.

du Lyonnat Lussac-St-Em. r. ★★ 82 83 85 86′
120-acre estate with well-distributed reliable wine.

Magdelaine St-Em. r. ★★★ 70′ 71′ 73 75 76 78 79 80 81 82 83′ 85′ 86 87 Leading first-growth of the Côtes, 28 acres next to AUSONE owned by J-P MOUEIX. Beautifully balanced wine. On top form.

Magence Graves r. w. dr. ★★ (r.) w. dr.
Go-ahead 45-acre property at St Pierre de Mons, in the s. of the Graves, well known for distinctly SAUVIGNON-flavoured very dry white that ages well, and fruity red for drinking in 4-6 yrs.

Malartic-Lagravière Graves r. and (w. dr.) ★★★ (r.) 70′ 75′ 76′ 78 79 80 81 82′ 83 84 85 86′ 87 (w.) 75 76 79 81′ 82 83 84 85 86 87 Well-known Léognan classed-growth of 34 acres making well-structured red and a very little excellent fruity SAUVIGNON white, hard to resist young, but worth cellaring.

Malescasse Lamarque (Haut-Médoc) r. ★★ 78 79′ 81 82 83 85 86 87
Renovated Cru Bourgeois with 100 acres in a good situation, owned by M. Tesseron of Ch LAFON-ROCHET.

Malescot-St-Exupéry Margaux r. ★★★ 70′ 75′ 78′ 79′ 80 81 82′ 83′ 84 85 86 Third-growth of 84 acres. Long-lived, eventually fragrant and stylish Margaux.

de Malle Sauternes r. w. sw./dr. ★★★ (w. sw.). 75 76 78 79 80 81′ 82 83 85 86′ Famous and beautiful ch with Italian gdns. at Preignac. 124 acres. Good sweet and dry w. and r. (Graves) Ch de CARDAILLAN.

de Malleret Haut-Médoc r. ★★ 82 83 84 85 86
Big well-run Cru Bourgeois with beautiful château and park at Le Pian near Bordeaux. Reliable quality.

Maquin-St-Georges St-Em. r. ★★ 81 82 83 85 86
Steady producer of delicious "satellite" St-Em. at St-Georges.

de Marbuzet St-Est. r. ★★ 75 76 78 79 81 82 83 84 85 86 87
Effectively the second label of Ch COS D'ESTOURNEL, and correspondingly well made.

Margaux Margaux r. (w. dr.) ★★★★ 61 66 70 78′ 79 80 81′ 82′ 83′ 84 85′ 86′ 87 First-growth (with 209 acres of vines), the most resounding and fabulously perfumed of all in its best vintages. "Pavillon Rouge" (81 82′ 83′ 84 85 86 87) is the second wine. "Pavillon Blanc" is the best white (SAUVIGNON) wine of the Médoc, for 3-4 years' ageing.

Marquis-d'Alesme Margaux r. ★★ 75′ 78 79 80 81 82 83 84 85 86
Tiny (17-acre) third-growth, formerly made with Ch MALESCOT; independent since '79. Better than its reputation.

Marquis-de-Terme Margaux r. ★★★ 75′ 79 80 81′ 82 83 85 86
Renovated fourth-growth of 84 acres. Fragrant, fairly lean wines. Sells principally in France.

Martinens Margaux r. ★★ 75 78′ 79′ 81 82 83 84 85 86
75-acre Cru Bourgeois at Cantenac, recently much improved.

Maucaillou Moulis r. ★★ 70′ 75′ 78 79 80 81 82 83′ 84 85′ 86′ 87
130-acre Cru Bourgeois with cru classé standards, property of DOURTHE family. Full, richly fruity, "Cap de Haut-M." is second wine.

Meyney St-Est. r. ★★→★★★ 75′ 78′ 79 81 82′ 83 84 85 86
Big (125-acre) riverside property next door to Ch MONTROSE, one of the best of many steady Crus Bourgeois in St-Estèphe. Owned by CORDIER. Second label: Prieur de Meyney.

Millet Graves r. w. dr. ★★ 81 82 83 85 86
160-acre estate at Portets; useful Graves.

La Mission-Haut-Brion Graves r. ★★★★ 61 64 66 71′ 75′ 76 78′ 79 80 81 82′ 83 84 85′ 86 87 Neighbour and long-time rival to Ch HAUT-BRION, since 1984 in the same hands. Serious and grand old-style claret for long maturing, usually "bigger" than Haut-Brion. 30 acres. Ch Latour-H-B is its second-quality wine.

Monbousquet St-Em. r. ■■ 75 78′ 79′ 81 82 83 84 85 86 Fine 75-acre estate in the Dordogne valley below St-Emilion. Attractive early-maturing wine from deep gravel soil lasts well.

Montrose St-Est. r. ■■■ 61 66 70′ 75′ 78 79′ 80 81 82′ 83 84 85 86′ 87 158-acre family-run second-growth well known for deeply coloured, forceful, old-style claret. But recent vintages are lighter. 2nd wine: La Dame de Montrose.

Moulin-à-Vent Moulis r. ★★ 70′ 75′ 78′ 79 80 81 82′ 83 84 85 86 60-acre property now in the forefront of this up-and-coming appellation. Lively, forceful wine. La Tour Blanche (Médoc) has same owners.

Moulin des Carruades The second-quality wine of Ch LAFITE.

Moulin du Cadet St-Em. ■■ 75′ 78′ 79 80 81 82′ 83 85 86 87 First-class little v'yd on the Côtes managed by MOUEIX.

Moulinet Pomerol r. ★★★ 75 78 79 81 82 83 85 86 One of Pomerol's bigger ch'x, 43 acres on lightish soil; wine ditto.

Mouton-Baronne-Philippe Pauillac r. ★★★ 70′ 75′ 78′ 79 81 82′ 83 84 85 86 87 Substantial fifth-growth nurtured by the late Baron Philippe de Rothschild, 125 acres making fine but much gentler, less rich and tannic wine than MOUTON.

Mouton-Rothschild Pauillac r. ■■■■ 61 66 67 70′ 71 73 75′ 76 78′ 79 80 81 82′ 83 84 85 86′ 87 Officially a first-growth since 1973, though for 40 years worthy of the title. 175 acres (87% CABERNET SAUVIGNON) making wine of majestic richness (82 and 86 are Imperial). Also the world's greatest museum of works of art relating to wine. Baron Philippe, the greatest champion of the Médoc, died in 1988.

Nairac Sauternes w. sw. ■■ 73 75 76′ 78 79 80 81 82 83′ 85 86′ Barsac classed-growth with perfectionist owner. Fascinating wines to lay down.

Nenin Pomerol r. ★★★ 70′ 75′ 78 81 83 85 86 Well-known 66-acre estate; currently below par.

Olivier Graves r. and w. dr. ★★★ (r.) 79′ 81 82 83 84 85 86 90-acre classed-growth, surrounding a moated castle at Léognan. 9,000 cases r., 12,000 w., both in need of a promised upgrade. Recent wines are intended for longer maturing.

Les Ormes-de-Pez St-Est. ■■ 75′ 78′ 79 80 81′ 82′ 83′ 84 85 86′ 87 Outstanding 72-acre Cru Bourgeois managed by Ch LYNCH BAGES. Increasingly notable full-flavoured St-Estèphe.

Les Ormes Sorbet Médoc r. ■■ 81 82 83 85 86′ Emerging smaller producer of good solid red aged in new oak at Couquèques. 2nd label: Ch de Conques.

Palmer Cant-Mar. r. ■■■■ 61′ 66′ 70 71′ 75′ 76 78′ 79′ 80 81 82 83′ 84 85 86 87 The star ch of CANTENAC; a third-growth often on a level just below the first-growths. Wine of power, flesh and delicacy. 110 acres with Dutch, British and French owners. 2nd wine: Réserve du Général (value).

Pape-Clément Graves r. and (w. dr.) ★★★ 70 75′ 78′ 79′ 81 82′ 83 84 85′ 86 87 Ancient v'yd at Pessac, with record of seductive, scented not ponderous reds, but recent vintages less even. New resolve since '85 (and more white).

Patache d'Aux Bégadan (Médoc) r. ★★ 79′ 81 82′ 83′ 85 86′ 90-acre Cru Bourgeois of the n. Médoc. Fragrant, lightish wine.

Paveil-de Luze Margaux r. ■■ 75′ 78 79 81 82′ 83 84 85 86′ Old family estate at Soussans. Small but highly regarded.

Pavie St-Em. r. ★★★ ▮▮▮ 70 71' 75' 76 78 79' 80 81 82' 83' 84 85' 86
Splendidly sited first-growth of 100 acres on the slope of the Côtes.
Typically rich and tasty St-Em., particularly since '82. The family
owns the smaller Ch'x Pavie-Decesse and La Clusière.

Pavie-Decesse St-Em. r. ▮▮

Pavie-Macquin St-Em. r. ▮▮ 75 78 79 82 83 85' 86
Reliable 25-acre Côtes v'yd e. of St-Em. Replanting and enlarging.

Pedesclaux Pauillac r. ★★ 70' 75' 78 79 80 81 82' 83 84 85 86
50-acre fifth-growth on the level of a good Cru Bourgeois. Solid strong
wines loved by Belgians. Grand-Duroc-Milon and Bellerose are
second labels.

Petit-Village Pomerol r. ★★★ 70 71' 75' 76' 78 79 81 82' 83 84 85 86
One of the best-known little properties: 26 acres next to VIEUX-CH-
CERTAN, same owner as Ch COS D'ESTOURNEL. Powerful plummy wine.

Petrus Pomerol r. ★★★★ 61 64 66 67 70' 71' 73 75' 76' 78 79' 80 81
82' 83 84 85' 86 87 The great name of Pomerol. 28 acres of gravelly
clay giving massively rich and concentrated wine. 95% Merlot vines.
Each vintage adds lustre (84 and 87 were in tiny quantities). The
price, too, is legendary.

Peyrabon St-Sauveur r. ▮▮ 75 78 79 81 82 83 84 85 86
Serious 82-acre Cru Bourgeois popular in the Low Countries.

Peyreau St-Em. r. ★★
Sister-ch of CLOS L'ORATOIRE.

de Pez St-Est. r. ▮▮▮ 66 70' 71' 73 75' 76 78' 79 80 81 82' 83 84 85
86 Outstanding Cru Bourgeois of 60 acres. As reliable as any of the
classed growths of the village, and nearly as fine. Needs v. long
storage. (e.g. '66 was ideal in '88.)

Phélan-Ségur St-Est. r. ▮▮ 70' 75' 76' 78 79 81 82' 85 86
Big and important Cru Bourgeois (125 acres) with some fine old
vintages. New owners in 1985 have put their foot down hard.

Pichon-Longueville Pauillac r. ▮▮▮ 70' 75 78' 79' 80 81 82' 83 84
85 86' 87 77-acre second-growth whose wines have varied widely.
Under new and highly ambitious management since '87.

Pichon-Longueville, Comtesse de Lalande Pauillac r. ▮▮▮▮ 61 66
70' 75' 76 78' 79' 80 81' 82' 83' 84 85 86 87 Second-growth
neighbour to Ch LATOUR. 148 acres. Consistently among the very top
performers; classic long-lived wine of fabulous breed, even in lesser
years. 2nd wine: Réserve de la Comtesse.

Pique-Caillou Graves r. ▮▮
Little-known 40-acre neighbour of HAUT-BRION in the Bordeaux
suburbs. Worth watching.

Pindefleurs St-Em. r. ★★ 75 78 79 81 82' 83 85 86
Up and coming 25-acre v'yd on the St-Emilion plateau.

Piron Graves (r.) w. dr. ▮▮
Producer of seductively fruity modern white Graves at St Morillon.

de Pitray Castillon r. ★★ 81 82 83 85 86
Substantial (62 acre) v'yd on the Côtes de Castillon e. of St-Emilion.
Good light wines.

Plagnac Médoc r. ★★
Cru Bourgeois at Bégadan restored by Cordier, owners of GRUAUD-
LAROSE, etc.

Plince Pomerol r. ★★ 75 79 80 81 82 83 85 86
Reputable 20-acre property near Libourne. Attractive, perhaps
rather simple wine from sandy soil.

La Pointe Pomerol r. ★★★ 70' 75' 78 79 81 82 83' 85 86
Prominent 63-acre estate, well made, but relatively spare of flesh. Ch
LA SERRE is in the same hands.

Pontac-Monplaisir Graves r. (w. dr.) ▮▮
Another Graves property suddenly offering delicious white wine.

Pontet-Canet Pauillac r. ★★★ 70 75′ 78′ 79′ 80 81′ 82′ 83′ 85 86
One of the biggest classed-growths. 182 acres, neighbour to MOUTON, potentially better than its official rank of fifth-growth, but dragged its feet for many years. Current owners (same as LAFON-ROCHET) are trying hard. 2nd label: Les Hauts de Pontet.

Potensac Potensac (Médoc) r. ■■ 75′ 78′ 79 81′ 82′ 83 84 85′ 86 87 The best-known Cru Bourgeois of the n. Médoc. The neighbouring Ch'x Lassalle and Gallais-Bellevue belong to the same family, the Delons, owners of LEOVILLE-LAS CASES. Class shows.

Pouget Margaux ★★ 70′ 75 78 79 80 81 82′ 83 85 86
19-acre v'yd attached to Ch BOYD-CANTENAC. In 1983 separate chais were built. Similar, rather lighter, wines.

Poujeaux (Theil) Moulis r. ■■ 70′ 75′ 76 78 79′ 80 81 82′ 83′ 84 85 86 87 Family-run Cru Exceptionnel of 120 acres selling its powerful, concentrated wine largely direct to an appreciative French public. 2nd label: La Salle de Poujeaux. Also Ch Arnauld (83′).

Prieuré-Lichine Cant-Mar. r. ■■■ 70 75 76 78′ 79′ 80 81 82′ 83′ 84 85 86′ 143-acre fourth-growth brought to the fore by Alexis Lichine since 1952. Excellent full-bodied and fragrant Margaux.

Puy-Blanquet St-Em. r. ★★ 75′ 78 79 81 82′ 83 85
The major property of St-Etienne-de-Lisse, e. of St-Emilion, with over 50 acres. Early-maturing St-Em., if below the top class.

Puy-Razac St-Em. r. ★★ 78 79 81′ 82′ 83 85 86
Tiny brother to MONBOUSQUET at the foot of the Côtes near Ch PAVIE.

Puygueraud Côte de Francs r. ★★ 82 83 85
Leading ch of this rising district. Wood-aged wines of surprising class.

Rabaud-Promis Sauternes w. sw. ★★ 71 75 76 78 79 81 83 85
74-acre classed-growth at Bommes. Little seen outside France.

Rahoul Graves r. and w. dr. ■■ (r.) 78′ 81 82 83 84 85 86 (w.) 85 86′ 87 37-acre v'yd at Portets making particularly good wine from maturing vines; 80% red. White is aged in oak, too.

Ramage-la-Batisse Haut-Médoc r. ■■ 75′ 78 79 81 82 83′ 85 86
Outstanding Cru Bourgeois of 130 acres at St-Sauveur, west of Pauillac. Increasingly attractive since '80.

Rausan-Ségla Margaux r. ★★★ 70′ 78 79 81 82 83′ 84 85 86′
106-acre second-growth; famous for its fragrance; a great Médoc name trying hard to regain its rank. New British owners in '89.

Rauzan-Gassies Margaux r. ★★ 61 75′ 76 78′ 79′ 80 81 82 83 85 86 87 75-acre second-growth neighbour of the last with little excitement to report for two decades, now seemingly perking up – but still far to go.

Raymond-Lafon Sauternes w. sw. ■■■ 75′ 76 78 79 80′ 81′ 82 83′ 85 86′ Serious Sauternes estate run by the manager of Ch D'YQUEM. Splendid wines for long ageing. Among the top Sauternes today.

de Rayne-Vigneau Sauternes w. sw. ★★★ 67 71′ 76′ 78 81 83 85 86
164-acre classed-growth at Bommes. Standard sweet wine and a little dry, "Raynesec". New equipment in 1980.

Respide-Médeville Graves (r.) w. dr. ★★ (w.) 81 83 84′ 85 86 87
One of the best white-wine ch'x. Full-flavoured wines for ageing. (N.B. '85 Cuvée Kauffman)

Reynon Premières Côtes de Bordeaux r. and w. dr. ■■
100 acres producing extraordinary dry white from very old Sauvignon vines ("Vieilles Vignes": 85 86 87). Also "Clos Floridène" barrel-fermented white (85 86 87′) and red since '85, D.Y.A. white and serious red (81 82 83 85 86).

Reysson Vertheuil Haut-Médoc r. ★★ 81 82′ 83 84 85 86
Recently replanted, up-and-coming 120-acre Cru Bourgeois with the same owners as Ch CHASSE-SPLEEN.

Ricaud Loupiac w. sw. (or dr.) or r. ■■ 81 82 83′ 85 86′
Substantial grower of Sauternes-like dessert wine, just across the river. New owners are working hard.

Rieussec Sauternes w. sw. ★★★ 70 71' 75' 76' 78 79 80 81' 82 83' 85 86 Worthy neighbour of Ch D'YQUEM with 136 acres in Fargues, bought in 1984 by the (Lafite) Rothschilds. Not the sweetest; can be exquisitely fine. Also a dry wine: "R" and super-wine "Crème de Tête".

Ripeau St-Em. r. ★★ 75 78 79 81 82 83 85 86 Increasingly high-performance Grand Cru in the centre of the plateau. 49 acres.

La Rivière Fronsac r. ★★ The biggest and most impressive Fronsac property. Tannic wines repay long ageing.

de Rochemorin Graves r. (w. dr.) ★★ 81 82 83 84 85 86 An important restoration at Martillac by the owner of ch LA LOUVIERE. 135 acres of new vines promise great things.

Romer du Hayot Sauternes w. sw. ★★ 79 80 81 82 83 85 86' A minor-classed growth with a growing reputation.

Roquetaillade-la-Grange Graves r. w. dr. ★★ Substantial estate establishing a name for fine red (s.) Graves.

Roudier Montagne-St-Em. r. ★★ 75-acre "satellite" St-Em. with the flavour of the real thing. Sister-ch of BALESTARD. To follow.

Rouget Pomerol r. ★★ 70 71 75' 76' 78 79 81 82' 83 85' 86 Attractive old estate with rising standards on the n. edge of Pomerol. Good vintages need 10 years +.

Royal St-Emilion Brand name of the important and dynamic growers' cooperative. See also Haut Quercus, Berliquet.

Ruat-Petit-Poujeaux Moulis r. ★★ 79 81 82 83 84 85 86 45-acre v'yd gaining in reputation for sound wine.

St-André Corbin St-Em. r. ★★ 75' 78 79' 81 82' 83 85 86 Considerable 54-acre property in Montagne-St-Emilion with a long record of above-average wines.

St-Bonnet Médoc r. ★★ Big n. Médoc estate at St-Christoly. V. flavoury wine.

St-Estèphe, Marquis de St-Est. r. ★ 81 82 83 84 85 86 The growers' cooperative; over 200 members. Good value.

St-Georges St-Geo., St-Em. r. ★★ 75 78 79 81 82 83 85 86 Noble 18th-century ch overlooking the St-Emilion plateau from the hill to the n. 125 acres; v. good wine sold direct to the public.

St-Georges-Côte-Pavie St-Em. r. ★★ 79 81 82 83' 85' 86 Perfectly placed little v'yd on the Côtes. To watch.

Saint-Pierre St-Jul. r. ★★★ 70' 75' 76 78' 79 80 81' 82' 83' 84 85 86 87 Small (50-acre) fourth-growth many years in Belgian ownership; bought in 1982 by Henri Martin of Ch GLORIA. A name to watch.

St-Pierre Graves (r.) w. dr. ★★ 81 84 85 86 87 Estate at St Pierre de Mons making classic Graves of notable character and flavour.

de Sales Pomerol r. ★★★ 70' 75' 78' 79 81 82' 83 85 86 The biggest v'yd of Pomerol (116 acres), attached to the grandest château. Not poetry but certainly excellent prose. Second labels: Ch Chantalouette and Ch du Delias.

Sénéjac Haut-Médoc r. (w. dr.) ★★ 75 76' 78 79 81 82' 83' 84 85 86' 43-acre Cru Bourgeois in s. Médoc run with increasing skill.

La Serre St-Em. r. ★★ 70 75' 78 79 81 82 83 85 86 Well-run small Grand Cru with same owner as LA POINTE.

Sigalas-Rabaud Sauternes w. sw. ★★★ 76' 78 79 81 82 83' 85 86 The lesser part of the former Rabaud estate: 34 acres in Bommes, making first-class sweet wine in a fresh, grapey style.

Siran Lab-Mar. r. ★★★ 61 66 70 71' 75' 78' 79 80 81' 82' 83 84 85 86 74-acre property of Cru Classé quality. Elegant, long-lived wines, consistently well made.

Smith-Haut-Lafitte Graves r. and (w. dr.) ★★→★★★ (r.) 78 79 81 82′
83 84 85 86 (w: age 2-3 years.) Run-down old classed-growth at
Martillac restored in the '70s. New British owners (same as RAUSAN-
SEGLA) in '89. 122 acres (14 of white). The white wine is light and
fruity; the red light. Recent efforts should improve it.

Sociando-Mallet Haut-Médoc r. ★★ 70 75 78 79 81 82 83 84 85 86
Splendid Cru Grand Bourgeois at St-Seurin in the n. 65 acres.

Soutard St-Em. r. ★★ 70′ 71 75′ 76 78′ 79 80 81 82′ 83 85′ 86
Reliable 48-acre classed-growth n. of the town. A long-term keeper.

Suduiraut Sauternes w. sw. ★★★ 67 70 75 76′ 78 79′ 81 82′ 83 84
85 86 One of the best Sauternes – though rarely super-rich. Over
173 acres of the top class, under capable management. Selection:
Cuvée Madame (82, 85).

Taillefer Pomerol r. ★★ 70 75 78 79 81 82′ 83 85 86
24-acre property on the edge of Pomerol owned by another branch
of the MOUEIX family. Give it time.

Talbot St-Jul. r. (w.) ★★★ 70′ 75′ 78′ 79 81 82′ 83 84 85 86 87
Important 240-acre fourth-growth, sister-ch to GRUAUD-LAROSE, wine
similarly attractive: rich, satisfying, reliable and good value. (V.g.)
second label: Connétable Talbot. White is called "Caillou Blanc".

Tayac Sou-Mar. r. ★★ 81 82 83 85 86
Margaux's biggest Cru Bourgeois. Reliable if not noteworthy.

Terrefort-Quancard Bordeaux r. w. dr. ★★ 82 83 84 85 86
Huge producer of good value wines at St-André-de-Cubzac. Rocky
sub-soil contributes to surprising quality. 33,000 cases.

du Tertre Ar-Mar. r. ★★★ 70′ 75 78 79′ 80 81 82′ 83′ 84 85 86 87
Fifth-growth, isolated s. of Margaux; restored to excellence by the
owner of CALON-SEGUR. Fragrant and long-lived.

Tertre-Daugay St-Em. r. ★★★ 78 79 81 82′ 83′ 85 86
Small, spectacularly sited, Grand Cru. Restored to its proper place
since purchase in '78 by the owner of LA GAFFELIERE.

Thieuley Entre-Deux-Mers r. p. w. dr. ★★
Substantial supplier, esp. of "clairet" (rosé) and grapey SAUVIGNON.

Timberlay Bordeaux r. (w. dr.) ★ 82 83 85 86
The biggest property of Cubzac; 185 acres. Pleasant light wines.

Toumilon Graves r. w. dr ★★
Notable ch in St-Pierre-de-Mons. Fresh and charming r. and w.

La Tour-Blanche Sauternes w. sw. (r.) ★★★ 75′ 76 79 81′ 83′ 85 86
Top-rank 57-acre estate at Bommes with a state wine-growing
school. Not among the leaders for a long time. But '83 is v.g.

La Tour-Carnet St-Lau. r. ★★ 79 80 81 82′ 83 84 85 86
Fourth-growth reborn from total neglect in the '60s. Medieval tower
with 79 acres just w. of St-Julien. Lightish, pretty wine.

La Tour de By Bégadan (Médoc) r. ★★ 78′ 79′ 80 81 82′ 83 84 85
86 Very well-run 144-acre Cru Bourgeois in the n. Médoc steadily
increasing its reputation for sturdy, impressive yet appealing wine.

La Tour-de-Mons Sou-Mar r. ★★ 70′ 75′ 78 79 80 81 82′ 83 85 86
Distinguished Cru Bourgeois of 75 acres, three centuries in the same
family. Sometimes excellent claret with a long life.

La Tour-du-Pin-Figeac St-Em. r. ★★
26-acre Grand Cru worthy of restoration.

La Tour-du-Pin-Figeac-Moueix St-Em. r. ★★★ 78 79 81 82 83 85 86
Another 26-acre section of the same old property, owned by a branch
of the famous MOUEIX family. Looking very good.

La Tour-Figeac St-Em. r. ★★ 75 78 79 81 82′ 83 85 86
34-acre Grand Cru between Ch FIGEAC and Pomerol, not quite showing
the form that such a site suggests.

La Tour-Haut-Brion Graves r. ★★★ 70 75 78 79 80 81 82′ 83 85 86 87
The second label of Ch LA MISSION-HAUT-BRION. Up to '83 a plainer, very
tannic wine for long life. Now more accessible.

La Tour-Martillac Graves r. and w. dr. ★★ (r.) 75′ 78 79 81 82′ 83 84 85 86 Small but serious property at Martillac. 10 acres of white grapes; 37 of black. The white can age admirably. The owner, Jean Kressmann, is resurrecting the neighbouring Ch Lespault.

La Tour St-Bonnet Médoc r. ■■ 78′ 79 81 82′ 83 85 86 Consistently well-made n. Médoc from St-Christoly. 100 acres.

La Tour du Haut Moulin Cussac (Haut-Médoc) r. ■■ 78 79 80 81 82 83 84 85 86 Little-known property; concentrated wines to age.

Tournefeuille Lalande de Pomerol r. ■■ 75′ 78 81′ 82′ 83′ 85′ 86 The star of Néac, overlooking Pomerol from the n. A small property (43 acres), but excellent long-lived wine.

des Tours Montagne-St-Em. r. ★★ 82 83 85 86 Spectacular ch with modern 170-acre v'yd. Sound, easy wine.

Toutigeac, Domaine de Entre-Deux-Mers r. (w. dr) ★ Enormous producer of useful Bordeaux at Targon.

Tronquoy-Lalande St-Est. r. ★★ 70 71 75 76 78 79 80 81 82′ 83 85 86 40-acre Cru Bourgeois making typical high-coloured St-Estèphe needing long ageing. Distributed by DOURTHE.

Troplong-Mondot St-Em. r. ■■ 70′ 75′ 78 79 81 82′ 83 85 86 One of the bigger Grand Crus of St-Emilion. 70 acres well sited on the Côtes above Ch PAVIE. To watch.

Trotanoy Pomerol r. ■■■■ 61 70 71′ 73 75′ 76′ 78 79 80 81 82′ 83 84 85 86′ 87 Perhaps the 2nd Pomerol after PETRUS, from the same stable. Only 27 acres but a glorious fleshy perfumed wine.

Trottevieille St-Em. r. ★★★ 75′ 79′ 81 82′ 83 85 86 Grand Cru of 27 acres on the Côtes e. of the town. Dragged its feet for years. '83 '85 '86 look better. Same owners as BATAILLEY.

Le Tuquet Graves r. and w. dr. ★★ 81 82 83 85 86 Big estate at Beautiran. Light fruity wines; the white better.

Verdignan Médoc r. ■■ 79 81 82 83 85 86 Substantial Grand Bourgeois sister property to Ch COUFRAN. More Cabernet than Coufran; Jack Sprat and his wife.

Vieux-Château-Certan Pomerol r. ■■■ 75 78 79 80 81 82 83 84 85 86 Traditionally rated close to PETRUS in quality, but totally different in style; almost Médoc build. 34 acres. Same (Belgian) family owns LABEGORCE-ZEDE and another tiny Pomerol, Le Pin.

Vieux-Château-Landon Médoc r. ★★ 82 83 85 86 Up-to-date grower of vigorous wine worth keeping 3-4 years.

Vieux-Château-St-André St-Em. r. ■■ 75′ 78 79′ 81 82′ 83 85′ 86 Small v'yd in Montagne-St-Emilion owned by the leading winemaker of Libourne. To follow. 2,500 cases.

Villegeorge Avensan r. ■■ 75′ 78′ 79 81 82 83′ 85 86 87 24-acre Cru Exceptionnel to the n. of Margaux with the same owner as Ch BRANE-CANTENAC. Enjoyable full-bodied wine.

Villemaurine St-Em. r. ■■ 70′ 75′ 78 79′ 80 81 82′ 83 84 85′ 86 Small Grand Cru with splendid cellars well sited on the Côtes by the town. Firm wine with a high proportion of Cabernet. Recently v.g.

Vraye-Croix-de-Gay Pomerol ★★★ 70′ 71′ 75′ 78 81 82′ 83 85 86 Very small ideally situated v'yd in the best part of Pomerol.

Yon-Figeac St-Em. r. ■■ 79 81 82 83 85 86 59-acre Grand Cru to follow for savoury and scented wine.

d'Yquem Sauternes w. sw. (dr.) ★★★★ 67′ 71′ 73 75′ 76′ 77 78 79 80 81 82 83′ 84 86 The world's most famous sweet-wine estate. 250 acres making only 500 bottles per acre of very strong, intense, luscious wine kept 4 years in barrel. Most vintages improve for at least 15 yrs. Also dry "Ygrec" in 78 79 80 84 85 86 (v. little) 87 88.

More Bordeaux châteaux are listed under Canon-Fronsac, Côtes de Bourg, Cubzac, Fronsac, Côtes-de-Castillon, Lalande de Pomerol, Loupiac, Ste-Croix-du-Mont, Premières Côtes de Blaye, Premières Côtes de Bordeaux in the A-Z of France, pages 26-56.

Switzerland

Switzerland has no truly great wines, but almost all (especially whites) are enjoyable and satisfying – and very expensive. Switzerland has some of the world's most efficient and productive vineyards. Costs are high and nothing less is viable. All the most important are lined along the south-facing slopes of the upper Rhône valley and Lake Geneva, respectively the Valais and the Vaud. For other areas see the map. Wines are known by place-names, grape-names, and legally controlled type names. All three, with those of leading growers and merchants, appear in the following list. On the whole, D.Y.A.

Aigle Vaud w. dr. ★★→★★★
  Principal town of CHABLAIS, between L. Geneva and the VALAIS. Dry CHASSELAS whites of appropriately transitional style: at best strong and well balanced.

Amigne Traditional white grape of the VALAIS. Heavy but tasty wine, usually made dry.

Arvine Another old VALAIS white grape, similar to the last; perhaps better. Makes good dessert wine. Petite Arvine is similar.

Auvernier Neuchâtel r. p. w. dr. (sp.) ★★
  Village s. of NEUCHATEL known for light PINOT NOIR, CHASSELAS and OEIL DE PERDRIX.

Blauburgunder One of the names given to the form of PINOT NOIR grown in German-speaking Switzerland.

Bonvin Old-established growers and merchants at SION.

Chablais Vaud (r.) w. dr. ★★→★★★
  The district between Montreux on L. Geneva and Martigny where the Rhône leaves the VALAIS. Good DORIN whites. Best villages: AIGLE, YVORNE, Bex, VILLENEUVE.

Chasselas The principal white grape of Switzerland, neutral in flavour but taking remarkable local character. Known as FENDANT in VALAIS, DORIN in VAUD and PERLAN round Geneva.

Clevner (or Klevner) Another name for BLAUBURGUNDER.

Completer Rare Grisons (see map) grape giving liquorous wine.

Cortaillod Neuchâtel r. (p. w.) ★★
  Village near NEUCHATEL specializing in light PINOT NOIR reds.

Côte, La The n. shore of L. Geneva from Geneva to Lausanne. V. good DORIN and SALVAGNIN. Best villages incl. Féchy and Rolle.

Dézaley Vaud w. dr. ★★★
　Best-known village of LAVAUX, between Lausanne and Montreux. Steep s. slopes to the lake make fine, strong, fruity DORIN. Dézaley-Marsens is equally good.

Dôle Valais r. ★★
　Term for red VALAIS wine of PINOT NOIR or GAMAY or both grapes, reaching a statutory level of strength and quality.

Dorin Vaud w. dr. ★→★★
　Obsolescent name for CHASSELAS wine in the VAUD, the equivalent of FENDANT from the VALAIS. Most wines are known by village names.

Epesses Vaud w. dr. and r. ★★
　Well-known lakeside village of LAVAUX. Good dry DORIN.

Ermitage VALAIS name for white wine from MARSANNE grapes. Rich, concentrated and heavy; usually dry.

Fendant Valais w. dr. ★→★★★
　The name for CHASSELAS wine in the VALAIS, where it reaches its ripest, strongest and smoothest. SION is the centre. All too easy to swallow.

Flétri Withered grapes for making sweet wine, often MALVOISIE.

Gamay The Beaujolais grape; makes pretty thin wine.

Glacier, Vin du Almost legendary long-matured white stored at high altitudes. Virtually extinct today.

Goron Red VALAIS wine that fails to reach the DOLE standard.

Grand Cru Vaudois term for estate wines from top areas.

Hammel Major merchant and grower of LA COTE at Rolle with wide range of good value wines. One of the few exporters.

Herrschaft Grisons r. (w. sw.) ★→★★★
　District near the border of Austria and Liechtenstein. Small amount of light PINOT NOIR reds and a few sweet whites.

Humagne Old VALAIS grape. Some red Humagne is sold: decent country wine. The strong white is a rare speciality.

Johannisberg The Valais name for SYLVANER, which can make excellent stiff, dense and high-flavoured dry wine here, comparable to Frankenwein (see Germany).

Lausanne, Ville de Producer of fine wines in surrounding villages for centuries, now incl. late-harvest CHARDONNAY.

Lavaux Vaud r. w. dr. ★→★★★
　The n. shore of L. Geneva between Lausanne and Montreux. The e. half of the VAUD. Best villages for CHASSELAS, lively and generous, incl. DEZALEY, EPESSES, Villette, Lutry, ST-SAPHORIN.

Légèrement doux Most Swiss wines are dry. Any with measurable sugar must be labelled thus or as "avec sucre résiduel".

Malvoisie VALAIS name for PINOT GRIS. Makes some wonderful late-picked sweet wines.

Mandement Geneva r. (p.) w. dr. ★
　Wine district just w. of Geneva, (see Vin-Union-Genève). Very light reds, chiefly GAMAY, and whites (PERLAN).

Marsanne The white grape of Hermitage on the French Rhône, used in the VALAIS to make ERMITAGE.

Merlot Bordeaux red grape (see Grapes for red wine) used to make the better wine of Italian Switzerland (TICINO). See also Viti.

Mont d'Or, Domaine du Valais w. dr. sw. ★★★★
　Often considered the best wine estate of Switzerland: 60 acres of steep hillside near SION. Good FENDANT, JOHANNISBERG, AMIGNE, etc., and real Riesling. Very rich concentrated wines.

Montreux The town's v'yds make some of the best CHASSELAS of the Vaud, juicy, ripe and resonant.

Neuchâtel Neuchâtel r. p. w. dr. sp. ★→★★★
　City and the wine from the n. shore of its lake. Pleasant light PINOT NOIR and attractive sometimes sparkling CHASSELAS.

Nostrano Word meaning "ours" applied to the lesser red wine of the TICINO, made from a mixture of native and Italian grapes, in contrast to MERLOT from Bordeaux.

Oeil de Perdrix Pale rosé of PINOT NOIR.

Orsat Long-established wine firm at Martigny, VALAIS, recently changed hands. See next entry.

Orsat, J. A. and P. L. Members of the original Orsat family have started this firm to maintain very high standards and good value in FENDANT, etc.

Perlan Geneva w. dr. ★
The MANDEMENT name for the ubiquitous CHASSELAS, here at its palest, driest and least impressive.

Provins The excellent central cooperative of the VALAIS.

Rèze The grape, now very rare, used for VIN DU GLACIER.

Riesling-Sylvaner Swiss name for MÜLLER-THURGAU, common in e. Switzerland (Thurgau), where it was bred by Dr. Müller. "A prophet is not without honour . . ."

Rivaz Vaud r. w. dr. ★★
One of the better known villages of LAVAUX.

St-Saphorin Vaud w. dr. ★★
One of the principal villages of LAVAUX: wines drier and more austere than DEZALEY or EPESSES.

Salvagnin Vaud r. ★→★★
Red VAUD wine of tested quality: the equivalent of DOLE.

Savagnin Swiss name for the TRAMINER, called Païen in the VALAIS.

Schafiser Bern (r.) w. dr. ★→★★
The n. shore of L. Bienne (Bielersee) is well known for very dry and light CHASSELAS sold as either Schafiser or Twanner.

Schenk, S.A. The biggest Swiss wine firm, based at Rolle in the VAUD, with 570 acres as well as other world-wide interests.

Sion Valais w. dr. ★→★★★
Centre of the VALAIS wine region, famous for its FENDANT.

Sierre Important centre for some of the best VALAIS wines.

Spätburgunder PINOT NOIR: by far the commonest grape of German-speaking Switzerland, making very light wines.

Testuz, V. & P. Well-known growers and merchants at Dézaley, LAVAUX.

Thun Source of some of Switzerland's best RIESLING

Ticino Italian-speaking s. Switzerland. See Merlot, Viti, Nostrano.

Twanner See Schafiser.

Valais The Rhône valley between Brig and Martigny. Its n. side is an admirable dry sunny and sheltered v'yd, planted mainly to the CHASSELAS grape, which here makes its most potent wine. Valais wines tend to be heady.

Vaud The region of L. Geneva. Its n. shore is Switzerland's biggest v'yd and in places as good as any. DORIN and SALVAGNIN are the main wines.

Vétroz Valais (r.) w. dr. ★★
Village near SION in the best part of the VALAIS.

Villeneuve Top-rate village for CHASSELAS between Montreux and the CHABLAIS slopes of YVORNE.

Vevey Town near Montreux with a famous wine festival once every 30-odd years. The last was in 1977.

Vin-Union-Genève Big growers' cooperative at Satigny in the MANDEMENT. Light reds and white PERLAN are Geneva's local wine.

Viti Ticino r. ★★
Legal designation of better-quality TICINO red, made of MERLOT and with at least 12% alcohol.

Yvorne Village near AIGLE with some of the best CHABLAIS v'yds.

Italy

Switzerland

VALLE D'AOSTA

Mila

Turin

PIEMONTE

LIGUR

Genoa

Italian wine on the threshold of the 1990s
is in a revolutionary state. The 30-year-old
DOC system, the basis of the country's wine
laws, is more or less discredited. Its original
purpose, of defining Italy's myriad winemaking
traditions, is increasingly seen more as hindrance
than help when most of the best winemakers are experimenting
with untraditional ideas, grape varieties and techniques.

A Denominazione di Origine Controllata (DOC) was granted by
the government in Rome to any grower or growers who could
plead convincingly for a distinctive regional style and claim that
it was "traditional". Once in place, a DOC stultifies progress –
and has very little bearing on quality. Most regions can make
more attractive (and saleable) wine by adopting the international top-selling grape varieties than by persisting with Italy's
indigenous but often degenerate types. Sangiovese and the rest
can be very good; but it takes time and trouble to select and
propagate the best vines. So to plant Cabernet is a short-cut.

Ironically the only appellation available to non-DOC wines,
however good, is the most basic of all: vino da tavola, or plain
table wine. The confidence of good growers in their new
products is such that they wear this apparent stigma as a
talisman. In these circumstances it is the maker's name that
matters most.

Meanwhile the DOC system remains, for all its faults, the only
general key to the Italian wine maze. It is the approximate
equivalent of France's Appellations Contrôlées. Most of Italy's
traditional wines have defined areas and standards under the
system. A few, like Chianti Classico, it must be said, had them
long before. An increasing number, however, have not – and
DOCs have been granted to many areas of only local interest: so
the mere existence of a DOC proves little. The entries in this
book ignore a number of unimportant DOCs and include
considerably more non-DOCs. They also include a larger
number of grape-name entries.

Italian wines are named in a variety of ways: some geographical like French wines, some historical, some folklorical, and
many of the best from their grapes. These include old "native"
grapes such as Barbera and Sangiovese and more and more
imported "international" grapes from France and Germany.
Many of the DOCs, particularly in the north-east, are area names
applying to widely different wines from more than a dozen
different varieties. No overall comment on the quality of such a
diversity is really possible, except to say that general standards
are rising steadily and a growing number of producers are
emerging as outstanding by international standards.

The single most important fact for buyers of Italian wine in
1990 is the quality of the vintages that are now generally in
circulation. 1985 and 1986 were years to please almost
everyone. And 1988 is an outstanding vintage to look forward to.

Austria

TRENTINO-ALTO-ADIGE

Bolzano
Trento

LOMBARDY

FRIULI-VENEZIA-GIULIA

Verona

VENETO

R. Po

Venice

Trieste

Yugoslavia

EMILIA-ROMAGNA

Bologna

Florence

TUSCANY

MARCHES

Siena

Perugia

Pisa

UMBRIA

Adriatic Sea

R. Tiber

ABRUZZI

Rome

LATIUM

MOLISE

CAMPANIA

APULIA

Naples

Bari

Alghero

BASILICATA

SARDINIA

Tyrrhenian Sea

CALABRIA

Cagliari

Palermo

Messina

Marsala

Mt Etna ▲

SICILY

The map is the key to the province names used for locating each entry. The following abbreviations are used in the text.

Abr.	Abruzzi	Camp.	Campania
Apu.	Apulia	Em-Ro.	Emilia-Romagna
Bas.	Basilicata	Fr-VG.	Fruili-Venezia-Giulia
Cal.	Calabria		

Lat.	Latium
Lig.	Liguria
Lom.	Lombardy
Mar.	Marches
M.	Molise
Piem.	Piemonte
Sard.	Sardinia
Sic.	Sicily
Tr-Aad.	Trentino-Alto-Adige
Tusc.	Tuscany
Umbr.	Umbria
V d'A.	Valle d'Aosta
Ven.	Veneto

Abbazia di Rosazzo Leading estate of COLLI ORIENTALI. White Ronco delle Acacie and Ronco di Corte and red Ronco dei Roseti are v.g. single v'yd wines.

Abboccato Semi-sweet.

Adanti Maker of v.g. Sagrantino di MONTEFALCO; also v.d.t. Rosso d'Arquata, outstanding BARBERA/Canaiolo/MERLOT blend.

Aglianico del Vulture Bas. DOC r. (s/sw. sp.) ✹✹✹ 82 85 86 88
Among the best wines of s. Italy. Ages well to rich aromas. Called Vecchio after 3 yrs, Riserva after 5. Top grower: Fratelli d'Angelo.

Alba Major wine-centre of PIEMONTE.

Albana di Romagna Em-Ro. DOCG w. dr. s/sw. (sp.) ✹✹✹ D.Y.A.
Produced for several centuries in Romagna from Albana grapes. Absurdly Italy's first DOCG for white wine. Cold fermentation now robs it of much character. Fattoria PARADISO makes some of the best. AMABILE is often better than dry. Fattoria ZERBINA's botrytis-affected PASSITO is outstanding.

Alcamo Sic. DOC w. dr. ✹
Soft neutral whites from w. Sicily. Rapitalà is the best brand.

Aleatico Red, slightly muscat-flavoured grape, chiefly of the south.

Aleatico di Gradoli Lat. DOC r. sw. or f. ✹✹
Aromatic, fruity; alcohol 17.5%. Made near Viterbo.

Aleatico di Puglia Apu. DOC r. sw. or f. ✹✹
Aleatico grapes make good dessert wine in limited quantities. Two distinct types have 15% or 18.5% alcohol.

Alezio Apu. DOC (r.) p. dr. ✹✹ 83 85 86 87 88
Recent Salento DOC, esp. for delicate rosé.

Allegrini High-quality producer of Veronese wines, incl. VALPOLICELLA.

Altesino Highly regarded estate producing BRUNELLO DI MONTALCINO and v.d.t. Palazzo Altese.

Alto Adige Tr-Aad. DOC r. p. w. dr. sw. sp. ✹✹→✹✹✹
A DOC covering some 19 different wines, usually named after their grape varieties, in 33 villages round Bolzano.

Ama, Castello di Modern CHIANTI CLASSICO estate nr. Gaiole. San Lorenzo and Bellavista are excellent top wines. V.g. CHARDONNAY, SAUVIGNON, PINOT NERO.

Amabile Semi-sweet, but usually sweeter than ABBOCCATO.

Amaro Bitter. When prominent on a label the content is a "bitters".

Amarone See Recioto.

Anghelu Ruju Port-like version of CANNONAU from Sella & Mosca in Sardinia.

Anselmi, Roberto A leader in SOAVE with his single v'yd Capitel Foscarino and exceptional sweet dessert RECIOTO dei Capitelli.

Antinori A long-established Tuscan house of the highest repute producing first-rate CHIANTI (esp. PEPPOLI) and ORVIETO, now also distinguished for pioneering new v.d.t. styles: e.g. TIGNANELLO, SOLAIA, CERVARO DELLA SALA.. See also Sassicaia.

Arneis Piem. w. dr. ✹✹ D.Y.A.
Revival of this ancient wine is much in vogue. DOC under Roero, a zone n. of Alba is imminent. Good producers incl. Bruno GIACOSA, Castello di Neive, Blangé (Ceretto), Montebertotto.

Artimino Ancient hill-town w. of Florence, known for its DOC CARMIGNANO.

Assisi Umbr. r. (w. dr.) ✹✹ D.Y.A.
Rosso di Assisi is a very attractive red v.d.t. Drink young and cool. BIANCO is also good.

Asti Major wine-centre of PIEMONTE.

Asti Spumante Piem. DOC w. sp. ✹✹✹ NV
Sweet and very fruity muscat sparkling wine. Low in alcohol.

Avignonesi MONTEPULCIANO house with range of good wines incl. VINO NOBILE, blended red Grifi, and superlative VIN SANTO.

Azienda agricola (or agraria) A farm producing crops, often incl. wine.

Azienda vinicola or casa vinicola Wine firm using bought-in grapes.

Azienda vitivinicola A (specialized) wine estate.

Badia a Coltibuono 71 75 79 82 83 85 86 88
Fine Chianti-maker at Gaiole with a restaurant and remarkable collection of old vintages. Also v.d.t. "Sangioveto" 80 81 82 83 85 86 88

Banfi See Villa Banfi.

Barbacarlo (Oltrepò Pavese) Lomb. DOC r. dr. or sw. sp. ★★→★★★ 82 83 85 86 88 Delicate wines with slightly bitter after-taste, from Broni.

Barbaresco Piem. DOCG r. dr. ★★★→★★★★ 78 79 82 83 85 86 87 88
Neighbour of BAROLO from the same grapes but lighter, ageing sooner. At best subtle and fine. At 4 yrs becomes Riserva. Best producers incl. GAJA, Bruno GIACOSA, Marchesi di Gresy, Produttori del B, Castello di Neive, Ceretto.

Barbera Dark acidic red grape, the second most planted in Italy after SANGIOVESE; a speciality of Piemonte also used in Lombardy, Emilia-Romagna and other northern provinces. Its best wines are:

Barbera d'Alba Piem. DOC r. dr. ■■ 82 83 85 86 87 88
Tasty, tannic, fragrant red. Superiore can age 7 years. Round ALBA, NEBBIOLO is sometimes added to make a VINO DA TAVOLA.

Barbera d'Asti Piem. DOC r. dr. ■■ 82 83 84 85 86 87 88
To many the best of the Barberas; all Barbera grapes; grapey and appetizing, drunk young or aged up to 7 years.

Barbera del Monferrato Piem. DOC r. dr. ★ 85 86 87 88
From a large area in the province of Alessandria and ASTI. Pleasant, slightly fizzy, sometimes sweetish.

Barberani Leading ORVIETO producer; Calcaia is sweet, botrytis-affected.

Bardolino Ven. DOC r. dr. (p.) ★★ D.Y.A.
Pale, light, slightly bitter red from e. shore of La Garda. Bardolino Chiaretto is even paler and lighter.

Berlucchi, Guido Italy's biggest producer of sparkling METODO CLASSICO, at FRANCIACORTA. Steady quality.

Barolo Piem. DOCG r. dr. ★★★→★★★★ 71 78 79 82 83 84 85′ 86 88
Small area s. of Turin with one of the highest-rated Italian red wines, dark, rich, alcoholic (minimum 13°), dry but deep in flavour. From NEBBIOLO grapes. Ages for up to 15 yrs, Riserva after 5. Best producers incl. VIETTI, GIACOSA, CONTERNO, Pio Cesare, Marcarini, MASCARELLO, CERETTO, PRUNOTTO, CORDERO, RATTI, Rinaldi, ROCCHE DEI MANZONI, FONTANA FREDDA, Sandrone, Voerzio, Altare, Clerico. The coop "Terre del Barolo" is also good.

Bell 'Agio Brand of sweet white MOSCATO from BANFI.

Bellavista Franciacorta estate rivalling CA'DEL BOSCO for sparkling wines (notable Crémant), with good v.d.t. reds from CABERNET and Pinot Noir.

Bertani Well-known producers of quality Veronese wines (VALPOLICELLA, VALPANTENA, SOAVE, etc.), including aged AMARONE.

Bianco White.

Bianco d'Arquata Umbr. w. dr. ■■ 85 86 87 88
A limpid and inspiring light and fruity white from near Perugia.

Bianco di Custoza Ven. DOC w. dr. (sp.) ■■ D.Y.A.
Twin of SOAVE from w. of Verona often rivals or surpasses it in quality.

Bianco di Pitigliano Tusc. DOC w. dr. ■ D.Y.A.
A soft, fruity, lively wine made near Grosseto.

Bianco Vergine della Valdichiana Tusc. DOC w. dr. ★ D.Y.A.
Pale dry light wine from Arezzo. But what music in the name.

Bigi, Luigi & Figlio Famous producers of ORVIETO and other wines of Umbria and Tuscany. Their Torricella v'yd produces v.g. dry Orvieto.

Biondi-Santi The original producer of BRUNELLO with cellars in MONTALCINO (Siena). His prices are v. high but ancient vintages unique. His Il Greppo v'yd is only 45 acres.

Boca Piem. DOC r. dr. ■■ 82 85 86 88
From same grape as BAROLO in n. of Piemonte. A coming name.

Bolla Famous Veronese firm producing VALPOLICELLA, SOAVE, etc. Top wines: Jago, Castellaro.

Bonarda Minor red grape widely grown in PIEMONTE and Lombardy.

Bonarda (Oltrepò Pavese) Lomb. DOC r. dr. ★★ 86 87 88
Soft, fresh, pleasant red from south of Pavia.

Bosca Wine-producers from PIEMONTE known for their ASTI SPUMANTE and Vermouths; also popular fizzy Caneï.

Boscarelli, Poderi Small estate with v.g. VINO NOBILE DI MONTEPULCIANO.

Botticino Lomb. DOC r. dr. ★★ 85 86 87 88
Strong, full-bodied rather sweet red from Brescia.

Brachetto d'Acqui Piem. DOC r. sw. (sp.) ★★ D.Y.A.
Sweet sparkling red with enticing muscat aroma.

Bramaterra Piem. DOC. r. dr. ★★★ 82 85 86 88
A stylish addition to Piemonte's reds. Nebbiolo grapes predominate.

Breganze Ven. DOC ★→★★★ 82 83 85 86 88
A catch-all for many varieties around Vicenza. CABERNET and PINOT BIANCO are best. Top producer: MACULAN.

Bricco dell'Uccellone Piem. r. dr. ★★★ 82 83 84 85 86 87 88
Barrique-aged BARBERA from firm of Giacomo Bologna.

Bricco Manzoni Piem. r. ★★★ 82 83 85 86 88
Excellent blend of NEBBIOLO and BARBERA from Monforte d'Alba.

Brolio One of the oldest (c. 1200) and most famous CHIANTI CLASSICO estates, now owned by a British group. Good whites as well as red.

Brunello di Montalcino Tusc. DOCG r. dr. ★★★★ 70 71 75 77 79 80 81 82 83 85 86 87 88 Italy's most celebrated red wine. Strong, full-bodied, high-flavoured and long-lived. After 5 yrs is called Riserva. Produced for over a century 25 miles s. of Siena. Top producers incl. BIONDI-SANTI, CAPARZO, Case Basse, Altesino, Costanti, Il Poggione, VILLA BANFI. Fattoria dei Barbi, Col d'Orcia, Lisini. ROSSO DI MONTALCINO is a less expensive alternative.

Brusco dei Barbi Piem. r. dr. ★★ 85 86 87 88
Lively variant on BRUNELLO, using old Chianti *governo* method.

Buttafuoco Lomb. ★
A potent foaming red of BARBERA and other grapes. Avoid.

Ca'del Bosco FRANCIACORTA estate making some of Italy's v. best sparkling wine, CHARDONNAY, and excellent reds (Pinot Noir, MAURIZIO ZANELLA and FRANCIACORTA).

Cabernet Bordeaux grape much used in n.e. Italy and increasingly in Tuscany and the south.

Cacchiano, Castello di First-rate CHIANTI CLASSICO estate at Gaiole.

Cafaggio, Villa A solid CHIANTI CLASSICO estate with a good red v.d.t. called Solatio Basilica.

Caldaro or Lago di Caldaro Tr-Aad. DOC r. dr. ★→★★ D.Y.A.
Alias KALTERERSEE. Light, soft, slightly bitter-almond red. Classico from a smaller area is better. From south of Bolzano.

Caluso Passito Piem. DOC w. sw. (f.) ★★ 74 76 78 79 80 82 85 86 88
Made from selected Erbaluce grapes left to partly dry; delicate scent, velvety taste. Tiny production from a large area.

Cannonau di Sardegna Sard. DOC r. (p.) dr. or s/sw. ★★ 85 86 87 88
Cannonau is Sardinia's basic red grape; its wine often formidably strong (min. 13.5% alc.). Less potent Cannonaus without the DOC can be easier to like.

Cantina 1. Cellar or winery. 2. Cantina Sociale = growers' coop.

Capannelle Good producer of Tuscan v.d.t. (formerly CHIANTI CLASSICO), though overrated and overpriced.

Caparzo, Tenuta MONTALCINO estate with excellent BRUNELLO La Casa; also CHARDONNAY and red blend Ca'del Pazzo.

Capezzana, Tenuta di (or Villa) The Tuscan estate of the ancient Contini Bonacossi family, producers of excellent CHIANTI MONTALBANO and CARMIGNANO. Also a Bordeaux-style red, GHIAIE DELLA FURBA.

Carpenè Malvolti Leading producer of classic PROSECCO and other sp. wines at Conegliano, Veneto.

Capri Camp. DOC r. w. p. ★
Widely abused name of the famous island in the Bay of Naples. Better to drink e.g. RAVELLO.

Carema Piem. DOC r. dr. ★★ 78 79 82 85 86 88
Old speciality of northern PIEMONTE, NEBBIOLO grapes traditionally fermented Beaujolais-style before crushing. (See France: macération carbonique.) More conventional today.

Carmignano Tusc. DOC r. dr. (p. br.) ★★★ 79 82 83 85 86 87 88
Section of CHIANTI using 10% of CABERNET to make increasingly good, and some very fine, wine. See Capezzana.

Carso Fr-VG. DOC r. w. dr. D.Y.A.
DOC near Trieste includes good MALVASIA. Terrano del C. is a soft REFOSCO-like red.

Casa fondata nel . . . Firm founded in . . .

Castel del Monte Apu. DOC r. p. w. dr. ★★ 81 83 84 85 86 87 88
Dry, fresh, well-balanced southern wines. The red becomes Riserva after 3 yrs. Rosé most widely known. Riserva's Il Falcone stands out.

Castel San Michele Tr-Aad. r. dr. ★★ 82 83 85 86 87
A good red made of CABERNET and MERLOT grapes by the Trentino Agricultural College near Trento.

Castellare Small but admired CHIANTI CLASSICO producer with first-rate Sangiovese v.d.t. I Sodi di San Niccoló and sprightly Governo del Castellare, a modern version of old-style Chianti.

Castello della Sala ANTINORI'S estate at ORVIETO and its fresh white. Cervaro della Sala top wine: CHARDONNAY and GRECHETTO aged in oak.

CAVIT CAntina VITicultori, a group of cooperatives near Trento, producing large quantities of table and sp. wines.

Cellatica Lomb. DOC r. dr. ★★ 87 88
Light red with slightly bitter after-taste of Schiava grapes.

Cerasuolo Abr. DOC p. dr. ★★
The rosato version of MONTEPULCIANO D'ABRUZZO.

Ceretto High-quality grower of v. expensive BARBARESCO, BAROLO, etc. Barb is called Bricco Asili, Barolo Bricco Rocche.

Cerveteri Lat. DOC w. dr. s/sw. ★ 85 86 87 88
Sound wines produced n.w. of Rome between Lake Bracciano and the Tyrrhenian Sea.

Chardonnay Has recently joined permitted varieties for several n. Italian DOCs. Some of the best (e.g. GAJA) are still only VINI DA TAVOLA.

Chianti Tusc. DOC r. dr. ★→★★★ 82 83 85 86 88
The lively local wine of Florence. Fresh but warmly fruity when young, still occasionally sold in straw-covered flasks. Variously age-worthy. Montalbano, RUFINA and Colli Fiorentini, Senesi, Aretini, Colline Pisane are sub-districts. RUFINA is recommended.

Chianti Classico Tusc. DOCG r. dr. ★→★★★★ 79 81 82 83 85 86 88 Senior Chianti from the central area. Many estates make fine powerful, slightly astringent wine. Riservas (after 3 yrs) often have the bouquet of age in oak. Members of the Consorzio use the badge of a black rooster, but several top firms do not belong.

Chianti Putto Tusc. DOCG r. dr. ★→★★★
Often high-quality Chianti from a league of producers outside the Classico zone. Neck-label is a pink and white cherub.

Chiaretto Very light reds, almost rosé (the word means "claret") produced around Lake Garda. See Bardolino, Riviera del Garda.

Cinqueterre Lig. DOC w. dr. or sw. or pa. ★★
Fragrant fruity white made for centuries near La Spezia. The PASSITO is known as Sciacchetrà.

Cinzano Major Vermouth company also known for its ASTI SPUMANTE from PIEMONTE. Its MONTALCINO estate is Col d'Orcia.

Cirò Cal. DOC r. (p.w.) dr. ★★ 83 84 85 86 87 88
   The wine of the ancient Olympic games. Very strong red, fruity white (to drink young).

Classico Term for wines from a restricted, usually central, area within the limits of a DOC. By implication, and often in practice, the best of the region.

Collavini, Cantina High-quality producers of COLLIO, COLLI ORIENTALI and GRAVE DEL FRIULI wines: PINOT GRIGIO, RIESLING, MERLOT, PINOT NERO and sparkling.

Colle Picchioni Estate s. of Rome making the best MARINO white; also red (CAB/MERLOT) v.d.t., Vigna del Vassallo, perhaps Latium's best.

Colli Means "hills" in many wine-names.

Colli Albani Lat. DOC w. dr. or s/sw. (sp.) ★→★★ D.Y.A.
   Soft fruity wine of the Roman hills.

Colli Berici Ven. DOC r. w. p. dr. ★★ 82 83 85 86 88
   CABERNET is the best of several promising products of these hills south of Vicenza.

Colli Bolognesi Em-Ro. DOC r. p. w. dr. ★★ D.Y.A. (w.) 83 85 86 87 88
   From the hills s.w. of Bologna. Six possible grape varieties. Terre Rosse is top estate.

Colli della Toscana Centrale Many Chianti makers use this name for table wines. (A future DOC? See Predicato.)

Colli del Trasimeno Umb. DOC r. w. dr. ★★ 85 86 87 88
   Lively wines from the province of Perugia.

Colli di Catone Reliable producer of FRASCATI.

Colli Euganei Ven. DOC r. w. dr. or s/sw. (sp.) ▓ 86 87 88
   A DOC applicable to 7 wines produced s.w. of Padua. Red is adequate; white soft and pleasant. The table wine of Venice.

Colli Orientali del Friuli Fr-VG. DOC r. w. dr. or sw. ▓ ★★→★★★ 82 83 85 86 88 18 different wines are produced under this DOC on the hills east of Udine and named after their grapes, esp v.g. whites.

Colli Piacentini Tusc. DOC r. p. w. dr. ★→★★★
   DOC incl. traditional GUTTURNIO and Monterosso Val d'Arda among 11 types grown round Piacenza. Good fizzy MALVASIA.

Collio (Goriziano) Fr-VG. DOC r. w. dr. ▓ ★★→★★★ 85 86 88
   12 different wines named after their grapes from a small area between Udine and Gorizia nr. the Yugoslav border. V.g. whites.

Colli Perugini Umbr. DOC r. p. w. dr. ★ 85 86 87 88
   DOC for light wines in the hills of Perugia.

Coltassala Tusc. r. dr. ▓ ★★★ 81 82 83 85 86 87 88
   Notable red of SANGIOVESE from the ancient CHIANTI CLASSICO estate of CASTELLO DI VOLPAIA at Radda. "Balifico" includes Cabernet.

Coltiva – Gruppo Italiano Vini Complex of coops and wineries, now apparently world's third largest producer. Sells 10% of all Italian wine.

Conterno, Aldo and Giacomo Highly regarded growers of BAROLO, etc, with separate estates at Monforte d'Alba.

Contratto Piemonte firm known for sparkling wines, ASTI SPUMANTE, BAROLO, etc.

Copertino Apu. DOC r. dr ★★ 82 83 84 85 86 87 88
   Age-worthy dark red of NEGROAMARO from the heel of Italy.

Cordero, Paolo, di Montezemolo Tiny producer of top-class Barolo.

Cori Lat. DOC w. r. dr./sw. ▓ 86 87 88
   Soft and well-balanced wines made 30 miles south of Rome.

Cortese di Gavi See Gavi.

Cortese (Oltrepò Pavese) Lomb. DOC w. dr. ★→★★ D.Y.A.
   Delicate fresh white from western Lombardy.

Corvo-Duca di Salaparuta Sic. r. w. dr. ★★ 83 84 85 86 87 88
   Popular Sicilian wines. Sound dry red, pleasant soft whites. Excellent new barrique red called Duca Enrico from Nero d'Avola grapes.

Costanti, Emilio Tiny estate producing top-quality BRUNELLO DI MONTALCINO.

d'Albola, Castello Formerly Pian d'Albola. Famous CHIANTI CLASSICO estate owned by ZONIN.

D'Ambra Well-known producer of ISCHIA and other wines of that island.

Darmagi Piem. r. dr. ★★★ 82 83 85 86 87
CABERNET SAUVIGNON grown in a choice plot in BARBARESCO by GAJA has become Piemonte's most discussed and admired "foreign" red.

Decugnano dei Barbi Top ORVIETO estate with an ABBOCCATO version known as "Pourriture Noble" and a good red v.d.t.

Di Majo Norante Molise's lone star with good MONTEPULCIANO and white Falanghina under the Ramitello label. Fine value.

Dolce Sweet.

Dolceacqua See Rossese di Dolceacqua.

Dolcetto Common low-acid red grape of PIEMONTE, the everyday wine of BAROLO and BARBARESCO-producing areas, giving its name to:

Dolcetto d'Acqui Piem. DOC r. dr. ★ 87 88
Good standard table wine from s. of ASTI.

Dolcetto d'Alba Piem. DOC r. dr. ★★ 87 88
Among the best Dolcetti, with a trace of bitter-almond.

Dolcetto di Diano d'Alba Piem. DOC ★★ 87 88
A rival to Dolcetto d'Alba; often more potent.

Dolcetto di Ovada Piem. DOC r. dr. ★★ 82 83 85 86 87 88
Reputedly the sturdiest and longest-lived of Dolcetti.

Donnafugata Sic. r. w. ★★★ 86 87 88
Sound red and zesty white from the Belici hills near Agrigento.

Donnaz Vd'A. DOC dr. ★★ 82 83 85 86 87 88
A mountain NEBBIOLO, fragrant, pale and faintly bitter. Aged for a statutory 3 yrs. Now part of the VALLE D'AOSTA regional DOC.

Elba Tusc. r. w. dr. (sp.) ★ 86 87 88
The island's white is drinkable with fish. Decent dry red.

Enfer d'Arvier Vd'A. DOC r. dr. ★★ 82 83 85 86 88
Alpine speciality (cf. DONNAZ); pale, pleasantly bitter, light red.

Enoteca Italian for "wine library", of which there are many in the country, the impressive original being the Enoteca Italica Permanente of Siena. Also used for wine shops.

Erbaluce di Caluso See Caluso Passito.

Est! Est!! Est!!! Lat. DOC w. dr. or s/sw. ★ D.Y.A.
Famous soft fruity white from Montefiascone, n. of Rome. The name is much more remarkable than the wine.

Etna Sic. DOC r. p. w. dr. ★→★★★ 85 86 87 88
Wine from the volcanic slopes. The red is warm, full, balanced and ages well; the white is distinctly grapey. See Villagrande.

Falerio dei Colli Ascolani Mar. DOC w. dr. ★★ D.Y.A.
Made in the province of Ascoli Piceno. Pleasant, fresh, fruity; a wine for the summer.

Falerno del Massico Camp. DOC r. w. dr. ★★ 88
As Falernum, one of the best-known wines of ancient times. Strong red from Aglianico, fruity white from Falanghina, improving in quality.

Fara Piem. DOC r. dr. ★★★ 82 83 85 86 88
Good NEBBIOLO wine from Novara, n. PIEMONTE. Fragrant; worth ageing. Small production.

Faro Sic. DOC r. dr. ★★ 86 87 88
Rare strong Sicilian red, made in sight of the Straits of Messina.

Favonio Apu. r. w. dr. ★★★ 83 84 85 86 87 88
Estate east of Foggia using CABERNET, CHARDONNAY and PINOT BIANCO.

Fazi-Battaglia Well-known producer of VERDICCHIO, etc.

Felluga Brothers Livio and Marco (Russiz Superiore) have separate companies in the COLLIO and COLLI ORIENTALI. Both highly esteemed.

Ferrari Firm making some of Italy's best dry sparkling wines by the champagne method near Trento, Trentino-Alto Adige.

Fiano di Avellino Cam. w. dr. ★★→★★★ 85 86 87 88
   Considered the best white of Campania, smooth, pale, dry but not
   otherwise remarkable. Ages well.

Fiorano Lat. r. w. dr. s/sw. ★★ 81 82 83 85 86 87 88
   Interesting Roman reds of CABERNET and MERLOT.

Flaccianello della Pieve See Fontodi.

Florio The major producer of Marsala, controlled by CINZANO.

Foianeghe Tr-Aad. r. ★★
   Trentino CABERNET/MERLOT red to age 7-10 years.

Folonari Large run-of-the-mill merchant at Brescia.

Fontana Candida One of the biggest producers of FRASCATI. Single v'yd
   Santa Teresa stands out.

Fontanafredda One of the biggest producers of Piemontese wines, incl.
   BAROLO from single v'yds and a range of ALBA DOCs. Also v.g. sp. wines.

Fonterutoli High-quality CHIANTI CLASSICO estate at Castellina with noted
   v.d.t. Concerto.

Fontodi Rising CHIANTI CLASSICO estate producing one of Italy's most highly
   regarded v.d.t. in Flaccianello della Pieve.

Franciacorta Pinot Lomb. DOC w. (p.) dr. (sp.) ★★→★★★
   Agreeable soft white and good sparkling wines made of PINOT BIANCO,
   NERO or GRIGIO. CA'DEL BOSCO is outstanding. Bellavista, Monterossa and
   Cavalleri also v.g.

Franciacorta Rosso Lomb. DOC r. dr. ★★ 82 83 85 86 88
   Lightish red of mixed CABERNET and BARBERA from Brescia.

Frascati Lat. DOC w. dr. s/sw. sw. (sp.) ★→★★★ D.Y.A.
   Best-known wine of the Roman hills: should be soft, ripe, golden,
   tasting of whole grapes. Most is disappointingly neutral today: look
   for dated wines from small producers (e.g. Conte Zandotti, Villa
   Simone, or single v'yd Santa Teresa from FONTANA CANDIDA). The sweet
   version is known as Cannellino.

Frecciarossa Lomb. DOC r. w. dr. ★→★★ 85 86 88
   Merely sound wines from estate nr. Casteggio in OLTREPO PAVESE.

Freisa d'Asti Piem. DOC r. dr. s/sw. or sw. (sp.) ★★ D.Y.A.
   Sometimes sweet, often FRIZZANTE red, said to taste of raspberries and
   roses. With enough acidity it can be highly appetizing.

Frescobaldi Ancient noble family, leading pioneers of CHIANTI RUFINA at
   NIPOZZANO, e. of Florence. Also white POMINO and PREDICATO SAUV BLANC
   (Vergena) and CABERNET (Mormoreto). See also Montesodi.

Friuli-Venezia Giulia The n.e. province on the Yugoslav border. Many
   wines, the DOCs COLLIO and COLLI ORIENTALI include most of the best.

Frizzante Semi-sparkling or "pétillant", a word used to describe wines
   such as LAMBRUSCO.

Gaja Old family firm at BARBARESCO with inspired direction. Top-quality
   Piemonte wines, esp. BARBARESCO (single v'yds Sorí Tildin, Sorí San
   Lorenzo, Costa Russi). Now setting trends with excellent CHARDONNAY
   (Gaia & Rey 84 85 86 87), CABERNET (Darmagi) and SAUV BLANC.

Galestro Tusc. w. dr. ★
   Name for light grapey white from Chianti country.

Gambellara Ven. DOC w. dr. or s/sw. (sp.) ★ D.Y.A.
   Neighbour of SOAVE. Dry wine similar. Sweet (known as RECIOTO DI
   GAMBELLARA), agreeably fruity. Also VIN SANTO.

Gancia Famous ASTI SPUMANTE house from Piemonte, also produces
   vermouth and dry sparkling wines. New Torrebianco estate in Apulia
   is making good v.d.t. whites; CHARDONNAY, SAUVIGNON, PINOT BIANCO.

Garganega The principal white grape of SOAVE.

Garofoli Notable style in VERDICCHIO Macrina and Serra Fiorese, as well
   as champenoise. ROSSO CONERO Piancarda is outstanding.

Gattinara Piem. DOC r. dr. ★★→★★★ 78 79 82 83 85 86 88
   Very tasty big-scale BAROLO-type red from northern PIEMONTE. Made
   from NEBBIOLO, locally known as Spanna.

Gavi (or Cortese di Gavi) Piem. w. dr. ★★→★★★ 86 87 88 (usually D.Y.A.) At best almost burgundian dry white of Cortese grapes. La Scolca is best known, Castello di Tassarolo top quality, La Giustiniana and Tenuta San Pietro admirable. But high prices rarely justified.

Ghemme Piem. DOC r. dr. ▓▓▓▓→▓▓▓▓ 82 83 85 86 88
Neighbour of GATTINARA, capable of Bordeaux-style finesse.

Ghiaie della Furba Tusc. r. dr. ★★★ 82 83 85 86 88
Bordeaux-style CABERNET blend from the admirable Tenuta di CAPEZZANA, CARMIGNANO.

Giacobazzi Well-known producers of LAMBRUSCO near Modena.

Giacosa, Bruno Inspired loner making excellent BARBARESCO, BAROLO and other Piemonte wines at Neive (Cuneo).

Girò di Cagliari Sard. DOC r. dr. or sw. ★ 86 87 88
A formidably alcoholic red, most sympathetic when some of its sugar content is left unfermented.

Goldmuskateller Aromatic grape made into wonderful dry white, esp. by TIEFENBRUNNER.

Gradi Degrees (of alcohol), i.e. percent by volume.

Grai, Giorgio Merchant and consultant to top ALTO-ADIGE and other estates. Own labels incl. Bellendorf.

Grave del Friuli Fr-VG. DOC r. w. dr. ★★ 85 86 87 88
A DOC covering 15 different wines named after their grapes, from near the Yugoslav border. Good MERLOT and CABERNET.

Gravner COLLIO estate with range of superb whites, led by CHARD and SAUV.

Grechetto A traditional white grape with far more flavour than the ubiquitous Trebbiano, increasingly used in Umbria. Greco ("Greek") is less specific.

Greco di Bianco (or Greco di Gerace) Cal. DOC w. sw. ★★ 83 85 86 87 88
An original smooth and fragrant dessert wine from Italy's toe. See also Mantonico.

Greco di Tufo Camp. DOC w. dr. (sp.) ★★★ 85 86 87 88
One of the best whites of the south, fruity and slightly "wild" in flavour. A character.

```
SOAVE
CLASSICO

VINO A DENOMINAZIONE DI
ORIGINE CONTROLLATA

IMBOTTIGLIATO DAL
PRODUTTORE ALL'ORIGINE

CANTINA SOCIALE DI SOAVE
```

Most Italian wines have a single name, in contrast to the combination village and vineyard names of France and Germany.

Soave is the name of this wine. It is qualified only by the word Classico, a legal term for the central (normally the best) part of many long-established wine regions.
"Denominazione di Origine Controllata" is the official guarantee of authenticity.
Imbottigliato . . . all'origine means bottled by the producer. Cantina Sociale di Soave means the growers' cooperative of Soave.

Grignolino d'Asti Piem. DOC r. dr. ★ D.Y.A.
Pleasant lively standard wine of PIEMONTE.

Grumello Lomb. DOC r. dr. ★★ 79 82 83 85 86 88
NEBBIOLO wine from VALTELLINA, can be delicate and fine.

Guerrieri-Rizzardi Top producer of BARDOLINO and other Veronese wines from various family estates (esp. Villa Rizzardi, 86').

Gutturnio dei Colli Piacentini Em-Ro. DOC r. dr. (s/sw.) ★★ 83 85 86 87 88 Full-bodied BARBERA/BONARDA blend from the hills of Piacenza. Ages admirably. (DOC is Colli Piacentini.)

Inferno Lomb. DOC r. dr. ★★ 79 82 83 85 86 88
Similar to GRUMELLO and like it classified as VALTELLINA Superiore.

Ischia Camp. DOC (r.) w. dr. ★ D.Y.A.
The wine of the island off Naples. Slightly sharp white Superiore is best.

Isole e Olena Up and coming CHIANTI CLASSICO estate with fine red v.d.t. called Cepparello. V.g. VIN SANTO.

Isonzo Fr-VG. DOC r. w. dr. ★★ 83 85 86 87
DOC covering 10 varietal wines in the extreme north-east. Best whites and CABERNET (esp. from Stelio Gallo) compare with top COLLIO wines.

Jermann Estate in Collio producing top-ranked v.d.ts., including the singular VINTAGE TUNINA white v.d.t.

Kalterersee German name for Lago di CALDARO.

Lacryma Christi del Vesuvio Camp. r. p. w. (f.) dr. (sw.) ★→★★ 86 87 88
Famous but usually ordinary wines in great variety from the slopes of Mount Vesuvius. (DOC is Vesuvio.) MASTROBERARDINO makes the only good example.

Lageder, Alois The senior producer of the Bolzano DOCs: STA MADDALENA, etc. Exciting wines, incl. barrel-aged CHARD Portico dei Leoni (alias Löwengang), Sauvignon Lehen-Montigal, and v.g. reds.

Lago di Caldaro See Caldaro.

Lagrein Tr-Aad. DOC r. p. dr. ★★ 82 83 85 86 87 88
A Tyrolean grape with a bitter twist. Good fruity wine – at best v. satisfying. The rosé is called Kretzer, the dark Dunkel.

Lamberti Producers of SOAVE, VALPOLICELLA and BARDOLINO at Lazise on the east shore of Lake Garda.

Lambrusco DOC (or not) r. p. (w.) s/sw. ■ D.Y.A.
Bizarre but popular fizzy red, generally drunk secco (dry) in Italy but best-known in its sweet version in the USA.

Lambrusco di Sorbara Em-Ro. DOC r. (w.) dr. or s/sw. sp. ★★ D.Y.A.
The best of the Lambruscos. From near Modena.

Lambrusco Grasparossa di Castelvetro Em-Ro. DOC r. dr. or s/sw. sp. ★★ D.Y.A. Often rivals above. Highly scented, pleasantly acidic; often drunk with rich food.

Lambrusco Salamino di Santa Croce Em-Ro. DOC r. dr. or s/sw. sp. ★ D.Y.A Similar to above. Fruity smell, high acidity and a thick "head".

Langhe The hills of central PIEMONTE, home of BAROLO, BARBARESCO. Candidate for its own DOC. The name is seen on many varietal v.d.t.

Latisana Fr-VG. DOC r. w. dr. ★★ 86 87 88
DOC for 7 varietal wines from some 50 miles n.e. of Venice. Particularly good TOCAI FRIULANO.

Leone de Castris Leading producer of Apulian wines with an estate at SALICE SALENTINO, near Lecce.

Lessona Piem. DOC r. d. ★★ 82 83 85 86 87 88
Soft, dry, claret-like wine produced in the province of Vercelli from NEBBIOLO, Vespolina and BONARDA grapes.

Liquoroso Strong and usually sweet (whether fortified with alcohol or not), e.g. Tuscan VIN SANTO.

Lisini Small estate producing some of the finest recent vintages of BRUNELLO DI MONTALCINO.

Locorotondo Apu. DOC w. dr. (sp.) ★ D.Y.A.
A pleasantly fresh southern white.

Lugana Lomb. DOC w. dr. (sp.) ★★★ D.Y.A.
One of the best white wines of s. Lake Garda: fragrant, smooth, full of body and flavour. Visconti is the best producer.

Lungarotti Leading producer of TORGIANO wine, with cellars and a wine museum near Perugia. Recently also fine CHARDONNAY.

Maculan The top producer of DOC BREGANZE. Also Torcolato, dessert VINO DA TAVOLA (★★★).

Malfatti Estate with modern methods, near Lecce, Apulia, producing Bianco, Rosso and SALICE SALENTINO of medium quality.

Malvasia Important white or red grape for luscious wines, incl. Madeira's Malmsey. Used all over Italy for dry and sweet, still and sp. wines.

Malvasia di Bosa Sard. DOC w. dr. sw. ★★ 85 86 87 88
A wine of character. Strong, aromatic finish.

Malvasia di Cagliari Sard. DOC w. dr. s/sw. or sw. (f. dr. s.) ★★ 85 86
87 88 Interesting strong Sardinian wine, fragrant and slightly bitter.

Malvasia di Casorzo d'Asti Piem. DOC r. sw. sp. ★★ D.Y.A.
Fragrant grapey sweet red, sometimes sparkling.

Malvasia di Castelnuovo Don Bosco Piem. DOC r. sw. (sp.) ★★
Peculiar method of interrupted fermentation gives very sweet
aromatic red.

Malvasia delle Lipari Sic. DOC w. sw. (pa. f.) ★★★ 82 83 84 85 86 87 88
Among the very best Malvasias, aromatic and rich, from the Lipari or
Aeolian Islands n. of Sicily. Top producer: Carlo Hauner.

Malvoisie de Nus Vd'A. DOC w. dr. s/sw. ★★★
Rare Alpine white, with a deep bouquet of honey. Small production
and high reputation. Can age remarkably well.

Mandrolisai Sard. DOC r. p. dr. ▨ 87 88
CANNONAU at a lower strength and more approachable style.

Manduria (Primitivo di) Apu. DOC r. s/sw. (f. dr. or sw.) ★★ 85 86 87 88
Heady red, naturally strong but often fortified. From nr. Taranto.
Primitivo is a southern grape related to ZINFANDEL.

Mantonico Cal. w. dr. or sw. f. ★★ 83 85 86 87 88
Fruity deep amber dessert wine from Reggio Calabria. Can age
remarkably well. See also Greco di Bianco.

Marino Lat. DOC w. dr. or s/sw. (sp.) ▨ D.Y.A.
A neighbour of FRASCATI with similar wine, often a better buy. Look
for COLLE PICCHIONI brand.

Marrano Umb. w. dr. ★★★
Pungent white from GRECHETTO grapes grown by BIGI near ORVIETO.

Marsala Sic. DOC br. dr. s/sw. or sw. f. ★★★ NV
Dark sherry-type wine invented by the Woodhouse Brothers from
Liverpool in 1773; excellent apéritif or for dessert. The dry ("virgin"),
sometimes made by the solera system, must be 5 years old. Top
producers: VECCHIO SAMPERI, Pellegrino, Diego RALLO, FLORIO.

Martina Franca Apu. DOC w. dr. (sp.) ★ D.Y.A.
Agreeable but rather neutral southern white, cousin to LOCOROTONDO.

Martini & Rossi Well-known vermouth and sparkling wine house, also
famous for its splendid wine museum in Pessione, near Turin.

Marzemino (del Trentino) Tr-Aad. DOC r. dr. ★ 86 87
Pleasant local red of Trento. Fruity fragrance; slightly bitter taste.
Mozart's Don Giovanni liked it and v.g. single v'yd AMARONE.

Mascarello The name of two top producers of BAROLO, etc.: Bartolo M.
and Giuseppe M. & Figli.

Masi, Agricola Well-known specialist producers of VALPOLICELLA, RECIOTO,
SOAVE, etc., including fine red Campo Fiorin.

Mastroberardino The leading wine-producer of Campania, incl. TAURASI,
LACRYMA CHRISTI DEL VESUVIO, GRECO DI TUFO and FIANO DI AVELLINO.

Melini Long-established important producers of CHIANTI CLASSICO at
Pontassieve. Inventors of the standard *fiasco*, or flask.

Melissa Cal. DOC r. w. dr. ★★ 82 83 84 85 86 87 88
Mostly made from Gaglioppo grapes in the province of Catanzaro.
Delicate, balanced, ages rather well. CIRO is identical.

Meranese di Collina Tr-Aad. DOC r. dr. ★ D.Y.A.
Light red of Merano, known in German as Meraner Hügel.

Merlot Adaptable red Bordeaux grape widely grown in n.e. Italy and
elsewhere. For example:

Merlot di Aprilia Lat. DOC r. dr. ★ 86 87 88
Harsh at first, softer after 2-3 yrs.

Merlot Colli Berici Ven. DOC r. dr. ★ 85 86 88
Pleasantly light and soft. Campo del Lago v.d.t. from Villa dal Ferro
is one of Italy's best merlots.

Merlot Colli Orientali del Friuli Fr-VG. DOC r. dr. ✴✴ **82 83 85 86 88**
Pleasant herby character, best at 2-3 yrs (Riserva). Some ages well; notably Vigne dal Leon.

Merlot Collio Goriziano Fr-VG. DOC r. dr. ✴✴ **85 86 88**
Grassy scent, slightly bitter taste. Best at 2-3 yrs.

Merlot Grave del Friuli Fr-VG. DOC r. dr. ✴✴ **83 85 86 88**
Pleasant light wine, usually best at 1-2 yrs, but potentially a keeper.

Merlot Isonzo Fr-VG. DOC r. dr. ✴✴ **83 85 86 88**
A DOC in Gorizia. Dry, herby, agreeable wine.

Merlot del Piave Ven. DOC r. dr. ✴✴ **85 86 88**
Sound tasty red, best at 2-4 yrs.

Merlot di Pramaggiore Ven. DOC r. dr. ✴✴ **83 85 86 88**
A cut above most other MERLOTS; improves in bottle. Riserva after 2 yrs.

Merlot (del Trentino) Tr-Aad. DOC r. dr. ✴ **83 85 86 88**
Full flavour, slightly grassy scent, Riserva after 2 yrs. (ALTO ADIGE has better; esp. from Margreid and Siebeneich v'yds.)

Metodo classico or tradizionale Terms increasingly in use to identify champagne method sparkling wines.

Monica di Cagliari Sard. DOC r. dr. or sw. (f. dr. or sw.) ✴✴ **86 87 88**
Strong spicy red, often fortified and comparable with Spanish Malaga. Monica is a Sardinian grape.

Monica di Sardegna Sard. DOC r. dr. ✴ **85 86 87 88**
Dry version of above, not fortified.

Monsanto Esteemed CHIANTI CLASSICO estate, esp. for IL POGGIO v'yd.

Montalcino Village in the province of Siena, Tuscany, famous for its deep red BRUNELLO and lighter ROSSO DI MONTALCINO.

Monte Vertine Top estate at Radda in Chianti. ✴✴✴ v.d.t. Le Pergole Torte and Sodaccio.

Montecarlo Tusc. DOC w. dr. r. ✴✴ D.Y.A.
One of Tuscany's best whites, smooth and delicate. Now applies to a CHIANTI-style red too.

Montecompatri Colonna Lat. DOC w. dr. or s/sw. ✴ D.Y.A.
A neighbour of FRASCATI. Similar wine.

Montefalco Umb. DOC r. dr. or sw. ✴✴ **83 85 86 87 88**
M. Rosso is standard red, Sagrantino (named for the grape) has sweetness and bite. Top producer ADANTI. Adanti's Rosso d'Arquata v.d.t. stands out.

Montepulciano, Vino Nobile di See Vino Nobile di Montepulciano.

Montepulciano d'Abruzzo (or Molise) Abr. & M. DOC r. p. dr. ✴✴✴ **82 83 85 86 87 88** At its best one of Italy's best reds, full of flavour and warmth, from the Adriatic coast round Pescara. See also Cerasuolo, Valentini.

Monterosso (Val d'Arda) Em-Ro. DOC w. dr. or sw. (sp.) ✴ D.Y.A.
Agreeable minor white from Piacenza. (DOC Colli Piacentini.)

Montesodi Tusc. r. ✴✴✴ **78 79 80 82 83 85 86 88**
Tip-top CHIANTI Rufina Riserva from FRESCOBALDI.

Moscadello di Montalcino Tusc. DOC w. sw./sp. ✴✴ D.Y.A.
Light, fizzy, not oversweet muscat. A refreshing speciality of MONTALCINO, esp. VILLA BANFI.

Moscato Fruitily fragrant grape grown all over Italy.

Moscato d'Asti Piem. DOC w. sw. sp. ✴✴ NV
Low-strength sweet fruity sparkler, delicious from Rivetti, Saracco, Iogliotti, Bera, Vignaioli di Santo Stefano. ASTI SPUMANTE is the (theoretically) superior version.

Moscato dei Colli Euganei Ven. DOC w. sw. (sp.) ✴✴ D.Y.A.
Golden wine, fruity and smooth, from near Padua.

Moscato (Oltrepò Pavese) Lomb. DOC w. sw. (sp.) ✴ D.Y.A.
The Lombardy equivalent of MOSCATO D'ASTI. Rarely as good.

Moscato di Pantelleria Sic. DOC w. sw. (sp.) (f. pa.) ★★★
Italy's best muscat, from the island of Pantelleria off the Tunisian coast; rich, fruity and aromatic. Ages well. Top wine: Bukkuram from De Bartoli.

Moscato di Sorso Sennori Sard. DOC w. sw. (f.) 🔳 D.Y.A.
Strong golden dessert wine from Sassari, n. Sardinia.

Moscato di Trani Apu. DOC w. sw. or f. ★ 83 84 85 86 87 88
Another strong golden dessert wine, sometimes fortified, with "bouquet of faded roses".

Müller-Thurgau Makes wine to be reckoned with in TRENTINO-ALTO ADIGE and FRIULI, esp. TIEFENBRUNNER's "Feldmarschall".

Nasco di Cagliari Sard. DOC w. dr. or sw. (f. dr. or sw.) ★ 87 88
Sardinian speciality, light bitter taste, high alcoholic content.

Nebbiolo The best red grape of PIEMONTE and Lombardy.

Nebbiolo d'Alba Piem. DOC r. dr. s/sw. (sp.) 🔳🔳 82 85 86 87 88
Like lightweight BAROLO; often easier to appreciate than the more powerful classic wine. Roero is a new DOC from n. of ALBA.

Negroamaro Literally "black bitter"; Apulian red grape with potential for quality. See Copertino.

Neive, Castello di Leading producer of BARBARESCO, in castle where Louis Oudart pioneered cask-ageing of NEBBIOLO in 1850s.

Nipozzano, Castello di The FRESCOBALDI estate nr. Florence producing Montesodi. The most important outside the CLASSICO zone.

Nozzole Famous estate in the heart of CHIANTI CLASSICO n. of Greve.

Nuragus di Cagliari Sard. DOC w. dr. 🔳 D.Y.A.
Lively Sardinian white, not too strong.

Oliena Sard. r. dr. ★★
Interesting strong fragrant CANNONAU red; a touch bitter.

Oltrepò Pavese Lomb. DOC. r. w. dr. sw. sp. ★→★★
DOC applicable to 15 wines produced in the province of Pavia, mostly named after their grapes.

Ornellaia New estate of Lodovico Antinori nr. Bolgheri on Tuscan coast. To watch for CAB/MERLOT and SAUV BLANC called Poggio delle Gazze.

Orvieto Umb. DOC w. dr. or s/sw. ★★→★★★ D.Y.A.
The classical Umbrian golden-white, smooth and substantial, formerly rather dull but recently more interesting, esp. in sweet versions. O. Classico is superior. Only the finest examples e.g. BIGI, DECUGNANO DEI BARBI, BARBERANI, age well. But see Castello della Sala.

Ostuni Apu. DOC r. or w. dr. ★ D.Y.A.
From the province of Brindisi. Nothing to write home about.

Pagadebit di Romagna Em-Ro. DOC w. dr./s.sw. D.Y.A.
Pleasant traditional "payer of debts" from round Bertinoro.

Paradiso, Fattoria Century-old family estate near Bertinoro (EM-RO). Good ALBANA, fine PAGADEBIT and unique red BARBAROSSA. SANGIOVESE is best.

Parrina Tusc. r. or w. dr. ★★ 86 87 88
Light red and fresh appetizing white from s. Tuscany.

Pasolini Dall'Onda Noble family with estates in CHIANTI Colli Forentini and ROMAGNA producing fine traditional style wines.

Passito Strong sweet wine from grapes dried on the vine or indoors.

Peppoli Estate owned by ANTINORI producing excellent CHIANTI CLASSICO in a full, round, youthful style – first vintage 85.

Per'e Palummo Camp. r. dr. ★★ 86 87 88
Appetizing red produced on the island of Ischia; delicate, slightly grassy, a bit tannic, balanced.

Petit Rouge Vd'A. 🔳🔳 82 83 85 86 88
Good dark lively REFOSCO-like red. Part of VALLE D'AOSTA DOC.

Piave Ven. DOC r. or w. dr. 🔳🔳 82 83 85 86 88 (w. D.Y.A.)
Flourishing DOC covering 8 wines, 4 red and 4 white, named after their grapes. CAB, MERLOT and RABOSO reds all need ageing.

Picolit (Colli Orientali del Friuli) Fr-VG. DOC w. s/sw. or sw. ★★★ 85 86 88   Delicate, well-balanced, very sweet dessert wine. Ages up to 6 years, but wildly overpriced.

Piemonte The most important Italian region for quality wine. Turin is the capital, Asti and ALBA the wine-centres. See Barolo, Barbera, Grignolino, Moscato, etc.

Pieropan Outstanding producers of SOAVE that deserves its fame.

Pigato New DOC under Riviera Ligure di Ponente. Often outclasses VERMENTINO as Liguria's finest white, with rich texture and structure.

Pighin, Fratelli Solid producers of COLLIO and GRAVE DEL FRIULI.

Pinot Bianco Popular in n.e., esp. good for sparkling wine.

Pinot Bianco (Alto Adige) Tr-Aad. DOC. w. dr. ▓▓ 85 86 88   Italy's best and longest-lived wine of this variety.

Pinot Bianco (dei Colli Berici) Ven. DOC w. dr. ★★ D.Y.A.   Straight, satisfying dry white.

Pinot Bianco (Colli Orientali del Friuli) Fr-VG. DOC w. dr. ★★ 87 88   Good white; smooth rather than showy.

Pinot Bianco (Collio Goriziano) Fr-VG. DOC w. dr. ★★ 86 88   Similar to the above.

Pinot Bianco (Grave del Friuli) Fr-VG. DOC w. dr. ★★ D.Y.A.   Not normally up to the standard of the last two.

Pinot Grigio Tasty, low-acid white grape increasingly popular in n.e. Italy. Best from A. ADIGE, COLLIO.

Pinot Grigio (Collio Goriziano) Fr-VG. DOC w. dr. ★★ D.Y.A.   Fruity, soft, agreeable dry white. The best age well.

Pinot Grigio (Grave del Friuli) Fr-VG. DOC w. dr. ★★ D.Y.A.   Second choice to Collio or Colli Orientali.

Pinot Grigio (Oltrepò Pavese) Lomb. DOC w. dr. (sp.) ★★ D.Y.A.   Lombardy's P.G. is usually at least adequate.

Pinot Nero Tr-Aad. DOC r. dr. ▓▓ 85 86 88   Pinot Nero (Noir) gives lively burgundy-scented light wine in much of n.e. Italy, incl. Trentino. Riserva after 2 yrs.

Pio Cesare A producer of top-quality red wines of PIEMONTE, incl. BAROLO.

Podere Il Palazzino Small estate with admirable CHIANTI CLASSICO and v.d.t. Grosso Senese.

Poggio al Sole CHIANTI CLASSICO estate. Less distinguished than formerly.

Poggione, Tenuta Il Perhaps the most consistent top estate for BRUNELLO and ROSSO DI MONTALCINO.

Pojer & Sandri Top producers of TRENTINO non-DOC MÜLLER-THURGAU, CHARDONNAY.

Pomino Tusc. DOC (r.) w. dr. (br.) ★★★ 85 86 88   Fine white, partly CHARDONNAY ("Il Benefizio" is 100%) and a SANGIOVESE/CABERNET blend. Also Vin Santo. From FRESCOBALDI.

Polyphemo Monster monocular Sicilian overfond of Greek red.

Predicato Name for four kinds of VINI DA TAVOLA from central Tuscany. They illustrate the headlong rush from tradition. P. del Muschio is CHARD, P BIANCO, P. del Selvante is SAUV BLANC, P. di Biturica is CAB SAUV with SANGIOVESE, P. di Cardisco is SANGIOVESE straight. RUFFINO's Cabreo brand are examples.

Primitivo di Apulia See Manduria.

Prosecco di Conegliano Ven. DOC w. dr. or s/sw. (sp.) ★★★ D.Y.A.   Popular sparkling wine of the n.e. Slight fruity bouquet, the dry pleasantly bitter, the sweet fruity; the best are known as Superiore di Cartizze. Carpené-Malvolti is famous old maker, now surpassed in quality by Pino Zardetto, Nino Franco, Canevel, Cardinal.

Prunotto, Alfredo Very serious ALBA company with v.g. BAROLO, BARBAR-ESCO, NEBBIOLO, etc.

Quintarelli, Giuseppe True artisan producer of VALPOLICELLA, RECIOTO and AMARONE, at the top in both quality and price.

Raboso del Piave (now DOC) Ven. r. dr. ★★ 82 83 85 86 88
Powerful, sharp, interesting country red; needs age.

Rallo, Diego & Figli A leader in MARSALA with 1st class Vergine and other
wines. (Giacomo Rallo is director. His wife runs DONNAFUGATA).

Ramandolo See Verduzzo Colli Orientali del Friuli.

Rampolla, Castello dei Top CHIANTI CLASSICO estate at Panzano; also
excellent Cabernet-based v.d.t. Sammarco.

Rapitalà See Alcamo.

Ratti, Renato Maker of v.g. BAROLO and other ALBA wines. Signor Ratti
(d. 1988) was a highly respected leader of the Piemonte industry.

Ravello Camp. r. p. w. dr. ★★ 86 87 88
Among the best wines of Campania: full dry red, fresh clean white.
Caruso is the best-known brand.

Recioto Wine made partly of half-dried grapes. Speciality of Veneto since
the great days of the Venetian empire.

Recioto di Gambellara Ven. DOC w. s/sw. sp. ★ D.Y.A.
Sweetish golden wine, often half-sparkling.

Recioto di Soave Ven. DOC w. s/sw. (sp.) ★★ 85 86 87 88
Soave made from selected half-dried grapes; sweet, fruity, fresh,
slightly almondy: high alcohol. Top maker: ANSELMI.

Recioto della Valpolicella Ven. DOC r. s/sw. sp. ★★ 80 81 83 85 86 88
Strong late-harvested red, sometimes sparkling. "Amabile" is sweet.

Recioto Amarone della Valpolicella Ven. DOC r. dr. ★★★★ 77 78 79 80
81 83 85 86 88 Dry version of the above; strong concentrated flavour,
rather bitter. Impressive and expensive.

Refosco (Colli Orientali del Friuli) Fr-VG. DOC r. dr. ★★ 82 83 85 86 88
Full-bodied dry red; Riserva after 2 yrs. Refosco is said to be the same
grape as the MONDEUSE of Savoie (France).

Refosco (Grave del Friuli) Fr-VG. DOC r. dr. ★★ 82 83 85 86 87 88
Similar to above but slightly lighter.

Regaleali Sic. w. r. p. ★★ 81 83 84 85 86 87 88
Perhaps the best Sicilian table wines, produced between Caltanissetta
and Palermo.

Ribolla (Colli Orientali del Friuli) Fr-VG. DOC w. dr. ★ D.Y.A.
Clean and fruity north-eastern white.

Ricasoli Famous Tuscan family, "inventors" of CHIANTI, whose Chianti
Classico is named after their BROLIO estate and castle.

Riecine Tusc. ★★★
First-class CHIANTI CLASSICO estate at Gaiole started by an Englishman,
John Dunkley. First wine 1973.

Riesling Formerly referred to Italian Riesling (R. Italico or "Welschriesling"). German Riesling, now ascendant, is R. Renano.

Riesling Alto Adige DOC w. dr. ★★ 85 86 88
Can often be Italy's best Riesling.

Riesling (Oltrepò Pavese) Lomb. DOC w. dr. (sp.) ★★
The Lombardy version, quite light and fresh. Occasionally sparkling.
Keeps well. Made of both types of Riesling.

Riesling (Trentino) Tr-Aad. DOC w. dr. ★★ D.Y.A.
Delicate, slightly acid, very fruity.

Riserva Wine aged for a statutory period, usually in barrels.

Riunite One of the world's largest coop cellars near Reggio Emilia
producing huge quantities of LAMBRUSCO and other wines.

Rivera Important and reliable winemakers at Andria, near Bari, with
good red Il Falcone and CASTEL DEL MONTE rosé. Also Vigna al Monte
label.

Riviera del Garda Chiaretto Ven. and Lom. DOC p. dr. ★★ D.Y.A.
Charming cherry-pink, fresh and slightly bitter, from s.w. Garda,
especially round Moniga del Garda.

Riviera del Garda Rosso Ven. DOC r. dr. ★★ 85 86 87 88
Red version of the above; ages surprisingly well.

Rocche dei Manzoni, Podere Go-ahead estate at MONFORTE D'ALBA. Excellent BAROLO, BRICCO MANZONI, ALBA wines and Valentino Brut sp.

Roero See Nebbiolo d'Alba.

Ronco del Gnemiz Tiny property with outstanding COLLIO ORIENTALI DOCs and v.d.t. CHARDONNAY made in barriques.

Rosa del Golfo Apu. p. dr. ★★ D.Y.A.
An outstanding v.d.t. rosato of ALEZIO.

Rosato Rosé.

Rosato del Salento Apu. p. dr. ★→★★ D.Y.A.
Strong but refreshing southern rosé from round Brindisi.

Rossese di Dolceacqua Lig. DOC r. dr. ★★ 85 86 87 88
Well-known fragrant light red of the Riviera, as clean as claret. Superiore is stronger.

Rosso Red.

Rosso Cònero Mar. DOC r. dr. ★★ 82 83 85 86 87 88
Limited production of some of the best MONTEPULCIANO (varietal) reds of Italy, i.e. Umani Ronchi's Cumaro and San Lorenzo, Garofoli's Piancarda.

Rosso d'Arquata See Adanti.

Rosso delle Colline Lucchesi Tusc. DOC r. dr. ★★ 85 86 88
Produced round Lucca but not greatly different from CHIANTI.

Rosso di Montalcino Tusc. DOC r. dr. ★★→★★★
Recent DOC for younger wines from BRUNELLO grapes. Still variable but potentially a winner.

Rosso Piceno Mar. DOC r. dr. ★→ ★★ 83 85 86 87 88
Adriatic red with a touch of style. Can be Superiore from classic zone near Asedi.

Rubesco The excellent popular red of TORGIANO.

Rubino di Cantavenna Piem. DOC r. dr. ★★ 86 87 88
Lively red, principally BARBERA, from a well-known coop s.e. of Turin.

Rufina A sub-region of CHIANTI in the hills east of Florence.

Ruffino The biggest and best known of all CHIANTI merchants. Riserva Ducale is the top wine. N.B. New PREDICATO wines.

Sagrantino See Montefalco.

Salice Salentino Apu. DOC r. ★★ 79 80 81 83 85 86 87 88
Strong red from Negroamaro grapes, Riserva after 2 yrs, ages to smooth full wine. Top makers: Taurino, De Castris.

San Felice Rising star in CHIANTI with fine Classico Poggio Rosso and prize-winning red v.d.t. Vigorello and PREDICATO di Biturica.

Sangiovese or Sangiovete Principal red grape of Italy, esp. Tuscany. Many forms incl. the noble BRUNELLO and Prugnolo Gentile (of MONTEPULCIANO), also:

Sangiovese d'Aprilia Lat. DOC r. or p. dr. ★ D.Y.A.
Strong dry rosé from south of Rome.

Sangiovese di Romagna Em-Ro. DOC r. dr. ★★ 82 83 85 86 87 88
Pleasant standard red; gains character with a little age.

San Giusto a Rentennano One of the best CHIANTI CLASSICO producers; stunning '85 at very reasonable prices. Excellent v.d.t. red Percarlo.

San Polo in Rosso, Castello di CHIANTI CLASSICO estate with first-rate red v.d.t. Cetinaia, (aged in standard casks, not barriques).

San Severo Apu. DOC r. p. w. dr. ★ 87 88
Sound neutral southern wine; not particularly strong.

Santa Maddalena Tr-Aad. DOC r. dr. ★★ 86 88
Perhaps the best Tyrolean red. Round and warm, slightly almondy. From Bolzano.

Santa Margherita The Veneto winery that popularized PINOT GRIGIO, now on a broad base with many good wines.

Sassella (Valtellina) Lomb. DOC r. dr. ★★★ 78 79 80 82 83 85 86 88
Considerable NEBBIOLO wine, tough when young. Known since Roman times, mentioned by Leonardo da Vinci.

Sassicaia Tusc. r. dr. ★★★★ 72 75 76 77 78 79 80 81 82 83 84 85 86 87 88 Outstanding pioneer CABERNET from the Tenuta San Guido of the Incisa family, at Bolgheri near Livorno. Limited production.

Sauvignon The Sauvignon Blanc: excellent white grape used in n.e., perhaps best at TERLANO, ALTO ADIGE. Very good in COLLIO and COLLI ORIENTALI.

Sauvignon (Colli Berici) Ven. DOC w. dr. ★ D.Y.A.
Fresh white from near Vicenza.

Sauvignon (Colli Orientali del Friuli) Fr-VG. DOC w. dr. ★★ 85 86 88
Full, smooth, freshly aromatic n.e. white.

Sauvignon (Collio Goriziano) Fr-VG. DOC w. dr. ★★ 85 86 88
Very similar to the last; slightly higher alcohol.

Savuto Cal. DOC r. p. dr. ★★ 83 85 86 88
The ancient Savuto produced in the provinces of Cosenza and Catanzaro. Fragrant juicy wine.

Schiava Good red grape of TRENTINO-ALTO ADIGE with characteristic bitter after-taste, used for SANTA MADDALENA, etc.

Sciacchetrà See Cinqueterre.

Sebaste Young Barolo-maker to watch in joint venture with GANCIA.

Secco Dry.

Secentenario Tusc. r. ★★★★
Perhaps ANTINORI's best-ever red, bottled (in magnums) for the firm's 600th anniversary in 1985.

Sella & Mosca Major Sardinian growers and merchants at Alghero. Their port-like Anghelu Ruju is good.

Selvapiana RUFINA estate owned by Giuntini family. One of the finest Chiantis of all, rivalled by few Classicos.

Settesoli Sicilian growers' coop with range of sometimes v.g. table wines.

Sforzato (Valtellina) Lomb. DOC r. dr. ★★★ 78 79 80 82 83 85 86 88
Valtellina equivalent of RECIOTO AMARONE made with partly dried grapes. Velvety, strong, ages remarkably well. Also called Sfursat.

Sfursat See Sforzato.

Sizzano Piem. DOC r. dr. ★★ 82 83 85 86 87 88
Attractive full-bodied red produced at Sizzano in the province of Novara, mostly from NEBBIOLO. Ages up to 10 years.

Soave Ven. DOC w. dr. ★★★ D.Y.A.
Famous, if not very characterful, Veronese white. Fresh with attractive texture. S. Classico is more restricted and better.

Solaia Tusc. r. ★★★ 79 82 83 85
Very fine Bordeaux-style wine of CAB. SAUV and now 25% SANGIOVESE from ANTINORI, first made in 1979.

A top category, DOCG, Denominazione Controllata e Garantita, is gradually being added to the Italian wine classification. It is awarded only to certain wines from top-quality zones which have been bottled and sealed with a government seal by the producer. The first five areas to be "guaranteed" were Barolo, Barbaresco, Brunello di Montalcino, Chianti and Vino Nobile di Montepulciano. The sixth (and first white) was Albana di Romagna, for no discernible reason. But it should be remembered that many of Italy's best wines are not covered by the DOC system and are officially only vino da tavola – v.d.t. in this book. Examples are Sassicaia, Tignanello, Venegazzù, Bricco Manzoni.

Solopaca Camp. DOC r. w. dr. ★★ 85 86 87 88
Up-and-coming from near Benevento; rather sharp when young, the white soft and fruity.

Sorni Tr-Aad. r. w. dr. ★★ D.Y.A.
Made in the province of Trento. Light, fresh and soft. Drink young.

Spanna See Gattinara.

Spumante Sparkling, as in sweet Asti or many good dry wines, incl. both METODO CLASSICO and tank-made cheapos.

Squinzano Apu. DOC r. p. dr. * 82 83 84 85 86 87 88
Strong southern red from Lecce. Riserva after 2 yrs.

Stravecchio Very old.

Sylvaner German white grape successful in ALTO ADIGE.

Taurasi Camp. DOC r. dr. *** 75 77 79 80 81 82 83 85 86 87 88
The best Campanian red, from Avellino, has a cult following in the
USA. Harsh when young. Riserva after 4 yrs.

Tedeschi, Fratelli Leading small producer of VALPOLICELLA, RECIOTO and
AMARONE. V.g. Capitel San Rocco red and white v.d.t.

Terlano Tr-Aad. DOC w. dr. ** 86 88
A DOC for 7 white wines from the province of Bolzano, named by their
grapes, esp. outstanding SAUVIGNON. Terlaner in German.

Teroldego Rotaliano Tr-Aad. DOC r. p. dr. **→*** 83 85 86 88
The attractive local red of Trento. Blackberry-scented, slight bitter
after-taste, can age v. well. Top maker: Foradori.

Terre Rosse Distinguished small estate near Bologna. CABERNET, CHARD,
SAUV BL, PINOT GRIGIO, etc., are the best of the region.

Tiefenbrunner Distinguished grower of some of the very best ALTO ADIGE
white and red wines at Schloss Turmhof, Kurtatsch (Cortaccio).

Tignanello Tusc. r. dr. *** 75 78 79 80 81 82 83 85 86 88
One of the leaders of the new style of Bordeaux-inspired Tuscan reds,
made by ANTINORI.

Tocai Friulano (Collio). ** 86 88
North-east Italian white grape; no relation of Hungarian or Alsace
Tokay. Light dry wine. The Tocais of the COLLI ORIENTALI DEL FRIULI and
COLLIO GORIZIANO are best.

Tocai di Lison Ven. DOC w. dr. ** D.Y.A.
From e. Veneto, delicate scent, fruity taste. Classico is better.

Tocai (Colli Berici) Ven. DOC w. dr. * D.Y.A.
A more modest wine altogether.

Tocai (Grave del Friuli) Fr-VG. DOC w. dr. ** D.Y.A.
Similar to TOCAI DI LISON, generally rather milder.

Tocai di S. Martino della Battaglia Lomb. DOC w. dr. ** D.Y.A.
Small production s. of Lake Garda. Light, slightly bitter.

Torbato di Alghero Sard. w. dr. (pa.) ** D.Y.A.
Good n. Sardinian table wine. Top maker: SELLA & MOSCA.

Torgiano (Rubesco di) Umb. DOC r. w. dr. *** 75 77 78 79 80 81
82 83 85 86 87 88 The creation of the LUNGAROTTI family. Excellent
red from near Perugia comparable with top CHIANTI CLASSICO. RUBESCO
is the standard quality. Riserva Monticchio is superb. Keep 10 years.
White Torre di Giano is good, but not as outstanding as reds.

Torricella Tusc. w. dr. *** 81 82 83 85 86 87 88
Remarkable aged, soft, buttery MALVASIA dry white from BROLIO.

Traminer Aromatico Tr-Aad. DOC w. dr. ** D.Y.A.
Delicate, aromatic, rather soft Gewürztraminer.

Trebbiano The principal white grape of Tuscany, found all over Italy.
Ugni Blanc in French. Rarely remarkable unless blended.

Trebbiano d'Abruzzo Abr. & M. DOC w. dr. *→** 79 88
Gentle, rather neutral, slightly tannic. From round Pescara. Valentini
is much the best producer (also of MONTEPULCIANO D'ABRUZZO).

Trebbiano d'Aprilia Lat. DOC w. dr. * D.Y.A.
Heady, mild-flavoured, rather yellow. From south of Rome.

Trebbiano di Romagna Em-Ro. DOC w. dr. or s/sw. (sp.) * D.Y.A.
Clean, pleasant white from near Bologna.

Trentino Tr-Aad. DOC r. w. dr. or sw. *→***
DOC for as many as 20 different wines, mostly named after their
grapes. Best are CHARD, P BIANCO, MARZEMINO and esp. VIN SANTO.

Umani Ronchi A leading producer of quality wines of the Marches;
notably VERDICCHIO, Casal di Serra and Villa Bianchi and ROSSO CONERO,
Cùmaro and San Lorenzo.

Uzzano, Castello di Fine old CHIANTI CLASSICO estate at Greve.
Valcalepio Lomb. DOC r. w. dr. ★ 86 88
From nr. Bergamo. Pleasant red; lightly scented, fresh white.
Valdadige Tr-Aad. DOC r. w. dr. or s/sw. ★
Name for the table wines of the Adige valley – in German Etschtal.
Val d'Arbia Tusc. DOC w. dr. ★ D.Y.A.
Another DOC for a pleasant white and VIN SANTO from CHIANTI country.
Valentini, Edoardo Outstanding traditionalist maker of TREBBIANO and
MONTEPULCIANO D'ABRUZZO.
Valgella (Valtellina) Lomb. DOC r. dr. ★★ 78 79 80 82 83 85 86 88
One of the VALTELLINA NEBBIOLOS: good dry red. Riserva at 4 yrs.
Vallana, Antonio & Figlio The protagonist of the "SPANNA" (Nebbiolo)
near Novara, Piem. Uses the DOC name BOCA. Rich-flavoured reds.
Valle d'Aosta/Vallée d'Aosta Vd'A. DOC
Regional DOC for 15 Alpine wines including DONNAZ, etc. A mixed bag.
Valle Isarco Tr-Aad. DOC w. dr. ★→★★ 86 88
A DOC applicable to 5 varietal wines made n.e. of Bolzano.
Outstanding MÜLLER-THURGAU, SYLVANER.
Valpantena Valley in the VALPOLICELLA zone. Rival to CLASSICO. See Bertani.
Valpolicella Ven. DOC r. dr. ★→ ★★★ 85 86 88
Attractive light red from nr. Verona; most attractive when young.
Delicate nutty scent, slightly bitter taste. (None of this is true of
Valpolicella sold in litre and bigger bottles.) Classico more restricted;
Superiore has 12% alcohol and 1 yr of age.
Valtellina Lomb. DOC r. dr. ★★→★★★ 82 83 85 86 88
A DOC applicable to wines made principally from Chiavennasca
(NEBBIOLO) grapes in the province of Sondrio, n. Lombardy. V.
Superiore is GRUMELLO, INFERNO, SASSELLA or VALGELLA.
Vecchio Samperi Sic. des. ★★★
The outstanding wine of MARSALA today, although not DOC. A dry
apéritif not unlike Amontillado sherry.
Velletri Lat. DOC r. w. dr. or s/sw. ★★ (r.) 86 87 88
Agreeable Roman dry red and smooth white. Drink young.
Vendemmia Harvest or vintage.
Venegazzù Ven. r. w. dr. sp. ★★★ 78 79 82 83 85 86 88
Remarkable rustic Bordeaux-style red produced from CABERNET
grapes nr. Treviso. Rich bouquet, soft, warm taste, "della Casa" is
best quality. Also sparkling white.
Verdicchio dei Castelli di Jesi Mar. DOC w. dr. (sp.) ★→★★★ D.Y.A.
Ancient, famous and very pleasant fresh pale white from nr. Ancona.
Goes back to the Etruscans. Classico more restricted. Traditionally
comes in amphora-shaped bottles: today also standard bottles of
notable class from Umani Ronchi, Garofoli, Brundri, Bucci, Monte
Schiaro; also Fazi-Battaglia.
Verdicchio di Matelica Mar. DOC w. dr. (sp.) ★★ D.Y.A.
Similar to the last, though less well known. Bigger wines than Jesi.
Verdiso Rare native white grape of n.e. Italy, used with PROSECCO.
Verduzzo (Colli Orientali del Friuli) Fr-VG. DOC w. dr. s/sw. or sw. ★★
85 86 88 Full-bodied white from a native grape. The best sweet is
called Ramandolo. (Top maker: Giovanni Dri.)
Verduzzo (Del Piave) Ven. DOC w. dr. ★ D.Y.A.
A dull little white.
Vermentino Lig. w. dr. DOC ★★ D.Y.A.
The best seafood white of the Riviera: from Pietra Ligure and San
Remo. DOC is Rivera Ligure del Ponente. See Pigato.
Vermentino di Gallura Sard. DOC w. dr. ★★ D.Y.A.
Soft, dry, rather strong white from northern Sardinia.
Vernaccia di Oristano Sard. DOC w. dr. (sw.) (f.) ★★★ 81 82 83 84
85 86 88 Sardinian speciality, like light sherry, a touch bitter, full-
bodied and interesting. Superiore with 15.5% alcohol and 3 yrs of age.
Top producer Contini.

Vernaccia di San Gimignano   Tusc. DOC w. dr. (f.) ★★ 87 88
Should be a distinctive strong high-flavoured wine from near Siena.
Michelangelo's favourite. Much today is light and bland but signs of
improvement. Try Teruzzi & Puthod, Falchini or (old-style) Pietrafitta.
Riserva after 1 yr.

Vernaccia di Serrapetrona   Mar. DOC r. s/sw. sp. ★★ D.Y.A.
Comes from the province of Macerata; aromatic; with pleasantly
bitter after-taste.

Vernatsch   German for SCHIAVA.

Vicchiomaggio   Important CHIANTI CLASSICO estate near Greve.

Vietti   Excellent small producer of some of Piedmont's most characterful
wines, incl. BAROLO. At Castiglione Falletto, Prov. Cuneo.

VIDE   An association of better-class Italian producers for marketing their
estate wines.

Vignamaggio   Historic and beautiful CHIANTI CLASSICO estate near Greve.

Villa Banfi   The production department of the biggest US importer of
Italian wine. Huge new plantings at MONTALCINO, incl. MOSCADELLO,
CABERNET, CHARDONNAY, are part of a drive for quality plus quantity.
BRUNELLO is proving excellent. Santa Costanza is v. fruity VINO NOVELLO.
In PIEMONTE Banfi produces sp. Banfi Brut, Principessa GAVI, BRACCHETO
D'ACQUI, Pinot Grigio.

Villagrande   Imposing old estate on the slopes of Mt. Etna, Sicily, DOC ETNA.

Vino da arrosto   "Wine for roast meat", i.e. good robust dry red.

Vino da pasto   "Mealtime" wine, i.e. nothing special.

Vino da tavola   "Table wine": intended to be the humblest class of Italian
wine, with one specific geographical or other claim to fame, but
increasingly the category to watch (with reasonable circumspection)
for top-class wines not conforming to DOC regulations. They are
referred to in the A-Z as v.d.t. It is the maker's name that counts.

Vino Nobile di Montepulciano   Tusc. DOCG r. dr. ★★★ 82 83 85 86
88 Impressive Chianti-like red with bouquet and style, rapidly
making its name and fortune. Aged for 3 yrs Riserva; for 4 yrs Riserva
Speciale. Best estates incl. BOSCARELLI, AVIGNONESI, Fognano, Poliziano.

Vino novello   Italy's equivalent of France's "primeurs", (as in BEAUJOLAIS).

Vinsanto or Vin Santo   Term for certain strong sweet wines esp. in
Tuscany: usually PASSITI. Can be v. fine, esp. in Tuscany and Trentino.

Vin Santo di Gambellara   Ven. DOC w. sw. ★★
Powerful velvety, golden: made near Vicenza and Verona.

Vin Santo Toscano   Tusc. w. s/sw. ★★→★★★
Aromatic bouquet, rich and smooth. Aged in very small barrels
known as Caratelli. Can be astonishing.

Vintage Tunina   Fr-VG. w. dr. ★★★ 85 86 88
A notable blended COLLIO white from the JERMANN estate.

Voerzio, Roberto   Young pace-maker in Barolo with refreshing wines.

Volpaia, Castello di   First-class CHIANTI CLASSICO estate at Radda. See
Coltassala.

VQPRD   Often found on the labels of DOC wines to signify "Vini di Qualita
Prodotti in Regioni Delimitate", or quality wines from restricted areas
in accordance with EEC regulations.

Zagarolo   Lat. DOC w. dr. or s/sw. ★★ D.Y.A.
Neighbour of FRASCATI, similar wine.

Zanella, Maurizio   Owner of CA'DEL BOSCO. His name is on top CAB/MERLOT
blend, one of Italy's best (82 83 84 85 86 87 88).

Zerbina, Fattoria   New leader in Romagna with best Albana DOCG to date
(a rich passita), good SANGIOVESE and a SANGIOVESE-CABERNET v.d.t. in
barrique called Marzeno di Marzeno.

Zonin   One of Italy's biggest privately owned estates and wineries, based
at GAMBELLARA, with DOC VALPOLICELLA, etc. Other large estates are at
ASTI and in CHIANTI, San Gimignano and FRIULI. Also at Barboursville,
Virginia, USA.

Germany

Of all the fine wines of the world those of Germany are currently most underrated (and best value for money). Yet to the regret of those who admire the many fine examples of her unique style of wine that truly reflect her traditions, her climate and her soil, Germany is considered to have betrayed herself by offering the world a mass of watery wine at bucket-shop prices.

Some of it is imported wine dressed up to look German. Alas, much of it is genuinely German, but made to the minimum standards allowed by a too-liberal wine law. The minimum requirements for the status of Qualitätswein b.A. (see below) are such as to allow the most dreary commodity to benefit from this apparently elevated denomination.

Active debate has started about overhauling the wine law of 1971, which is largely to blame for this and other problems in the German wine industry. Restrictions on quantities of wine per hectare, plus upgrading minimum standards of ripeness, will for the moment be all the Government does about it. But meanwhile many of the best producers in certain areas have formed themselves into associations (such as "Charta" in the Rheingau) pledged to uphold high standards of their own definition, and to ignore as irrelevant the minimum standards set up by the Government.

Meanwhile wine-drinkers very reasonably call for a revision of the labelling system which they find over-complicated: long on logic but short on practical help for the consumer. Traditional German labels do indeed need very close scrutiny. The differences between the fine long-lived Riesling wines of conscientious growers and the bulk of Liebfraumilch and the like are far greater than their labels, and even their official denominations, suggest. Major moves are being made to simplify labels and the lead is coming from the top. Some of today's best German wines are deliberately unspecific about their precise origins. The guarantee of the producer is replacing the worthless warranty of the official system.

Meanwhile German taste has changed dramatically. The role of wine in Germany up to very recent times has been as refreshment between meals, as an apéritif before or a succulent throatful after. To the grower delicacy and balance have been ends in themselves, with sweetness and fruity acidity counterpoised; the wine a drink to be enjoyed and contemplated alone.

The new trend is for dry wines made for drinking with meals. More than half the production of most good growers is now in the "trocken" (dry) category. This change is beneficial; drinkers rapidly realize that a poor-quality wine without even a veil of sugar to hide its nakedness is a miserable drink. The move to dry wines is therefore already raising winemaking standards.

Consumers familiar with the old pattern, in which, for example, a Spätlese was expected to be a moderately sweet wine, now need to understand the concept of a *dry* Spätlese, in which all the sugar is converted to alcohol with an effect closer to (though still not quite as strong as) a wine from Alsace.

The following
abbreviations of
regional names
are used in the text.

Bad.	Baden
Frank.	Franken
M-M	Mittel-Mosel
M-S-R	Moselle Saar Ruwer
Na.	Nahe
Rhg.	Rheingau
Rhh.	Rheinhessen
Rhpf.	Rheinpfalz
Wurtt.	Württemberg

The labels and the law

German wine law is based on the ripeness of the grapes at harvest time. Vintages vary, but most German wine, like most French wine, needs sugar added before fermentation to increase its strength, and make up for missing sunshine.

Unlike in France, wine from grapes ripe enough not to need sugar is kept apart as Qualitätswein mit Prädikat or QmP. Within this top category its natural sugar content is expressed by traditional terms – in ascending order of ripeness: Kabinett, Spätlese, Auslese, Beerenauslese, Trockenbeerenauslese.

But good wine is also made by good growers from grapes that fail to reach the natural sugar content required for a QmP label. This category is called Qualitätswein as well, but with the different qualification of bestimmter Anbaugebiete (i.e. QbA) instead of mit Prädikat. "Prädikat" is therefore (theoretically) the key word to look for. Matters are complicated, though, by growers who add sugar even to Prädikat standard juice, believing, as the French do, that slightly more alcohol gives better balance. Do not assume that *all* QbA wines are inferior.

The third level, Tafelwein, has no pretensions to quality and is not allowed to give itself airs beyond the name of the general region or sub-region it comes from. (But see Landwein).

Though there is very much more detail in the laws this is the gist of the quality grading. Where it differs completely from the French system is in ignoring geographical differences. There are no Grands Crus, no VDQS. In theory all any German vineyard has to do to make the best wine is to grow the ripest grapes.

The law distinguishes only between degrees of geographical exactness. In labelling quality wine the grower or merchant is given a choice. He can (and almost always will) label the relatively small quantities of his best wine with the name of the precise vineyard or Einzellage where it was grown. Germany has about 2,600 Einzellage names. Obviously only particularly good ones are famous enough to help sell the wine. Therefore the 1971 law created a second class of vineyard name: the Grosslage. A Grosslage is a group of neighbouring Einzellages of supposedly similar character. Because there are fewer Grosslage names, and far more wine from each, they have the advantage of familiarity. The law was thus responsible for confusing the public, and the industry is now suffering as a result.

<table>
<tr><td>

MOSEL-SAAR-RUWER

BERKASTELER

SCHLOSSBERG

RIESLING AUSLESE

1987

Qualitätswein mit Prädikat

A.P. NR. 12345678

ERZEUGERABFÜLLUNG

MOZARTHOF TRIER

</td><td>

The traditional German label

The order of wording on traditional German quality wine labels usually follows a pattern. The first mention is the Anbaugebiet or wine region. The second is the town or parish, with the suffix – er. The third is the vineyard (either Einzellage or Grosslage – see introduction and footnote). The fourth (optional) is the grape variety, the fifth the quality in terms of ripeness. For Qualitätswein mit Prädikat see page 114. For A.P. Nr. see page 105. Erzeugerabfüllung means bottled by the producer.

</td></tr>
</table>

Thirdly the grower or merchant (more likely the latter) may choose to sell his wine under a regional name: the word is Bereich. To cope with the vast demand for "Bernkasteler" or "Niersteiner" or "Johannisberger" these world-famous names have been made legal for considerable districts. "Bereich Johannisberg" is the whole of the Rheingau; "Bereich Bernkastel" the whole of the Mittelmosel. By the same logic the whole of the Médoc could be called Margaux. Beware the Bereich.

A fourth alternative, now gaining ground, is to use the community (or village) name only, not mentioning the vineyard. Do not confuse these with Bereich wines; they are far more specific, in a higher quality category, but the only visible difference is the absence of the word "Bereich" on the label. This is only allowed for QbA or QmP wines. With simplification of nomenclature very much on merchants' minds, we will see more and more of this style of labelling, and also of labels stressing the style of wine, rather than its origin. "Riesling Dry" is a new concept which is already making an impact. One golden rule remains true: the name of the producer is the key.

Recent vintages

Mosel-Saar-Ruwer

Mosels (including Saar and Ruwer wines) are so attractive young that their keeping qualities are not often enough explored, and wines older than seven years or so are unusual. But well-made wines of Kabinett class gain from three or more in bottle, Spätleses by longer, and Ausleses and Beerenausleses by anything from 10 to 20 years.

As a rule, in poor years the Saar and Ruwer make sharp, thin wines, but in the best years they can surpass the whole of Germany for elegance and "breed".

1988 Excellent vintage. Much ripe QmP, esp. in Mittelmosel. For long keeping.
1987 Rainy summer but warm Sept/Oct. 90% QbA wines, crisp and lively, to drink in 1990-93. The few QmPs will continue to improve.
1986 Fair Riesling year despite autumn rain: 13% QbA wines, mostly Kabinett. Keeping well.
1985 A modest summer but beautiful autumn. 40% of the harvest was QmP. Very good Riesling vintage from best v'yds, incl. Eiswein. Drinking well.
1984 A late and rainy year. Two-thirds QbA, one-third Tafel- or Landwein. Almost no QmP. But good acidity means some wines (esp. Ruwers) have kept well.
1983 The best since 1976; much good QbA, a little Kabinett, 31% Spätlese, Ausleses few but some fine, others have off-odours. Drinking well.
1982 A huge ripe vintage marred by rain which considerably diluted the wines. Most is plain QbA but good sites made Kabinett, Spätlese and Auslese. Drink up.
1981 A wet vintage but some good middle Mosels up to Spätlese. Also Eiswein. Drink up.
1980 A terrible summer. Some pleasant wines but little more. Avoid.
1979 A patchy vintage after bad winter damage. But several excellent Kabinetts and better. Light but well-balanced wines should be drunk up.
1978 A similar vintage to '77, though very late and rather small. Very few sweet wines but many with good balance. Drink up.
1977 Big vintage of serviceable quality, mostly QbA. Drink up.
1976 Very good small vintage, with some superlative sweet wines and almost no dry. Most wines now ready; the best will keep a little longer.
1975 Very good; many Spätleses and Ausleses. Almost all now ready.
1971 Superb, with perfect balance. At its peak.
Older fine vintages: '69, '67, '64, '59, '53, '49, '45.

Rheinhessen, Nahe, Rheinpfalz, Rheingau

Even the best wines can be drunk with pleasure after two or three years, but Kabinett, Spätlese and Auslese wines gain enormously in character by keeping for longer. Rheingau wines tend to be longest-lived, improving for 10 years or more, but wines from the Nahe and Palatinate can last nearly as long. Rheinhessen wines usually mature sooner, and dry Franconian wines are best at 3-6 years.

1988 Not so outstanding as the Mosel, but comparable with 1983.
1987 Good average quality: lively, round and fresh. 80% QbA (keep 2-4 years), 15% QmP (keep 3-6 years).
1986 Well-balanced Rieslings, mostly QbA but some Kabinett and Spätlese, esp. in Rheinhessen and Nahe. No hurry to drink.
1985 Frost, hail and drought led to sadly small crops, but good quality, esp. Riesling. Average 65% QmP. Comparable quality to 1983. Keeping well.
1984 Poor flowering and ripening. Three-quarters QbA, with QmP only in Rheinhessen, Rheinpfalz, Baden and Nahe. But flavour can be good. Drink soon.
1983 Very good Rieslings, esp. in the Rheingau and central Nahe. Generally about half QbA, but plenty of Spätleses. No hurry to drink.
1982 A colossal vintage gathered in torrential rain. Spätleses and even Kabinett are rare, but all '82s should be drunk up.
1981 Poor conditions in the Rheingau but better in Nahe and Rheinhessen and good in Palatinate. Generally ready.
1980 Bad weather from spring to autumn. Only passable wines. Avoid.
1979 Uneven and reduced in size. Few great wines but many typical and good, esp. in Palatinate. Drink up.
1978 Satisfactory vintage saved by late autumn. 25% QmP, but very few Spätleses. Some excellent wines in the south. Drink up.
1977 Big and useful; few Kabinett wines or better. Drink up.
1976 The richest vintage since 1921 in places. Very few dry wines. Balance less consistent than 1975. Generally mature.
1975 A splendid Riesling year, a high percentage of Kabinetts and Spätleses. Drink soon.
1971 A superlative vintage, now at its peak.
Older fine vintages: '69, '67, '66, '64, '59, '57, '53, '49, '45.

N.B. On the German vintage notation

Vintage notes after entries in the German section are given in a different form from those elsewhere, to show the style of the vintage as well as its quality. Three styles are indicated: The classic, super-ripe vintage with a high proportion of natural (QmP) wines, including Spätleses and Ausleses. Example: **83**

The "normal" successful vintage with plenty of good wine but no great preponderance of sweeter wines. Example: 79

The cool vintage with generally poor ripeness but a fair proportion of reasonably successful wines, tending to be over-acid. Few or no QmP wines, but correspondingly more selection in the QbA category. Such wines sometimes mature better than expected. Example: *84*

Where no mention is made the vintage is generally not recommended, or most of its wines have passed maturity.

Achkarren Bad. (r.) w. **★★**
 Well-known wine village of the KAISERSTUHL, esp. for SILVANER, RULÄNDER. Best site: Schlossberg.

Adelmann, Graf Famous grower with 37 acres at Kleinbottwar, WÜRTTEMBERG. Uses the name "Brussele". Light reds; good RIESLINGS.

Affental An area, not a village, just s. of Baden-Baden, producing a popular red Affentaler SPÄTBURGUNDER in a bottle moulded with a monkey ("Affe") climbing it.

Ahr Ahr r. ★→★★ 76 83 85 86 87 88
 Germany's best-known red-wine area, s. of Bonn. Very light pale SPÄTBURGUNDERS.

Amtliche Prüfungsnummer See Prüfungsnummer.

Anheuser Name of two distinguished growers of the NAHE.

Annaberg Rhpf. w. ★★★ 75 76 79 83 *84* 85 86 87 88
 18-acre v'yd at Dürkheim famous for stylish and pungent wines, with prodigious keeping qualities.

A.P.Nr. Abbreviation of AMTLICHE PRÜFUNGSNUMMER.

Assmannshausen Rhg. r. ★→★★★ 71 75 76 83 85 86 87 88
 RHEINGAU village known for its pale, sometimes sweet, reds. Top v'yd: Höllenberg. Grosslagen: Steil and Burgweg. Growers incl. the State Domain at ELTVILLE.

Auslese Specially selected wine with high natural sugar content, all the best affected by "noble rot" and correspondingly unctuous in flavour.

Avelsbach M-S-R (Ruwer) w. ★★★ 71 75 76 79 83 *84* 85 86 87 88
 Village near TRIER. Supremely delicate wines. Growers: Staatliche Weinbaudomäne (see Staatsweingut), BISCHÖFLICHE WEINGÜTER. Grosslage: Römerlay.

Ayl M-S-R (Saar) w. ★★★ 71 75 76 79 83 *84* 85 86 87 88
 One of the best villages of the SAAR. Top v'yds: Kupp, Herrenberger. Grosslage: Scharzberg. Growers incl. BISCHÖFLICHE WEINGÜTER.

Bacchus Modern highly perfumed grape variety, best for sweet wines.

Bacharach Romantic old town, a tourist centre of the MITTELRHEIN.

Bacharach (Bereich) ★→★★
 District name for the s. Mittelrhein v'yds downstream from the RHEINGAU. Steely, racy wines, some v. pleasant.

Baden Huge area of scattered wine-growing. The style is substantial, relatively low in acid, well adapted for mealtimes. Best areas are KAISERSTUHL and ORTENAU.

Badische Bergstrasse/Kraichgau (Bereich) Widespread district of n. BADEN. RIESLING and RULÄNDER are best.

Bad Dürkheim See Dürkheim, Bad.

Badischer Winzerkeller New name for the former ZBW, Germany's (and Europe's) biggest ultra-modern cooperative, at Breisach, BADEN, with 25,000 grower-members with 12,000 acres, producing 80% of Baden's wine at all quality levels.

Badisches Frankenland (Bereich) Minor district name of n. BADEN; Franconian-style wines.

Bad Kreuznach Nahe w. ★★→★★★ 75 76 79 83 *84* 85 86 87
Main town of the NAHE with some of its best wines. Many fine v'yds, incl. Brückes, Kahlenberg, Steinweg, Krötenpfuhl. Grosslage: Kronenberg.

Balbach Erben, Bürgermeister One of the best NIERSTEIN growers. 44 acres, 80% Riesling. Best v'yds: Pettenthal, Ölberg.

Barriques A few German growers are experimenting with fashionable new-oak small-barrel ageing. Higher prices are only positive result.

Basserman-Jordan 117-acre MITTELHAARDT family estate with many of the best v'yds in DEIDESHEIM, FORST, RUPPERTSBERG, etc.

Becker, J.B. Excellent family estate and brokerage house at WALLUF, Rheingau.

Beerenauslese Extremely sweet and luscious wine from exceptionally ripe selected individual bunches, their sugar and flavour concentrated by "noble rot".

Bereich District within an Anbaugebiet (region). See introduction and under Bereich names, e.g. Bernkastel (Bereich). The word on a label should be treated as a warning.

Bergweiler-Prüm Erben (Dr. Pauly-Bergweiler), Zach., Weingut Fine 24-acre estate based at BERNKASTEL. V'yds there and in WEHLEN, etc. Also Nicolay wines from ÜRZIG and ERDEN.

Bergzabern, Bad Rhpf. (r.) w. ★→★★ 76 79 83 *84* 85 86 87 88
Town of SÜDLICHE-WEINSTRASSE. Pleasant light wines. Grosslage: Liebfrauenberg.

Bernkastel M-M w. ★★→★★★★ 71 75 76 79 83 *84* 85 86 87 88
Top wine-town of the Mosel; the epitome of RIESLING. Best v'yds: Doctor (8 acres), Graben, Bratenhöfchen, etc. Grosslagen: Badstube (★★★) and Kurfürstlay (★★). Top growers incl. FRIEDRICH WILHELM GYMNASIUM, VEREINIGTE HOSPITIEN, THANISCH, PRÜM, WEGELER-DEINHARD, BERGWEILER, etc.

Bernkastel (Bereich) Wide area of mixed quality but decided flowery character. Includes all the Mittelmosel.

Bingen Rhh. w. ★★→★★★ 71 75 76 79 83 *84* 85 86 87 88
Town on Rhine and Nahe with fine v'yds, incl. Scharlachberg. Grosslage: Sankt Rochuskapelle.

Bingen (Bereich) District name for w. Rheinhessen.

Bischöfliche Weinguter der Verwaltung Famous M-S-R estate at TRIER, a union of the Cathedral properties with two other famous charities, the Bischöfliches Priesterseminar and the Bischöfliches Konvikt. 230 acres of top v'yds in AVELSBACH, WILTINGEN, SCHARZHOFBERG, AYL, KASEL, EITELSBACH, PIESPORT, TRITTENHEIM, ÜRZIG, etc.

Blankenhornsberg Outstanding KAISERSTUHL estate; 62 acres based at IHRINGEN.

Blue Nun The best-selling brand of LIEBFRAUMILCH, from SICHEL.

Bodenheim Rhh. w. ★★
Village nr. NIERSTEIN with delicate wines, esp. from Silberberg.

Bodensee (Bereich) Minor district of s. BADEN, on Lake Constance.

Bocksbeutel Flask-shaped bottle used for FRANKEN wines.

Braunberg M-M w. ★★★ 71 75 76 79 83 *84* 85 86 87 88
Village near BERNKASTEL with 750 acres. Excellent full-flavoured Rieslings. Best v'yd: Juffer. Grosslage: Kurfürstlay. Growers incl, BERGWEILER, Pauly, Paulinshof, RICHTER, HAAG.

Breisach Baden
Frontier town on Rhine nr. KAISERSTUHL. Seat of the largest German cooperative, the BADISCHER WINZERKELLER.

Breisgau (Bereich) Minor district of BADEN, just n. of KAISERSTUHL. Best known for very pale pink WEISSHERBST.

Brentano, von 25-acre old family estate in WINKEL, Rheingau.

Breuer, G. Weingut Family estate of 36 acres in RÜDESHEIM, with 6 acres of Berg Schlossberg. Artists' labels on these wines. See also Scholl & Hillebrand.

Buhl, von, Reichsrat Great RHEINPFALZ family estate. 250+ acres in DEIDESHEIM, FORST, RUPPERTSBERG, etc. In the very top class.

Bullay M-S-R ★→ ■■■ 76 83 85 86 87 88
Lower Mosel village. Good light wines. Growers incl. Drathen.

Bundesweinprämierung The German State Wine Award, organized by the DLG (see below): a gold, silver or bronze medallion on bottles of wines of a sufficiently high standard.

Bürgerspital zum Heiligen Geist Ancient charitable estate at WÜRZBURG. 333 acres in WÜRZBURG, RANDERSACKER, etc., make rich dry wines.

Bürklin-Wolf, Dr Great RHEINPFALZ family estate. 247 acres in WACHENHEIM, FORST, DEIDESHEIM and RUPPERTSBERG, with rarely a dull, let alone poor, wine.

Castell'sches, Fürstlich Domänenamt Historic 142-acre princely estate in STEIGERWALD. Good FRANKEN wines: SILVANER, RIESLANER. Also SEKT.

Chardonnay A small acreage of Chardonnay has been experimentally, and sometimes illegally, planted – e.g. on an island in the Rhine. It is the wrong grape for Germany.

Charta Organization of top RHEINGAU estates selling HALBTROCKEN RIESLINGS. The wines are made to considerably higher standards than the legal minima.

Crown of Crowns Popular brand of LIEBFRAUMILCH from LANGENBACH & CO.

Crusius 30-acre family estate at TRAISEN, Nahe. Excellently made, fresh RIESLINGS from Bastei and Rotenfels v'yds age v. well. Also SEKT of high quality and recently freshly fruity SPÄTBURGUNDER dry rosé.

Dahlem Erben, Dr Long-established 67-acre estate in OPPENHEIM. Some fine RIESLING and SYLVANER.

Deidesheim Rhpf. w. (r.) ■■★★→★★★★ 71 75 76 79 83 *84* 85 86 87 88
Biggest top-quality wine-village of RHEINPFALZ with 1,000 acres. Rich, high-flavoured, lively wines. V'yds incl. Grainhübel, Herrgottsacker, Leinhöhle, Hohenmorgen, Kieselberg, Paradiesgarten, etc. Grosslagen: Hofstück (★★), Mariengarten (★★★).

Deinhard Famous old Koblenz merchants and growers of top-quality wines in RHEINGAU, MITTELMOSEL, RUWER and RHEINPFALZ (see Wegeler-Deinhard), also makers of v.g. SEKT (brand name: Lila). Launched in '88 the Heritage range of single-village TROCKEN wines.

Deinhard, Dr 62-acre family estate in DEIDESHEIM with many of best v'yds.

Deutscher Tafelwein TAFELWEIN from Germany (only). See also Tafelwein.

Deutsches Weinsiegel A quality "seal" (i.e. neck label) for wines that have passed a statutory tasting test. Seals are yellow = dry, green = medium dry, red = sweet.

Deutsche Weinstrasse Popular tourist road of the southern Palatinate, Bockenheim to Schweigen.

DLG (Deutsche Landwirtschaft Gesellschaft) The German Agricultural Society at Frankfurt. Awards national medals for quality.

Dhron See Neumagen-Dhron.

Diabetiker Wein Wine with minimal residual sugar (less than 4gms/litre); thus suitable for diabetics – or those who like *very* dry wine.

Diel auf Burg Layen, Schlossgut 47 acre NAHE estate specializing in RIESLING and ROTBERGER, a Riesling cross making good rosé.

Dienheim Rhh. w. ★★ 76 83 85 86 87 88
Southern neighbour of OPPENHEIM. Mainly run-of-the-mill wines. Best v'yds: Kreuz, Herrenberg, Schloss. Grosslagen: Güldenmorgen, Krötenbrunnen.

Dom German for Cathedral. Wines from the famous TRIER Cathedral properties have "Dom" before the v'yd name.

Domäne German for "domain" or "estate". Sometimes used alone to mean the "State domain" (Staatliche Weinbaudomäne).

Durbach Baden w. (r.) ★★→ ▨▨▨ 76 83 *84* 85 86 87
775 acres of the best v'yds of BADEN. Top growers: Schloss Staufenberg, Wolf-Metternich, von Neveu. Choose their KLINGELBERGERS (Rieslings) and KLEVNERS (Traminers). Grosslage: Fürsteneck.

Dürkheim, Bad Rhpf. w. or (r.) ★★→★★★ 76 79 83 *84* 85 86 87
Main town of the MITTELHAARDT with the world's biggest barrel (converted into a tavern). Top v'yds: Hochbenn, Michelsberg. Grosslagen: Feuerberg, Schenkenböhl, Hochmess.

Edel Means "noble". Edelfäule means "noble rot": the condition which gives the greatest sweet wines (see p. 49).

Edenkoben Rhpf. w. (r.) ★→ ▨▨ 76 79 83 85 86 87 88
Important village of n. SÜDLICHE WEINSTRASSE. Grosslage: Ludwigshöhe. The best wines have plenty of flavour.

Egon Müller zu Scharzhof Top Saar estate of 32 acres at WILTINGEN. His delicate, racy SCHARZHOFBERGER Rieslings are among the worlds greatest wines, esp. in vintages that produce AUSLESES.

Eiswein Wine made from frozen grapes with the ice (e.g. water content) rejected, thus very concentrated in flavour and sugar, of Beerenauslese ripeness or more. Rare and expensive. Sometimes produced as late as the January or February following the vintage. Alcohol content can be as low as 5.5%.

Eitelsbach Ruwer w. ★★→★★★ 71 75 76 83 *84* 85 86 87 88
RUWER village now part of TRIER, incl. superb Karthäuserhofberg estate. Grosslage: Römerlay.

Elbling Traditional but generally inferior grape widely grown on upper Mosel but capable of great freshness and vitality in the best conditions (e.g. at MENNIG or in the Mittelmosel).

Eltville Rhg. w. ▨▨ →★★★ 71 75 76 79 83 *84* 85 86 87 88
Major wine-town with cellars of the Rheingau State domain, FISCHER and VON SIMMERN estates. Excellent wines. Top v'yds: Sonnenberg, Taubenberg. Grosslage: Steinmächer.

Enkirch M-M w. ★★→ ▨▨▨ 71 76 83 *84* 85 86 87 88
Minor MITTELMOSEL village, often overlooked but with lovely light tasty wine. Grosslage: Schwarzlay. Best v'yds: Steffensberg, Herrenberg.

Erbach Rhg. w. ★★★→★★★★ 71 76 79 83 *84* 85 86 87 88
One of the best parts of the Rheingau with powerful, perfumed wines, incl. the great MARCOBRUNN; other top v'yds: Schlossberg, Siegelsberg, Honigberg, Michelmark. Grosslage: Deutelsberg. Major estates: SCHLOSS REINHARTSHAUSEN, VON SCHÖNBORN.

Erden M-M w. ★★→★★★ 71 75 76 83 *84* 85 86 87
Village between Ürzig and Kröv with full-flavoured vigorous wine. Top v'yds: Prälat, Treppchen. Leading growers: BISCHÖFLICHE WEINGÜTER, BERGWEILER-PRÜM, Nicolay. Grosslage: Schwarzlay.

Erzeugerabfüllung Estate-bottled; bottled by the producer.

Escherndorf Frank. w. ★★→★★★ 76 83 86 87 88
Important wine-town near WÜRZBURG. Similar tasty dry wine. Top v'yds: Lump, Berg. Grosslage: Kirchberg.

Remember that vintage information about German wines is given in a different form from the ready/not ready distinction applying to other countries. Read the explanation on page 105.

Fischer, Dr. Weingut 60-acre estate of top quality at OCKFEN, incl. whole of WAWERNER Herrenberg.

Fischer Erben, Weingut 18-acre RHEINGAU estate with highest traditional standards. Immensely long-lived classic wines.

Forst Rhpf. w. ★★→★★★★ 71 75 76 79 83 *84* 85 86 87 88
MITTELHAARDT village with 500 acres of Germany's best v'yds. Ripe, richly fragrant, full-bodied but subtle wines. Top v'yds: Kirchenstück, Jesuitengarten, Ungeheuer. Grosslagen: Mariengarten, Schnepfenflug.

Franken Franconia: region of excellent distinctive dry wines, esp. SILVANER. The centre is WÜRZBURG. BEREICH names: MAINDREIECK, STEIGERWALD.

Freiburg Baden w. (r.) ★→★★ D.Y.A.
Wine centre in n. of MARKGRÄFLERLAND. Good GUTEDEL.

Freinsheim Rhpf.
Well-known village of Lower Haardt with high proportion of Riesling. Earthy, spicy wines.

Friedrich Wilhelm Gymnasium Superb 111-acre charitable estate based in TRIER with v'yds in BERNKASTEL, ZELTINGEN, GRAACH, TRITTENHEIM, OCKFEN, etc., all M-S-R.

Geheimrat 'J' Brand-name of v.g. dry Riesling Spätlese from WEGELER-DEINHARD, Oestrich. Epitomizes new thinking in German wine.

Geisenheim Rhg. w. ★★→★★★ 71 76 83 *84* 85 86 87 88
Village famous for Germany's leading wine-school and fine aromatic wines. Best v'yds incl. Rothenberg, Kläuserweg. Grosslagen: Burgweg and Erntebringer.

Gemeinde A commune or parish.

Gewürztraminer Spicy grape, speciality of Alsace, used a little in s. Germany, esp. RHEINPFALZ and BADEN. See Traminer. ![G]

Gimmeldingen Rhpf. w. ★→★★ 76 83 *84* 85 86 87 88
Village just s. of MITTELHAARDT. At their best, similar wines. Grosslage: Meerspinne.

Goldener Oktober Brand of Rhine and Mosel blends from ST URSULA.

Graach M-M w. ★★→ ![***] 71 75 76 83 *84* 85 86 87 88
Small village between BERNKASTEL and WEHLEN. Top v'yds: Himmelreich, Domprobst, Abstberg, Josephshöfer. Grosslage: Münzlay.

Green Label Germany's best-selling MOSEL (BEREICH BERNKASTEL). Brandname of DEINHARD.

Grosslage See Introduction, p.103.

Guntersblum Rhh. w. ★→★★ 76 83 *84* 85 86 87 88
Big wine-town s. of OPPENHEIM. Grosslagen: Krötenbrunnen, Vogelsgärten.

Guntrum, Louis Fine 164-acre family estate in NIERSTEIN. OPPENHEIM, etc., and merchant house with high and reliable standards.

Gutedel German for the Chasselas grape, used in s. BADEN.

Gutsverwaltung Estate administration.

Haag, Fritz Top-quality little (12 acres) estate at BRAUNEBERG.

Halbtrocken Medium-dry. Containing less than 18 but more than 9 grams per litre unfermented sugar. An increasingly popular category of wine intended for meal-times, often better-balanced than TROCKEN.

Hallgarten Rhg. w. ★★→★★★ 71 76 83 *84* 85 86 87 88
Important little wine-town behind HATTENHEIM. Robust, full-bodied wines. Top v'yds incl. Schönhell, Jungfer. Grosslage: Mehrhölzchen.

Hallgarten, House of Well-known London-based wine-merchant.

Hanns Christof Estimable Rhine-wine brand from DEINHARD.

Hattenheim Rhg. w. ★★→★★★★ 71 75 76 83 *84* 85 86 87 88
Superlative 500-acre wine-town. V'yds incl. STEINBERG, NUSSBRUNNEN, MANNBERG, HASSEL, etc. Grosslage: Deutelsberg. MARCOBRUNN lies on the ERBACH boundary.

Heilbronn Württ. w. r. ★→★★ 76 83 85 86 87 88
Wine-town with many small growers and a big coop. Seat of DLG competition.

Hessische Bergstrasse w. ★★→★★★ 76 83 84 85 86 87 88
Germany's smallest wine-region (1,000 acres) n. of Heidelberg. Pleasant Riesling from State domain v'yds in Heppenheim and Bensheim.

Hessische Forschungsanstalt für Wein-Obst-& Gartenbau . . .
Germany's top wine-school and research establishment, at GEISENHEIM, Rheingau.

Heyl zu Herrnsheim Fine 72-acre estate at NIERSTEIN, 55% Riesling.

Hochgewächs Term for a superior level of QbA, esp. in MOSEL-SAAR-RUWER.

Hochheim Rhg. w. ★★→★★★ 71 75 76 79 83 *84* 85 86 87 88
600-acre wine-town 15 miles e. of the main part of the RHEINGAU. Similar fine wines with an extra "earthy" touch. Top v'yds.: Domdechaney, Kirchenstück, Hölle, Königin Viktoria Berg. Grosslage: Daubhaus. Growers incl.: Aschrott, RESS, SCHÖNBORN, WERNER.

Hock English term for Rhine-wine, derived from HOCHHEIM.

Huesgen, Adolph Important merchant house at TRABEN-TRARBACH.

Huxelrebe Modern very aromatic grape variety; mainly for sweet wines.

Ihringen Bad. r. w. ★→★★★ 81 83 *84* 85 86 87 88
One of the best villages of the KAISERSTUHL, BADEN. Proud of its SPÄTBURGUNDER red, WEISSHERBST and v.g. SILVANER.

Ilbesheim Rhpf. w. ★→★★ 83 85 86 87 88
Base of important growers' cooperative of SÜDLICHE WEINSTRASSE. See also Schweigen.

Ingelheim Rhh. r. or w. ★ 85 86 87 88
Town opposite the RHEINGAU historically known for red (SPÄTBURGUNDER) wine.

Iphofen Frank. w. ★★→★★★ 75 76 *83* 85 87 88
Village e. of WÜRZBURG. Superb top v'yd: Julius-Echter-Berg. Grosslage: Burgweg.

Jahrgang Year – as in "vintage".

Jesuitengarten 15-acre vineyard in FORST. One of Germany's best.

Johannisberg Rhg. w. ★★→★★★★ 71 75 76 79 83 *84* 85 86 87 88
260-acre village with superlative subtle RIESLINGS. Top v'yds incl. SCHLOSS JOHANNISBERG, Hölle, Klaus, etc. Grosslage: Erntebringer.

Johannisberg (Bereich) District name of the entire RHEINGAU.

Josephshöfer Fine v'yd at GRAACH, the property of von KESSELSTATT.

Juliusspital Ancient charity at WÜRZBURG with 374 acres of top FRANKEN v'yds. Look for SYLVANERS.

Kabinett The term for the lightest category of natural unsugared (QmP) wines. Low in alcohol (average 7-9%).

Kaiserstuhl-Tuniberg (Bereich) One of the top districts of BADEN. Villages incl. ACHKARREN, IHRINGEN.

Kallstadt Rhpf. w. (r.) ★★→★★★ 75 76 83 *84* 85 86 87 88
Village of n. MITTELHAARDT. Fine rich wines. Top v'yd: ANNABERG. Grosslagen: Feuerberg, Kobnert.

Kammerpreismünze See Landespreismünze.

Kanzem M-S-R (Saar) w. ▓▓▓ 71 75 76 83 *84* 85 86 87 88
Small but excellent neighbour of WILTINGEN. Top v'yds: Sonnenberg, Altenberg. Grosslage: Scharzberg.

Kasel M-S-R (Ruwer) w. ▓▓→▓▓▓▓ 71 75 76 83 *84* 85 86 87 88
Village with wonderfully attractive light wines. Best v'yd: Nies'chen. Grosslage: Römerlay.

Keller Wine-cellar.

Kellerei Winery.

Kerner Modern grape variety, earlier-ripening than Riesling, of good quality but without the lingering flavour of Riesling.

Kesselstatt, von The biggest private Mosel estate, 600 years old. Over 200 acres in GRAACH (Josephshöfer), PIESPORT, KASEL, MENNIG, WILTINGEN, etc., plus substantial rented or managed estates, making light and fruity typical Mosels. Now belongs to Gunther Reh of Leiwen.

Kesten M-M w. ★→★★★ 71 75 76 79 83 *84* 85 86 87 88
Neighbour of BRAUNEBERG. Best wines (from Paulinshofberg v'yd) similar. Grosslage: Kurfürstlay.

Kiedrich Rhg. w. ★★→★★★ 71 75 76 79 83 *84* 85 86 87 88
Neighbour of RAUENTHAL; almost as splendid and high-flavoured. Top v'yds: Gräfenberg, Wasseros, Sandgrub. Grosslage: Heiligenstock.

Klevner (or Clevner) Red Klevner (synonym, Blauer Frühburgunder), grown in WÜRTTEMBERG, is supposedly either a mutation of Pinot Noir or Italian Chiavenna, an early-ripening black Pinot. Also an ORTENAU (BADEN) synonym for TRAMINER.

Klingelberger BADEN term for the RIESLING, esp. at DURBACH.

Kloster Eberbach Glorious 12th-century Abbey in HATTENHEIM, Rheingau, now State domain property and H.Q. of the German Wine Academy.

Klüsserath M-M w. ★★→ ▓▓▓ 76 83 *84* 85 86 88
Minor Mosel village worth trying in good vintages. Best v'yds: Bruderschaft, Königsberg. Grosslage: St Michael.

Kraichgau Small BADEN region s. of Heidelberg. Best-known wines are from Neckarzimmern and Wiesloch.

Kreuznach (Bereich) District name for the entire northern NAHE. See also Bad Kreuznach.

Kröv M-M w. ★→★★★ 76 83 85 86 87 88
Popular tourist resort famous for its Grosslage name: Nacktarsch, meaning "bare bottom".

Landespreismünze Prizes for quality at state, rather than national, level. Considered by some more discriminating than DLG medals.

Landgräflich Hessisches Weingut Wide-ranging 75-acre estate in JOHANNISBERG, WINKEL, KIEDRICH and ELTVILLE.

Landwein A category of better quality TAFELWEIN (the grapes must be slightly riper) from 15 designated regions. It must be TROCKEN or HALBTROCKEN. Similar in intention to France's Vins de Pays.

Lauerburg One of the four owners of the famous Doctor v'yd, with 10 acres, all in Bernkastel. Excellent racy wines.

Liebfrauenstift 26-acre v'yd in the city of Worms, said to be the origin of the name LIEBFRAUMILCH.

Liebfraumilch A much-abused name, accounting for 50% of all German wine exports – much to the detriment of Germany's better products. Legally defined as a QbA "of pleasant character" from RHEINHESSEN, RHEINPFALZ, NAHE or RHEINGAU, of a blend with at least 51% of RIESLING, SILVANER, KERNER *or* MÜLLER-THURGAU. Most is mild semi-sweet wine from Rheinhessen and Rheinpfalz. The rules now say it must have more than 18 gms. per litre unfermented sugar. Sometimes very cheap and of inferior quality, depending on brand/shipper. Its definition makes a mockery of the term "Quality wine".

Lieser M-M w. ★→ ▓▓ 71 76 83 *84* 85 86 87 88
Little-known neighbour of BERNKASTEL. Best v'yd: Schlossberg. Grosslage: Kurfürstlay.

Lingerfelder Weingut Small innovative estate at Grosskalbach (Rhpf.) making v.g. Burgundy-style SPÄTBURGUNDER and full-bodied RIESLING etc.

Lorch Rhg. w. (r.) ★→★★ 71 76 83 85 86 87 88
At extreme w. end of Rheingau. Some fine light RIESLINGS more like MITTELRHEIN wines. Best grower: von Kanitz.

Löwenstein, Fürst 66-acre FRANKEN estate: classic dry powerful wines. HALLGARTEN property rented by MATUSCHKA-GREIFFENCLAU.

Maikammer Rhpf. w. (r.) ★→ ▓▓ 83 85 86 87 88
Village of n. SÜDLICHE WEINSTRASSE. Very pleasant wines incl. those from coop at Rietburg. Grosslage: Mandelhöhe.

Maindreieck (Bereich) District name for central part of FRANKEN, incl. WÜRZBURG.

Marcobrunn Historic RHEINGAU v'yd; one of Germany's best. See Erbach.

Markgräflerland (Bereich) District s. of Freiburg (BADEN). GUTEDEL wine is delicious refreshment when drunk very young.

Martinsthal Rhg. w. ★★→ ▓▓▓ 71 75 76 83 *84* 85 86 87 88
Little-known neighbour of RAUENTHAL. Top v'yds: Langenberg, Wildsau. Grosslage: Steinmächer.

112

Matuschka-Greiffenclau, Graf Erwein Owner of the ancient SCHLOSS VOLLRADS estate and tenant of the Fürst Löwenstein Weingut at Hallgarten. President of the VDP association.

Maximin Grünhaus M-S-R (Ruwer) w. ★★★★ 71 75 76 79 83 *84* 85 86 87 88 Supreme RUWER estate of 80 acres at Mertesdorf. Wines to mature 20 years+.

Maximinhof Top-quality 12-acre estate in WEHLEN, GRAACH, BERNKASTEL. Owner: Stephan Studert-Prüm.

Mennig M-S-R (Saar) w. ★★ 71 75 76 79 82 83 *84* 85 86 87 88 Village between TRIER and the SAAR. Its v'yds (once called Falkenstein) are more famous than the village (Nieder-Obermennig).

Mertesdorf See Maximin Grünhaus.

Mittelheim Rhg. w. ★★→ ★★★ 71 75 76 79 83 *84* 85 86 87 88 Minor village between WINKEL and OESTRICH. Top grower: WEGELER-DEINHARD. Grosslage: Honigberg.

Mittelhaardt The north-central and best part of RHEINPFALZ, incl. FORST, DEIDESHEIM, RUPPERTSBERG, WACHENHEIM, largely planted with RIESLING.

Mittelhaardt-Deutsche Weinstrasse (Bereich) District name for the northern and central part of RHEINPFALZ.

Mittelmosel The central and best part of the Mosel, incl. BERNKASTEL, WEHLEN, PIESPORT, etc. Its best sites are entirely RIESLING.

Mittelrhein Northern Rhine area of domestic importance, incl. BACHAR-ACH. Some attractive steely RIESLINGs, esp. in 1983, 1985, 1986, 1988.

Mönchhof, Weingut Top-quality 12-acre estate in ÜRZIG, Erden, ZELTINGEN and WEHLEN.

Morio-Muskat Stridently aromatic grape variety now on the decline.

Mosel The TAFELWEIN name of the area. All quality wines from the area must be labelled MOSEL-SAAR-RUWER. (Moselle is the French – and English – spelling for this beautiful river.)

Moselland, Winzergenossenscaft The biggest coop of the M-S-R, based at Bernkastel, incl. Saar-Winzerverin at WILTINGEN. Its 5,200 members produce 25% of the M-S-R wines. Formerly Zentralkellerei M-S-R.

Moseltaler New registered name for MOSEL-SAAR-RUWER QbA, intended to simplify selection (cf. LIEBFRAUMILCH) but maintain a higher standard than the latter.

Mosel-Saar-Ruwer 31,000-acre QUALITÄTSWEIN region between TRIER and KOBLENZ. Includes MITTELMOSEL, SAAR, RUWER and lesser areas. Grows more RIESLING than any region on earth.

Müller, Felix Fine small SAAR estate with delicate SCHARZHOFBERGER, now run by VON KESSELSTATT.

Müller zu Scharzhof, Egon See Egon Müller.

Müller-Thurgau Fruity, early-ripening, usually low-acid grape variety; the commonest in RHEINPFALZ and RHEINHESSEN, the NAHE, BADEN and FRANKEN, and increasingly planted in all areas, including the Mosel; generally to the detriment of quality.

Mumm, von 173-acre estate in JOHANNISBERG, RUDESHEIM, etc. Under the same control as SCHLOSS JOHANNISBERG.

Munster Nahe w. ★→★★★★ 71 75 76 83 *84* 85 86 87 Best village of northern NAHE, with fine delicate wines. Top grower: State Domain. Grosslage: Schlosskapelle.

Nackenheim Rhh. w. ★→ ★★★ 75 76 79 83 85 86 87 Neighbour of NIERSTEIN; best wines (Engelsberg, Rothenberg) similar. Grosslagen: Spiegelberg (★★★), Gutes Domtal (★).

Nahe Tributary of the Rhine and high quality wine region. Balanced, fresh and clean but full-flavoured wines, the best are RIESLING. Two Bereiche: KREUZNACH and SCHLOSS BÖCKELHEIM.

Nahesteiner Brand name of new NAHE HALBTROCKEN blend of RIESLING, SILVANER and MÜLLER THURGAU. Distinctive bottle and modern label.

Neef M-S-R w. ★→ ★★ 71 76 83 85 86 87 Village of lower Mosel with one fine v'yd: Frauenberg.

Neipperg, Graf 71-acre top WÜRTTEMBERG estate at Schwaigern, esp. known for red wines and TRAMINER.

Nell, von (Weingut Thiergarten) 40-acre family estate at TRIER and AYL.

Neumagen-Dhron M-M w. ★★→★★★ 71 75 76 83 *84* 85 86 87
Neighbours of PIESPORT. Top v'yd: Hofberger. Grosslage: Michelsberg.

Neustadt Central town of RHEINPFALZ, with a famous wine school.

Niederhausen Nahe w. ★★→★★★★ 71 75 76 79 83 *84* 85 86 87
Neighbour of SCHLOSS BÖCKELHEIM and H.Q. of the Nahe State Domain. Wines of grace and power. Top v'yds incl. Hermannshöhle, Steinberg. Grosslage: Burgweg.

Niedermennig See Mennig.

Niederwalluf See Walluf.

Nierstein (Bereich) Large e. RHEINHESSEN district of very mixed quality.

Nierstein Rhh. w. ★→★★★ 71 75 76 83 *84* 85 86 87 88
Famous but treacherous name. 1,300 acres incl. superb v'yds: Hipping, Ölberg, Pettenthal, etc., and their Grosslagen Rehbach, Spiegelberg, Auflangen: ripe aromatic wines with great "elegance". But beware Grosslage Gutes Domtal: no guarantee of anything.

Germany's Quality Levels

The range of qualities in ascending order is

1) *Deutscher Tafelwein; sweetish light wine of no special character.*
2) *Landwein: dryish Tafelwein with some regional style.*
3) *Qualitätswein: dry or sweetish wine with sugar added before fermentation to increase the strength, but tested for quality and with distinct local and grape character.*
4) *Kabinettwein: dry or dryish natural (unsugared) wine of distinct personality and distinguishing lightness. Can be very fine.*
5) *Spätlese: stronger, often sweeter than Kabinett. Full bodied. The trend today is towards drier or even completely dry Spätleses.*
6) *Auslese: sweeter, sometimes stronger than Spätlese, often with honey-like flavours, intense and long.*
7) *Beerenauslese: very sweet and usually strong, intense, can be superb.*
8) *Eiswein: (Beeren-or Trockenbeerenauslese) concentrated, sharpish and very sweet. Extraordinary and everlasting.*
9) *Trockenbeerenauslese: intensely sweet and aromatic; alcohol slight.*

Nobling New white grape variety giving light fresh wine in BADEN, esp. Markgräflerland.

Norheim Nahe w. ★→★★★ 71 76 79 83 *84* 85 86 87 88
Neighbour of NIEDERHAUSEN. Top v'yds: Klosterberg, Kafels, Kirschheck. Grosslage: Burgweg.

Novum Completely new style of wine from Sichel, softened by malolactic fermentation. Aromatic, gentle, full and v.g.

Oberemmel M-S-R (Saar) w. ★★→★★★ 71 75 76 83 85 86 87 88
Next village to WILTINGEN. Very fine wines from Rosenberg, Hütte, etc. Grosslage: Scharzberg.

Obermosel (Bereich) District name for the upper Mosel above TRIER. Generally uninspiring wines from the Elbling grape unless v. young.

Ockfen M-S-R (Saar) w. ★★→★★★ 71 75 76 83 *84* 85 86 87 88
200-acre village with superb fragrant austere wines. Top v'yds: Bockstein, Herrenberg. Grosslage: Scharzberg.

Oechsle Scale for sugar-content of grape-juice (see page 19).

Oestrich Rhg. w. ★★→★★★ 71 75 76 83 *84* 85 86 87 88
Big village; variable but capable of splendid Riesling Ausleses. V'yds incl. Doosberg, Lenchen, Klosterberg. Grosslage: Gottesthal. Major grower: WEGELER-DEINHARD.

Oppenheim Rhh. w. ★→★★★ 71 75 76 79 83 *84* 85 86 87 88
Town S. of NIERSTEIN with a famous 13th-century church. Best wines (Kreuz, Sackträger) similar. Grosslagen: Guldenmorgen (★★★), Krötenbrunnen (★).

Ortenau (Bereich) District just s. of Baden-Baden. Good KLINGELBERGER (Riesling) and RÜLANDER. SPÄTBURGUNDER (not so good) is a speciality. Best village DURBACH.

Palatinate English for RHEINPFALZ.

Perlwein Semi-sparkling wine.

Pfalz See Rheinpfalz.

Piesport M-M w. ★★→★★★★ 71 75 76 83 *84* 85 86 87 88
Tiny village with famous amphitheatre of vines giving (at best) glorious, gentle, fruity RIESLINGS. Top v'yds: Goldtröpfchen, Falkenberg. Treppchen is on flatter land and inferior. Grosslage: Michelsberg (much planted with MÜLLER-THURGAU).

Plettenberg, von Fine 100-acre Nahe estate at BAD KREUZNACH.

Pokalwein Wine by the glass. A pokal is a big glass.

Portugieser Second-rate red-wine grape now often used for WEISSHERBST.

Prädikat Special attributes or qualities. See QmP.

Prüfungsnummer The official identifying test-number of a quality wine.

Prüm, J. J. Superlative 34-acre Mosel estate in WEHLEN, GRAACH, BERNKASTEL. Delicate, long-lived wines, esp. in Wehlener Sonnenuhr.

Prüm, S. A., Erben Small separate part of the Prüm family estate making fine Wehleners, etc.

Qualitätswein bestimmter Anbaugebiete (QbA) The middle quality of German wine, with sugar added before fermentation (as in French "chaptalization"), but strictly controlled as to areas, grapes, etc.

Qualitätswein mit Prädikat (QmP) Top category, incl. all wines ripe enough to be unsugared, from KABINETT to TROCKENBEERENAUSLESE.

Rappenhof, Weingut 90-acre Rheinhessen estate at Alsheim with wide range of varieties and techniques, incl. barrique-ageing, Chardonnay and deep-coloured SPÄTBURGUNDER.

Randersacker Frank. w. ★★→★★★ 76 79 *83* 86 87 88
Leading village for distinctive dry wine. Top v'yds incl. Teufelskeller. Grosslage: Ewig Leben.

Rauenthal Rhg. w. ★★★ →★★★★ 71 75 76 79 83 *84* 85 86 87 88
Supreme village for spicy complex wine. Top v'yds incl. Baiken, Gehrn, Wulfen. Grosslage: Steinmächer. The State Domain is an important grower.

Rautenstrauch Erben Owners of the Karthäuserhof, EITELSBACH.

Reh, Franz & Sohn Thriving wine-merchant at Leiwen (Mosel) with two small estates.

Ress, Balthasar RHEINGAU grower with 50 acres of good land, cellars in HATTENHEIM. Also runs SCHLOSS REICHARTSHAUSEN. Fine fresh wines; highly original artists' labels.

Restsüsse Unfermented sugar remaining in wine to give it sweetness. New-style TROCKEN wines have very little, if any.

Reverchon, Eddie Substantial SAAR estate in Filzen, WILTINGEN, etc.

Rheinart Erben 26-acre SAAR estate known for its OCKFENER BOCKSTEIN.

Rheinburgengau (Bereich) District name for v'yds of the MITTELRHEIN round the Rhine gorge. Wines with "steely" acidity needing time to mature.

Rheingau The best v'yd region of the Rhine, near Wiesbaden. 7,000 acres. Classic, substantial but subtle RIESLING. Bereich name, for the whole region, JOHANNISBERG.

Rheinhess New name for blended HALBTROCKEN Rheinhessen wines.

Rheinhessen Vast region (61,000 acres of v'yds) between Mainz and Worms, bordered by the river NAHE, mostly second-rate, but incl. top wines from NIERSTEIN, OPPENHEIM, etc.

Rheinhessen Silvaner (RS) New uniform label for dry wines from Silvaner designed to give a modern quality image to the region.

Rheinpfalz 56,000-acre v'yd region s. of Rheinhessen. (See Mittelhaardt and Südliche Weinstrasse.) This and RHEINHESSEN are the chief sources of LIEBFRAUMILCH. Grapes ripen to relatively high degrees. The classics are rich wines, but TROCKEN and HALBTROCKEN increasingly fashionable.

Rhodt Village of SÜDLICHE WEINSTRASSE with well-known cooperative. Agreeable fruity wines. Grosslage: Ordensgut.

Richter, Max Ferd, Weingut 37-acre MITTELMOSEL family estate based at Müllheim. Fine barrel-aged RIESLINGS from WEHLEN, GRAACH, BRAUNE-BERG (Juffer), Mülheim (Helenenkloster).

Rieslaner Cross between SILVANER and RIESLING; has made fine Auslesen in FRANKEN, where most is grown.

Riesling The best German grape: fine, fragrant, fruity, long-lived. Only Chardonnay can compete as the world's best white grape.

Roseewein Rosé wine made of red grapes fermented without their skins.

Rotwein Red wine.

Rüdesheim Rhg. w. ★★–★★★★★ 71 75 76 79 *81* 82 83 *84* 85 86 87 88 Rhine resort with 650 acres of excellent v'yds; the three best called Rüdesheimer Berg... Full-bodied wines, fine-flavoured, often remarkable in "off" vintages. Grosslage: Burgweg.

Rüdesheimer Rosengarten Rüdesheim is also the name of a NAHE village near BAD KREUZNACH. Do not be misled by the ubiquitous blend going by this name. It has nothing to do with Rheingau RÜDESHEIM.

Ruländer The PINOT GRIS: grape giving soft, full-bodied wine, alias Grauburgunder. Best in BADEN.

Ruppertsberg Rhpf. w. ★★→★★★ 75 76 79 83 *84* 85 86 87 88 Southern village of MITTELHAARDT. Top v'yds incl. Hoheburg. Reiter-pfad, Linsenbusch. Grosslage: Hofstück.

Ruwer Tributary of Mosel near TRIER. Very fine delicate but well-structured wines. Villages incl. EITELSBACH, MERTESDORF, KASEL.

Saar Tributary of Mosel s. of RUWER. Brilliant, austere, "steely" RIESLINGS. Villages incl. WILTINGEN (SCHARZHOFBERG), AYL, OCKFEN, SERRIG. Grosslage: Scharzberg.

Saar-Ruwer (Bereich) District incl. the two above.

Salem, Schloss 188-acre estate of Margrave of Baden near L. Constance in s. Germany. MÜLLER-THURGAU and WEISSHERBST.

St Ursula Well-known merchants at BINGEN; owners of VILLA SACHSEN.

Scharzberg Grosslage name of WILTINGEN and neighbours.

Scharzhofberg Saar w. ★★★★ 71 75 76 79 83 *84* 85 86 87 88 Superlative 67-acre SAAR v'yd: austerely beautiful wines, the perfection of RIESLING. Do not confuse with above. Top estate: EGON MÜLLER.

Schaumwein Sparkling wine.

Scheurebe Fruity grape of good quality used in RHEINHESSEN and RHEINPFALZ.

Schillerwein Light red or rosé QbA, speciality of WÜRTTEMBERG (only).

Scholl & Hillebrand RÜDESHEIM merchants with fine BREUER estate wines and highly succesful "Riesling Dry".

Schlossböckelheim Nahe w. ★★→★★★★ 71 75 76 79 83 *84* 85 86 87 88 Village with the best NAHE v'yds, incl. Kupfergrube, Felsenberg. Firm yet delicate wine. Grosslage: Burgweg.

Schloss Böckelheim (Bereich) District name for the whole southern NAHE.

Schloss Groenesteyn Top-grade Rheingau estate (80 acres) in KIEDRICH and RÜDESHEIM, owned by Baron von Ritter zu Groenesteyn.

Schloss Johannisberg Rhg. w. ★★★ 76 79 83 *84* 85 86 87 88 Famous RHEINGAU estate of 86 acres owned by Prince Metternich and the Oetker family, and now run in conjunction with VON MUMM. Wines incl. fine SPÄTLESE and KABINETT TROCKEN. Formerly one of Germany's undoubted "first growths". Wines still need at least 3 yrs. storing.

Schloss Reichartshausen 10-acre HATTENHEIM v'yd run by RESS.

Schloss Reinhartshausen Fine 165-acre estate in ERBACH, HATTENHEIM, etc. Changed hands in 1987.

Schloss Vollrads Rhg. w. ★★★→★★★★ 71 76 83 85 86 87 88 Great estate at WINKEL, since 1300. 116 acres producing classical RHEINGAU RIESLING, esp. since 1977. TROCKEN and HALBTROCKEN wines a speciality. The owner, Graf MATUSCHKA GREIFFENCLAU, leads the "German wine with food" campaign.

Schmitt, Gustav Adolf Merchant house with fine old 250-acre family estate at NIERSTEIN.

Schmitt, Franz Karl Even older 74-acre ditto.

Schönborn, Schloss One of the biggest and best Rheingau estates, based at HATTENHEIM. Full-flavoured wines, at best excellent. Also v.g. SEKT.

Schoppenwein Café wine: i.e. wine by the glass.

Schorlemer, Freiherr von Historically important MOSEL estate of 116 acres in 5 parts. Current financial and other problems have clouded its reputation.

Schubert, von Owner of MAXIMIN GRÜNHAUS.

Schweigen Rhpf. w. ★→ ■■ ★★ 83 *84* 85 86 87 88
Southernmost Rheinpfalz village with important cooperative, Deutsches WEINTOR. Grosslage: Guttenberg.

Sekt German (QbA) sparkling wine, best when RIESLING is on the label. SEKT B.A. is the same thing, but from a specified area.

Senfter, Reinhold One of the best growers in NIERSTEIN, with 32 acres. Best v'yds: Niersteiner Hipping and Oppenheimer Sackträger.

Serrig M-S-R (Saar) w. ★★→★★★ 71 75 76 79 83 *84* 85 86 87 88
Village known for "steely" wine, excellent in hot years. Top growers: VEREINIGTE HOSPITIEN and State Domain. Grosslage: Scharzberg.

Sichel H., Söhne Famous wine-merchants of London and Mainz with new KELLEREI in Alzey, Rhh. Owners of "Blue Nun" LIEBFRAUMILCH and creators of revolutionary NOVUM.

Silvaner The third most-planted German white grape, best in FRANKEN and the KAISERSTUHL. But look for good Silvaners from RHEINHESSEN.

Simmern, Langwerth von Top 120-acre family estate at ELTVILLE. Famous v'yds: Mannberg, MARCOBRUNN, Baiken etc. Some of the very best, most typical RHEINGAU RIESLINGS.

Sonnenuhr "Sun-dial." Name of several v'yds, esp. the famous one at WEHLEN.

Spätburgunder PINOT NOIR: the best red-wine grape in Germany esp. in BADEN and WÜRTEMBERG – though its wines are not widely appreciated outside Germany.

Spätlese "Late gathered." One better (stronger/sweeter) than KABINETT. Wines to age *at least* three years. Dry Spätleses can be v. fine.

Spindler, Wilhelm Fine 33-acre family estate at FORST, Rheinpfalz.

Staatlicher Hofkeller The Bavarian State Domain. 287 acres of finest FRANKEN v'yds with spectacular cellars under the great baroque Residenz at WÜRZBURG.

Staatsweingut (or Staatliche Weinbaudomäne) The State wine estate or domain.

Staufenberg, Schloss 69-acre DURBACH estate of the Margrave of Baden. Fine "Klingelberger" (RIESLING).

Steigerwald (Bereich) District name for eastern part of FRANKEN.

Steinberg Rhg. w. ■■■ →★★★★ 71 75 76 79 83 *84* 85 86 87 88
Famous 79-acre v'yd at HATTENHEIM walled by Cistercians 700 yrs. ago. Now property of the State Domain, ELTVILLE.

Steinwein Wine from WÜRZBURG's best v'yd, Stein. In the past the term was loosely used for all Franconian wine.

Stuttgart Chief city of WÜRTEMBERG, producer of some pleasant wines (esp. Riesling), recently beginning to be exported.

Südliche Weinstrasse (Bereich) District name for the S. RHEINPFALZ. Quality has improved tremendously in the last 25 years.

Tafelwein "Table wine." The vin ordinaire of Germany. Mostly blended with other EEC wines. But DEUTSCHER TAFELWEIN must come from Germany alone. See also Landwein.

Thanisch, Weingus Wwe. Dr. H 16-acre BERNKASTEL family estate of top quality, incl. part of Doctor v'yd. Are standards slipping? Another 16 acres changed hands in 1987; the new name is Erben Müller-Burggref.

Traben-Trarbach M-M w. ★★ 76 83 85 86 87 88
Secondary wine-town, some good light wines. Top v'yds incl.
Würzgarten, Schlossberg. Crosslage: Schwarzlay.

Traisen Nahe w. ★★★ 71 75 76 79 83 *84* 85 86 87 88
Small village incl. superlative Bastei and Rotenfels v'yds, making
RIESLINGS of great concentration and class.

Traminer See Gewürztraminer.

Trier M-S-R w. ★★→★★★
Important wine city of Roman origin, on the Mosel, adjacent to RUWER,
now incl. AVELSBACH and EITELSBACH. Grosslage: Römerlay.

Trittenheim M-M w. ★★ 71 75 76 83 *84* 85 86
Attractive light wines from the s. end of the Mittelmosel. Top v'yds
Apotheke, Altärchen. Grosslage: Michelsberg.

Trocken Dry. On labels Trocken *alone* means with a statutory maxiumum
of unfermented sugar (9 grams per litre). But see next entry. See also
Halbtrocken.

Trockenbeerenauslese The sweetest and most expensive category of
wine, extremely rare and with concentrated honey flavour, made
from selected withered grapes (esp. Riesling). See also Edel.

Trollinger Common red grape of WÜRTTEMBERG: locally very popular.

Ungstein Rhpf. w. ★★→ ★★★ 71 75 76 83 *84* 85 86 87 88
MITTELHAARDT village with fine harmonious wines. Top v'yd Herren-
berg. Top growers: Fuhrmann (Weingut Pfeffingen), Fitz-Ritter,
BASSERMANN-JORDAN. Grosslages: Honigsäckel, Kobnert.

Ürzig M-M w. ★★★ 71 75 76 79 87 83 *84* 85 86 87 88
Village famous for lively spicy wine. Top v'yd: Würzgarten. Grosslage:
Schwarzlay. Growers incl. MÖNCHHOF.

Valckenburg, P.J. Major merchants at Worms, with Madonna LIEB-
FRAUMILCH and a small estate with good Rieslings. Also Riesling Dry.

VdP Verband Deutscher Prädikats und Qualitätsweinguter, an association of premium growers.

Vereinigte Hospitien "United Hospitals." Ancient charity at Trier with
large holdings in SERRIG, WILTINGEN, TRIER, PIESPORT, etc.

Verwaltung Administration (of property/estate etc.).

Villa Sachsen 67-acre BINGEN estate belonging to ST URSULA Weingut.

Wachenheim Rhpf. w. ★★★ →★★★★ 71 75 76 79 83 85 86 87 88
840 acres, incl. exceptionally fine Rieslings. V'yds incl. Gerümpel,
Böhlig, Rechbächel. Top grower: BÜRKLIN-WOLF. Grosslagen: Schenkenböhl, Schnepfenflug, Mariengarten.

Waldrach M-S-R (Ruwer) w. ★★ 75 76 79 83 *84* 85 87 88
Some charming light wines. Grosslage: Römerlay.

Wallhausen, Schloss The 25-acre estate of the Prince Zu Salm at
Dalberg, Nahe, one of Germany's oldest. 50% Riesling. V.g. TROCKEN.

Walluf Rhg. w. ★★ 75 76 79 83 *84* 85 87
Neighbour of ELTVILLE; formerly Nieder-and Ober-Walluf. Underrated
wines. Grosslage: Steinmächer.

Walporzheim Ahrtal (Bereich) District name for the whole AHR valley.

Walthari-Hof Much-discussed estate at Edenkoben, Rheinpfalz, making
wine without recourse to sulphur dioxide.

Wawern M-S-R (Saar) w. ★★→★★★ 71 75 76 83 *84* 85 86 87 88
Small village with fine RIESLINGS. Grosslage: Scharzberg.

Wegeler-Deinhard 136-acre RHEINGAU estate. V'yds in OESTRICH, MIT-
TELHEIM, WINKEL, GEISENHEIM, etc. Consistent quality; dry
SPÄTLESES, classic AUSLESES, finest EISWEIN. Also 67 acres in MITTEL-
MOSEL, incl. major part of BERNKASTELER DOCTOR (WEHLENER, SONNENUHR
etc.) and 46 acres in MITTELHAARDT (FORST, DEIDESHEIM, RUPPERTSBERG).

Wehlen M-M w. ★★★ 71 75 76 79 83 *84* 85 86 87 88
Neighbour of BERNKASTEL with equally fine, somewhat richer, wine.
Best v'yd: Sonnenuhr. Top growers: PRÜM family. Grosslage: Münzlay.

Weil, Dr. Fine 46-acre estate at KIEDRICH, owned by Suntory of Japan.

Weinbaugebiet Viticultural region for TAFELWEIN (e.g. Mosel, Rhein, Saar).

Weingut Wine estate. Can only be used on the label by estates that grow all their own grapes, make their wines from these grapes and bottle these same wines.

Weinkellerei Wine cellars or winery. See Keller.

Weinstrasse "Wine road." Scenic route through v'yds. Germany has several, the most famous the Deutsche Weinstrasse in RHEINPFALZ.

Weintor, Deutsches See Schweigen.

Weissherbst Very pale pink or "blush" wine of QbA standard or above, even occasionally BEERENAUSLESE, the speciality of BADEN, WÜRTTEMBERG, and RHEINPFALZ. Currently v. popular in Germany.

Werner, Domdechant Fine 25-acre family estate on the best slopes of HOCHHEIM. 95% Riesling.

Werner Klein (Mosbacher Hof) 25-acre estate, 90% Riesling, in FORST and DEÏDESHEIM. Good TROCKEN wines.

Remember that vintage information about German wines is given in a different form from the ready/not ready distinction applying to other countries. Read the explanation on page 105.

Wiltingen Saar w. ★★→★★★★ 71 75 76 79 83 85 86 87 88
The centre of the Saar. 790 acres. Beautiful subtle austere wine. Top v'yds incl. SCHARZHOFBERG, Braune Kupp, Braunfels, Klosterberg. Grosslage (for the whole Saar): Scharzberg.

Winkel Rhg. w. ★★★→★★★★ 71 75 76 79 83 *84* 85 86 87 88
Village famous for fragrant wine, incl. SCHLOSS VOLLRADS. V'yds incl. Hasensprung, Jesuitengarten. Grosslagen: Honigberg, Erntebringer.

Winningen M-S-R. w. ★★
Village of lower Mosel near Koblenz with some fine delicate RIESLING. Best v'yds: Uhlen, Röttgen.

Wintrich M-M w. ★★→★★★ 71 75 76 83 *84* 85 86 87 88
Neighbour of PIESPORT; similar wines. Top v'yds: Grosser Herrgott, Ohligsberg, Sonnenseite. Grosslage: Kurfürstlay.

Winzergenossenschaft Wine-growers' cooperative, usually making good and reasonably priced wine.

Winzerverein The same as the last.

Wirsching, Hans Well-known estate in IPHOFEN, FRANKEN. Robust, full-bodied wines. 100 acres in top v'yds: Julius-Echter-Berg, Kalb, etc.

Wonnegau (Bereich) District name for s. RHEINHESSEN.

Württemberg Vast s. area little known for wine outside Germany. Some good RIESLINGS, esp. from Neckar valley. Also TROLLINGER.

Würzburg Frank. ★★→★★★★ 71 76 81 *83* 85 86 87 88
Great baroque city on the Main, centre of Franconian (FRANKEN) wine: fine, full-bodied and dry. Top v'yds: Stein, Leiste, Schlossberg. No Grosslage. See also Maindreieck.

Zell M-S-R w. ★→★★ 76 83 85 86 87 88
The best-known lower Mosel village, esp. for its Grosslage name Schwarze Katz ("Black Cat"). RIESLING on steep slate gives aromatic light wines.

Zell (Bereich) District name for the whole lower Mosel from Zell to Koblenz.

Zeltingen-Rachtig M-M w. ★★ →★★★★ 71 75 76 79 83 *84* 85 86 87 88 Important Mosel village next to WEHLEN. Typically lively crisp RIESLING. Top v'yds: Sonnenuhr, Schlossberg. Grosslage: Münzlay.

Zilliken, Forstmeister Geltz Former estate of the Prussian royal forester at Saarburg, Saar. 21 acres of Riesling make old-style wines for maturing.

Zwierlein, Freiherr von 55-acre family estate in Geisenheim. 100% Riesling. Best v'yds: Rothenberg, Kläuserweg.

Spain & Portugal

The following abbreviations of regional names are used in the text.

Alen.	Alton Alentejo	**Est'a.**	Estremadura	**N.Cas.**	New Castile
Alg.	Algarve	**Ext.**	Extremadura	**O.Cas.**	Old Castile
And.	Andalucia	**Gal.**	Galicia	**R'a.A.**	Rioja Alta
Ara.	Aragon	**g.**	see Vino generoso	**R'a.Al.**	Rioja Alavesa
B'a.al.	Beira Alta	**Gui.**	Guipuzcoa	**R'a.B.**	Rioja Baja
Bei. Lit.		**Lev.**	Levante	**Res.**	Reserva
Beira Littoral		**M'o.**	Minho	**Trás-os-m.**	
Cat.	Catalonia	**Nav.**	Navarra	Trás-os-Montes	

In 1986 Spain and Portugal joined the European Common Market, a move which stimulated the rapidly growing scope and quality of their wine industries. Modern ideas have arrived to enrich (and often replace) their traditions. The state of ferment is highly productive, and some splendid new wines are appearing, both in their few traditional quality areas, and in former bulk-wine regions.

Currently in Spain (apart from sherry country), Catalonia, Rioja, Navarra, Rueda and Ribera del Duero still hold most interest; in Portugal (apart from port and madeira) Bairrada, the Douro, the Ribatejo, Alentejo and Estremadura, and the Minho. In Portugal especially, new delimited ("VQPRD") areas are tending to overshadow the old-fashioned appellations.

The listing here includes the best and most interesting types and regions of each country, whether legally delimited or not. Geographical references (see map) are to the traditional divisions of Spain into kingdoms and Portugal into provinces.

Sherry, port and madeira are listed separately on pp. 133-138.

Spain

A.G.E., Bodegas Unidas R'a.A. r. (p.) w. dr. or sw. res. ★→★★ 73 74 75 78 80 81 82 83 84 Large bodega making a wide range of wines, of which the best are the red Marqués de Romeral and Siglo Gran Reserva.

Alavesas, Bodegas R'a.Al. r. (w. dr.) res ★★→★★★ 73 74 75 76 78 80 81 83 Pale orange-red SOLAR DE SAMANIEGO is one of the most delicate of the soft, fast-maturing Alavesa wines. Quality since 1983 has been seriously variable; some wines excessively light.

Albariño del Palacio Gal. w. dr. ★★
Flowery and pétillant young wine from FEFINANES near Cambados, made with the Albariño grape, the best of the region.

Alella Cat. r. (p.) w. dr. or sw. ★★
Small demarcated region just n. of Barcelona. Makes pleasantly fresh and fruity wines. (See Marfil and Marqués de Alella.)

Alicante Lev. r. (w.) ★
Demarcated region: wines tend to be "earthy" and overstrong.

Almansa Lev. r. ★
Demarcated region w. of ALICANTE, with similar wines.

Aloque N. Cas. r. ![symbol] D.Y.A.
A light (though not in alcohol) variety of VALDEPEÑAS, made by fermenting together red and white grapes.

Almendralejo Ext. r. w. ★
Commercial wine centre of the Extremadura. Much of its produce is distilled to make the spirit for fortifying sherry.

Alvear, S.A. And. g. ★★★
The largest producer of excellent sherry-like apéritif and dessert wines from MONTILLA-MORILES.

Ampurdán See Perelada.

Año 4° Año (or Años) means 4 years old when bottled.

Bach, Masia Cat. r. p. w. dr. or sw. res. ![symbol] →★★★ 70 74 78 80 81 82 83 85 Excellent villa-winery nr. SAN SADURNI DE NOYA, now owned by CODORNIU. Best known for luscious oaky white Extrisimo Bach. Now also a dry white Extrisimo and good red reservas.

Banda Azul R'a.A. r. ★★ 75 76 80 81 84
Big-selling wine, very variable in quality, from BODEGAS PATERNINA.

Barril, Masia Cat. r. res. br. ★★→★★★ 81 82 83 86 87
Tiny family estate in DO PRIORATO making powerful fruity reds – the 1983 was 18°! – and providing superb RANCIO to better-known firms.

Berberana, Bodegas R'a.A. r. (w. dr.) res. ★→★★★ 64 66 70 73 74 75 76 78 80 82 83 84 85 The fruity, full-bodied reds are best: the 3° año Carta de Plata, the 5° año Carta de Oro and the velvety reservas.

Beronia, Bodegas R'a.A. r. w. dr. res. ★★→★★★ 73 75 77 78 80 81 82 83 84 A small modern bodega making excellent reds in the traditional oaky style. Their light CRIANZA "Beron" is also very attractive.

Bilbainas, Bodegas R'a.A. r. (p.) w. dr. sw. or sp. res. ![symbol] →★★★ 66 69 70 72 73 75 76 78 81 82 Large bodega in HARO, with a wide reliable range including dark Viña Pomal, lighter Viña Zaco, Vendimia Especial Reservas and "Royal Carlton" CAVA.

Blanco White.

Bodega Spanish for 1. a wineshop; 2. a concern occupied in the making, blending and/or shipping of wine and 3. a cellar.

Campanas, Las See Vinicola Navarra.

Campo Nuevo Nav. r. p. w. dr. ![symbol]
Good value everyday red and white Navarra from the Coop Vinícola Murchantina.

Campo Viejo, Bodegas R'a.A. r. (w. dr.) res. ■ →★★★ 64 66 70 71 73 75 76 78 80 81 82 83 84 Branch of Savin S.A., one of Spain's largest wine companies. Makes the popular and tasty 2° año San Asensio and some big, fruity red reservas, esp. Marqués de Villamagna.

Can Rafols de Caus Cat. r. w. dr. ★★ 84 85 86
New small PENEDES bodega, growing its own fruity estate CAB SAUV and pleasant CHARD.

Cañamero Ext. w. ★
Remote village near Guadalupe whose wines grow FLOR and acquire a sherry-like taste.

Caralt, Cavas Conde de Cat. sp. r. w. res. ★★ 73 78 80 81 82 83 84 85
"CAVA" wines from SAN SADURNI DE NOYA; also pleasant still wines.

Carbonell And. br. ■■
Producer of good Montilla ("Sombra") and olive oil, at Cordoba.

Cariñena Ara. r. (p. w.) ■
Demarcated region and large-scale supplier of strong wine for everyday drinking, dominated by cooperatives but now being invigorated (and its wines lightened) by modern technology.

Casar de Valdaiga O.Cas. r. w. dr. ★★
Producer in El Bierzo, n. of LEON, with a light, very dry CLARETE.

Castellblanch Cat. sp. ■■
PENEDES CAVA firm, owned by FREIXENET. Recently much praised for Brut Zero and slightly sweeter Cristal Seco.

Castillo Ygay See Marqués de Murrieta.

Cava Any Spanish sparkling wine made by the champagne method. Also the bodega making it.

Cenalsa Nav. r. w. dr. ■■
A marketing organization shipping a range of Navarra wines, incl. a flowery new-style and a fruity red "Agramont".

Cenicero Wine township in the RIOJA ALTA with ancient Roman origins.

Cepa Wine or grape variety.

Chacolí Gui. (r.) w. ★ D.Y.A.
Alarmingly sharp, often fizzy, wine from the Basque coast. It contains only 9% to 11% alcohol.

Chaves, Bodegas Gal. w. dr. ★★→★★★ 81 82 84 (D.Y.A.)
Small family firm making a good and fragrant, though slightly acidic, ALBARINO; arguably the best Galician wine exported.

Chivite, Bodegas Julián Nav. r. (p.) w. dr. or sw. res. ■■ 81 82 83 84 86 Biggest bodega in NAVARRA, producing full-bodied, fruity red wines and a flowery, well-balanced white.

Clarete Term frowned upon by the EEC describing light red wine (occasionally dark rosé).

Codorníu, S.A. Cat. sp ■★→★★★★
One of the two largest and best known of the firms in SAN SADURNI DE NOYA making good CAVA by the champagne method. Non Plus Ultra is matured, Ana de Codorníu a fresher style.

Compañía Vinicola del Norte de España (CVNE) R'a.A. r. (p.) w. dr. or sw. res. ■★→★★★★ 66 70 73 74 75 76 78 80 81 82 83 84 85
The 3° año is among the best young red Riojas and Monopole one of the best slightly oaky whites. Excellent red Imperial and Viña Real reservas. CVNE is pronounced "Coonay."

Conca de Barberá Cat. (r. p.) w. dr.
Demarcated region supplying Parellada grapes for making CAVA. Its best wine is the TORRES Milmanda Chardonnay.

Consejo Regulador Official organization for the defence, control and promotion of a DENOMINACION DE ORIGEN.

Contino R'a.Al. r. res. ★★★ 74 75 76 78 80 81 82 84
Superior single-vineyard red wine made by a subsidiary of COMPANIA VINICOLA DEL NORTE DE ESPANA.

Corral S.A., Bodegas   R'a.A. r. (p. w. dr.) res. ★★ 71 73 75 78
Long-established bodega now operating from new premises at Navarrete. Best-known for red Don Jacobo.

Cosecha   Crop or vintage.

Criado y embotellado por . . .   Grown and bottled by . . .

Crianza   Literally, "nursing", the ageing of wine. New or unaged wine is "sin crianza". Wines labelled crianza are at least 2 years old, with 1 year in oak.

Cumbrero   See Montecillo, Bodegas.

De Muller   Cat. (r. w. dr.) br. ★★→★★★
Old TARRAGONA firm famous for altar wines, making a good PRIORATO and superb v. old solera-aged dessert wines, incl. PRIORATO DULCE and PAXARETE. Also fragrant Moscatel Seco.

Denominación de origen   Officially regulated wine region. (See p. 119).

Domecq. S.A.   R'a.Al. r. (w. dr.) res. ■★★→★★★★ 73 74 76 78 80 82 84
Rioja outpost of Pedro Domecq (see Sherry). Best wines are the fruity red Domecq Domain, exceptional in '76, and Marqués de Arienzo RESERVAS.

Dulce   Sweet.

Elaborado y añejado por . . .   Made and aged by . . .

El Coto, Bodegas   R'a.Al. r. (w. dr.) res. ★★→★★★ 73 76 78 80 81 82 84 85   Bodega in which Alexis Lichine has recently taken an interest, best-known for light, soft red El Coto and Coto de Imaz.

Espumoso   Sparkling (but see Cava).

Fariña, Bodegas   O.Cas. r. res. w. dr. ★★→★★★ 82 85 86
Rising star of the new DO TORO, making good spicy reds. Gran Colegiata is aged in cask; Colegiata is not.

Faustino Martínez, S.A.   R'a.Al. r. w. dr. (p.) res. ■★★ →★★★ 64 70 72 73 74 75 76 78 80 81 82 83   Good red wines and light, fruity white Faustino V. Gran Reserva is Faustino I. Do not be put off by the repellent bottles.

Ferrer, José L.   Majorca r. res. ★★
His bodega in Binisalem is still the only one to note in Majorca.

Flor   A wine yeast peculiar to FINO sherry and certain other wines that oxidize slowly and tastily under its influence.

Franco-Españolas, Bodegas   R'a.A. r. w. dr. or sw. res. ★→★★ 64 68 70 73 74 75 76 78 79 82 83   Reliable wines from LOGROÑO. Bordón is a fruity red. The semi-sweet white Diamante is a favourite in Spain.

Freixenet, S.A., Cavas   Cat. sp. ■★★→★★★
CAVA, rivalling CODORNIU in size through recent acquisitions, making a range of good sparkling wines. Also owns GLORIA FERRER in California and the Champagne house of Henri Abelé in Reims. Paul Cheneau is a low-price brand.

Gonzalez y Dubosc, S.A., Cavas   Cat. sp. ■★★
A branch of the sherry giant GONZALES BYASS. Pleasant sparkling wines exported as "Jean Perico".

Gran Vas   Pressurized tanks (*cuves closes*) for making inexpensive sparkling wines; also used to describe this type of wine.

Gurpegui, Bodegas   R'a.B. (p. w. dr.) res. ★★→★★ 70 73 75 78 81 82
Large family firm making some of the best wines from the RIOJA BAJA, labelled as Berceo. They incl. a fresh rosé.

Haro   The wine centre of the RIOJA ALTA, a small but stylish old town.

Huelva   And. r. w. br. ★→★★
Demarcated region w. of Cadiz. White table wines and sherry-like *generosos*, formerly sent to JEREZ for blending.

Irache, S.L.   Nav. r. p. (w. dr) res. ★★ 64 70 73 78 81 82
Well-known bodega with substantial exports.

Jean Perico   See Gonzalez Dubosc.

Jerez de la Frontera The capital city of sherry. (See p. 135).

Jumilla Lev. r. ★ (w. dr. p.) ★→★★
Demarcated region in the mountains n. of MURCIA. Its overstrong wines (up to 18% alcohol) are being lightened by earlier picking and better winemaking. Rosés are best.

Juvé y Camps Cat. sp. ★★→★★★
Family CAVA firm aiming for and achieving top quality wines, made with free-run juice, esp. Reserva de la Familia.

Labastida, Cooperativa Vinícola de R'a.Al. r. res ★★ →★★★ 66 70 75 78 82 Makers of very drinkable Manuel Quintano, fruity, well-balanced Montebuena, Gastrijo and Castillo Labastida reservas and gran reservas, and a fresh dry white with masses of flavour.

La Granja Remélluri R'a.Al. r. res. ★★★ 74 76 79 80 81 83 84
Small firm (since 1970), making good traditional red Riojas.

Laguardia Picturesque walled town at the centre of LA RIOJA ALAVESA.

Lagunilla, Bodegas R'a.A. r. ★★ 73 75 78 81 83
Modern firm owned by the British Grand Met. Co. Easy oaky light reds incl. Viña Herminia and Gran Reserva.

Lan, Bodegas R'a.A. r. (p. w.) res. ★★→★★★ 73 75 78 82 85
Huge modern bodega, lavishly equipped and making aromatic red Riojas, incl. the good Lancorta and fresh white Lan Blanco.

La Rioja Alta, Bodegas R'a.A. r. (p.) w. dr. (or sw.) res. ★★→★★★ 64 68 70 73 76 78 80 81 83 84 Excellent wines, esp. the red 3° año Viña Alberdi, the velvety 5° año Ardanza, the lighter 6° año Araña, the splendid Reserva 904 and marvellous Reserva 890. In future this bodega will be making only reservas and gran reservas.

León O.Cas. r. p. w. ★→★★ 78 81 82 83 84
Northern region on the move. Its wines, esp. those from the unfortunately named V.I.L.E. (e.g. the young Coyanza and full-blooded Don Suero reserva), are fruity, dry and refreshing.

León, S.A., Jean Cat. r. w. dr. res ★★★ 74 75 77 78 79 80 81 82 83
Small firm owned by a Los Angeles restaurateur. Good oaky CHARDONNAY and deep, full-bodied CABERNET that repays long bottle-ageing, though less so since 1980.

Rioja Vintages

Thanks to a more consistent climate and the blending of a proportion of wine from better vintages in poor years, Riojas do not vary to the same extent as the red wines from Bordeaux and Burgundy. With few exceptions the '72 and '77 vintages were a disaster, owing to high rainfall and the onset of rot and oidium. Of other recent years, the best were: 52 55 58 64 66 68 70 73 76 78 80 81 82 83 85 86 and 87. (Those in bold type were outstanding.)

Riojas are put on the market when they are ready to drink. The best reservas of the best vintages, however, have very long lives and improve with more bottle age. The best '64s are now at their peak.

Logroño Principal town of the RIOJA region. (I prefer HARO.)

López de Heredia, S.A. R'a.A. r. (p.) w. dr. or sw. res. ★★→ ★★★★ 64 68 70 73 76 78 80 81 82 83 84 85
Superb old established bodega in HARO with typical and good dry red Viña Tondonia of 6° año or more. Its wines are exceptionally long-lasting, and the Tondonia whites can also be very impressive.

Lopez Hermanos Malaga ★★
Large bodega making commercial Malaga wines, incl. popular Malaga Virgen and Moscatel Flor de Malaga.

Los Llanos N.Cas. r. (w. dr.) res. ★★ 75 78 81
One of the few VALDEPEÑAS bodegas to age wine in oak. Señorío de Los Llanos Gran Reserva is remarkably scented and silky. Also a clean and fruity white "Armonioso".

124

Magaña, Bodegas Nav. r. res. 80 81 82 ★★
 Small new bodega making vigorous red with MERLOT (vines bought from Pétrus) and CABERNET SAUVIGNON.

Majorca No wine of interest except from José FERRER.

Málaga And. br. sw. ★★→★★★
 Demarcated region around the city of Málaga. At their best, its dessert wines yield little to tawny port.

Mancha, La N.Cas. r. w. ★
 Large demarcated region n. and n.e. of VALDEPEÑAS. Mainly white wines, lacking the lively freshness of the best Valdepeñas, but showing marked signs of improvement. To watch.

Marfil Cat. r. (p.) w. ★★
 Brand name of Alella Vinicola (Bodegas Cooperativas), best known of the producers in ALELLA. Means "ivory".

Marqués de Alella Cat. w. dr. (sp.) ★★→★★★ 83 84 85 86 87 (D.Y.A.) Small bodega making light and fragrant white ALELLA wines, some from CHARDONNAY, by modern methods. Also a little CAVA.

Marqués de Cáceres, Bodegas R'a.A. r. p. w. dr. res. ★★→★★★ 70 73 75 76 78 80 81 82 83 84 85 Good red Riojas of various ages made by French methods from CENICERO (R'a.A.) grapes and also a surprisingly light and fragrant white (D.Y.A.).

Marqués de Griñon O.Cas. (r.) w. dr. ★★★ (r.) 82 83 84 85
 Enterprising nobleman making very fine CABERNET nr. Toledo, not a recognized wine region. Also refreshing white from Verdejo grapes in RUEDA.

Marqués de Monistrol, Bodegas Cat. w. r. (dr. or sw.) sp. res. ★★→★★★ 75 77 78 80 Old bodega now owned by Martini & Rossi. Refreshing whites, esp. the Vin Nature, a good red reserva and an odd sweet red wine.

Marqués de Murrieta, S.A. R'a.A. r. p. w. dr. res. ★★→ ★★★★ 34 42 60 62 64 68 70 73 74 75 76 78 79 80 81 82 83 84 85 Highly reputed bodega near LOGROÑO making some of the yield of all Riojas. Makes 4° año Etiqueta Blanca, superb red Castillo Ygay, an "old-style" oaky white, dry, fruity, and worth bottle-ageing, and a wonderful old-style ROSADO.

Marqués de Riscal, S.A. R'a.Al. r. (p. and w. dr.) res. ★★→★★★ 64 65 68 71 73 75 76 78 80 81 82 83 84 The best-known bodega of the RIOJA ALAVESA. Its red wines are relatively light and dry. Old vintages are very fine; some recent ones disappointing. Its white wines from RUEDA, incl. a v.g. SAUV BLANC, are some of the best from this region.

Marqués de Romeral R'a.A. r. w. dr. ★★ 76 78
 Everyday Romeral and Gran Reserva are both v.g. value.

Marqués del Puerto R'a.A. r. (p. w. dr.) res. ★★→★★★ 73 76 81 83
 Small concern, founded as Bodegas Lopez Agos, making a red reserva Señorio de Agos highly praised in Spain.

Martinez-Bujanda R'a.Al. r. w. dr. res ★★★ 73 75 80 81 82 83
 Refounded (1985) family-run RIOJA bodega, remarkably equipped. Excellent wines, incl. fruity SIN CRIANZA as well as Valdemar reservas.

Mascaró, Cavas Cat. sp. (w. dr. r.) ★★→ ★★★
 Maker of some of the best Spanish brandy, good sparkling wine and a refreshing dry white Viña Franca.

Mauro, Bodegas O.Cas. r. ★★★ 81 83 84
 New bodega in Tudela del Duero nr. Valladolid with v.g. round, fruity Tinta Fina red.

Méntrida N.Cas. r. w. ★
 Demarcated region w. of Madrid, source of everyday red wine.

Milmanda See Conca de Barberá, Torres.

Monopole See Compania Vinicola del Norte de España (CVNE).

Montánchez Ext. r. g. ★
 Village near Mérida, interesting because its red wines grow FLOR.

Montecillo, Bodegas   R'a.A. r. w. (p.) res. ★★★ 75 76 78 80 81 82 84
"State of the art" Rioja bodega owned by Osborne (see Sherry). Red and fresh dry white Cumbrero are currently among the best of the 3° año wines. Viña Monty is the worthy Reserva, also a rare but first rate "Gran Reserva Especial".

Montecristo, Bodegas ★★
Well-known brand of MONTILLA-MORILES wines.

Monterrey   Gal. r. ★
Region near the n. border of Portugal, making strong wines like those of VERIN.

Montilla-Moriles   And. g. ★★→★★★
Demarcated region near Cordoba. Its crisp, sherry-like FINO and AMONTILLADO contain 14% to 17.5% natural alcohol and remain unfortified and singularly toothsome.

Muga, Bodegas   R'a.A. r. (w.) res. (sp.) ★★★ 70 73 75 76 78 80 81 82 84   Small family firm in HARO, making some of the best red Rioja now available by strictly traditional methods. Wines are light but intensely aromatic, with long complex finish. The best is Prado Enea. Whites not so good.

Navarra   Nav. r. p. (w.) ★→ ★★
Demarcated region; mainly fresh and fruity rosés and sturdy red wines, but some reservas up to Rioja standards. See Cenalsa, Chivite, Magaña, etc.

Nuestro Padre Jésus del Perdón, Coop de   N.Cas. r. w. dr. ★ D.Y.A.
Bargain Yuntero, Casa la Teja and fresh white Lazarillo.

Olarra, Bodegas   R'a.A. r. (w. p.) res. ★★→★★★ 70 73 75 76 78 80 81 82 85   Vast modern bodega near LOGRONO, one of the show-pieces of RIOJA, making good red and white wines and excellent Cerro Añon reservas. Since '81, Añares is the top reserva.

Palacio de Arganza   O.Cas. r. p. w. dr. res. ★★→★★★ 65 70 74 76 79
Best-known bodega in El Bierzo, between LEON and GALICIA. White Vega Burbia; red Almeña del Bierzo.

Palacio de Fefiñanes   Gal. w. res. ★★★
Best of all the ALBARINO wines, though without appreciable pétillance, since it is aged in oak for 3-5 yrs.

Rioja's Characteristic Style
To the Spanish palate the taste of luxury in wine is essentially the taste of oak. Oak contains vanillin, the taste of vanilla. Hence the characteristic vanilla flavour of all mature Spanish table wines of high quality – exemplified by the reservas of Rioja (red and white).

Historically the reason for long oak-ageing was to stabilize the best wines while their simple fruity flavours developed into something more complex and characteristically winey. Fashion has swung (perhaps too far) against the oaky flavour of old Rioja whites. But the marriage of ripe fruit and oak in red Rioja is still highly appreciated.

Paternina, S.A., Bodegas   R'a.A. r. (p.) w. dr. or sw. res. ★→★★★ 28 59 67 68 71 73 75 76 78 82 83   A household name, esp. for Banda Azul red and Banda Dorada white. Fine older wines, but recent vintages disappointing. Most consistent red is Viña Vial.

Paxarete   Traditional dark brown almost chocolaty speciality of Tarragona. See De Muller.

Pazo   Gal. r. p. w. dr. ★ D.Y.A.
Brand name of the cooperative at RIBEIRO, making wines akin to Portuguese VINHOS VERDES. The rasping red is the local favourite. The pleasant slightly fizzy Pazo and Xeiro whites are safer, and the Viña Costeira has real quality.

Peñafiel   O.Cas. r. and w. dr. res. ★★ 64 74 76 79 80 82 83 85 86
Village on the R. Duero near Valladolid. Best wines are fruity reds from the Coop de RIBERO DEL DUERO, incl. the tasty 5° año PROTOS.

Penedès Cat. r. w. dr. sp. ★→★★★
Demarcated region including Vilafranca del Penedès SAN SADURNI DE NOYA and SITGES. See also Torres.

Perelada Cat. (r. p.) w. sp. ★★
In the demarcated region of Ampurdán on the Costa Brava. Best known for sparkling wines made both by the champagne and tank or CUVE CLOSE systems.

Pérez Pascua Hnos. O.Cas. r. (p.) res. ★★★ 81 83 85 86
Immaculate tiny family bodega in Ribera del Duero. In Spain its fruity and complex red Viña Pedrosa is rated one of the country's best.

Pesquera O.Cas. r. ★★★ 80 82 84 85 86
RIBERA DEL DUERO red made in small quantity by Alejandro Fernandez. Robert Parker rates it a match for Bordeaux GRANDS CRUS. Janus is an (even more expensive) special bottling.

Piqueras, Bodegas N.Cas. r. ▓
Makers of inexpensive and drinkable red Castillo de Almansa with more style than most of the region's wines.

Priorato Cat. br. dr. r. ★★
Demarcated region, an enclave in that of TARRAGONA, known for its alcoholic "rancio" wines and also for almost black full-bodied reds, often used for blending. Lighter blended Priorato is a good carafe wine in Barcelona. See De Muller, Scala Dei, Masia Barril.

Protos See Peñafiel.

Raimat Cat. r. w. p. sp. ★→★★ (Cab) 76 81 82 83 84 85
Intriguing, well-made wines from old v'yds near Lérida, recently replanted by CODORNIU and CABERNET, CHARDONNAY and other foreign vines. Also a good 100% CHARD CAVA.

René Barbier Cat. r. w. dr. res. ★★
Part of the FREIXENET group known for fresh white Kraliner and red R.B. Reservas.

Reserva Good-quality wine matured for long periods. Red reservas must spend at least 1 year in cask and 2 in bottle; Gran Reservas 2 in cask and 3 in bottle.

Ribeiro Gal. r. (p.) w. dr. ★→★★
Demarcated region on the n. border of Portugal making wines similar to Portuguese VINHO VERDE – and others.

Ribera del Duero Historic demarcated region e. of Valladolid, potentially excellent for Tinto Fino (TEMPRANILLO) reds. See Vega Sicilia, Peñafiel, Mauro, Torremilanos, Pesquera, Pérez Pascua.

Rioja O.Cas. r. p. w. sp. esp. 64 66 68 70 73 75 76 78 80 81 82 83 85 86 87
This upland region along the R. Ebro in the n. of Spain produces most of the country's best table wines in some 50 BODEGAS DE EXPORTACION. It is sub-divided into:

Rioja Alavesa North of the R. Ebro, the R'a.Al. produces fine red wines, mostly light in body and colour.

Rioja Alta South of the R. Ebro and w. of LOGRONO, the R'a.A. grows most of the finest red and white wines; also some rosé.

Rioja Baja Stretching e. from LOGRONO, the Rioja Baja makes coarser red wines, high in alcohol and often used for blending.

Riojanas, Bodegas R'a.A. r. (w. p.) res. ★★→★★★ 34 42 56 64 66 68 70 73 74 75 76 78 80 81 82 83 One of the older bodegas, making a good traditional Viña Albina. Monte Real reservas are big and mellow.

Rioja Santiago, S.A. R'a.A. r. (w. dr. or sw. p.) res. ★→★★★ 78 82
Bodega at HARO with well-known wines. The flavour sometimes suffers from pasteurization, and appropriately, as until recently it belonged to Pepsi-Cola, it makes the biggest-selling bottled SANGRIA. Top reds: Condal and Gran Enologica.

Rosada Rosé.

Rovellats S.A. Cat. sp. ★★→★★★
  Small family firm producing limited amounts of exclusive and expensive CAVA, stocked in some of Spain's leading restaurants.

Rovira S.A., Pedro Cat. r. p. w. dr. or sw. br. res. ★→★★
  Large firm with branches in the DOs TARRAGONA, TERRA ALTA and PENEDES, making beverage, apéritif and dessert wines.

Rueda O.Cas. br. w. dr. ★→★★
  Small demarcated area w. of Valladolid. Traditional producer of flor-growing sherry-like wines up to 17° alcohol, now making fresh whites incl. those of the MARQUES DE RISCAL and MARQUES DE GRINON.

Ruiz, Santiago Gal. w. dr. ★★★ D.Y.A.
  Small but prestigious bodega in the new Galacia DO Rias Baixas, whose Albariño is of the very best.

Salceda, S.A., Bodegas Viña R'a.Al. r. res. ★★→★★★ 73 75 78 80 81 82 83 84 Makes fruity, well-balanced red wines.

Sangre de Toro Brand name for a rich-flavoured red wine from TORRES.

Sangría Cold red wine cup traditionally with citrus fruit, fizzy lemonade, ice and brandy. Also cheap commercial fizz.

Sanlúcar de Barrameda Centre of the Manzanilla district. (See Sherry.)

San Sadurní de Noya Cat. sp. ████████
  Town s. of Barcelona, hollow with cellars where dozens of firms produce sparkling wine ("CAVA") by the champagne method. Standards are high, even if the taste of champagne is lacking.

San Valero, Bodega Cooperative Ara. r. p. (w.) res. ████████
  Large CARINENA coop with some modern wines. Good red CRIANZA Villalta; fresh Perceval rosado with slight spritz; and good value young, unoaked Don Mendo red.

Sarría, Señorio de Nav. r. (p. w. dr.) res. ████████ 64 73 74 75 76 78 81 82 84 The vineyards and model winery near Pamplona produce wines up to (high) RIOJA standards.

Scala Dei, Cellers de Cat. r. res. ★★
  One of the few bodegas in the tiny DO PRIORATO. Wines are full-bodied reds replete with fruit, body and alcohol though less so than formerly.

Scholtz, Hermanos, S.A. And. br. ★★→ ████
  Makers of the best MALAGA, including a good, dry 10-year-old amontillado, excellent Moscatel and traditional Dulce y Negro. Best is the dessert Solera Scholtz 1885.

Seco Dry.

Segura Viudas, Cavas Cat. Sp. ★★→★★★
  CAVA of PENEDES. Buy the Brut Reserva.

Serra, Jaume Cat. w. dr. r. res. ★★→★★★ 84
  With establishments in both ALELLA and the PENEDES, the firm makes fresh white wines and fruity, well-balanced reds.

Siglo Popular sack-wrapped RIOJA brand of Bodegas A.G.E.

Sin Crianza See Crianza.

Sitges Cat. w. sw. ★★
  Coastal resort s. of Barcelona formerly noted for sweet dessert wine made from Moscatel and MALVASIA grapes.

Tarragona Cat. r. w. dr. or sw. br. ★→★★★
  1. Table wines from the demarcated region; of little note. 2. Dessert wines from the firm of DE MULLER.

Tinto Red.

Toro O.Cas. r. ★→★★
  Newly demarcated region 150 miles n.w. of Madrid, traditionally making powerful (up to 16°) red wines, but now producing some superior reds. See Bodega Fariña.

Torremilanos O.Cas. r. res. ████ 76 79 81 82 83 85 86
  Label of Bodegas López Peñalba, a fast-expanding family firm near Aranda de Duero. Their Tinto Fino (TEMPRANILLO) reds are lighter and more Rioja-like than most. Also labelled "Peñalba".

SP

Torres, Bodegas Cat. r. w. dr. or semi-sw. p. res. ★★→★★★★ 64 70 71 73 74 75 76 77 78 79 80 81 82 83 84 85 86 87 Distinguished family firm making the best wines of PENEDES, esp. flowery white Viña Sol and Gran Viña Sol, MILMANDA oak-fermented CHARD, semi-dry aromatic Esmeralda, Waltraud RIESLING, red Tres Torres and Gran Sangredetoro, superlative Gran Coronas (Cabernet) reservas, and Santa Digna Pinot Noir. The family now also has vineyards in Chile and California.

Utiel-Requeña Lev. r. (w.) p.
Demarcated region w. of Valencia. Sturdy reds and chewy vino de doble pasta for blending; also really light and fragrant rosé.

Valbuena O.Cas. r. ★★★ 75 76 77 78 79 80 82 83
Made with the same grapes as VEGA SICILIA but sold as 3° año or 5° año. Best at about 10 years. Some prefer it to its elder brother.

Valdeorras Gal. r. w. dr. ★→★★
Demarcated region e. of Orense. Dry and refreshing wines.

Valdepeñas N.Cas. r. (w.) ★→ ★★
Demarcated region near the border of Andalucia. Its mainly red wines, though high in alcohol, are sometimes surprisingly light in flavour. Some superior wine is now being matured in oak.

Valencia Lev. r. w. ★
Demarcated region producing earthy high-strength wine.

Vega Sicilia O.Cas. r. res. ★★★★ 41 48 53 59 61 62 64 66 67 69 72 73 76
One of the very best Spanish wines, full-bodied, fruity, piquant and fascinating. Contains up to 16% alcohol. VALBUENA is the same wine with less time in oak (78 79 80 82).

Vendimia Vintage.

Verín Gal. r. ★
Town near n. border of Portugal. Its wines are the strongest from Galicia, without a bubble, and up to 14% alcohol.

Vicente, Suso y Pérez, S.A. Ara. r. ★★
A bodega s. of Saragossa producing superior CARINENA.

Viña Literally, a vineyard. But wines such as Tondonia (LOPEZ DE HEREDIA) or Zaco (BILBAINAS) are not necessarily made with grapes exclusively from the vineyard named.

Vinícola de Castilla N.Cas. r. p. w. dr. ★
One of the largest firms in LA MANCHA, marketing its wines under the labels of "Castillo de Manza" and Gran Verdad.

VINIVAL Lev. r. w. ★
Huge Valencian consortium marketing the most widely drunk wine in the region, Torres de Serrano.

Vino Blanco White wine.

Vino comun/corriente Ordinary wine.

    clarete Light red wine.

    dulce Sweet wine.

    espumoso Sparkling wine.

    generoso Apéritif or dessert wine rich in alcohol.

    rancio Maderized (brown) white wine.

    rosado Rosé wine.

    seco Dry wine.

    tinto Red wine.

    verde Wine akin to Portuguese VINHO VERDE.

Yecla Lev. r. w. ★
Demarcated region n. of Murcia. Its cooperative, "La Purisima", is said to be Spain's biggest. Its wines, formerly all heavy-weight bruisers, have been lightened for export.

Ygay See Marqués de Murrieta.

Portugal

For port and madeira see pages 133-138.

Adega A cellar or winery.

Alentejo Alen. r. (w.) ★→★★★
> Vast tract of southern Portugal with only sparse vineyards near the Spanish border. The great bulk of its wine is cooperative-made. Estate wines from ROSADO FERNANDES, Quinta de Mouchão and ESPORAO show remarkable potential. Best coops are at Redondo, BORBA and REGUENGOS DE MONSARRAZ. Expect excitement here.

Algarve Alg. r. w. ★
> Newly demarcated region in the holiday area. Its wines are nothing to write home about.

Aliança, Caves r. w. dr. sp. res. ★★→★★★
> Large BAIRRADA-based firm, making champagne-method sparkling wines. Reds and whites include good BAIRRADA wines and mature DAOS. Tinta Velha is the best-selling red in Portugal.

Almodovar, Casa Agricola Alen. w. dr. r. res. ★★ 84 86 87
> Based in Vidigueira, best known for its white wines, this concern also makes worthwhile reds.

Amarante Sub-region in the VINHOS VERDES area. Rather heavier and stronger wines than those from farther north.

Arruda, Adega Cooperative de B'a.al. r. res. ★
> Vinho Tinto Arruda is a best buy. Avoid the Reserva.

Aveleda Douro w. dr. ★★ D.Y.A.
> A first-class VINHO VERDE made on the Aveleda estate of the Guedes family. Sold dry in Portugal but sweetened for export.

Bacalhoa, Quinta da Est'a. r. res. ★★★ 81 82 83 84 85
> American-owned estate near Setúbal, whose harmonious, fruity, mid-weight CABERNET SAUVIGNON wine is vinified by João PIRES.

Bairrada Bei. Lit. r. w. dr. and sp. ★→ ★★★ 66 70 75 76 77 82
> Recently demarcated region supplying much of Oporto's carafe wine and some excellent GARRAFEIRAS. Also good-quality sparkling wines by the champagne method. A potential star.

Barca Velha ("Ferreirinha") Trás-os-m. r. res. ★★★★ 57 64 65 66 78
> Perhaps Portugal's best red, made in very limited quantity by the port firm of FERREIRA. Powerful and fine with deep bouquet.

Barrocão Cavas do Bei. Lit. r. w. dr. res. ★→ ★★★
> Based in the BAIRRADA, the firm blends good red DAOS and makes first-rate old BAIRRADA garrafeiras, such as 60 and 64.

Basto A sub-region of the VINHOS VERDES area on the R. Tamego, producing more astringent red wine than white.

Borba Alen. r. ★
> Small VQPRD area nr Evora, making some of best wine from ALENTEJO.

Borba, Adega Cooperative de Alen. r. res. (w. dr.) ★★ 82
> A producer of big, fruity, mouth-filling wines, often at best when young.

Borges & Irmão Merchants of port and table wines at Vila Nova de Gaia. Brands incl. Gatâo and (better) Gamba VINHOS VERDES. Also Fita Azul sparkling.

Braga Sub-region of the VINHOS VERDES area, good red and white.

Buçaco B'a.al. r. (p.) w. res. ★★★★ r. 51 53 57 58 60 63 67 70 72 75 77; w. 56 65 66 70 72 75 The legendary speciality of the luxury Palace hotel at Buçaco nr. Coimbra, not seen elsewhere. Variable, at best incredible quality.

Bucelas Est'a. w. dr. ★★★ 79
> Tiny demarcated region just n. of Lisbon. CAVES VELHAS make delicate, perfumed wines with 11% to 12% alcohol.

Camarate, Quinta de Est'a. r. ★★ 74 78 80 82
> Notable CLARETE from FONSECA at Azeitão, s. of Lisbon, incl. detectable CABERNET SAUVIGNON.

Carcavelos Est'a. br. sw. ★★★

Minute demarcated region w. of Lisbon. Its excellent sweet apéritif or dessert wines average 19% alcohol and are drunk cold.

Cartaxo Ribatejo r. w. ★

A district in the Ribatejo n. of Lisbon, now a VQPRD area making everyday wines popular in the capital.

Carvalho, Ribeiro & Ferreira B'a. al. r. w. des. ▓▓ ★★→★★★

Large merchants bottling and blending SERRADAYRES and excellent RIBATEJO GARRAFEIRAS.

Casa de Sezim M'o. w. dr. ★★→★★★ D.Y.A.

One of the best estate-bottled VINHO VERDES from a member of the new association of private producers, APEVV.

Casal García Douro w. dr. ★★ D.Y.A.

One of the biggest-selling VINHOS VERDES in Portugal, made by SOGRAPE.

Casal Mendes M'o. w. dr. ★★ D.Y.A.

The VINHOS VERDES from CAVES ALIANCA.

Casaleiro Trademark of Caves Dom Teodosio-João T. Barbosa, who make a variety of reliable wines: DAO, VINHOS VERDES, etc.

Caves Velhas Bei. Lit. r. w. dr. res ★★→★★★

Only maker of BUCELAS; also good DAO and Romeira GARRAFEIRAS.

Cepa Velha M'o. (r.) w. dr. ★★★

Brand name of Vinhos de Monção, Lda. Their Alvarinho, from the grape of that name, is one of the best VINHOS VERDES.

Clarete Light red wine.

Colares Est'a. r. ★★★

Small demarcated region on the coast w. of Lisbon. Its classical dark red wines, rich in tannin, are from vines which survived the phylloxera epidemic. Drink the oldest available: it needs ten years.

Conde de Santar B'a. al. r. (w. dr.) res. ★★→★★★ 70 73 78

The only estate-grown DAO, later matured and sold by the port firm of CALEM. Reservas are fruity, full-bodied and exceptionally smooth.

Dão B'a. al. r. w. res. ★→ ▓▓▓ ★★★ 66 67 69 70 71 74 75 80 83

Demarcated region round Viseu on the R. Mondego. Produces some of Portugal's best table wines: solid reds of some subtlety with age: substantial dry whites. All are sold under brand names.

Douro The northern river whose valley produces port and more than adequate demarcated table wines.

Esporão Heredade do Based on Alentejo vineyards dating from the 13th century, the owners are currently planting CAB SAUV and Touriga Nacional on a large scale and constructing one of the largest wineries in Portugal.

Evelita Trás-os-m. r. ▓▓★★★ 75

Reliable middle-weight red made near VILA REAL by Real Companhia Vinícola do Norte de Portugal. Ages well.

Fonseca, J.M. da Est'a. r. w. dr. br. res. ▓▓→★★★

Large, old-established family firm in Azeitão making a wide range of good wines, incl. the red PERIQUITA, PASMADOS and QUINTA DE CAMARATE (formerly known as Palmela) and Terras Altas DAO, as well as the famous MOSCATEL DE SETUBAL.

Fonseca Internacional J.M. da Est'a p. ★

Formerly part of the last, now owned by Grand Met. Produces LANCERS rosé and sparkling LANCERS Brut (which see).

Gaeiras Est'a. r. ★★

Dry, full-bodied and well-balanced red made near Obidos.

Garrafeira The "private reserve" aged wine of a merchant aged for a minimum of 2 years in cask and 1 in bottle, but often much longer; usually his best, though often of indeterminate origin.

Gatão M'o. w. dr. ★★ D.Y.A.

Reliable "GREEN WINE" from the firm of Borges & Irmão, fragrant but sometimes a little sweetened.

Gazala M'o. w. dr. ★★ D.Y.A.
A new VINHO VERDE made at Barcelos by SOGRAPE since the AVELEDA estate went to a different branch of the Guedes family.

Grão Vasco B'a.al. r. w. res. ★★→★★★ 70 73 75 78 80 81 83
One of the best brands of DAO, blended and matured at Viseu by SOGRAPE. Fine red reservas; fresh young white (D.Y.A.)

Lagoa See Algarve.

Lagosta M'o. w. dr. ★★ D.Y.A.
Well-known VINHO VERDE from the Real Companhia Vinícola do Norte de Portugal.

Lancers Est'a. p. w. sp. ★
Sweet carbonated rosé and sparkling white extensively shipped to the USA by FONSECA INTERNACIONAL.

Lima Sub-region in the n. of the VINHOS VERDES area making mainly astringent red wines.

Madeira Island br. dr./sw. ★★→★★★★
Source of famous apéritif and dessert wines. See pp. 133-138.

Magrico M'o. w. dr. ★★ D.Y.A.
Many VINHOS VERDES are slightly sweetened for export. This is a genuinely dry one.

Mateus Rosé Trás-os-m. p. (w.) ★
World's biggest-selling medium-sweet carbonated rosé, made by SOGRAPE at VILA REAL and Anadia in the BAIRRADA.

Monção Sub-region of the VINHOS VERDES area on R. Minho, producing the best of them from the ALVARINHO grape.

Palacio de Brejoeira M'o. (r.) w. dr. ★★★
Outstanding estate-made VINHOS VERDE from MONCAO, with astonishing fragrance and full, fruity flavour.

Penafiel Sub-region in the s. of the VINHOS VERDES area.

Periquita Est'a. r. ★★ 71 74 77 78 80 84
One of Portugal's most enjoyable robust reds, made by FONSECA at Azeitão s. of Lisbon from a grape much used in the ALENTEJO.

Pinhel B'a.al. (r.) w. sp. ★
VQPRD region e. of the DAO, making similar white wine, mostly processed into sparkling.

Planalto Douro w. dr. ★★
Good white wine from SOGRAPE.

Pires, João Est'a r. w. dr./sw. res. ★★→★★★
Producers of red TINTO DE ANFORA, a young red Quinta de Santo Amoro made by maceration carbonique, white dry Moscato, Catarina CHARDONNAY and CAB SAUV. (See Bacalhoa, Quinta da.)

Ponte de Lima, cooperativa de M'o. r. ★★
Maker of one of the best bone dry *red* VINHOS VERDES and also of a first-rate dry and fruity white.

Quinta da Insua Ba.al. r. w. ★★
One of the very few single estate DAOS, made with a proportion of CAB SAUVIGNON in an old cellar recently re-equipped and modernized.

Quinta da Pacheca Trás-os-m. r. w. ★★ 82
Superior Douro table wines, estate-grown, made and bottled.

Quinta de Ribeirinho Bei. Lit. r. sp. ★★→★★★
Luis Pato makes some of the best estate-grown BAIRRADA wines: fruity red and fresh méthode champenoise sparkling.

Quinta de S. Claudio M'o. w. dr. ★★★ D.Y.A.
Estate at Esposende and maker of some of the best VINHO VERDE outside MONCAO.

Quinta do Côtto Trás-os-m. r. w. dr. res. ★★→★★★ 82 85
Red Grande Escolha and Q. do Côtto are dense, fruity, tannic wines that will repay long keeping. Also port.

Quinta do Corval Trás-os-m. r. ★★
Estate near Pinhão making good light CLARETES.

Raposeira B'a.al. sp. ★★
  One of the best-known Portuguese sparkling wines, made by the champagne method at Lamego. Ask for the Bruto.

Redondo See Alentejo.

Reguengos de Monsarraz, Cooperativa de Alen. r. res. (w. dr.) ★★ 82 83 87 Important cooperative making steadily better wines, the best of them red, since modernization.

Ribalonga, Vinícola B'a.al. r. res. ★★ 71 74 76 78 80 82 83
  Makers of a sound and very reasonably priced red DAO.

Ribatejo Region on the R. Tagus n. of Lisbon. Source of several good GARRAFEIRAS, etc.

Rosado Fernandes, José de Sousa Alen. r. res. ★★ 71 75 79 83 86
  Small private firm, recently acquired by J. M. da FONSECA, producing the most sophisticated of the full-bodied wines from the Alentejo, fermenting them in *tinajas* and ageing them in oak.

Santola B'a. al. w. dr. ★★ D.Y.A.
  A refreshing dry VINHO VERDE from Vinhos Messias.

São João, Caves Bei. Lit. r. w. dr. sp. res. ★★→ ★★★ 70 75 76 78 80
  One of the best firms in the BAIRRADA, known for its fruity and full-bodied reds and Porto dos Cavaleiros DAOS. Also fizz.

Serradayres Est'a. r. (w.) res. ★★
  Blended RIBATEJO table wines from CARVALHO, RIBEIRO & FERREIRA. Usually sound and very drinkable, but recently very tart.

Setúbal Est'a. br. ★★★
  Small demarcated region s. of the R. Tagus, where J. M. da FONSECA make an aromatic dessert muscat, 6 and 25 yrs old.

Sogrape Sociedad Comercial dos Vinhos de Mesa de Portugal. Largest wine concern in the country, making VINHOS VERDES, DAO, MATEUS ROSE, VILA REAL red, etc., and now owners of FERREIRA port.

Terras Altas B'a. al. r. w. res. ★★ 75 76 78 79 80 82 83 84
  Good DAO wines made by J. M. da FONSECA.

Tinto de Anfora Est'a r. ★★★ 78 80 81 82 84 85 86
  Deservedly popular juicy and fruity red from JOAO PIRES.

Torres Vedras Est'a r. w. dr. ★
  Area n. of Lisbon famous for Wellington's "lines". Major supplier of bulk wine with one of the biggest coops in Portugal.

Vila Real Trás-os-m. r. ★→ ★★
  Town in the demarcated DOURO region, now making some good red table wine.

Vinho branco White wine.
  consumo Ordinary wine.
  doce Sweet wine.
  espumante Sparkling wine.
  garrafeira A reserve with min. 2 years in cask and 1 in bottle.
  generoso Apéritif or dessert wine rich in alcohol.
  maduro A mature table wine – as opposed to a VINHO VERDE.
  rosado Rosé wine.
  seco Dry wine.
  tinto Red wine.
  verde See under Vinhos Verdes.

Vinhos Verdes M'o. and Douro. r. ★ w. dr. ★→★★★
  Demarcated region between R. Douro and n. frontier with Spain, producing "green wines": wine made from barely ripe grapes and undergoing a special secondary fermentation which leaves it with a slight sparkle. Ready for drinking in the spring after the harvest. It may be white or red. "Green wine" is not an official term.

Remember that vintage years generally ready for drinking in 1990 are printed in **bold type.** *Those in light type will benefit from being kept.*

Sherry, Port & Madeira

The original true sherries of Spain, ports of Portugal and madeiras of Madeira are listed below. References to their many imitators in South Africa, California, Australia, Cyprus, Argentina will be found under their respective countries. (N.B. "British Sherry" is an outrageous theft of the name to describe a drink made of dehydrated must and water – not legally wine at all.)

The map on page 119 locates the port and sherry districts. Madeira is an island 400 miles out in the Atlantic from the coast of Morocco, a port of call for west-bound ships: hence its historical market in North America.

In this section most of the entries are shippers' names followed by a brief account of their wines. The names of wine-types are included in the alphabetical listing.

Almacenista Individual old unblended sherry; high-quality, usually dark dry wines for connoisseurs. Often superb quality and value. See Lustau. **SPM**

Amontillado In general use means medium sherry; technically means a FINO which has been aged in oak to become more powerful and pungent.

Amoroso Type of sweet sherry, not much different from a sweet OLOROSO.

Barbadillo, Antonio The largest SANLUCAR firm, with a range of 50-odd MANZANILLAS and sherries, incl. Sanlucar Fino, Solera Manzanilla Pasada, Fino de Balbaina, etc. Also fresh young Castillo de San Diego table wines.

Barbeito Shippers of good-quality madeira, the last independent family firm in the business. Wines include one of the driest and best apéritif madeiras "Island Dry". Also Crown range and vintage wines, e.g. Malmsey 1901.

Bertola Sherry shippers, best known for their Bertola Cream Sherry.

Blandy Historic family firm of Madeira shippers. Duke of Clarence Malmsey is their most famous wine. 10-year-old Reserve Malmsey is v. popular.

Blazquez Sherry bodega at JEREZ (owned by DOMECQ) with outstanding FINO, "Carta Blanca", and "Carta Oro" amontillado "al natural" (unsweetened).

Brown sherry British term for a style of dark sweet sherry.

Bual One of the best grapes of Madeira, making a soft smoky sweet wine, not usually as sweet as Malmsey.

Caballero Sherry shippers at Puerto de Santa Maria best known for Pavon Fino, Oloroso Mayoral Cream, excellent "Burdon" sherries and Ponche orange liqueur.

Cálem Old Portuguese house with a good reputation, esp. for vintage wines. Owning the excellent Quinta da Foz (82 84). Vintages: 50 58 60 63 70 75 77 80 83 85. Adequate light tawny.

Churchill The only recently-founded port shipper, already respected for excellent vintages '82 and '85. Also a good crusted.

Cockburn British-owned port shippers with a range of good wines incl. 20-year-old "Directors' Reserve". Fine vintage port from very high v'yds can look deceptively light when young, but has great lasting power. Vintages: 55 60 63 67 70 75 77 83 85.

134

Cossart Gordon Leading firm of Madeira shippers founded 1745, best known for their "Good Company" range of wines but also producing old vintages (latest, 1952) and soleras (esp. superb Sercial Duo Centenary).

Cream Sherry A style of amber sweet sherry made by sweetening a blend of well-aged OLOROSOS.

Crofts One of the oldest firms shipping vintage port: 300 years old in 1978. Bought early this century by Gilbey's. Well-balanced vintage wines last as long as any. Vintages: **55 60 63 66** 70 75 77 82 85, and lighter vintage wines under the name of their Quinta da Roeda in several other years (**78** 80 83). Also now in the sherry business with Croft Original (PALE CREAM), Croft Particular (medium), Delicado (FINO), and good PALO CORTADO.

Crusted Term for a vintage-style port, but blended from several vintages not one, bottled young and aged in bottle, so forming a "crust" in the bottle. Needs decanting.

Delaforce Port shippers owned by I.D.V., particularly well known in Germany. "His Eminence's Choice" is an excellent tawny. "Vintage Character" is also good. Vintage wines are very fine, among the lighter kind: **55 58 60 63 66 70 75** 77 82 85. "Quinta da Corte" in '78 '80.

Delgado Zuleta Old-established Sanlùcar firm best-known for its marvellous La Goya Manzanilla Pasada.

Diez-Merito S.A. Fast-growing JEREZ firm owned by BODEGAS INTER-NACIONALES specializing in "own-brand" sherries. Latest acquisition is Zoilo Ruiz Mateus, formerly part of the ill-fated Rumasa empire. Its own Fino Imperial and Oloroso Victoria Regina are excellent. DON ZOILO wines are superb.

Domecq Giant family-owned sherry bodegas at JEREZ. Double Century Original Oloroso is their biggest brand, La Ina their excellent FINO. Other famous wines incl. Celebration Cream, Botaina (old amontillado) and the magnificent Rio Viejo (dry oloroso). Recently introduced a range of old solera sherries. Now also in Rioja.

Don Zoilo Luxury sherries, incl. velvety FINO, sold by DIEZ-MERITO.

Dow Old name used on the British market by the port shippers Silva & Cosens, well known for their relatively dry but nonetheless splendid vintage wines, said to have a faint "cedarwood" character. Also v.g. "Vintage Character" and Boardroom Tawny. 15-year-old Tawny Quinta do Bomfim is their single-quinta port. Vintages: **55 60 63 66** 70 72 75 77 80 83 85. Dow, WARRE, GRAHAM, GOULD CAMPBELL, QUARLES HARRIS and SMITH WOODHOUSE all belong to the Symington family.

Dry Fly A household name in the UK, this crisp, nutty AMONTILLADO is made in Jerez for its British proprietors, Findlater, Mackie, Todd & Co.

Dry Sack See Williams & Humbert.

Duff Gordon Sherry shippers best known for their El Cid AMONTILLADO. Also good Nina dry OLOROSO. Owned by the big Spanish firm Bodegas Osborne.

Duke of Wellington Luxury range of sherries from BODEGAS INTER-NACIONALES.

Eira Velha, Quinta da Small port estate with old-style vintage wines shipped by HARVEY's of Bristol. Vintages: **72** 78 80 82 85.

Ferreira The biggest Portuguese-owned port growers and shippers (since 1751) recently bought by Sogrape; well-known for old tawnies and good, relatively light, vintages: **60 63 66 70 75** 77 78 80 82 83 85. Also Dona Antónia Personal Reserve and sublime tawny Duque de Braganza.

Findlater's Old established London wine merchant shipping own very successful brand of medium sherry: Dry Fly amontillado.

Fino   Term for the lightest and finest of sherries, completely dry, very pale and with great delicacy. Fino should always be drunk cool and fresh: it deteriorates rapidly once opened. TIO PEPE is the classic example.

Flor   The characteristic natural yeast which gives FINO sherry its unique flavour.

Fonseca Guimaraens   British-owned port shipper of stellar reputation, connected with TAYLOR. Robust, deeply coloured vintage wine, sometimes said to have a slight "burnt" flavour. Vintages: 55 60 63 66 70 75 77 80 83 85. Quinta de Panascal 78 is a new single-quinta wine. Also popular Vintage Character "Bin 27".

Forester   Port shippers and owners of the famous Quinta Boa Vista. Their vintage wines tend to be round, "fat" and sweet, good for relatively early drinking. Vintages: 60 62 63 66 67 70 72 75 77 80 82 83 85.

Garvey's   Famous old sherry shippers at JEREZ. Their finest wines are Fino San Patricio, Tio Guillermo Dry Amontillado and Ochavico Dry Oloroso. San Angelo Medium Amontillado is the most popular. Also Bicentenary Pale Cream.

Gonzalez Byass   Enormous concern shipping the world's most famous and one of the best FINO sherries: Tio Pepe. Other brands incl. La Concha Medium Amontillado, Elegante Dry Fino, San Domingo Pale Cream, Nectar Cream and Alfonso Dry Oloroso. Matusalem and Apostoles are respectively sweet and dry old olorosos of rare quality.

Gould Campbell   See Smith Woodhouse.

Graham   Port shippers famous for one of the richest and sweetest of vintage ports, largely from their own Quinta Malvedos, also excellent brands, incl. "Six Grapes" Ruby, Late Bottled, and 10- and 20-year-old tawnies. Vintages: 55 58 60 63 66 70 75 77 80 83 85.

Harvey's   Probably the largest sherry firm, having recently bought PALOMINO and DE TERRY. World-famous Bristol shippers of Bristol Cream and Bristol Milk sweet sherries, Club Amontillado and Bristol Dry, which are medium. Luncheon Dry and Bristol Fino, which are dry, and excellent PALO CORTADO. Also a very good new range: "1796". Harvey's also control COCKBURN.

Sherry & Food

By a quirk of fashion the wines of sherry, madeira and to some extent port are currently being left on the sidelines by a world increasingly hypnotized by a limited range of "varietal" wines. Yet all three include wines with every quality of "greatness", and far more gastronomic possiblities than the world seems to realize. It is notorious that for the price of e.g. a bottle of top-class white burgundy you can buy three of the very finest fino sherry, which with many dishes (see Wine & Food) will make an equally exciting accompaniment. Mature madeiras give the most lingering farewell of any wine to a splendid dinner. Tawny port is a wine of many uses. Perhaps it is because the New World cannot rival these Old World classics that they are left out of the headlines.

Henriques & Henriques   Well-known independent Madeira shippers of Funchal. Their wide range includes a good dry apéritif wine: Ribeiro Seco and (sometimes) fine old reservas.

Internacionales, Bodegas   Once the pride of RUMASA and incorporating such famous houses as BERTOLA, Varela and DIEZ-MERITO, Internacionales is now the cornerstone of a new empire embracing PATERNINA and FRANCO ESPANOLES in Rioja. Its own best-known sherries are the Duke of Wellington range.

Jerez de la Frontera   Centre of the sherry industry, between Cadiz and Seville in s. Spain. The word sherry is a corruption of the name, pronounced in Spanish "Hereth". In French, Xérés.

Late-bottled vintage Port of a single vintage kept in wood for twice as long as vintage port (about 5 years). Therefore lighter when bottled and ageing quicker. A real "L.B.V." will "throw a crust" like vintage port. Few qualify.

Leacock One of the oldest Madeira shippers. 10-year-old Special Reserve Malmsey and 13-year-old Bual are excellent.

Lustau One of the largest independent family-owned sherry bodegas in JEREZ, making many wines for other shippers, but with a very good "Dry Lustau" range (particularly the OLOROSO) and "Jerez Lustau" PALO CORTADO. Also shippers of excellent ALMACENISTA and "landed age" wines.

Macharnudo One of the best parts of the sherry v'yds, n. of Jerez, famous for wines of the highest quality, both FINO and OLOROSO.

Malmsey The sweetest form of madeira; dark amber, rich and honeyed yet with madeira's unique sharp tang.

Manzanilla Sherry, normally FINO, which has acquired a peculiar bracing salty character from being kept in bodegas at Sanlucar de Barrameda, on the Guadalquivir estuary near JEREZ.

Manzilla Pasada A mature MANZILLA half-way to an amontillado-style wine.

Morgan A subsidiary of CROFT port, best known in France.

Offley Forester See Forester.

Oloroso Style of sherry, heavier and less brilliant than FINO when young, but maturing to greater richness and pungency. Naturally dry, but generally sweetened for sale, as CREAM.

Osborne Well-known brandy but also good sherries include Fino Quinta, Coquinero, dry AMONTILLADO, 10 R.F. Oloroso.

Pale Cream Increasingly popular style of sherry made by sweetening FINO, pioneered by CROFTS "Original".

Palo Cortado A style of sherry close to OLOROSO but with some of the character of an AMONTILLADO. Dry but rich and soft. Not often seen.

Palomino & Vergara Sherry shippers of JEREZ bought in 1986 by HARVEY'S, best known for Palomino Cream, Medium and Dry. Best FINO: Tio Mateo.

Ponche An aromatic digestif made with old sherry and brandy, flavoured with herbs and orange, and presented in eye-catching silvered bottles. See Caballero and De Soto.

Puerto de Santa Maria Second city of the sherry area, with important bodegas.

P.X. Short for Pedro Ximénez, the grape part-dried in the sun used in JEREZ for sweetening blends.

Quarles Harris One of the oldest port houses, since 1680, now owned by the Symingtons (see Dow). Small quantities of L.B.V. mellow and well-balanced. Vintages: **60** 63 66 70 **75** 77 **80** 83 85.

Quinta Portuguese for "estate".

Quinta do Côtto Single vineyard port from Miguel Champalimaud, best-known of a new association of grower-bottlers. V.g. vintage '82.

Quinta do Noval Great Portuguese port house making intensely fruity, structured and elegant vintage port; a few pre-phylloxera vines still at the Quinta make a small quantity of "Nacional" – very dark, full and slow-maturing wine. Also v.g. 20-year-old Tawny. Vintages: 55 **58** 60 63 66 **67** 70 75 78 82 83 85.

Rainwater A fairly light, not very sweet blend of madeira – in fact of VERDELHO wine – traditionally popular in N. America.

Real Tesoro, Marqués de One of the smaller family firms of JEREZ, with excellent MANZANILLA La Bailadora and a range of good sherries, esp. their AMONTILLADO.

Rebello Valente Name used for the vintage port of ROBERTSON. Their vintage wines are light but elegant and well-balanced, maturing rather early. Vintages: **55 60 63 66 67** 70 72 **75 77** 80 83 85.

La Riva Distinguished firm of sherry shippers making one of the best FINOS, Tres Palmas, among many good wines.

Rivero, J.M. The famous "C.Z." brand of the oldest sherry house now belongs to Antonio Niñez who makes and markets Rivero sherries as well as his own.

Passing the Port
Vintage port is almost as much a ritual as a drink. It always needs to be decanted with great care (since the method of making it leaves a heavy deposit in the bottle). The simplest and surest way of doing this is by filtering it through clean muslin or a coffee filter-paper into either a decanter or a well-rinsed bottle. All except very old ports can safely be decanted the day before drinking. At table the decanter is traditionally passed from guest to guest clockwise. Vintage port can be immensely long-lived. Particularly good vintages older than those mentioned in the text include 1950, '48, '45, '35, '34, '27, '20, '11, '08, '04.

Robertson Subsidiary of SANDEMAN, shipping REBELLO VALENTE vintage and L.B.V. and Robertson's Privateer Reserve, 10-year-old Pyramid and 20-year-old Imperial.

Rozes Port shippers controlled by Moët-Hennessy. Tawny very popular in France; also Ruby. Vintages: **63 67** 77 78 81 83 85.

Ruby The youngest (and cheapest) style of port: very sweet and red. The best are vigorous and full of flavour. Others can be merely strong and rather thin.

Rutherford & Miles Madeira shippers with one of the best known of all Bual wines: Old Trinity House. Also Old Custom House Sercial and Old Artillery House Malmsey.

Sanchez Romate Family firm in JEREZ since 1781. Best known in Spanish-speaking world esp. for their brandy, Cardinal Mendoza. Makes good sherry – Fino Cristal, Oloroso Don Antonio, Amontillado N.P.U. ("Non Plus Ultra").

Sandeman Giant of the port trade and a major figure in the sherry one, owned by Seagrams. Founder's Reserve is their well-known vintage character; their vintage wines are robust – some of the old vintages were superlative (**55 60 63 66 67** 70 75 77 **80 82 85**). Of the sherries, Medium Dry Amontillado is best-seller, Don Fino is v.g. and a new range of wonderful luxury dry old sherries incl. Royal Ambrosante, Imperial Corregidor, Character Oloroso, etc. Not to be missed.

Sanlucar Seaside sherry-town (see Manzanilla).

Sercial Grape (reputedly a RIESLING) grown in Madeira to make the driest of the island's wines – a good apéritif.

Smith Woodhouse Port firm founded in 1784, now owned by the Symington family (see Dow). GOULD CAMPBELL is a subsidiary. Wines incl. His Majesty's Choice 20-year-old, Old Lodge Tawny **60 70 75** 77 80 83 85.

Solera System used in making both sherry and (in modified form) madeira, also some port. It consists of topping up progressively more mature barrels with slightly younger wine of the same sort: the object to attain continuity in the final wine. Most commercial sherries are blends of several solera wines.

Soto, José de Best-known for inventing PONCHE, this family firm also makes a range of excellent sherries.

Tarquinio Lomelino Madeira shippers famous for their collection of antique wines. Standard range is Don Henriques; top range, "Lomelino".

Tawny A style of port aged for many years in wood (in contrast to vintage port, which is aged in bottle) until tawny in colour. Low-price tawnies are blends of red and white ports. Taste the difference.

Taylor Perhaps the best port shippers, particularly for their full, rich, long-lived vintage wine and tawnies of stated age (40-year-old, 20-year-old, etc.). Their Quinta de Vargellas is said to give Taylor's its distinctive scent of violets. Vintages: **55 60 63 66 70 75 77 80 83 85**. Vargellas is shipped unblended in certain (lesser) vintages (**67 72 74 76 78**). Their L.B.V. is also better than most.

Terry, Fernando A. de Bodega at PUERTO DE SANTA MARIA with a good range of sherries (and famous brandies), bought in 1986 by HARVEY'S.

Tio Pepe The most famous of FINO sherries (see Gonzalez Byass).

Valdespino Famous family-owned bodega at JEREZ, owner of the Inocente v'yd, making the excellent FINO of the same name. Tio Diego is their splendid dry AMONTILLADO, Solera 1842 a ditto oloroso, Matador the name of their popular range.

Varela Sherry shippers best known for their Medium and Cream.

Verdelho Madeira grape making fairly dry wine without the distinction of SERCIAL. A pleasant apéritif. Some fine old vintage wines.

Vintage Port The best port of exceptional vintages is bottled after only 2 years in wood and matures very slowly, for up to 20 years or even more, in its bottle. It always leaves a heavy deposit and therefore needs decanting.

Vintage Character Somewhat misleading term used for a good-quality full and meaty port like a first-class RUBY made by the solera system. Lacks the splendid "nose" of vintage port.

Warre Probably the oldest of all port shippers (since 1670), now owned by the Symington family (see Dow). Fine long-maturing vintage wines, a good TAWNY, Nimrod and Vintage Character Warrior. Their single-v'yd Quinta da Cavadinha is a new departure. Vintages: **55 58 60 63 66 70 75 77 80 83 85**

White Port Port made of white grapes, golden in colour. Formerly made sweet, now more often dry: a good apéritif but a heavy one.

Williams & Humbert Famous and first-class sherry bodega, recently bought by Antonio Barbadillo. Dry Sack (medium AMONTILLADO) is their best-selling wine. Pando is an excellent FINO. Canasta Cream and Walnut Brown are good in their class. Dos Cortados is their famous PALO CORTADO.

Masters of Wine

The Institute of Masters of Wine was founded in London in 1953 to provide an exacting standard of qualification for the British wine trade. A small minority pass its very stiff examinations, even after rigorous training, both theoretical and practical. (They must be able to identify wines "blind", know how they are made, and also know the relevant EEC and Customs regulations). In all, only 130 people have qualified to become Masters of Wine. Fourteen "Masters" are women.

In 1988 the Institute, aided by a grant from the Madame Bollinger Foundation, opened its examinations for the first time to non-British candidates. "Master of Wine" (or M.W.) should eventually become the equivalent of a Bachelor of Arts degree in the worldwide wine trade.

England

The English wine industry started again in earnest in the late 1960s after a pause of some 400 years. Well over a million bottles a year are now being made from over 1,200 acres; almost all white and generally Germanic in style, many from new German and French grape varieties designed to ripen well in cool weather. Natural acidity is high, which means that good examples have a built-in ability (and need) to age. Four years is a good age for many, and up to ten for some. Mature wines can be really excellent. The annual Gore-Brown Trophy is a awarded for the best English wine. N.B. Beware "British Wine", which is neither British nor wine, and has nothing to do with the following.

Adgestone nr. Sandown, Isle of Wight.
> Prize-winning 8½-acre v'yd on chalky hill site. Vines are MÜLLER-THURGAU, Reichensteiner, SEYVAL BLANC. First vintage 1970. Light, fragrant, dryish wines age exceedingly well.

Astley Stourport-on-Severn, Worcestershire.
> 4 acres producing good KERNER. Won prizes for its '85s.

Barkham Manor Vineyard Uckfield, Sussex.
> 23 acres of MÜLLER-THURGAU, KERNER etc.

Barnsgate Manor nr. Uckfield, Sussex.
> A showpiece 21 acres of MÜLLER-THURGAU, Reichensteiner, KERNER, Seyval, P NOIR, CHARD.

Barton Manor East Cowes, Isle of Wight.
> 10-acre v'yd producing an aromatic medium-dry blend, regular prize-winner. Consistently good.

Beaulieu nr. Lymington, Hampshire.
> 6-acre v'yd, principally of MÜLLER-THURGAU established in 1960 by the Gore-Brown family on an old monastic site.

Biddenden nr. Tenterden, Kent.
> 22-acre mixed v'yd planted in 1970, making crisp medium-dry white of MÜLLER-THURGAU and Ortega; also a rosé with PINOT NOIR. Also makes wine for other growers. Gold medal winner in 1983 and 1986.

Bosmere nr. Chippenham, Wiltshire.
> 16 acres of MÜLLER-THURGAU and SEYVAL BLANC; GAMAY and PINOT NOIR.

Bothy Vineyard Abingdon, Oxfordshire.
> 3-acre v'yd producing two wines since 1983.

Breaky Bottom nr. Lewes, Sussex.
> Good dry wines from 4-acre vineyard.

Broadfield Bodenham, Herefordshire.
> 10-acre vineyard producing wines sold under Bodenham label.

Bruisyard nr. Saxmundham, Suffolk.
> 10 acres of MÜLLER-THURGAU making medium-dry wines since 1976.

Carr Taylor Vineyards nr. Hastings, Sussex.
> 21 acres, planted 1974. Gutenborner, Huxelrebe, KERNER and Reichensteiner. Also a KERNER/Reichenstiener méthode champenoise. Exports to France.

Cavendish Manor nr. Sudbury, Suffolk.
> 10½-acre v'yd of MÜLLER-THURGAU planted on a farm. Fruity dry wine has won several awards at home and abroad since 1974.

Chalkhill Bowerchalke, Wiltshire.
> 6½-acre vineyard producing range of impressive wines. The wine-maker, Mark Thompson, advises the WELLOW vineyard in Hampshire.

Chilford Hundred Linton, nr. Cambridge.

18 acres of MÜLLER-THURGAU, Schönburger, Huxelrebe, Siegerrebe and Ortega making fairly dry wines since 1974.

Chilsdown nr. Chichester, Sussex.

10 acres of MÜLLER-THURGAU, Reichensteiner and SEYVAL BLANC making full dry French-style white since 1974.

Chiltern Valley Wines Henley-on-Thames, Oxfordshire.

Small, modern winery drawing on 3 acres of own v'yds and neighbouring growers; producing four white wines. Gold medal winner in 1988. Impressive quality.

Cranmore Cranmore, Isle of Wight.

12-acre vineyard planted with MÜLLER-THURGAU and GUTENBORNER.

Ditchling nr. Hassocks, Sussex.

5-acre v'yd well reputed for consistency. Good MÜLLER-THURGAU.

Downers Vineyard Henfield, Sussex.

6 acres of MÜLLER-THURGAU, planted 1976.

Elmham Park nr. East Dereham, Norfolk.

3-acre v'yd of a wine-merchant/fruit farmer, planted with MÜLLER-THURGAU, Madeleine-Angevine, etc. "Mosel-style" light, dry, flowery wines. First vintage 1974. Also a fine dry cider.

Felsted (formerly Felstar) Felsted, Essex.

A pioneer 10½-acre v'yd planted 1966. MÜLLER-THURGAU, Seyval, P NOIR, Madeleine-Angevine. The CHARD/SEYVAL BLANC blend is notable.

Gamlingay nr. Sandy, Bedfordshire.

8½ acres of MÜLLER-THURGAU, Reichensteiner and SCHEUREBE since 1970.

Great Shoesmiths Farm Wadhurst, Sussex.

17 acres planted with Regner, Huxelrebe, KERNER, Schönberger, SEYVAL BLANC and MÜLLER-THURGAU.

Hambledon nr. Petersfield, Hampshire.

The first modern English v'yd, planted in 1951 on a chalk slope with advice from Champagne. Grapes are CHARDONNAY, PINOT NOIR and SEYVAL BLANC. Now 7½ acres. Fairly dry wines.

Harden Farm Penshurst, Kent.

18 acres of Schönburger, Bacchus, Reichensteiner, Regner and Huxelrebe.

Highwaymans nr. Bury St Edmunds, Suffolk.

25 acres, planted 1974. MÜLLER-THURGAU and PINOT NOIR.

Lamberhurst Priory nr. Tunbridge Wells, Kent.

England's biggest producing v'yd with 55 acres, planted 1972. Largely MÜLLER-THURGAU, SEYVAL BLANC, also Reichensteiner, Schönburger. Their Huxelrebe Dry 1986 was awarded high marks at a recent international tasting. Production capacity approx. half a million bottles a year including winemaking for other small v'yds. Also makes Horam Manor, 8 acres at Heathfield, Sussex. A regular prize-winner.

Leeford Vineyards nr. Battle, Sussex.

17-acre vineyard producing wines under Saxon Valley label.

Lexham Hall nr. King's Lynn, Norfolk.

8-acres, planted 1975. MÜLLER-THURGAU, SCHEUREBE, Reichensteiner and Madeleine-Angevine.

New Hall nr. Maldon, Essex.

29½ acres of a mixed farm planted with Huxelrebe, MÜLLER-THURGAU and PINOT NOIR. Makes award-winning whites. Experimental reds.

Nutbourne Manor nr. Pulborough, Sussex.

14 acres producing elegant and tasty Schönburger, Bacchus and Huxelrebe.

Penshurst nr. Tunbridge Wells, Kent.

12 acres of the usual varieties in production since 1976.

Pilton Manor nr. Shepton Mallet, Somerset.

22-acre hillside v'yd, chiefly of MÜLLER-THURGAU and SEYVAL BLANC, planted 1966. Also méthode champenoise sp.

Pulham nr. Norwich, Norfolk.

6-acre v'yd planted 1973; principally MÜLLER-THURGAU, Auxerrois and experimental Bacchus. Award-winning wines using the Magdalen label.

Rock Lodge nr. Haywards Heath, Sussex.

7-acre v'yd of MÜLLER-THURGAU and Reichensteiner making dry white since 1970.

St Etheldreda nr. Ely, Cambridgeshire.

2-acre mixed v'yd making a MÜLLER-THURGAU and a CHARDONNAY since 1974.

St George's Waldron, Heathfield, E. Sussex.

20 acres planted 1979. MÜLLER-THURGAU etc. and some GEWÜRZ. Well-publicized young venture has sold wine to Japan, etc.

Sedlescombe Robertsbridge, Sussex.

10 acres which claims to be England's first organic vineyard.

Stanlake Park Twyford, Berkshire.

17-acre vineyard of MÜLLER-THURGAU, PINOT NOIR, Schönburger etc.

Staple nr. Canterbury, Kent.

7 acres, mainly MÜLLER-THURGAU. Some Huxelrebe and Reichensteiner. Dry and fruity wines.

Stocks nr. Suckley, Worcestershire.

Successful 11-acre v'yd. All MÜLLER-THURGAU.

Tenterden nr. Tenterden, Kent.

18 acres of a 100-acre fruit farm. Planted 1977. Six wines from very dry to sweet, incl. MÜLLER-THURGAU, SEYVAL BLANC and rosé.

Three Choirs nr. Newent, Gloucestershire.

20 acres of MÜLLER-THURGAU and Reichensteiner.

Wellow nr. Romsey, Hampshire.

Ambitious new venture which at 80 acres is England's biggest. 12 varieties, incl. CHARDONNAY, predominantly MÜLLER-THURGAU and BACCHUS. First (2,000 bottles) vintage 1987. Successful wines include a Late Harvest Huxelrebe. Expects 100 acres to be planted by 1992.

Westbury nr. Reading, Berkshire.

12½ acres of a mixed farm. 11 varieties in commercial quantities since 1975, incl. England's only real PINOT NOIR red. MÜLLER-THURGAU-SEYVAL 1982 awarded gold medal.

Wootton nr. Wells, Somerset.

6-acre v'yd of Schönburger, MÜLLER-THURGAU, SEYVAL BLANC, etc., making award-winning fresh and fruity wines since 1973.

Wraxall nr. Shepton Mallet, Somerset.

6 acres of MÜLLER-THURGAU and SEYVAL BLANC. Planted 1974.

Not too Strong

The current trend towards "low-alcohol" wines and beers, from which most alcohol has been removed by artificial means, should be a golden opportunity for the producers of wines that are naturally lower in alcohol than the 12 or 13 degrees expected in most table wines. Germany is the prime example. England is another. Their best wines with plenty of fruity acidity do not need high alcohol to make an impact. They are today's logical choice.

Central &
South-East Europe

LANGENLOIS   WEINVIERTEL
WACHAU   Vienna
MATRAA
Austria   SOMLÓ
SOPRON   Budapest
BURGENLAND
Graz   Hungary
STYRIA   BALATON
LUTOMER   VILLÁNYI-PÉCS
Ljubljana
Italy   SLAVONIA
SLOVENIA   VOJVODIN
Trieste   Zagreb
CROATIA
BOSNIA-HERZEGOVINA
Yugoslavia
DALMATIA   Sarajevo
Adriatic Sea   Split
MONTENEG
Dubrovnik

The countries covered by this map, on both sides of the Iron
Curtain, offer some very good value for money, complete with
off-the-beaten-track characters which true wine-lovers will
enjoy exploring. The range of quality widens as (e.g.) Bulgaria
develops and Romania totters. Greece has a lot of revision to do.

The references are arranged country by country, with all
geographical references back to the map on this page.

Labelling in all the countries involved, except Greece and
Cyprus is broadly based on the now international, pattern of
place-name plus grape-variety. The main grape-varieties are
therefore included alongside areas and other terms in the
alphabetical listings. Quality ratings in this section are given
where experience justifies more than a single, everyday, star.

Austria

A run of small harvests, and thus low exports, have obscured to
the outside world the progress made by Austria since the
scandal of 1985. New legislation should now ensure that nothing
of the kind happens again. The laws include curbs on yields
(Germany please copy) and impose higher levels of ripeness for
each category than their German counterparts. Many regional
names, introduced under the 1986 law, will still be unfamiliar
to international consumers. 1988's decent-sized crop gives
exporters a new impetus.

Recent vintages:

1988 Good quantity, some excellent wines.
1987 A third small harvest, but quality is good.
1986 An outstanding vintage in most cases, though small.
1985 A small but excellent-quality harvest.
1984 Good wines for early drinking.
1983 Outstandingly ripe; many sweet wines though some are low in acidity.

Apetlon Burgenland (r.) w. s./sw. or sw. ★→ ▮▮
  Village of the SEEWINKEL making good whites and some reds on sandy
  soil, incl. very good sweet wines, esp. Prädikat wines from SEPP
  MOSER.
Ausbruch Term used for very sweet wines between Beerenauslese and
  Trockenbeerenauslese (see Germany) in richness.
Baden Vienna (r.) w. dr. or sw. ★→★★★
  Town and wine region S. of VIENNA incl. GUMPOLDSKIRCHEN. Some good
  lively high-flavoured wines, whites best from ROTGIPFLER and ZIERF-
  ÄNDLER grapes.
Blaufränkisch Reputedly the GAMAY grape; gives adequate reds.
  Kékfrankos in Hungary.
Bouvier Native Austrian grape giving soft but aromatic wine esp. for
  Beerenauslese and Trockenbeerenauslese.
Burgenland Burgenland r. w. dr. sw. ★→ ▮▮▮
  Region on the Hungarian border with ideal conditions for sweet wines
  and 45,000 acres. Four wine-regions: NEUSIEDLERSEE (e. of the lake),
  Neusiedlersee-Hügelland (w. shore and around EISENSTADT) and
  Mittel- and Südburgenland. "Noble rot" occurs regularly and
  AUSBRUCH, Beerenausleses, etc., are abundant. (See Oggau, Rust, etc.)
Donauland-Carnuntum Unwieldly new name for Danube (Donau) valley
  wine region incl. KLOSTERNEUBURG.
Dürnstein w. dr. sw. ★★→★★★
  Wine centre of the WACHAU with a famous ruined castle and the
  important WINZERGENOSSENSCHAFT WACHAU. Some of Austria's best
  whites, esp. Rheinriesling and GRÜNER VELTLINER.
Eisenberg Old name for the Südbergenland.
Eisenstadt Burgenland (r.) w. dr. or sw. ★★→★★★
  Capital of BURGENLAND and historic seat of the ESTERHAZY.
Esterházy Noble and historic family (patrons of Haydn) whose AUSBRUCH
  and other BURGENLAND wines are often of superlative quality.
Falkenstein See Weinviertel.
Grinzing Vienna w. ★★ D.Y.A.
  Suburb of VIENNA with delicious lively HEURIGE wines.
Grüner Veltliner Austria's most characteristic white grape (32% of her
  white v'yds) making short-lived but marvellously spicy and flowery,
  racy and vital wine – ideal HEURIGE, in fact.

Gumpoldskirchen Vienna (r.) w. dr. or sw. ★★→★★★
Pretty resort s. of VIENNA with wines of great character from ROTGIPFLER and ZIERFÄNDLER grapes. See Thermenregion.

Heiligenkreuz, Stift Cistercian Monastery at THALLERN making some of Austria's best wine, particularly RIESLING from a fine steep v'yd: Wiege.

Heurige Means both new wine and the tavern where it is drunk.

Kahlenberg Vienna w. ★★→★★★
Village and v'yd hill n. of VIENNA, famous for HEURIGEN.

Kamptal-Donauland (r.) w. dr. or sw. ★→★★
Wine region around KREMS and the Kamp valley, a tributary of the Danube (Donau), with pleasant Veltliner (see Grüner Veltliner) and RIESLING.

Klöch Steiermark (r.) p. w. ★→★★
The chief wine town of Styria, the s.e. province. No famous wines, but several agreeable ones, esp. Traminer.

Klosterneuburg Danube r. w. ★→★★★
District just n. of VIENNA, with a famous monastery, which is a major producer, a wine college and a research station.

Kloster Und New wine college and tasting centre in restored Capuchin monastery at KREMS.

Krems Danube w. ★→★★★
Town and district just e. of the WACHAU with good GRÜNER VELTLINER and Rheinriesling (see Riesling) esp. from Austria's biggest WINZER-GENOSSENSCHAFT.

Langenlois Langenlois r. w. ★→★★
Chief town of the KAMPTAL with many modest and some good wines, esp. peppery GRÜNER VELTLINER and Rheinriesling (see Riesling) from its loess soil. Reds less interesting.

Lenz Moser Major wine grower, recently purchased by a big retail chain. Invented a high vine system amd makes good to excellent wine at Röhrendorf near KREMS, APETLON and elsewhere. Owns the Schlossweingut Malteser Ritterorden (formerly the estate of the Knight of Malta) at MAILBERG. Experiments with CAB SAUV, MERLOT and P NOIR. Took over SIEGENDORF in 1988.

Mailberg Weinviertel w. ★★
Town of the WEINVIERTEL known for lively light wine.

Mörbisch Burgenland r. w. dr. or sw. ★→ ███ ★★★
Leading wine-village of BURGENLAND. Good sweet wines. Reds and dry whites not inspiring.

Müller-Thurgau Far less interesting than GRÜNER VELTLINER, represents 10% of all Austria's vines.

Muskat-Ottonel The strain of muscat grape grown in e. Europe, incl. Austria. Can be dry and pungent.

Neuberger Popular white grape: pleasant wine in KREMS/LANGENLOIS but soft and coarse in BURGENLAND.

Neusiedlersee A broad shallow lake in flat sandy country on the Hungarian border, creating autumn mists and giving character to the sweet wines of BURGENLAND. Under the new law, centre of two wine regions: see Burgenland.

Niederösterreich Lower Austria: i.e. all the n.e. corner of the country, with 5 wine regions: DONAULAND-CARUNTUM, KAMPTAL-DONAULAND, WACHAU, WEINVIERTEL.

Nussdorf Vienna w. ★★
Suburb of VIENNA with well-known HEURIGEN.

Oggau Burgenland (r.) w. sw. ★★→ ███ ★★★
One of the wine-centres of BURGENLAND, famous for Beerenausleses (see Germany) and AUSBRUCH.

Portugieser With BLAUFRANKISCH, one of the two main red-wine grapes of Austria, giving dark but rather characterless wine.

146

Retz Weinviertel (r.) w. ★

Leading wine-centre of the WEINVIERTEL, known for pleasant GRÜNER VELTLINER, etc.

Ried Single vineyard: when named on the label it is usually a good one.

Riesling When used alone is German Riesling. Wälschriesling, which is always inferior, is labelled as such.

Rotgipfler Good and high-flavoured grape peculiar to BADEN and GUMPOLDSKIRCHEN. Used with ZIERFANDLER to make powerful but lively whites. Very heavy/sweet on its own.

Rust Burgenland (r.) w. dr. or sw. ★→★★★

Most famous wine centre of BURGENLAND, long and justly famous for its AUSBRUCH, often made of mixed grapes.

St-Laurent Traditional Austrian red grape, faintly muscat-flavoured.

Saloman, Fritz ★★→★★★★

Top grower of oak-aged RIESLING and Gewürztraminer at Weinkelleri Undhof in the Danube valley near KREMS.

Schilcher Pleasant sharp rosé, a speciality of STYRIA.

Schloss Grafenegg w. dr./sw. ★★→★★★★

Famous castle and estate of the Metternich family near KREMS. Good standard whites and excellent Ausleses, some dry (trocken).

Seewinkel "Sea corner": the sandy district around the NEUSIEDLERSEE.

Sepp Hold Well-known BURGENLAND grower and merchant.

Siegendorf, Klosterkeller First-class 50 acre BURGENLAND wine estate experimenting with CAB SAUV and MERLOT.

Sievering Vienna w. ★★

Picturesque suburb of VIENNA with notable HEURIGEN.

Spätrot Another name for the ZIERFANDLER grape.

Spitzenwein Top wines – as opposed to TISCHWEIN: ordinary table wines.

Steiermark (Styria) Province in the s.e., not remarkable for wine but well supplied with it. Three wine regions: Süd (south), Süd-Ost (south-east) and West-Steirmark. Sauvignon Blanc showing promise here. See Klöch.

Stift The word for a monastery. Monasteries have been, and still are, very important in Austria's wine-making, combining tradition and high standards with modern resources.

Südbergenland Wine region in south of Burgenland, away from the lake. Some steep slopes. Grapes include RIESLING and Blauburgunder.

Thallern Vienna (r.) w. dr. or sw. ★★→★★★★

Village near GUMPOLDSKIRCHEN and trade-name of wines from Stift HEILIGENKREUZ.

Thermenregion New name for region s. of VIENNA, incl. GUMPOLDSKIRCHEN.

Tischwein Everyday wine, as opposed to SPITZENWEIN.

Traiskirchen Vienna (r.) w. ★★

Village near GUMPOLDSKIRCHEN with similar wine.

Veltliner See Grüner Veltliner.

Vöslau Baden r. (w.) ★

Spa town s. of BADEN (and WIEN) known for its reds made of PORTUGIESER and BLAUFRANKISCH: refreshing but no more.

Wachau Wine region on the bank s. of the Danube round DÜRNSTEIN with cliff-like slopes giving some of Austria's best whites, esp. Rheinriesling (see Riesling) and GRÜNER VELTLINER.

Weinviertel "The wine quarter": name given to the huge and productive district between VIENNA and Czech border. Mainly light white wines. Formerly divided into Falkenstein-Matzen (east) and Retz (west).

Wien (Vienna) The capital city, with 1,800 acres of v'yds in its suburbs to supply its cafés and HEURIGEN.

Weissburgunder Alias Pinot Blanc. Increasingly for solid, often dry wines.

Winzergenossenschaft Growers' cooperative.

Zierfändler White grape of high flavour peculiar to the BADEN area. Used in a blend with ROTGIPFLER.

Hungary

The traditional and characteristic firmness and strength of character which used to make Hungarian wine the most exciting of Eastern Europe have been modified by modern ideas. Average quality is still high; whites are generally lively and at least some reds made to last, but much of the drama has gone at least from the standard exported lines. Foreign buyers seem frightened of real character. Visitors to the country will find plenty of excellent wines in the old style. They are distinguished by numbered bottles (and higher prices).

Alföld Hungary's Great Plain, producer of much everyday wine. See also Hajós.

Aszú Word meaning "shrivelled" applied to very sweet wines, esp. Tokay (TOKAJI), where the "aszú" is late-picked and "nobly rotten" as in Sauternes. (See p. 49)

Aszú Eszencia Tokaji br. sw. ★★★★
The highest quality of Tokay commercially available: superb amber wine of Yquem-like quality.

Badacsony Balaton w. dr. sw. ★★→★★★
Famous 1,400 ft. hill on the n. shore of Lake BALATON whose basalt soil can give rich high-flavoured white wines, among Hungary's best.

Balatonfüred Balaton (r.) w. dr. sw. ★★
Town on the n. shore of Lake BALATON, centre of the Balatonfüred-Csopak district. Good but softer, less fiery wines.

Balaton Balaton r. w. dr. sw. ★
Hungary's inland sea and Europe's largest lake. Many wines take its name and most are good. The ending "i" (e.g. Balatoni, Egri) is the equivalent of -er in Londoner.

Bikavér Eger r. ★
"Bulls Blood". The historic name of the best-selling red wine of EGER: formerly full-bodied and well-balanced, but disconcertingly variable in its export version today.

Csopak Village next to BALATONFÜRED, with similar wines but drier.

Debrö Mátraalya w. sw. ★★
Important centre of the MATRAALYA famous for its pale, aromatic and sweet HARSLEVELÜ.

Eger Eger district r. w. dr. sw. ★→★★
Best-known red wine centre of n. Hungary; fine baroque city of cellars full of BIKAVER. Also delicate white LEANYKA (perhaps its best product today) TRAMINI and dark sweetish MEDOC NOIR.

Eszencia The fabulous quintessence of Tokay (TOKAJI): intensely sweet grape-juice of very low, if any, alcoholic strength, reputed to have miraculous properties. Now almost unobtainable.

Ezerjó The grape grown at MOR to make one of Hungary's best dry white wines: potentially distinguished, fragrant and fine.

Furmint The classic grape of Tokay (TOKAJI), with great flavour and fire, also grown for table wine on Lake BALATON, sometimes with excellent results.

Hajós Alföld r. ★
Village in s. Hungary known as a centre for good lively CAB SAUV reds of medium body and ageing potential. Also a good PINOT NOIR.

Hárslevelü The "lime-leaved" grape used at DEBRO and as the second main grape of TOKAJI. Gentle sweet wine.

Hungarovin Largest wine traders with huge cellars at Budafok near Budapest.

Kadarka The commonest red grape of Hungary, grown in vast quantities for light everyday wine on the plains in the s.; capable (e.g. at SZEKSZARD and VILLANY) of ample flavour and interesting maturity.

Kékfrankos Hungarian for Blaufränkisch; reputedly related to Gamay. Makes good light and full-bodied reds at SOPRON on the Austrian border and goes into "Bulls Blood" at EGER.

Kéknyelü High-flavoured white grape making the best and "stiffest" wine of Mt. BADACSONY. It should be fiery and spicy stuff, like a distant cousin to Pinot Gris from Alsace.

Különleges Minöség Special vintage. Wines generally worth trying.

Leányka Old Hungarian white grape also grown in Transylvania. Makes admirable pale soft dry wine at EGER.

Mátraalja Wine-district in the foothills of the Mátra range in n. Hungary, incl. DEBRO, GYONGYOS and NAGYREDE.

Mecsekalja District in the foothills of the Mecsek range in s. Hungary, known for the good whites of PECS.

Médoc Noir Grape apparently similar to MERLOT, used to make sweet red and in the blend of BIKAVER, at EGER.

Monimpex The main Hungarian wine-export company.

Mór North Hungary w. dr. ★★
Town in n. Hungary famous for its fresh dry EZERJO.

Muskotály Makes light though long-lived Muscat wine at Tokay (TOKAJI) and EGER. Very occasionally made ASZU at Tokay.

Nagyburgundi Literally "great burgundy" – an indigenous grape and not P NOIR as sometimes thought. Makes sound solid wine in s. Hungary, esp. round VILLANY and SZEKSZARD.

Olaszrizling The Hungarian name for the Italian, or Welschriesling.

Pécs Mecsek (r.) w. dr. ■ →★★
Town in the Mecsek hills known in the West for its agreeable well-balanced (if rather sweet) OLASZRIZLING.

Puttonyos The measure of sweetness in Tokay (TOKAJI). A 7-gal. container from which ASZU is added to SZAMORODNI. One "putt" makes it sweetish; 6 (the maximum) very sweet indeed. Each "putt" is a 20-25 kilo hod of ASZU grapes added to 136 litres of base wine. The minimum now made is 3 putts, the maximum 6.

Sauvignon Blanc A stranger in Hungary, but recent results at BALATON have been impressive – with plenty of Hungarian vigour.

Siklos Southern district known for its white wines.

Siller Pale red or rosé. Usually made from KADARKA or KEKFRANKOS grapes.

Somló North Hungary w. dr. ★★
Isolated small v'yd district n. of BALATON making white wines formerly of high repute from FURMINT.

Sopron West Hungary r. ★★
Little Hungarian enclave in Burgenland s. of the Neusiedlersee (see Austria) specializing in light KEKFRANKOS reds and some Austrian-style sweet whites.

Szamorodni Word meaning "as it comes"; used to describe TOKAJI without the addition of ASZU grapes. Can be dry or (fairly) sweet depending upon the proportion of ASZU grapes naturally present.

Szürkebarát Literally means "grey friar": Hungarian for PINOT GRIS, which makes rich (not nec. sweet) heavy wine in the BADACSONY v'yds.

Szekszárd r. ■
District in south-central Hungary. Dark strong KADARKA red wine which needs age (say 3-4 years).

Tokaji (Tokay) Tokaji w. dr. sw. ■ →★★★★
The ASZU is Hungary's famous strong sweet wine, comparable to a maderized Sauternes, from hills in the n.e. close to the Soviet Union. See Aszu, Eszencia, Furmint, Puttonyos, Szamorodni.

Tramini The TRAMINER grape; increasingly grown in Hungary.

Villány Siklos r. p. (w.) ■
Southernmost town of Hungary and well-known centre of red wine production. Villnyi Burgundi is largely KEKFRANKOS and rather good. See also Nagyburgundi.

Welschriesling Austrian name sometimes used for Olasz (Italian) Rizling.

Romania

The wine industry is orientated towards Russia as its biggest customer, and consequently specializes in the sweet wines that Russians like. Recent Soviet moves to discourage drinking threaten this trade. The need for foreign currency makes export to the West highly desirable, so the best qualities are available at subsidized prices. They include sound and cheap reds and whites, including dry ones, but at present nothing memorable.

Alba Iulia Town in the TIRNAVE area in Transylvania, known for off-dry whites blended from Italian RIESLING, FETEASCA and MUSKAT-OTTONEL.

Aligoté The junior white burgundy grape makes pleasantly fresh white wine in Romania.

Babeasca Traditional red grape of the FOCSANI area: agreeably sharp wine tasting slightly of cloves.

Banat The plain on the border with Serbia. Workaday Italian RIESLING and light red CADARCA.

Cabernet Increasingly grown, particularly at DEALUL MARE, to make dark intense wines, though often too sweet for Western palates.

Cadarca Romanian spelling of the Hungarian Kadarka.

Chardonnay Used at MURFATLAR to make sweet dessert wine.

Cotesti Part of the FOCSANI area making reds of PINOT NOIR, MERLOT, etc., and dry whites claimed to resemble Alsace wines.

Cotnari Romania's most famous historical wine but rarely seen: light dessert wine from MOLDAVIA. Rather like very delicate Tokay.

Dealul Mare Important up-to-date v'yd area in the s.e. Carpathian foothills. Red wines from CABERNET, MERLOT, PINOT NOIR, etc.

Dobruja Black Sea region round the port of Costanta. MURFATLAR is the main vineyard area.

Dragasani Region on the river Olt s. of the Carpathian Mts. Both traditional and "modern" grapes. Good MUSKAT-OTTONEL.

Feteasca Romanian white grape of mild character, the same as Hungary's Leanyka (and some say Switzerland's Chasselas).

Focsani Important eastern wine region including those of COTESTI, ODOBESTI and NICORESTI.

Grasa A form of the Hungarian Furmint grape grown in Romania and used in, among other wines, COTNARI.

Mehana Branded wines shipped to Britain, tending to sweetness.

Moldavia The n.e. province, now largely within the USSR.

Murfatlar Big modern v'yds near the Black Sea specializing in sweet wines, incl. CHARDONNAY. Now also dry reds and whites.

Muskat-Ottonel The e. European muscat, a speciality of Romania.

Nicoresti Eastern area of FOCSANI best known for its red BABEASCA.

Odobesti The central part of FOCSANI; mainly white wines of FETEASCA, Italian RIESLING, etc.

Oltenia Wine region including DRAGASANI. Sometimes also a brand name on labels.

Perla The speciality of TIRNAVE: a pleasant blended semi-sweet white of Italian RIESLING, FETEASCA and MUSKAT-OTTONEL.

Pitesti Principal town of the Arges region s. of the Carpathian Mtns. Traditionally whites from FETEASCA, TAMIIOASA, RIESLING.

Premiat Reliable range of higher-quality wines for export.

Riesling Italian Riesling. Very widely planted. No exceptional wines.

Sadova Town in the SEGARCEA area exporting a sweetish rosé.

Segarcea S. wine area near the Danube. Exports rather sweet CABERNET.

Tamîioasa Traditional white-wine grape variety of no very distinct character.

Tîrnave Important Transylvanian wine region, known for its PERLA and MUSKAT-OTTONEL.

Trakia Branded wines shipped to USA. Better judged for Western palates than most other Romanian wines.

Valea Calugareasca "The Valley of the Monks", part of the DEALUL MARE v'yd with a well-known research station. CABERNET, MERLOT and PINOT NOIR are generally made into heavy sweetish wines.

Yugoslavia

A well-established supplier of wines of international calibre if not generally exciting quality. Yugoslav "Riesling" was the pioneer, now followed by Cabernet, Pinot Blanc and Traminer, as well as such worthwhile specialities as Zilavka Plavać and Prokupać. All parts of the country except the central highlands make wine, almost entirely in giant cooperatives. Tourists on the Dalmatian coast and in Macedonia will find more original products all worth trying.

Amselfelder German marketing name for the Red Burgundac (Spätburgunder or PINOT NOIR) wine of KOSOVO. Disagreeably sweet.

Babic Standard red of the Dalmatian coast, ages better than ordinary PLAVAC.

Banat Sandy north-eastern area, partly in Romania, with up-to-date wineries making adequate RIESLING.

Beli Pinot The PINOT BLANC, a popular grape in SLOVENIA.

Bijelo White.

Blatina The red grape and wine of MOSTAR. Not in the same class as the white ZILAVKA.

Bogdanusa Local white grape of the Dalmatian islands, esp. Hvar and Brac. Pleasant refreshing faintly fragrant wine.

Burgundac Bijeli The CHARDONNAY, grown a little in SLAVONIA and VOJVODINA.

Cabernet Now introduced in many places with usually pleasant, occasionally exciting, results. See Kosovo.

Crno Black – i.e. red wine.

Cvićek Traditional pale red or dark rosé of the Sava valley, SLOVENIA.

Dalmaciajavino Important cooperative based at Split and selling a full range of Dalmatian coastal and island wines.

Dalmatia The middle coast of Yugoslavia from Rijeka to Dubrovnik. Has a remarkable variety of wines of character.

Dingac Heavy sweetish red from the local PLAVAC grape, speciality of the mid-Dalmatian coast.

Faros Substantial age-worthy PLAVAC red from the island of Hvar.

Fruska Gora Hills in VOJVODINA, on the Danube n.w. of Belgrade, with modern v'yds and a wide range of wines, incl. rather higher strength Traminer and Sauvignon Blanc.

Grasevina Slovenian for Italian Riesling (also called Wälschriesling, LASKI RIZLING, etc.). The normal Riesling of Yugoslavia.

Grk White grape, speciality of the island of Korcula, giving strong, even sherry-like wine (and also a lighter pale one).

Istria Peninsula in the n. Adriatic, Porec its centre, with a variety of pleasant wines, the MERLOT as good as any.

Jerusalem Yugoslavia's most famous v'yd, at LJUTOMER. Its best wines are late-picked RAJNSKI RIZLING, LASKI RIZLING.

Kadarka The major red grape of Hungary, widely grown in SERBIA.

Kosovo (or Kosmet) Region in the south between SERBIA and Macedonia, with modern v'yds. The source of AMSELFELDER and some lively CABERNET.

Kraski Means grown on the coastal limestone "karst" of SLOVENIA.

Laski Rizling Yet another name for Italian Riesling.

Ljutomer (or Lutomer)-Ormoz Yugoslavia's best known and probably best white-wine district, in n.e. SLOVENIA, famous for its LASKI RIZLING: full-flavoured, full-strength and at its best rich and satisfying wine. Export qualities can be variable.

Malvasia White grape giving luscious wine, used in W. SLOVENIA.

Maraština Strong dry white of the Dalmatian islands, best from Cara Smokviča on Hvar.

Maribor Important centre of n. SLOVENIA. White wines, mainly from VINAG, incl. LASKI RIZLING, RIESLING, SAUV BLANC, PINOT BLANC, TRAMINER.

Merlot Grown in SLOVENIA and ISTRIA with reasonable results.

Mostar Islamic-looking little city inland from DALMATIA, making admirable dry white from the ZILAVKA grape. Also BLATINA.

Muskat-Ottonel The East European muscat, grown in VOJVODINA.

Navip The big growers' cooperative of SERBIA, with its headquarters at Belgrade.

Opol Pleasantly light pale red made of PLAVAC grapes round Split and Sibenik in DALMATIA.

Plavać Mali Native red grape of SLOVENIA and DALMATIA; capable of great body and strength and ageing well. See Dingac, Postup, Opol, etc. Ordinary reds are often called "Plavać". There is also a white Plavać Beli.

Plavina Light red of the DALMATIAN coast round Zadar.

Plovdina Native red grape of Macedonia in the south, giving mild wine. Generally blended with tastier PROKUPAC.

Portugizac Austria's Portugieser: plain red wine.

Pošip Pleasant, not-too-heavy white wine of the Dalmatian islands, notably Korcula.

Postup Sweet and heavy DALMATIAN red from the Peljesać peninsula near Korcula. Highly esteemed locally.

Prokupać Principal native red grape of s. SERBIA and Macedonia: 85% of the production. Makes good dark rosé (RUZICA) and full-bodied red of character. Some of the best comes from ZUPA. PLOVDINA is often added for smoothness.

Prošek The dessert wine of DALMATIA, of stupefying natural strength but variable quality. The best is excellent, but hard to find.

Radgonska Ranina Ranina is Austria's BOUVIER grape (see Austria). Radgona is near MARIBOR. The wine is sweet and carries the trade name TIGROVO MLJEKO (Tiger's Milk).

Rajnski Rizling The Rhine Riesling, rare in Yugoslavia but grown a little in LJUTOMER-ORMOZ.

Refosco Italian grape grown in e. SLOVENIA and ISTRIA under the name TERAN.

Renski Rizling Alternative spelling for Rhine Riesling.

Riesling Used without qualification formerly meant Italian Riesling. Now legally limited to real Rhine Riesling.

Ruzića Rosé, usually from PROKUPAC. Darker than most; and better.

Serbia The e. state of Yugoslavia, with nearly half the country's v'yds, stretching from VOJVODINA to Macedonia.

Sipon Yugoslav name for FURMINT of Hungary, grown in SLOVENIA.

Slamnak A late-harvest LJUTOMER estate Reisling.

Slavonia Northern Croatia, on the Hungarian border between SLOVENIA and SERBIA. A big producer of standard wines, mainly white, including most "Yugoslav Riesling".

Slovenia The n.w. state, incl. Yugoslavia's most European-style v'yds and wines: LJUTOMER, etc. Slovenija-vino, the sales organization, is Yugoslavia's biggest.

Smederevka Important white grape of SERBIA and KOSOVO. Fresh dry wines.

Teran Stout dark red of ISTRIA. See Refosco.

Tigrovo Mljeko See Radgonska Ranina.

Tocai The PINOT GRIS, making rather heavy white wine in SLOVENIA.

Traminać The TRAMINER. Grown in SLOVENIA and VOJVODINA. Particularly successful in the latter.

Vinag Huge production cellars at MARIBOR.

Vojvodina An autonomous province of n. SERBIA developing substantial v'yds. Wide range of grapes, both European and Balkan.

Vranać Red grape making attractive vigorous wine in Montenegro.

Vugava Rare white variety of Vis in DALMATIA. Linked in legend with the VIOGNIER of the Rhône valley.

Zilavka The white wine of MOSTAR in Hercegovina. Can be one of Yugoslavia's best: dry, pungent and memorably fruity, with a faint flavour of apricots. Exported samples are disappointing.

Zupa Central SERBIAN district giving its name to above-average red and rosé (or dark and light red) of PROKUPAC and PLOVDINA: respectively Zupsko Crno and Zupsko Ruzića.

Bulgaria

Bulgaria has, in a decade, become one of the top four wine exporters. Enormous new vineyards and industrial-sized wineries have been grafted onto an old, if embattled, wine tradition. The state-run and state-subsidized wineries have learnt a great deal from the New World and offer Cabernet, Chardonnay and other varieties at bargain prices. Controlled appellation ("Controliran") wines, introduced in 1985, are being joined by wood-aged "Reserve" bottlings. A drop in sales to the USSR has led to renewed emphasis on quality wines, somewhat higher prices and a ban on planting outside the 24 Controliran regions. Despite the Russian cutbacks Bulgaria still exports 85% of its wine production.

Asenovgrad Main MAVRUD-producing cellar on the outskirts of Plovdiv, Bulgaria's second city.

Cabernet The Bordeaux grape is highly successful in n. Bulgaria. Dark, vigorous, fruity and well-balanced wine drinks well young, but top qualities mature well for 5-6 years.

Chardonnay The white burgundy grape is scarcely less successful. Very dry but full-flavoured wine improves with a year in bottle. Recent oak-aged examples are developing real quality.

Controliran See introductory note.

Dimiat The common native white grape, grown in the east towards the coast. Agreeable dry white without memorable character.

Euxinograd (Château) Ageing cellar on the coast, part of the ex-King's palace. Wines reserved for State functions and top restaurants.

Fetiaska The same grape as Romania's Feteasca and Hungary's Leanyka. Pleasant pale wine, best a trifle sweet, sold as Donau Perle.

Gamza Good red grape, Hungary's Kadarka. Aged examples, esp. from PAVLIKENI, can be delicious.

Han Krum The most modern white-wine plant, near Varna in the east.

Iskra The national brand of sparkling wine, normally sweet but of fair quality. Red, white or rosé.

Kadarka Grape (also found in Hungary) and a popular brand of GAMZA red from n. Bulgaria.

Karlovo Town in central Bulgaria famous for the "Valley of Roses" and its very pleasant white MISKET.

Lozitza "Controliran" CABERNET from the north; perhaps Bulgaria's most elegant red wine yet.

Mavrud Grape variety and resulting darkly plummy red from s. Bulgaria, esp. ASENOVGRAD. Improves with age. Traditionally considered the country's best.

Melnik City of the extreme s.e. and its highly prized grape. Such concentrated red wine that locals say it can be carried in a handkerchief. Needs at least 5 years and lasts for 15.

Merlot Soft red grape variety grown mainly in Haskovo in the south.

Misket Muscat-flavoured local grape used for sweet whites.

Muscat Ottonel Normal muscat grape, grown in eastern Bulgaria for medium-sweet, fruity whites.

Novi Pazar Controlled appellation CHARDONNAY winery near VARNA. Finer wines than VARNA.

Novo Selo "Controliran" red MISKET from the north.

Orjahoviza Major south area for "Controliran" CABERNET/MERLOT. Rich savoury red best at 4-5 years. Recent RESERVE CABERNET releases have been good, especially '80.

Pamid The light soft everyday red of the south-west and north-west.

Pavlikeni Northern wine town with a prestigious estate specializing in GAMZA and CABERNET of high quality.

Pleven Northern cellar important for PAMID, GAMZA and CABERNET. Also Bulgaria's wine research station.

Plovdiv Southern wine town and region, source of good CABERNET.

Provadya East of SHUMEN, near the coast, another centre for good white wines, especially dry CHARDONNAY.

Rcatzitelli One of Russia's favourite white grapes for strong, sweet wine. Grown in north-east Bulgaria to produce bulk dry or medium white wines.

Reserve Used on labels of selected and oak-aged "controliran" wines.

Riesling Normally refers to Italian Riesling. Some Rhine Riesling is grown and is now made into Germanic-style whites.

Sauvignon Blanc Grown in eastern Bulgaria, recently released as dry white wine on export markets.

Shumen Eastern Bulgaria's largest white wine-producing cellar specializing in dry wines. Also makes rather good brandy.

Sonnenkuste Brand of medium-sweet white sold in Germany.

Suhindol PAVLIKENI's neighbour, site of Bulgaria's first cooperative (1909). Good cellar for GAMZA, CABERNET and PAMID.

Sungarlare E. town giving its name to a dry "controliran" MISKET.

Svishtov CABERNET-producing winery by the Danube in the north. The front-runner in Bulgaria's controlled appellation wines.

Sylvaner Some pleasant dry Sylvaner is exported as "Klosterkeller".

Tamianka Sweet white; sweeter than HEMUS.

Targovichte Independent (non-VINPROM) white wine cellar near SHUMEN that concentrates on medium and sweet wines.

Tirnovo Strong sweet dessert red wine.

Trakia "Thrace". Brand name of a good export range.

Varna Major coastal appellation for CHARDONNAY.

Vinimpex The "State Commercial Enterprise for Export and Import of Wines and Spirits".

Vinprom State body controlling all 145 cooperative cellars and responsible for dramatic quality improvements over last decade. Owns 10% of the country's vineyards and 3 research institutes.

Greece

Despite entry into the EEC, little has happened to modernize a wine industry that has been up a backwater for two thousand years. The pace of change is far faster in, say, Portugal (also a recent EEC member) and in Bulgaria to the north. A new EEC-style system of 29 appellations is now in place in Greece and much is spoken of the hopeful future for Greek wines. So far evidence is scarce. Athenian waiters try to sell over-priced brands and look snooty when you ask for Retsina (which is always the best value). But look for local wines in the country, esp. in the north.

Achaia-Clauss The best-known Greek wine merchant, with cellars at Patras, n. PELOPONNESE, makers of DEMESTICA, etc.

Agioritikos Mount Athos, the monastic peninsula in Chalkidiki. Source of CABERNET and other grapes for TSANTALI wines. Brand name of a good dry rosé.

Aminteion (Appellation) Crisp red or rosé from the mountains of Macedonia.

Attica Region round Athens, the chief source of RETSINA.

Boutari Merchants and makers with high standards in Macedonian and other wines, esp. NAOUSSA. Grand Réserve is the best wine.

Calliga Modern winery with 800 acres on CEPHALONIA. ROBOLA white and reds from indigenous grapes are adequately made but grossly over-dressed.

Cambas, Andrew Important Athenian wine-growers and merchants.

Carras, John Hotelier at Sithonia, Chalkidiki, n. Greece, producing interesting red and white wines under the names Château Carras, Porto Carras and COTES DU MELITON. Ch Carras is a Bordeaux-style barrel-aged red, worth bottle-age.

Castel Danielis One of best brands of dry red wine, from ACHAIA-CLAUSS.

Cephalonia (Kephalonia) Ionian (western) island with good white ROBOLA and red Thymiatiko. Also MAVRODAPHNE. See Gentilini, Calliga.

Corfu Adriatic island with wines scarcely worthy of it. Ropa is the traditional red.

Côtes du Meliton (Appellation) Thracian red, white and rosé of fair quality, made by CARRAS.

Courtakis, D. Athenian merchant with good dark NEMEAN red.

Crete Island with the name for some of Greece's better red wine. Appellations are: Archanes, Daphnes, Peza and Sitia. But Cretan white can also be very good.

Demestica A reliable brand of dry red and white from ACHAIA-CLAUSS.

Gamalafka Speciality of Mykonos. Alarmingly like sherry vinegar.

Gentilini New ('84) up-market white from CEPHALONIA, a Robola blend, soft and appealing. To watch.

Goumenissa (Appellation) Good-quality, oak-aged mid-weight red from BOUTARI.

Hymettus Standard brand of red and dry white without resin.

Kokkineli The rosé version of RETSINA: like the white. Drink cold.

Lac des Roches Sound, blended Dodecanese white from BOUTARI.

Lindos Name for the higher quality of RHODES wine, whether from Lindos itself or not. Acceptable; no more.

Malvasia The famous grape is said to originate from Monemvasia in the S. PELOPONNESE.

Mantinia (Appellation) A fresh white from the PELOPONNESE by CAMBAS.

Mavro "Black" – the word for dark (usually sweet) red wine.

Mavrodaphne (Appellation) Literally "black laurel": dark sweet concentrated red; a speciality of the Patras region, n. PELOPONNESE.

Mavroudi (Appellation) The red wine of Delphi and the n. shore of the Gulf of Corinth: dark and plummy.

Metsovo (Appellation) CABERNET red from Epirus in the north.

Minos Popular Cretan brand; the Castello red is best.

Naoussa (Appellation) Above-average strong dry red from Macedonia in the north, esp. from BOUTARI and TSANTALI.

Nemea (Appellation) Town in the e. PELOPONNESE famous for its lion (a victim of Hercules) and its fittingly forceful MAVRO.

Patras (Appellation) Important wine town on the Gulf of Corinth.

Peloponnese The south landmass of mainland Greece, with a half of the whole country's vineyards.

Pendeli Reliable brand of dry red from ATTICA, grown and bottled by Andrew CAMBAS.

Retsina White wine with Aleppo pine resin added, tasting of turpentine and oddly appropriate with Greek food. The speciality of ATTICA. Drink very cold.

Rhodes Easternmost Greek island. Its sweet MALVASIAS are its best wines. LINDOS is the brand name for tolerable table wines.

Robola (or Rombola) (Appellation) The fashionable dry white of Cephalonia; island off the Gulf of Corinth. Can be a pleasant soft wine of some character.

Samos (Appellation) Island off the Turkish coast with a reputation for its sweet pale-golden muscat. The normal quality is nothing much.

Santorini Dramatic volcanic island north of Crete, making sweet Vinsanto from sun-dried grapes, and dry white Thira. Unrealized potential here.

Tsantali Producers at Agios Pavlos with a wide range of table wines, including Macedonian Cabernet, wine from the monks of Mt. Athos, NAOUSSA and Muscat from PATRAS. "Cava" is a blend.

Verdea The dry white of Zakinthos, the island just west of the PELOPONNESE. The red is Byzantis.

Xynomavro The best Greek red grape, basis for NAOUSSA and other northern wines.

Cyprus

A well-established exporter of strong wines of reasonable quality, best known for very passable Cyprus sherry, though old Commandaria, a treacly dessert wine, is the island's finest product. Until recently only traditional grape varieties of limited potential were available; now better kinds are beginning to improve standards, but regrettably slowly.

Afames Village at the foot of Mt. Olympus, giving its name to one of the better red (MAVRON) wines from SODAP.

Aphrodite Full-bodied medium-dry white from KEO, named after the Greek goddess of love.

Arsinöe Dry white wine from SODAP, named after an unfortunate female whom Aphrodite turned to stone.

Bellapais Fizzy medium-sweet white from KEO named after the famous abbey near Kyrenia. Essential refreshment for holidaymakers.

Commandaria Good-quality brown dessert wine made since ancient times in the hills north of LIMASSOL, named after a crusading order of knights. The best (sold as "100 yrs old") is superb, of incredible sweetness. Most is standard Communion wine.

Domaine d'Ahera Modern-style lighter red from KEO.

Emva Cream Best-selling sweet sherry from Etko, a HAGGIPAVLU subsidiary.

Etko See Haggipavlu.

Haggipavlu Well-known wine-merchant at LIMASSOL. Trades as Etko.

Hirondelle The sweet white and some of the other wines of this popular brand are produced by Etko (see Emva).

Keo One of the biggest and most go-ahead firms in the wine trade at LIMASSOL.

Khalokhorio Principal COMMANDARIA village, growing only XYNISTERI.

Kokkineli Rosé: the name is related to "cochineal".

Kolossi Red and white table wines from SODAP.

Limassol "The Bordeaux of Cyprus". The wine-port in the south.

Loel Major producer. Amathus and Kykko brands, Command Cyprus sherry and good Negro red.

Mavron The black grape of Cyprus (and Greece) and its dark wine.

Mosaic KEO's brand of Cyprus sherries. Includes a fine dry wine.

Othello A good standard dry red: solid, satisfying wine from KEO.

Palomino Soft dry white made of this (sherry) grape by LOEL. Very drinkable ice-cold.

Pitsilia Region south of Mt. Olympus producing the best white and COMMANDARIA wines.

Rosella Brand of strong medium-sweet rosé.

St Panteleimon Brand of strong sweet white from Keo.

Semeli Good traditional red from HAGGIPAVLU.

Sherry Cyprus makes a full range of sherry-style wines, the best (particularly the dry) of very good quality.

SODAP Major wine cooperative at LIMASSOL.

Xynisteri The native white grape of Cyprus.

Zoopiyi Principal COMMANDARIA village, growing MAVRON grapes.

Asia & North Africa

Algeria The massive v'yds of Algeria have dwindled in the last decade from 860,000 acres to under 500,000. Red, rosé and white wines of some quality are made in the coastal hills of Tlemcen, Mascara, Haut-Dahra, Zaccar and Ain-Bessem. Most goes for blending (much of it to the USSR).

China Germans and Russians started making wine on the Shantung (now Shandong) peninsula in the early 1900s. Since 1980 a modern industry, initiated by Rémy Martin, has produced the adequate white Dynasty and Tsingtao wines, and new more sophisticated plantings of better varieties in Shandong and Tianjin, further north, promise more interest in the future. Basic table wines are made of the local Dragon Eye and Muscat Hamburg grapes (esp. in Tianjin). In Quingdao Italian Riesling has been followed by Chardonnay and the Hua Dong winery started experimental plantings of many varieties in 1985.

India In 1985 a Franco-Indian firm launched a Chardonnay-based sparkling wine, Omar Khayyam, made at Narayangoan, s.e. of Bombay. Plans are to export up to 2m. bottles. It is remarkably good.

Israel Israeli wine, since the industry was re-established by a Rothschild in the 1880s, has been primarily of Kosher interest until recently, when CABERNET, SAUVIGNON BLANC, SÉMILLON, PETITE SIRAH and GRENACHE of fair quality have been introduced. Carmel is the principal brand. Since 1986 Yarden wines from the Golan Heights has set a higher standard esp. for SAUV BLANC.

Japan Japan has a small wine industry in Yamanashi Prefecture, w. of Tokyo. Wines are here blended with imports from Argentina, E. Europe, etc. Premium wines of SEMILLON, CHARDONNAY, CABERNET and the local white grape, Koshu, are light but can be good, though expensive. Perhaps the most interesting (and expensive) is Suntory's Sauternes-like Château Lion. Château Lumiére leads the way with high-quality CHARD, CABERNET, etc. The main producers are Suntory, Mercian, Mann's. In 1985 tainted Austrian wine was discovered being sold as Japanese by a major company. Regrettably, Japanese labelling laws are so lax that misrepresentation of imported wines as "Japanese" has been the rule rather than the exception. There are increasing signs of more honourable conduct but still much confusing labelling.

Lebanon The small Lebanese wine industry, based on Ksara in the Bekaa valley n.e. of Beirut, continues against all odds to make red wine of real vigour and quality. Château Musar ▮▮▮ produces splendid matured reds, largely of CABERNET SAUVIGNON, a full-blooded white, and recently a lighter red "Tradition", which is 75% Cinsaut, 25% Cabernet Sauvignon.

Morocco Morocco today makes North Africa's best wine from v'yds along the Atlantic coast and round Meknes. In ten years the v'yds have declined from 190,000 to 54,000 acres. Chante Bled and Tarik are the best reds, Gris de Guerrouane a very pale dry rosé.

Tunisia Tunisia now has 75,000 acres compared with 120,000 ten years ago. Her speciality is sweet muscat, but reasonable reds and rosés come from Carthage, Mornag and Cap Bon.

Turkey Most of Turkey's huge v'yds produce table grapes. But her wines, from Thrace, Anatolia and the Aegean, are remarkably good. Trakya (Thrace) white and Buzbag (Anatolian) red are the well-known standards of the State wineries. Doluca and Kavaklidere are private firms of good quality. Villa Doluca red from Thrace is very well made. Buzbag is a (sometimes rough and ready) bargain.

USSR With over 3 million acres of v'yds the USSR is the world's fourth-biggest wine-producer – almost entirely for home consumption. Ukraine (incl. the Crimea) is the biggest v'yd republic, followed by Moldavia, the Russian Republic and Georgia. The Soviet consumer has a sweet tooth, for both table and dessert wines. Of the latter the best come from the Crimea (esp. Massandra). Moldavia and Ukraine use the same grapes as Romania, plus CABERNET, RIESLING, PINOT GRIS, etc. The Russian Republic makes the best Rieslings (Arbau, Beshtau, Anapa) and sweet sparkling Tsimlanskoye "Champanski". Georgia uses antique methods to make extremely tannic wines for local consumption, and (relatively) modern methods to make blended products for export (e.g. Tsinandali, Mukuzani). Kakheti (e. Georgia) is historically famous for both reds and whites of withering tannin content. Imeteria (w. Georgia) makes milder, highly original wines. When the equipment (e.g. good bottles) becomes available Georgia will be a hit on the export market. Georgian sparkling is extremely cheap and drinkable.

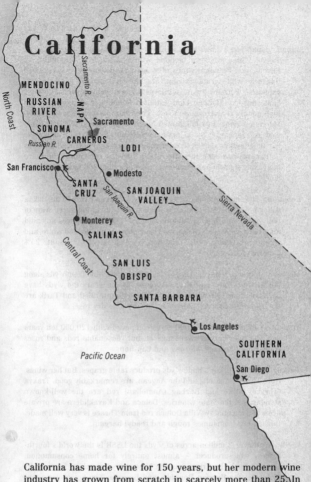

California

California has made wine for 150 years, but her modern wine industry has grown from scratch in scarcely more than 25. In the past ten it has challenged the world with good-quality cheap wines and a growing number of luxury wines of brilliant quality. The industry has expanded and altered at a frenzied pace. Many of the wineries listed here have a history shorter than ten years. Quality ratings must therefore be tentative. The star-ratings attempt to give a picture of the international standing of a winery. Some new entries have provisional ratings (in brackets).

Appellation areas are an important new fact of life in California. They are being registered thick and fast; the current total is more than thirty with five in the Napa Valley alone and four more proposed. It is still too soon to use them as a useful guide to style. Listed below are the broad regions traditionally referred to.

Grape varieties combined with brand-names are the key to California wine. Since grapes in California play many new roles they are listed separately over.

Principal vineyard areas

Amador County in the Sierra foothills e. of Sacramento. Grows very good Zinfandel, esp. in Shenandoah Valley.

Central Coast A long sweep of coast with increasing though scattered wine activity, from San Francisco Bay s. to Santa Barbara.

Central Coast/Santa Barbara Some of the most promising vineyard land (esp. for white wines) in the state is in the Santa Ynez Valley n. of Santa Barbara, where coastal fog gives particularly cool conditions.

Central Coast/Santa Cruz Mts. Wineries are scattered round the Santa Cruz Mts. s. of San Francisco Bay, from Saratoga down to the HECKER PASS.

Central Coast/Hecker Pass Pass through the Santa Cruz Mts. s. of San Francisco Bay with a cluster of small old-style wineries.

Central Coast/Salinas Valley/Monterey The Salinas Valley runs inland s.e. from Monterey. After frenzied expansion in the '70s, many vines were removed. What are left make wines of great character.

Central Coast/San Luis Obispo Edna Valley just s. of San Luis Obispo and new more scattered v'yds nr. Paso Robles.

Livermore Valley e. of San Francisco Bay long famous for white wines but now largely built over.

Lodi Town and district at the n. end of the San Joaquin Valley, its hot climate modified by a westerly air-stream.

Mendocino Northernmost coastal wine country; a varied climate coolest in Anderson Valley nr. the coast, warm around Ukiah inland.

Napa The Napa valley, n. of San Francisco Bay, long established as a top-quality wine area. Coolest at southern end (Los Carneros).

San Joaquin Valley The great central valley of California, fertile and hot, the source of most of the jug wines and dessert wines in the State.

Sonoma County n. of San Francisco Bay, between Napa and the sea. Most v'yds are in the north (see below). A few, historically important, are in the Valley of the Moon in the south. Vineyards extend south into Los Carneros. (See also Napa.)

Sonoma/Alexander Valley/Russian River Top-quality area from Alexander Valley (n. of Napa Valley) towards the sea (Russian River). Incl. Dry Creek Valley.

Temecula (Rancho California) New small area in s. California, 25 miles inland, halfway between San Diego and Riverside.

Ca

California has adopted the world's repertoire of "classic" grapes: for notes on these see pp. 6-9. Grapes specific to California include:

Emerald Riesling an original in the German manner. Clean, flowery/fruity and a touch tart.

Flora mildly flowery white, best made sweet and/or sparkling.

Gamay Beaujolais not true Gamay but a Pinot Noir clone.

Gray Riesling not Riesling, makes full-bodied but standard white.

Johannisberg Riesling real (also called white) Riesling.

Petite Sirah no relation to Syrah, a synonym for the obscure French Durif.

Ruby Cabernet California-bred cross between Carignan and Cabernet Sauvignon, with enough of the latter's character to be interesting. Good in hot conditions.

Zinfandel California's own red, open to many interpretations from light-weight and fruity to galumphing. The current fad is for white or "blush" Zin. The red is capable of ageing to high quality.

Recent vintages

The Californian climate is far from being as consistent as its reputation. Although on the whole the grapes ripen regularly, they are subject to severe spring frosts in many areas, sometimes a wet harvest-time, and such occasional calamities as the two-year drought of 1976-77. 1987 was a very early, rather small crop, with very good white wines. The size of the harvest has the useful effect of balancing supply and demand after a run of big vintages. 1988 was less special, but by no means poor.

Wines from the San Joaquin Valley tend to be most consistent year by year. The vintage date on these, where there is one, is more important for telling the age of the wine than its character.

Vineyards in the Central Coast are widely scattered; there is little pattern. The Napa and Sonoma valleys are the areas where comment can usefully be made on the last dozen vintages of the top varietal wines: Cabernet Sauvignon and Chardonnay. All Chardonnays can be considered "ready" at 2 years, though the best can develop for up to 10 years.

	Chardonnay	Cabernet Sauvignon
1988	Flavourful, perhaps early maturers	Variable weather, attractive at the v. least.
1987	Ideal weather: very good wines.	Considered extremely promising.
1986	Cool season; fine wines.	Good, but not as good as '85.
1985	Big crop, good acidity, excellent.	Coolish ripening season. Excellent balance; some great wines.
1984	Wonderfully perfumed when young, now fully mature. Drink up.	Exceptional; very ripe and fragrant. Will improve for years.
1983	Drink up.	Similar to '80 but maturing faster.
1982	Sound, agreeable; drink up	Many outstanding; now mostly mature.
1981	Good if not too strong. Drink.	Should be drunk soon.
1980	Should have been drunk.	Excellent, but drink soon.
1979	Excellent; drink up.	Rain; generally light.
1978	Very good but drink up.	Excellent. Generally ready.
1977	Generally excellent. Drink up.	Attractive; fully mature.
1976	Should have been drunk.	Small crop but splendid. Mature.
1975	Very good; getting old.	Delicate: charming. Mature.
1974	Should have been drunk.	Difficult: but many superb. Mature.
1973	Very good, but drink up.	Big and good; drink up.
1970	Should have been drunk.	One of the best ever. Mature.

California wineries

Acacia Napa. ★★★ CH 81 83 84 85 86 87 PN 80 81 82 83 84 85 86
Carneros winery, now owned by CHALONE, specializing in CHARDONNAY and P NOIR. Both are fulfilling marvellous promise.

Adelaida Cellars Central Coast/San Luis Obispo. (★★)
Skilful maker of soft CHARD and supple CAB at Paso Robles.

Alderbrook Sonoma. ★★ CH 84 85 86
New ('82) winery using owner-grown and other grapes to make full-flavoured whites. CHARD, SAUV BLANC and SEMILLON all good.

Alexander Valley Vineyards Alexander Valley. ★★→★★★ CH 83 84 85 86 87 CS 81 82 83 84 85 86 Small winery best known for well-balanced CHARD, and J.R. CABERNET also v. well made.

Almaden San Joaquin.
Famous pioneer name bought in '87 by Heublein; now everyday brand operated from Madera.

S. Anderson Vineyard Napa. ★★ CH 83 84 85 86
Young winery with extensive caves. Good CHARDONNAY and recently good sparkling wine.

Baldinelli Amador ★★ CS 79 80 81 82 83 84
One of the more stylish producers of CABERNET and ZINFANDEL in Shenandoah Valley.

Balverne Sonoma/Russian River. ★★ CH 81 83 84 CS 82
Small winery near Windsor, started in '80 with fine CHARD, SAUV BLANC. CAB SAUV is above average. New managers in 1988.

Beaulieu Napa. ★★★ CS 74 76 77 78 79 80 81 82 83 84 85 86
Justly famous medium-size growers and makers of esp. CABERNET. Top wine: De Latour Private Reserve Cabernet. Crackerjack SAUV BLANC. Now owned by Grand Metropolitan. Beautour CAB SAUV is value ('86).

Bel Arbres A second label of FETZER.

Belvedere Wine Co. Sonoma. ★★ CS 82 83 84 CH 85 86 87
Born-1980 winery featuring single-v'yd wines. incl. Robert Young CAB from Alex Valley, York Mtn. Napa CAB, Bacigalupi Russian River CHARD. They go down well.

Beringer Napa. ■ ★★→★★★ CH 83 84 85 86 87 CS 80 81 82 83 84 85
Century-old winery recently restored to the front rank. Increasingly fine wines incl. esp. CHARD (excellent Private Reserve), CABERNET (ditto) and "Nightingale", the winemaker's induced-botrytis dessert wine.

Boeger El Dorado. ★★ CS 79 80 81 82 83 CH 85
Small winery in Sierra foothills. Good ZIN.

Bonny Doon Vineyard Central Coast/Santa Cruz Mtns. ★★ CH 86 87
Small winery (since '81) with original ideas about Rhône grapes, incl. Syrah, Grenache, and even Roussanne and Marsanne. (E.g. Le Cigare Volant; Grenache spiced with Mourvèdre: 84 85 86.)

Bouchaine Napa/Carneros. ★★→★★★ CH 83 84 85 PN 85
New firm in old Carneros barn started with Acacia-style oaky PINOT NOIR. Now similar v.g. CHARDONNAY and SAUV BLANC.

Brander Central Coast/Santa Barbara. ★★
Small new winery specializes in excellent SAUVIGNON BLANC of Santa Ynez Valley grapes. Now also hitting high notes with CAB FRANC and MERLOT labelled "Bouchet" (84 85 86).

Bruce, David Central Coast. ★★ CH 83 84 85
Small luxury winery with heavy-weight wines. Improving.

Buena Vista Sonoma. ■ ★★ CH 83 84 85 86 87 CS 83 84 85
Historic pioneer winery with German owners and very sound recent record esp. in whites (CHARD, RIESLING, FUME BLANC).

Burgess Cellars Napa ★★ CH 83 84 85 86 CS 80 81 82 83 84 85 Z 81 82 83 84 85 Small hillside winery, in former Souverain cellars, making good CABERNET, very good ZIN, and CHARD.

B.V. Abbreviation of BEAULIEU VINEYARDS used on their labels.

Bynum, Davis Sonoma. ■ ★★ CH 83 84 85 86 CS 82 83
Well-established maker of standard varieties, w. of Healdsburg. Esp. GEWÜRZ, CHARD, P NOIR.

Byron Vineyards Santa Barbara. (★★★) CH 84 85 86 PN 85 86
Long-time Zaca Mesa winemaker Ken Brown is off to excellent start with his own Santa Maria Valley winery. P NOIR memorable.

Cain Cellars Napa (★★) CH 84 85 86 CS 84 85
Young (1984) winery draws on estate v'yd on Spring Mountain for ambitious Bordeaux-blend Cain Five. Also CAB SAUV, CHARDONNAY.

Cakebread Napa. ★★★ CH 83 84 85 86 CS 80 81 82 83 84 85
Started 1973. Increasing reputation, esp. for SAUVIGNON BLANC and CABERNET (79 N.B.); also CHARDONNAY.

Calera Monterey-San Benito. ★★ PN 80 81 82 83 84 85 86 CH 85 86
1975 winery ambitious with PINOT NOIR; Now owned by Allied-Hiram Walker. To watch.

Callaway S. California. ★★ CH 83 84 85 86
Mid-sized winery in new territory at TEMECULA. Sound whites.

Carmenet Sonoma. ★★→★★★ CS 84 85
Where CHALONE emulates Burgundy, the same owners have chased Bordeaux here since '82 with SAUV BL from Sonoma, and CAB/MERLOT from high above Sonoma town (83 84). Also "Gavilan" FRENCH COLOMBARD from Napa.

Carneros Creek Napa. ★★★ CH 83 84 85 86 87 CS 74 77 80 81 82 83 84
The first winery in the cool Carneros area between Napa and San
Francisco Bay. Good P NOIR, CHARDONNAY and CABERNET. Good-value
MERLOT.

Caymus Napa. ███ →★★★★ CS 74 75 76 77 78 79 80 81 82 83 84
85 Outwardly modest small winery at Rutherford with v. high
standards, esp. for notably complex CAB and ZIN; also white P NOIR,
CHARD, SAUV BLANC, CAB FRANC. Second label: Liberty School (value).

Chalk Hill Sonoma/Russian River. ★★ CH 84 85 86 87 CS 83 84 85
Considerable vineyards in Chalk Hill near Windsor. Encouraging
early wines.

Chalone Central Coast/Salinas. ★★★★ CH 80 81 82 83 84 85 86 87 PN
80 81 82 83 84 Unique small hilltop v'yd/winery at the Pinnacles.
French-style CHARDONNAY and PINOT NOIR of super quality. Also
excellent PINOT BLANC. See also Acacia, Carmenet. In 1989 traded
shares with Ch Lafite-Rothschild.

Chappellet Napa. ███ CH 81 83 84 85 86 CS 74 75 76 78 79 80 81
82 83 84 85 Luxury winery and beautiful amphitheatrical hillside
v'yd. Excellent very long-lived CABERNET, CHARDONNAY and RIESLING:
very good dry CHENIN BLANC.

Château Montelena Napa. ★★★ CH 83 84 85 86 CS 75 77 78 79 80 81
82 83 Small 1969 winery making very good distinctive CHARDONNAY
and very tannic CABERNET SAUVIGNON.

Château St-Jean Sonoma. ★★★ CH 83 84 85 86 87
Impressive winery specializing in whites from individual v'yds, incl.
CHARD, P BLANC and esp. late harvest RIES. Also fine sparkling wine and
bargain "Vin Blanc". Owned by Suntory.

Château Souverain Alexander Valley. ★★ CH 83 84 85 86 CS 78 79 80 81
82 83 84 85 Luxurious mid-sized winery with a record of competent
wines, bought by BERINGER in 1986. '86 Carneros Reserve CHARD is
first-rate.

Christian Brothers Napa and San Joaquin. ███←→███ CH 85 86 87 CS 84
85 The biggest Napa winery, run by a religious order. Sound and
improving CABERNET (since 84), attractive CHARD, useful FUME BLANC,
sweet white Ch La Salle, very good brandy and ZIN "port".

Clos du Bois Sonoma. ███ →★★★ CH 83 84 85 86 87 CS 78 79 80 81
82 83 84 85 Healdsburg winery with v'yds in Dry Creek and
Alexander Valleys. V.g. GEWÜRZ, P NOIR, MERLOT, CHARD, SAUV BLANC.
Named-v'yd wines outstanding. Now owned by Allied-Hiram Walker.

Clos du Val Napa. ███ CH 83 84 85 86 87 CS 77 78 79 80 81 82 83
84 85 French-run. V.g bold ZIN, fine CAB, MERLOT, CHARD and SEM.

Clos Pegase Napa. (★★)
Amazing post-modernist building near STERLING. So far wines are
simply steady.

Concannon Livermore. Table. ★★ CH 83 84 86
Substantial winery first famous for whites, reds now prominent.
Owned by winemaker Sergio Traverso and Deinhard of Germany.

Congress Springs Santa Clara/Santa Cruz. ★★ CH 84 85 86
Tiny winery above Saratoga with growing reputation. Well-made
whites, e.g. SAUV BLANC, CHARD and esp. PINOT BLANC. Also CAB FRANC.

Conn Creek Napa. ★★→★★★ CH 83 84 85 CS 78 79 80 81 82 83 84
Winery built on Silverado Trail in 1979 has built a solid following.
Now owned by Ch Ste Michelle of Washington. Best known for CAB.

Cooks "Cooks Champagne" – See Guild.

Corbett Canyon Central Coast/San Luis Obispo. ███ CH 84 85 86 87
New ('83) Edna Valley winery to make sizeable amounts of varietal
and generic ("Coastal Classic") wines (value.)

Culbertson Temecula. ★★
Young sparkling-wine specialist using local grapes of an improbable
region with medal-winning results.

Cuvaison Napa. ★★→★★★ CH 83 85 86 87 CS 78 79 80 81 82 83 84
Small winery with expert new direction. Formerly austere CABERNET and CHARDONNAY now more approachable; CHARD from own Carneros v'yd is tops.

Dehlinger Sonoma. ★★→ ▓▓▓ CH 83 84 85 86 PN 79 80 81 82 83 84
Small winery and v'yd w. of Santa Rosa. Since 1976 CHARDONNAY, CABERNET and since '79 P NOIR all extremely well made.

DeLoach Vineyards Sonoma. ★★★ CH 83 84 85 86 87 PN 80 81 82 83 84 85 86 Russian River winery founded 1975 for CHARDONNAY, GEWÜRZ, P NOIR. Also good ZIN (v.g. white ZIN), and SAUV BLANC.

De Moor Napa. ★★ CH 83 84 85 86 CS 80 81 82 83 84
Small Yountville winery (formerly Napa Cellars) with steady record, esp. for CAB and ZIN. New (European) owners.

Diamond Creek Napa. ★★★ CS 74 75 76 77 78 79 80 81 82 83 84 85 86
Small winery since the 60s with austere, long-ageing CABERNET from hills w. of Calistoga, e.g. "Volcanic Hill", "Gravelly Meadow".

Domaine Carneros Napa.
Taittinger's highly visible cellar in CARNEROS is the newest sparkling producer with roots in Champagne. First wines due in 1990.

Domaine Chandon Napa. ▓▓▓
Californian outpost of Moët & Chandon Champagne. Launched 1976. Promise is being fulfilled. First Reserve wine (released in 1985) was a showstopper. So is second. Shadow Creek now its non-Napa label.

Domaine Laurier Sonoma. ▓▓▓ CH 83 84 85 86 CS 78 79 80 81 82 83 84 85 Small new winery with beautifully structured wines, esp. CABERNET and SAUVIGNON BLANC, using the new appellation Green Valley. A classic in the making. CHARD now equally fine.

Domaine M. Marion Central Coast/Santa Cruz Mts. ★→★★
Ex-merchant label now housed in historic Los Gatos winery to make its own mid-range, mostly Central Coast varietals.

Domaine Mumm Napa. (★★)
Seagram-owned. Sparkling-wine house near Rutherford. First wine released '86, promising, and promises kept: v. crisp and fine.

Dominus Napa. (★★★★) 84
First fruits (1984 vintage released '88) of partnership ("John Daniel Society") between inheritors of ex-Inglenook v'yd n. of Yountville and Christian Moueix of Pomerol. B'x-style Cabernets-Merlot blend shows immense promise.

Dry Creek Sonoma. ▓▓▓ CH 83 84 85 86 CS 79 80 81 82 83 84 85 86
Small winery with high ideals, making old-fashioned dry wines, esp. whites, incl. CHARDONNAY, CHENIN BLANC and FUME BLANC and outstanding CAB SAUV.

Duckhorn Vineyards Napa. ★★→★★★ M 79 80 81 82 83 84 85 CS 79 80 81 82 83 84 85 Small winery on Silverado Trail best known for reds, esp. v.g. MERLOT. Also SAUVIGNON BLANC.

Dunn Vineyards Napa. (★★★) 81 82 83 84 85
Randall Dunn (ex-Caymus) now makes small lots of dark, stern Howell Mountain CABERNET SAUVIGNON in his own winery.

Durney Vineyard Central Coast/Monterey. ★★ CS 79 80 81 82 83
Well-established source of robust CABERNET. Also CHENIN BL, RIESLING.

Eberle Winery Central Coast/San Luis Obispo. ★★
Most stylish and consistent CAB producer in Paso Robles area since '79. Also CHARD.

Edna Valley Vineyard Central Coast/San Luis Obispo. ★★→★★★ CH 84 85 86 87 Joint venture of grape-grower with CHALONE winemakers. Fat CHARDONNAY full of character.

Estancia See Franciscan.

Estrella River San Luis Obispo/Santa Barbara. ★★ CH 83 84 85 86 87 CHARDONNAY, RIESLING, MUSCAT, SYRAH from Paso Robles v'yds are competent and satisfying.

Far Niente Napa. ★★ CH 83 84 85 86 87 CS 84 85
> Founded 1885; reactivated in 1979. Full-flavoured CHARDONNAY first; now similar CABERNET.

Ferrari-Carano Sonoma. (★★)
> New (1985), family-owned major player with 1,000 acres of v'yd land in ALEXANDER, Dry Creek, Knights Valley. CHARD, SAUV BL well received. CAB SAUV, MERLOT in the works.

Fetzer Mendocino. ■■★★→★★★★ CH 83 84 85 86 CS 79 80 81 82 83 84 85 Rapidly expanding winery with interesting reliable wines, esp. CHARD and CAB. Also FUMÉ BLANC, RIES and strong dark ZIN. A byword for value.

Ficklin San Joaquin. ★★★
> Family firm making California's best "port".

Field Stone Sonoma (Alexander Valley). ★★
> Small subterranean winery founded by mechanical harvester maker. Good wines incl. delicious CABERNET rosé.

Firestone Central Coast/Santa Barbara. ★★★ CH 83 84 85 86 CS 81 82 83 84 85 86 Ambitious 1973 winery n. of Santa Barbara. Cool conditions are producing full spectrum of unusual, gentle wines.

Fisher Napa. (★★)
> Small mountain estate nr. Calistoga for v.g CAB and CHARD.

Flora Springs Wine Co. Napa. ★★ CH 83 84 85 86 87 CS 80 81 82 83 84 85
> Old stone cellar in St-Helena reopened 1979. CHARDONNAY and SAUV BLANC are v. successful, CABERNET less certain.

Folie à Deux Napa. ■■★★
> Tiny producer of impeccable Chardonnays, v. good CHENIN BL, CAB, from bought-in grapes.

Foppiano Sonoma. ■■★★
> Old winery at Healdsburg refurbished with estate varieties incl. FUME BLANC, CAB, PETITE SYRAH. Second label, Riverside Farms, has good value ZIN.

Franciscan Vineyard Napa. ★★ CH 83 84 85 86 CS 80 81 82 83
> Growing enterprise with a meet-the-folks approach. Good ZIN, CAB, CHARD and RIES. Wines from own SONOMA and Monterey v'yds are labelled "Estancia" (value).

Franzia San Joaquin. ★
> Large old winery with well-distributed brands. Various labels, but all say "made and bottled in Ripon".

Freemark Abbey Napa. ★★★★ CH 83 84 85 86 CS 74 75 76 77 78 79 80 81 82 83 84 85 Small connoisseur's winery with high reputation for CABERNET, CHARDONNAY and RIESLING (esp. late-harvest "Edelwein"). Top Cab is "Bosché" (74 75 78 79 80′ 81 82 83 84). Also "Sycamore".

Frog's Leap Napa. ★★
> Little St Helena winery as charming as its name. Now CAB SAUV and CHARD outclass the original SAUV BL and ZIN.

Gainey Vineyard Santa Barbara. (★★)
> Promising young winery in Santa Ynez Valley has done well with SAUV BLANC; poised to make a mark with named-v'yd PINOT NOIRS.

Gallo, E. & J. San Joaquin. ■■★→★★ CS 78 81
> The world's biggest winery, pioneer in both quantity and quality. Family owned. Hearty Burgundy and Chablis Blanc set national standards. Varietals incl. SAUV BLANC (esp.), GEWÜRZ, RIES, CABERNET. CHARD not so good. Vintage-dated CAB has won wide approval. Drink it fairly young. Also "André" fizz and many others.

Gan Eden Sonoma. (★★)
> Kosher producer of serious CHARD, CAB SAUV has won wide critical acclaim in each vintage since 1985.

Geyser Peak Sonoma. ★★
> Old winery revived by Schlitz Brewery then sold to local grower Henry Trione. Wines are increasingly from his 700 acres.

Giumarra San Joaquin. ★★
Modern installation in hottest part of San Joaquin Valley with broad range from valley and Central Coast grapes.

Glen Ellen Sonoma. ★★→★★★ CH 84 85 86 87 CS 83 84 85 86
Father-and-son team making restrained elegant wines from own-grown and other Sonoma grapes under Benziger of Glen Ellen label. SAUV BLANC, CHARD and CABERNET. "Proprietor's Reserve" indicates bought-in wines.

Gloria Ferrer Sonoma. ★★
Big new sparkling winery launched in '85 by FREIXENET of Spain. An impressive start.

Grand Cru Sonoma. ★★ CS 78 79 80 81 82 83 84 85
Small 1971 winery making good GEWÜRZ and increasingly CABERNET, CHENIN and SAUVIGNON BLANC. Now CHARD.

Green and Red Napa. ★★
Tiny Pope Valley winery with vigorous ZIN.

Grgich Hills Cellars Napa. ★★★ CH 83 84 85 Z 77 78 79 80 81 82 83 84
Grgich (formerly of Ch Montelena) in winemaker, Hills grows the grapes – esp. CHARDONNAY and RIESLING. Lively wines include high-strength ZINFANDEL and (esp.) CABERNET.

Groth Vineyards Napa. (★★) CS 84 85
Estate at Oakville is challenging leaders with polished, subtle CAB SAUV. Also CHARD.

Guenoc Vineyards Lake County. ★★ CH 84 85 86
Ambitious new vineyard/winery venture just beyond the Napa county line. CHENIN BLANC ZIN and PETITE SIRAH are esp. appealing.

Guild San Joaquin. ★
Big growers' cooperative. B. Cribari is table wine label, "Cooks Champagne" a runaway success.

Gundlach-Bundschu Sonoma. ★★ CH 83 84 85 86 CS 79 80 81 82 83 84
Very old small family winery revived by the new generation. Excellent CABERNET, MERLOT, ZIN and good whites: CHARDONNAY, GEWÜRZ, RIESLING.

Hacienda Sonoma. ★★ CH 83 84 85 86 CS 79 81 84
Small winery at Sonoma specializing in high-quality CHARDONNAY and GEWÜRZ. CABERNET has wobbled recently.

Handley Cellars Mendocino. (★★)
Small family-owned Anderson Valley cellar specializes in impressive sparkler, CHARDONNAY. Also refreshing Brightlighter (Gewürz-based).

Hanzell Sonoma. ★★★ CH 83 84 85 86 PN 80 81 82 83 84
Small winery whose (late) founder revolutionized Californian CHARDONNAYs in the '50s. CHARD and P NOIR are both huge wines. CABERNET first released in 1986.

Haywood Vineyard Sonoma. ★★ CH 83 84 85 86 CS 83 84 85
Small new estate on hills above SEBASTIANI. First wines were lovely fruity CHARDONNAY and RIESLING and gutsy ZIN. Now CABERNET.

Heitz Napa. ★★★★ CH 83 84 85 86 CS 76 77 78 79 80 81 82 83 84
An inspired individual winemaker who has set standards for the whole industry. His CABERNETS (esp. "Martha's Vineyard" and "Bella Oaks") are dark, deep and emphatic, his best CHARDONNAYs potent and long-lived. But Chard and other wines can be eccentric. Added substantial new v'yds in 1984.

Hill, William Winery Napa. ★★→★★★ CH 83 84 85 86 CS 80 81 82 83 84
Huge new plantings in the Mayacamas Mts. and a new winery have yielded very emphatic (but well-received) early wines.

Hop Kiln Sonoma/Russian River. ★★ CH 83 84 85
Small winery. Individual, tasty PETITE SIRAH, ZIN, GEWÜRZ.

Husch Vineyards Mendocino. ★★ CH 86 CS 84 85
Reliable CHARD, P NOIR and GEWÜRZ from Anderson Valley; CAB and SAUV BLANC from Ukiah.

Inglenook Napa. ★★→★★★ CH 85 CS 76 77 78 79 80 81 82 83 84
One of the great old Napa wineries much changed by current owners: Heublein (now Grand Metropolitan). Inglenook Napa Valley is Napa label, with two qualities: "Cask" (Reserve) and Estate, now joined ('83) by hugely tannic "Reunion". CAB SAUV, MERLOT, CHARD and SAUV BLANC now v. well made. PETITE SIRAH is tasty. (Inglenook Navalle are good-value Central Valley wines, only nominally related.)

Iron Horse Vineyards Sonoma. ★★★ CH 83 84 85 86 CS 79 80 81 82 83 84 85 Stylish Russian River property with CHARDONNAY, CABERNET, P NOIR and SAUV BLANC of vivid flavours. Sparkling IRON HORSE is v. dry and fine. Tin Pony is second label.

(Italian Swiss) Colony San Joaquin. ★
Honourable old name from Sonoma now a brand owned by something called The Beverage Source. Standards have been recovering.

Jekel Vineyards Central Coast/Monterey. ★★→★★★ CH 83 84 85 CS 78 79 81 82 83 84 Well-made RIESLING, CHARDONNAY, and CABERNET have rich resounding flavours. Wines (esp. whites) mature fast but tastily.

Jepson Vineyards Mendocino. (★★)
A Chicago industrialist owns 100 acres of CHARD, SAUV BLANC near Ukiah. They produce varietals, a sparkler, and a little pot-still brandy.

J. Lohr Central Coast. ★★
Substantial winery in San José and Paso Robles with its own v'yds in SALINAS Clarksburg, San Luis Obispo, Napa. Reliable RIESLING, CABERNET rosé and CHENIN BLANC.

Johnson-Turnbull Napa. ★★ CS 80 81 82 83 84 85 86
Very small new estate producing balanced and distinguished, not overweight, CABERNETS from next door to MONDAVI.

Johnsons of Alexander Valley Sonoma. ★★ CS 79 80 81 82 83 84
Small winery with good v'yd land. CABERNET best.

Jordan Sonoma. ★★★ CH 83 84 85 86 CS 76 77 78 79 80 81 82 83 84
Extravagant winery. CABERNET modelled on Bordeaux, smooth CHARDONNAY. Polished wines to please sophisticates.

Karly Amador. ★★
Stylish producer of esp. ZIN from Sierra foothills.

Keenan, Robert Napa. ★★ CH 83 84 85 86 CS 83 84 85
V'yds on Spring Mountain started with over-strong and tannic wines. More polite recent style is winning approval.

Kendall-Jackson Lake County. ★★→★★★ CH 84 85 86 87 CS 84 85 86
Young (1980) and growing maker of good uncomplicated CHARD. RIES, SAUV BLANC, CABERNET and ZIN show real promise. V.g. SYRAH in '86.

Kenwood Vineyards Sonoma. ★★→★★★ CH 83 84 85 86 CS 78 79 80 81 82 83 84 85 Growing producer of steadily stylish reds, esp. CABERNET and ZIN also v.g. SAUV BLANC, good CHARD and CHENIN.

Kistler Vineyards Sonoma. ★★ CH 83 84 85 86 87 CS 80 81 82 83
Young small winery in hills. First CHARDONNAY ('79) was overwhelming; recent wines show more restraint. Now also CAB and P NOIR.

Konocti Cellars Lake County ★★
Mid-sized cooperative winery in remote north, half-owned by John PARDUCCI. RIESLING, Fumé Blanc, CAB SAUV are consistently attractive.

Korbel Sonoma ★★
Long-established sparkling wine specialists. "Natural" and "Brut" are among California's best standard "champagnes". Also brandy.

Kornell, Hanns Napa. ★★
Independent-minded sparkling wine house using RIES to make full-flavoured dry Sehr Trocken.

Krug, Charles Napa. ★→★★ CS 74 77 78 79 80 81 82 83 84 CH 86
Historic old winery with generally sound wines. Good CABERNET (incl. releases of mature vintages), sweet CHENIN BLANC and very sweet Muscat Canelli. C.K. Mondavi is the jug-wine brand.

La Crema Sonoma. ★★ CH 83 84 85 86 87 PN 79 80 81 82
Founded 1979 at Petaluma. CHARD has been huge; P NOIR impressive.

Lakespring Winery Napa. ★★ CS 84 85 SB 87
Steady small winery for well-made MERLOT, CAB SAUV. Powerful whites.

Lambert Bridge Sonoma. ★★ CS 80 81 82 83 84 85
Small 1975 winery nr. Healdsburg. CHARD less oaky than formerly; CABERNET austere, needs ageing.

Landmark Sonoma. ★★★ CH 83 84 85 86
Young winery nr. Windsor; sound CHARD. Signs of class.

Laurel Glen Sonoma. ★★ CS 81 82 83 84 85
Splendid '81 CABERNET was first wine of tiny Glen Ellen winery. '83 and '84 look very good.

Leeward Winery Central Coast/Ventura. ★★ CH 83 84 85 86 87 CS 83 84 85 86 CHARDONNAY from Monterey and San Luis Obispo grapes started this new venture near Santa Barbara well in 1980.

Long Vineyards Napa. ★★ CH 83 84 85 86 CS 79 80 81 82 83 84 85
Tiny winery in eastern hills nr. CHAPPELLET. First good CHARDONNAY and late-harvest RIESLING, now CABERNET.

Lyeth Vineyard Sonoma. ★★ 84 85
New winery with ambitions for Bordeaux-style red and white. Red is 78% CAB SAUV, 12% MERLOT, etc. – and promising.

Lytton Springs Sonoma. ★★ Z 83 84 85 86
Small specialist in Russian River ZIN; thick, heady, tannic.

Madrona El Dorado. (★★)
Winery with loftiest v'yd in Sierra Foothills and impressive CHARD.

Maison Deutz Sonoma. (★★)
New sp. winery with Champagne parentage. Promising first wines.

Mark West Sonoma. ★★→★★★ CH 83 84 85 86 87 PN 79 80 81 82 83 84 85 Young winery in cool sub-region. Very satisfactory GEWÜRZ, CHARDONAY. Now P NOIR and sparkling Blanc de Noirs.

Markham Napa. ★★ CS 78 79 80 81 82 83 84 CH 85 86
1979 winery with 300 acres. CAB very sound, not thrilling. Good bone dry CHENIN BLANC. CHARD gaining a reputation. Now Japanese owned.

Martin Bros Central Coast/San Luis Obispo. ★★
Excellently crisp CHENIN BL and CHARD. The small family winery aims to justify Nebbiolo in Paso Robles.

Martini, Louis Napa. ★★→ ★★★ CS 78 79 80 81 82 83 84 85 Z 78 79 80 81 82 83 84 85 Large but individual winery with very high standards at every level. CABERNET "Vineyard Selection" one of California's best. BARBERA, MERLOT, PETITE SIRAH, P NOIR, ZIN, GEWÜRZ, FOLLE BLANCHE and Moscato Amabile are all well made. Second label: "Glen Oaks". **Ca**

Masson, Vineyards Central Coast. ★←→★★
Famous old name sold by Seagram's in '87, moved to Monterey. New owners have raised their sights.

Matanzas Creek Sonoma. ★★ CH 85 86 M 79 80 81 82 83 84
Young winery now settled in with well-balanced CHARD, SAUV BL, and MERLOT.

Mayacamas Napa. ★★★ CH 81 83 84 85 CS 76 77 78 79 80 81 82 83 84
First-rate very small v'yd and winery offering CABERNET, highly eccentric monster CHARD, also SAUV BLANC and ZINFANDEL (sometimes).

McDowell Valley Vineyards Mendocino. ★★ CS 80 81 82 83 84
Big new development using old-established v'yd to make wide range. To watch, esp. for ZIN and real SYRAH.

Merry Vintners Sonoma. (★★)
Merry Edwards (ex-MOUNT EDEN, MATANZAS CREEK) made her name with CHARDONNAYS (regular, reserve bottlings), but is branching out into P NOIR.

Milano Winery Mendocino. ★★ CH 83 84 85 86 CS 79 80 81 82 83 84
Very small winery worth noting for CHARD. CAB is overweight.

Mill Creek Sonoma. ★★ CH 84 85

1974 winery near Healdsburg with pleasant, easy-going CHARDONNAY, MERLOT, CABERNET.

Mirassou Central Coast. ★★

Dynamic mid-sized growers and makers, the fifth generation of the family. Pioneers in SALINAS v'yds. Notable GAMAY BEAUJOLAIS, GEWÜRZ and very plesant sparkling.

Mondavi, Robert Napa. ★★★ →★★★★ CH 83 84 85 86 87 CS 74 75 76 77 78 79 80 81 82 83 84 85 Winery with a brilliant quarter-century record of innovation in styles, equipment and technique. Solid successes incl. CABERNET, SAUV BLANC (sold as Fumé Blanc), CHARDONNAY, PINOT NOIR. "Reserves" are marvellous – regularly among California's best. Also useful table wines. See also Opus One.

Monterey Peninsula Central Coast/Salinas. ★★ CH 83 84 85 CS 78 80 81 82 Very small winery near Carmel making chunky v. long-living ZINFANDEL and CABERNET from SALINAS and other grapes.

Monterey Vineyard Central Coast/Salinas. ★★

The first big modern winery of SALINAS, opened 1974. Now owned by Seagrams. Good ZIN, GEWÜRZ and SYLVANER and fruity feather-weight GAMAY BEAUJOLAIS. "Classic Red" is value.

Monteviña Amador. ★★ CS 79 80 81 82 83 Z 80 81 82 83

Pioneer small winery in revitalized area: the Shenandoah Valley, Amador County, in the Sierra foothills. ZINFANDEL, BARBERA and SAUVIGNON BLANC are achieving balance. Now owned by Sutter Home.

Monticello Cellars Napa. ★★★ CH 83 84 85 86 CS 80 81 82 83 84 85

Ultra-modern new winery near TREFETHEN. Outstanding GEWÜRZ and SAUVIGNON BLANC first caught the eye. Now v.g. CHARDONNAY, fine tannic CABERNET, and SEMILLON (called Chevrier Blanc).

Mont St John Napa. (★★) CS 80 81 82 83 84

Old-line Bartolucci family makes solid, good value varietals from their Carneros v'yd.

Morgan Central Coast/Salinas. (★★)

Ex-JEKEL winemaker now making his own v.g. CHARD.

J. W. Morris Sonoma. ★★★

Small former specialist in high-quality port-types from SONOMA grapes. Now in Healdsburg, with best table wines under Black Mtn. label, lesser bottlings under J.W.Morris.

Mount Eden Vineyards Central Coast. ★★ CH 80 81 82 83 84 85 86 CS 84

Company owning a major share of what were MARTIN RAY vineyards. Expensive wines.

Mount Veeder Napa. ★★ CS 74 75 77 78 79 80 81 82 83 84

Ambitious little 1973 winery. High prices but good CABERNET.

Navarro Vineyards Mendocino. ★★

Grower of first-rate CHARD, P NOIR, outstanding GEWÜRZ and RIESLING in cool Anderson Valley.

Newton Vineyards Napa. ★★★ CH 85 86 CS 84 85

Luxurious estate. Big oak-scent CAB SAUV, MERLOT, CHARD, SAUV BL.

Opus One Napa. ★★★★ CS 79 80 81 82 83 84

Not a winery but a wine; the joint venture of Robert Mondavi and Baron Philippe de Rothschild. So far, in effect, a Mondavi Reserve of Reserves at a far-fetched price, however good.

Papagni, Angelo San Joaquin. ★★

Long-established grower with a technically outstanding modern winery at Madera. Dry coastal-style varietals incl. ZIN, CHARD, and enjoyable Alicante Bouschet.

Parducci Mendocino. ★★ →★★★ CH 83 84 85 86 87 CS 78 79 80 81 82 83 84 85 Well-established mid-sized winery with v'yds in several locations. Good sturdy reds: CABERNET (and an excellent Cab/ Merlot blend), PETITE SIRAH, ZIN, "Burgundy". Also pleasant CHENIN BLANC and FRENCH COLOMBARD. N.B. The no-oak CHARD.

Pat Paulsen Vineyards Sonoma. ★★
Property of T.V. comedian offers thoroughly well-made range, esp. SAUV BLANC, and incl. a near-dry Muscat.

Pecota, Robert Napa. ▓▓ CH 83 84 85 86 CS 84 85
Small cellar of ex-BERINGER man with high standards. Wines are CABERNET, SAUV BLANC, CHARD, good light GAMAY.

Pedroncelli Sonoma/Russian River. ▓▓→▓▓▓ CH 83 84 85 86 87 CS 78 79 80 81 82 83 84 Long-established family business with recent reputation for well-above-average ZIN and CHARDONNAY, all growing more stylish with practice.

Pepi, Robert Napa. ★★ CH 83 84 85 86 CS 82 83
Young stone hilltop winery between Oakville and Yountville has launched well, esp. as a SAUVIGNON BLANC specialist.

Phelps, Joseph Napa. ▓▓▓ →★★★★ CH 80 81 83 84 85 86 87 CS 74 75 76 77 78 79 80 81 82 83 84 85 De-luxe mid-size winery and v'yd. Late harvest RIESLING exceptional. Very good CHARDONNAY, CABERNET, SYRAH. The "Reserve" wine, "Insignia", can be monstrously tannic. Whites age v. well, too. (e.g. '80 GEWÜRZ perfection in '88.)

Pine Ridge Napa. ★★ CH 83 84 85 86 87 CS 79 80 81 82 83 84 85
Small winery near STAG'S LEAP has made constantly stylish CHARD, MERLOT and CAB. Also mild but fresh, off-dry CHENIN BLANC.

Piper-Sonoma Sonoma. ★★★
A venture of Piper-Heidsieck of Champagne which released its first (very good) sparkling cuvée in 1980. Benefits from bottle-age.

Preston Sonoma. ★★ CS 83 84
Tiny winery with very high standards in Dry Creek Valley, Healdsburg, esp. for SAUV BLANC, ZIN and now blended SIRAH–SYRAH..

Quady Winery Central Valley. ★★
Imaginative dessert wines from Madera since '75. Celebrated orangey "Essencia"; "Elysium" from Black Muscat.

Quail Ridge Napa. ★★ CH 84 85 86
Small specialist in barrel-fermented CHARD. Also CAB. Good, if pricey. Owned by the CHRISTIAN BROTHERS.

Quivira Sonoma. (★★)
New ('86) winery with highly promising SAUV BL and ZIN from Dry Creek Valley.

Rafanelli, A. Sonoma. ▓▓
Tiny cellar specializing in outstanding ZIN; also CABERNET.

Raymond Vineyards Napa. ▓▓▓ CH 83 84 85 86 87 CS 77 78 79 80 81 82 83 84 85 Small 1974 winery near St Helena with experienced owners. CHARD, RIESLING and CABERNET all excellent.

Ridge Central Coast/Santa Cruz. ★★★★ CS 77 78 79 80 81 82 83 84 85 Small winery of high repute among connoisseurs for concentrated reds needing long maturing in bottle. Notable CAB and ZIN from named v'yds; esp. Montebello and York Creek, Napa.

River Oaks Sonoma. ★→★★
Sound commercial wines from same winery as CLOS DU BOIS, but different vineyards.

Roederer USA Mendocino. (★★★)
The Anderson Valley branch of the Reims Champagne house. First wine, released in 1988, is impressive.

Rombauer Vineyards Napa. ★★ CH 85 86 87 CS 84 85
Young ('80) small winery buying Napa grapes for impressive CHARD and CAB SAUV.

Roudon-Smith Santa Clara/Santa Cruz. ★★→ ▓▓▓ CH 83 84 CS 78 79 81 82 Small winery offering stylish CHARDONNAY.

Round Hill Napa. ▓▓→▓▓▓ CH 83 84 85 86 87 CS 80 81 82 83 84 85 86 Consistent good value, esp. GEWÜRZ and FUME BLANC, from big new winery in St Helena. Rutherford Ranch is label for best wines.

Ca

Rutherford Hill Napa. ▓▓▓ CH 83 84 85 86 CS 79 80 81 82 83 84 85
Larger stable-mate of FREEMARK ABBEY. Good GEWÜRZ. Excellent CHARD, MERLOT and CABERNET.

Rutherford Ranch See Round Hill.

Rutherford Vintners, Inc. Napa. ▓▓ CH 83 84 85 CS 77 78 79 80 81 82 83 Small winery started in 1977 by Bernard Skoda. "Chateau Rutherford" is "Reserve" label.

St Andrews Napa. ✶✶ CH 83 84 85 86 CS 83 84
Small CHARDONNAY estate on Silverado Trail near Napa city. Steadily excellent wine.

St Clement Napa. ✶✶→✶✶✶ CH 83 84 85 86 CS 78 79 80 81 82 83
Small production. Good CABERNET, powerful CHARD and delicious SAUVIGNON BLANC.

St Francis Sonoma. ✶→✶✶ CH 83 84 85 86 87
New small winery is using excellent CHARD, CABERNET, GEWÜRZ grapes from older v'yd. Wines have been disappointing so far.

Saintsbury Napa. ▓▓▓ CH 83 84 85 86 87 PN 81 82 83 84 85 86
Young winery using Carneros grapes to make perhaps the best P NOIR and CHARD of this region.

Sanford Santa Barbara. ✶✶✶ CH 84 85 86 87
New winery started with striking 1982 SAUV BLANC and CHARDONNAY in the toast and oak school. P NOIR is beautifully made; also P Noir Blanc.

San Martin Central Coast. ✶✶ CH 81 82 83 84 85 86 87
Restructured old company using Salinas and San Luis Obispo grapes to make correct varietals. Also pioneers in "soft" (low-alcohol) wines.

Santa Barbara Winery Santa Barbara. (✶✶)
One-time jug-wine producer showing even greater turns of speed, esp. with estate CHARD

Santa Cruz Mountain V'yd. Central Coast. ✶✶ CS 78 79 80 81 82 83 PN 79 80 81 82 83 84 Small winery in the hills with hopes for fine PINOT NOIR, but problems with overbearing alcohol. Now CABERNET too.

Santa Ynez Valley Winery Santa Barbara. ✶✶ CH 83 84 85 86
Established producer of very good SAUV BLANC and CHARD.

Sausal Sonoma. ✶✶
Small specialist in stylish ZIN, etc.

Scharffenberger Mendocino. ✶✶
The major pioneer of champagne method sparkling Mendocino. Move planned from Ukiah to Anderson Valley.

Schramsberg Napa. ✶✶✶✶
A dedicated specialist using historic old cellars to make California's best "champagne", incl. splendid "Reserves". "Blanc de Noirs" is outstanding, deserves 2-3 years' ageing.

Schug Cellars Napa. ✶✶ CH 83 84 85 PN 80 81 82 83 84 85
New (1982) enterprise of PHELPS' ex-winemaker. Very tough PINOT NOIR at outset; recently moderated. Also dense dry CHARD.

Sebastiani Sonoma. ▓◀▶▓▓ CS 78 79 80 81 82 83 84 85 86
Substantial and distinguished old family firm with robust appetizing wines, incl. BARBERA. Top wines have SONOMA appellation. Keep under observation.

Seghesio Sonoma. ▓▓
Old Healdsburg bulk producer offers notable value in P NOIR and ZIN.

Sequoia Grove Napa. ✶✶✶ CH 83 84 85 86 87 CS 83 84 85
Small winery nr. Oakville. CHARD since '79 has been well-balanced. CAB SAUV (Napa and Alexander Valleys) is tannic and meant to age.

Shadow Creek See Domaine Chandon.

Shafer Vineyards Napa. ✶✶→✶✶✶ CH 81 83 84 85 86 CS 80 81 82 83 84 85 Young winery and vineyard near STAG'S LEAP is making polished CHARDONNAY and very stylish CABERNET and MERLOT.

Shaw, Charles F., Vineyards and Winery Napa. ★★ CH 83 84 85 86 87
St Helena specialist in GAMAY light red, has added CHARD, SAUV BLANC.

Sierra Vista El Dorado. (★★)
Steady producer of CHARD, CAB SAUV, ZIN; more recently SYRAH from
Sierra Foothills v'yds.

Silver Oak Napa. ★★→★★★ CS 78 79 80 81 82 83 84
Small 1972 winery succeeding with oaky CABERNETS, incl. v. expensive
"Bonny's Vineyard".

Silverado Vineyards Napa. ★★★ CH 84 85 86 87 CS 83 84 85
A showy new winery east of Yountville. Early CHARD and SAUV BLANC
made news. Now CAB is even better. The owner is Mrs. Walt Disney,
which suggests adequate capital.

Simi Alexander Valley. ███ CH 83 84 85 86 CS 78 79 80 81 82 83 84
85 Restored historic winery with expert direction of Zelma Long.
Some of America's best, most lively CHARDONNAY, delicate CABERNET
and (since '82) splendid SAUV BLANC. Also good CHENIN BLANC,
irresistible rosé.

Smith & Hook Central Coast/Monterey. ★★ CS 79 80 81 82 83 84 85
Specialist entirely dedicated to CAB SAUV from Salinas Valley w. hills.

Smith-Madrone Napa. ★★→★★★ CH 83 84 85 86 CS 79 80 81 82 83 84
New v'yd high on Spring Mountain made first good RIESLING in '77.
CHARD is now eye-catching. Also CAB.

Sonoma-Cutrer Vineyards, Inc. Sonoma. ★★★★ CH 81 82 83 84 85 86
Perhaps the ultimate (so far) in specialist estates, using new
techniques to display the characters individual v'yds give to CHARDS
(as in Burgundy). So far Les Pierres v'yd is No. 1.

Spottswoode Napa. (★★→★★★)
From a v'yd right at St Helena town, small lots of increasingly subtle,
stylish CAB SAUV, SAUV BLANC.

Spring Mountain Napa. ★★ CH 83 84 CS 75 77 78 79 81
Renovated small 19th-century property with winery noted for good
CHARDONNAY, SAUVIGNON BLANC and CABERNET.

Stag's Leap Wine Cellars Napa. ★★★→★★★★ CH 83 84 85 86 87 CS
74 75 76 77 78 79 80 81 82 83 84 85 Celebrated small v'yd and
cellar with the highest standards. Excellent CABERNET and MERLOT,
fresh GAMAY, fine CHARD.

Sterling Napa. ★★★ CH 83 84 85 86 CS 82 83 84 85
Extremely proficient (also scenic) winery owned by Seagrams. Strong,
tart SAUVIGNON BLANC and CHARDONNAY; oaky CABERNET and MERLOT. Also
"Three Palms" red from '85.

Stonegate Napa. ★★ CH 83 84 CS 78 79 80 81 82 83 84
Small privately owned winery and v'yd making CABERNET, CHARDONNAY
and better and better SAUV BLANC.

Stony Hill Napa. ████ CH 74 75 76 77 78 79 80 81 82 83 84 85
Many of California's very best whites have come from this minute
winery over 30 years. Owner Fred McCrea died in 1977; his widow
Eleanor carries on. Stony Hill CHARDONNAY, GEWÜRZ and RIESLING are all
delicate and fine. CHARD recently weightier.

Stratford Napa. ★★ CH 84 85 86 87 CS 83 84 85
First wine ('82) was an impressive blended CHARD. New winery nr.
Rutherford to provide more; also good SAUV BL (from '85).

Strong, Rodney, Vineyards Sonoma/Russian River. ███ →★★★ CH 85
86 CS 78 79 80 Formerly called Sonoma Vineyards. Well regarded,
esp. for CHARD. Range includes single-v'yd wines, esp. Alexander's
Crown CABERNET.

Sutter Home Napa. ██ z 77 78 79 80 81 82 83 84 85
Small winery revived and hugely expanded on the success of its sweet,
pink "white" ZINFANDEL. (1m. cases a year.)

Swan, J. Sonoma. ★★ z 74 76 77 78 80 81 82 83 84 85 PN 85
>One-man winery with a name for rich ZIN, CHARD, P NOIR.

Taft Street Sonoma (★★→★★★) CH 84 85 86 87
>After muddling along, the winery hit impressive stride with Russian River CHARDS.

Trefethen Napa. ███ ★★→★★★ CH 80 81 83 84 85 86 CS 74 75 76 77 78 79 80 81 82 83 84 Growing family-owned winery in Napa's finest old wooden building. Very good dry RIESLING, CABERNET, P NOIR. Tense CHARDONNAY for ageing and a notable low-price blend, Eshcol. Late-released "Library" wines demonstrate ageing potential.

Tudal Napa. ★★
>Small estate winery since '79 just n. of St Helena. Excellent dark age-worthy CABERNET.

Tulocay Napa. ★★ CS 80 81 82 83 84
>Tiny young winery at Napa City. PINOT NOIR and CABERNET can be really accomplished.

Ventana Central Coast/Monterey. ★★ CH 83 84 85 86 87
>New in '78 with flavoury PINOT BLANC and CHARDONNAY.

Vichon Winery Napa. ★★→★★★ CH 83 84 85 86 CS 77 78 79 80 81 82 83 84 85 Founded 1980; original and ambitious. Fine CHARDONNAY and blended (50/50) SAUVIGNON/SEMILLON "Chevrignon Blanc". Now promising CABS. Bought (1985) by Robert MONDAVI.

Villa Mount Eden Napa. ★★ CH 83 84 85 86 CS 77 78 79 80 81 82 Small Oakville estate has made excellent dry CH BLANC, good CHARD, outstanding CAB. Bought (1986) by CH STE MICHELLE.

Weibel Central Coast and Mendocino ███ ★→★★ ___
>Veteran mid-sized winery giving value in its class. Specialist in own-label sparkling wines.

Wente Livermore and Central Coast. ★→★★★ CH 84 85 86
>Important and historic specialists in Bordeaux-style whites. Fourth-generation Wentes are as dynamic as ever, CHARD, SAUV BLANC and RIESLING are all successful. Arroyo Secco Chard is v.g. Now also sparkling.

Whitehall Lane Napa. ★★
>Small St Helena producer to follow for fresh and lively P NOIR.

White Oak Sonoma. (★★)
>Small Healdsburg winery using Alexander Valley CHARD, SAUV BLANC, CHENIN BLANC for rich, ripe wines. Now CABERNET.

Wild Horse Winery San Luis Obispo. (★★)
>Small, young winery near Paso Robles draws on local Santa Barbara v'yds. Impressive P NOIR.

William Wheeler Winery Sonoma. ★★ CH 86 CS 82 83 84
>Young Dry Creek Valley family firm. Big CAB, good SAUV BLANC, CHARD to watch with interest.

Zaca Mesa Central Coast/Santa Barbara. ███ CH 81 82 83 84 85 86 CS 79 80 81 82 83 84 Santa Ynez Valley pioneer with good CHARD and RIESLING now scaling the heights with P NOIR.

Z D Wines Napa. ★★ CH 83 84 85 86 87 CS 79 80 81 82 83 84
>Very small winery (moved from Sonoma to Rutherford) with a name for powerful PINOT NOIR and CHARDONNAY.

The Pacific North-West

There are now over 16,000 acres of vines and over 100 wineries in the States of Washington, Oregon and Idaho.

Oregon's vines lie mainly in the cool-temperate Willamette and warmer Umpqua valleys between the Coast and Cascades ranges. Those of Washington and Idaho are mainly east of the Cascades in the semi-arid Yakima Valley and Columbia basin areas, with very hot days and cold nights. Most Oregon-grown wines are consequently more delicate, Washington's more intensive in flavour. Individual wineries, with some notable exceptions, can be hard to characterize. In Oregon most are small and have yet to establish a steady track-record. Vintages are also as uneven as in e.g. Burgundy, whose Pinot Noir is Oregon's most talked about grape. Drouhin of Burgundy has encouraged the talk by buying land. Yet whites remain in the majority, and a serious over-supply threatens the finances of the industry in the north-west. Its excellent Riesling is sadly out of fashion (and is consequently a first-rate bargain). The principal producers are:

Adelsheim Vineyard Willamette, Oregon.
Small winery: promising P NOIR, oaky CHARDONNAY, fresh PINOT GRIS.

Alpine Vineyards Willamette, Oregon.
Young small estate winery with high spots, incl. P NOIR, RIESLING.

Amity Vineyards Willamette, Oregon.
1976 70-acre winery; variable quality; PINOT NOIR best.

Arbor Crest Spokane, Washington.
Expanding and encouraging newcomer. Early CHARD and SAUV BLANC v.g. Reds also promising, if unpredictable.

Bethel Heights nr. Salem, Oregon.
Much praised newcomer, esp. for PINOT NOIR (85). Owned by Bonny Doon (see California).

Champs de Brionne George, Washington.
New winery. Fast start in whites but ? direction.

Château Benoit Oregon.
Sound producer of MÜLLER-THURGAU, CHARD, and P NOIR has acquired a winemaker from Chablis and is launching sparkling.

Château Ste Chapelle Caldwell, Idaho.
The first Idaho winery, near Boise. Early CHARD and RIESLING had intense flavours but beautiful balance. Now well settled in.

Château Ste Michelle Seattle, Columbia and Yakima valleys, Washington.
The largest north-west winery (550,000 cases), though now operating separately from COLUMBIA CREST. Wineries at Grandview and Woodinville offer wide range incl. v.g. CABERNET, SEMILLON, CHARDONNAY, MERLOT and sparkling. Second label: Farron Ridge.

Columbia Cellars (formerly Associated Vintners) Washington.
A Washington pioneer and still a leader, at Redmond, nr. Seattle. CABERNET, RIESLING, dry spicy GEWÜRZ and esp. SEMILLON have all been successful. Good value. Now good CHARDONNAY.

Columbia Crest Washington.
The label used by CHATEAU STE MICHELLE for a range of wines from River Run, the group's biggest and newest winery, in the Columbia Valley. Good delicately fruity CHARD.

Covey Run (formerly Quail Run) Yakima, Washington.
Admirable whites incl. ALIGOTE; reds are strong in alcohol and flavour.

Elk Cove Vineyards Willamette, Oregon.

Very small 1977 winery. Good CHARDONNAY and RIESLING from named v'yds. PINOT NOIR inconsistent.

The Eyrie Vineyards Willamette, Oregon.

Early (1965) winery with Burgundian ideas. Oregon's most famous and consistently good P NOIR, and v. oaky CHARD. Also Pinots Gris and Meunier and dry Muscat.

Hillcrest Vineyard Umpqua Valley, Oregon.

Early (1961) winery in warmer area. Inconsistent; CAB best.

Hogue Cellars Yakima Valley, Washington.

Expanding young winery outstanding for off-dry whites, esp. RIESLING, CHENIN BLANC, SAUV BLANC, and bold CHARD. Since '83 really stylish CAB, MERLOT. The leader in the region.

Kiona Vineyards Yakima Valley, Washington.

Small cellar and v'yd nr. Benton City attracting attention with RIESLING, and CHARD.

Knudsen Erath Willamette, Oregon.

Oregon's second-biggest winery with reliable good-value PINOT NOIR, esp. Vintage Select. Austere CHARDONNAY.

F. W. Langguth Winery Yakima Valley, Washington.

German Mosel-maker succeeded with German-style RIESLINGS, esp. late harvest, now owned by SNOQUALMIE.

Latah Creek Spokane, Washington.

Recent source of fruity, off-dry whites, esp. CHENIN BL, RIES, SAUV BL.

Mercer Ranch Columbia Valley, Washington.

New winery has made some outstanding CABERNET and (unusually) Limberger from established v'yds.

Oak Knoll Willamette, Oregon.

Fruit-winemaker making fair-value red and white wines, esp. P NOIR.

Preston Wine Cellars Yakima Valley, Washington.

Early winery with broad range of sound to very good wines.

Rex Hill Yamhill City, Oregon.

Well-financed assault on top levels of P NOIR from individual v'yds, incl. Reserve wines. Also RIES. Fine new winery.

Saddle Mountain Label first used for second wines by F.W. LANGGUTH.

Shafer Vineyard Cellars Willamette, Oregon.

Small meticulous P NOIR specialist. White P NOIR may be Oregon's best; CHARD almost certainly is.

Snoqualmie Yakima Valley, Washington.

Off to new start in 1988 after complete financial reorganization. Prospects seemingly bright.

Sokol Blosser Vineyards Willamette, Oregon.

Largest Oregon winery with wide range, incl. CHARD (esp. "Yamhill County"), SAUV BLANC, MERLOT and RIESLING. P NOIR is best effort.

Staton Hills Yakima Valley, Washington.

Reliable, occasionally excellent source of easy, not very dry whites.

Stewart Vineyards Yakima Valley, Washington.

New estate nr. Sunnyside. Early whites v. impressive.

Paul Thomas Seattle, Washington.

Former fruit winery nr. Seattle now making v.g varietals and CHARDONNAY. Reds hold promise.

Tualatin Vineyards Willamette, Oregon.

Third-largest Oregon winery. Mainly whites with emphasis on CHARD, P NOIR (red and white). Both Washington and home-grown grapes. Mixed reports.

Woodward Canyon Walla Walla, Washington.

New district, small cellar but first SEM, CAB SAUV v. stylish.

Yamhill Valley Oregon.

First wines, made at SOKOL BLOSSER, were good. Own v'yds may confirm prospects.

The North & East

New York State and its neighbours Ohio and Ontario have traditionally made their wine from grapes of native American ancestry. American grapes have a flavour known as "foxy"; a taste acquired by many easterners. Fashion is steadily moving in favour of hybrids between these and European grapes with less, or no, foxiness, and now rapidly towards true European varieties. Recent European-style wines both from old vineyards and areas such as Long Island promise a bright future. Chardonnays and Rieslings can both be excellent. The entries below include both wineries and grape varieties.

Andres Canada's second-largest wine-producer, with wineries in Ontario and British Columbia.

Aurora One of the best white French-American hybrid grapes, the most widely planted in New York. Good for sparkling wine.

Baco Noir One of the better red French-American hybrid grapes. High acidity but good clean dark wine.

Banfi 55-acre CHARDONNAY v'yd at Old Brookville, Long Island, released its first wine in 1986. First impressions v. favourable.

Benmarl Highly regarded and expanding v'yd and winery at Marlboro on the Hudson River. Wines are mainly from French-American hybrids (e.g. Seyval Blanc), but CHARD can be splendid.

Bridgehampton Wine Co. Tiny property on Long Island. RIESLING and CHARD.

Brights Canada's biggest winery, in Ontario, now tending towards French-American hybrids and experiments with European vines. Their BACO NOIR is a sound red, CHARDONNAY is steely, ALIGOTE pleasant. Now also in British Columbia.

Bully Hill FINGER LAKES winery founded 1970, using both American and hybrid grapes to make varietal wines.

Byrd Vineyards Maryland Winery with CABERNET intended for ageing.

Canandaigua Wine Co. Major traditional eastern winemaker ("the nation's third largest"). Bought WIDMERS in 1986. Also in California.

Catawba One of the first American wine-grapes, still the second most widely grown. Pale red and foxy flavoured.

Château des Charmes Smaller Ontario winery, doing well with CHARD, P NOIR, GAMAY, RIESLING.

Château Gai Big Canadian (Ontario) winery making European and hybrid wines, incl. v. light CHARD, GAMAY, MERLOT.

Chautauqua The biggest grape-growing district in the east, along the s. shore of Lake Erie from New York to Ohio. 20,000 acres.

Chelois Popular red hybrid. Dry wine with some richness, slightly foxy.

Delaware Old American white-wine grape making pleasant, slightly foxy dry wines. Used in "champagne" and for still wine.

De Chaunac A good red French-American hybrid grape, popular in Canada as well as New York. Full-bodied dark wine.

Finger Lakes Century-old wine district in upper New York State, best-known for its "champagne". The centre is Hammondsport.

Finger Lakes Wine Cellars Young winery making good CHARD, and (esp.) RIES.

Firelands CABERNET from Isle St George in Lake Erie, Ohio.

Glenora Wine Cellars Recent FINGER LAKES winery. Very successful RIES and CHARD.

Gold Seal One of New York's biggest and best wineries, makers of Charles Fournier "champagne" and the HENRI MARCHANT range. Recent CHARDONNAY has been excellent, winning major prizes.

Great Western The brand name of the PLEASANT VALLEY WINE CO's "champagne", one of New York's sound traditional wines.

Hargrave Vineyard Trend-setting winery planting extensively on North Fork of Long Island, N.Y. Well established with CHARDONNAY and PINOT NOIR.

Henri Marchant GOLD SEAL's range of mainly traditional American wines.

Heron Hill Vineyards Small FINGER LAKES estate with good RIES, CHARD, etc.

Inniskillin Leading quality Canadian winery at Niagara. European and hybrid wines, incl. good MARECHAL FOCH, also CHARDONNAY.

Phylloxera is an insect that lives on the roots of the vine. Its arrival in Europe from North America in the 1860s was an international catastrophe. It destroyed almost every vineyard on the Continent before it was discovered that the native American vine is immune to its attacks. The remedy was (and still is) to graft European vines on to American rootstocks. Virtually all Europe's vineyards are so grafted today. Whether their produce is just as good as the wine of pre-phylloxera days is a favourite debate among old-school wine-lovers.

Maréchal Foch Useful red French hybrid between PINOT NOIR and GAMAY.

Marrko Small Ohio winery with buttery CHARD.

Niagara Old American white grape used for sweet wine. Very foxy.

Pindar Vineyards Substantial young company on North Fork, Long Island. RIESLING has been successful.

Pleasant Valley Wine Co. Famous old winery at Hammondsport, FINGER LAKES, owned by TAYLOR's, producing GREAT WESTERN wines.

Seibel Celebrated French grape hybridist. Many successful French-American crosses originally known by numbers, since christened as AURORA, DE CHAUNAC, CHELOIS.

Seyve-Villard Another well-known French hybridist. His best-known cross, no. 5276, known as Seyval Blanc, is the most successful variety of its kind, making clean, aromatic wine with good acidity.

Taylor's The biggest wine-company of the E. States, based in the FINGER LAKES. Brands incl. GREAT WESTERN and lake country. Most vines are American. Also in California. Changed hands in 1987.

Vinifera Wines Small but influential winery of the late Dr Konstantin Frank, pioneer in growing European vines, incl. RIESLING, CHARDONNAY and PINOT NOIR, in the FINGER LAKES area. Some excellent wines.

Wagner Vineyards Excellent CHARD, also GEWÜRZ, AURORA from the FINGER LAKES.

Widmers Major FINGER LAKES winery selling native American varietal wines: DELAWARE, NIAGARA, etc. Now also good RIESLING.

Wiemer, Herman J. Creative and daring German FINGER LAKES winemaker. Fine RIESLINGS; ferments v.g. CHARDONNAY in oak.

Woodbury Vineyards Chatauque estate for CHARD, RIES and some P NOIR.

Texas

In the past few years a brand new Texan wine industry has sprung noisily to life. It already seems past the experimental stage, with some very passable wines, though such a short track record can only confirm the state potential. The biggest winery is Ste Genevieve, at Fort Stockton. Wines include SAUV BLANC, CHENIN BLANC, FRENCH COLOMBARD. But money problems have slowed its progress. Still, with 450 growers and 25 wineries now active, the state's wines have begun to show some form. Llano Estacado, with 220 acres near Lubbock, has been the consistent leader to date. Nearby and much smaller is Pheasant Ridge, which has made good CHARDONNAY and SEMILLON. Fall Creek, 80 miles n. of Austin, has become a name to watch, esp. for its v.g. CARNELIAN, the first Texan red to excite interest. Pressing these front-runners are Oberhellman, Taysha (esp. for GEWÜRZTRAMINER) and Slaughter-Leftwich. Total production is a relatively minute 220,000 cases per year, but growing swiftly.

Missouri

Has a small but long-established wine industry at Augusta, where Mount Pleasant Vineyards makes some very good white, esp. from Seyval Blanc. Their high acidity gives them the capacity to age remarkably: five years is not too long.

Virginia

Early successes with lean-bodied, fresh-flavoured CHARDONNAYS and RIESLINGS have given growers in Virginia the self-confidence to push into new territories with a broader range of European grape varieties. CHARDONNAY and RIESLING remain the most popular varieties in most of the state, with Barboursville Vineyards and Meredyth Vineyards trading the honours. North, around Charlottesville, Bordeaux red varieties are the focal point; Montdomaine Cellars appear to be showing the way.

South America

Argentina

Argentina has the world's fifth largest wine production, most of it gratefully and uncritically consumed within S. America. But things are stirring. The quality vineyards are concentrated in Mendoza province in the Andean foothills at about 2,000 feet. They are all irrigated. San Rafael, 140 miles s. of Mendoza city, is centre of a slightly cooler area. Salta, to the north, and Rio Negro, to the south, also produce interesting wines.

Bianchi, Bodegas Well-known premium wine producer at San Rafael owned by Seagrams. "Don Valentin" CABERNET and Bianchi Borgoña are best-sellers. "Particular" is their top Cabernet.

Canale, Bodegas Active winery in Rio Negro: good CABERNET and SEMILLON.

Crillon, Bodegas 1972-built winery owned by Seagram's, only for tank-method sparkling wines.

Esmeralda Producers of a good CAB and CHARD, St Felician, at Mendoza.

Etchart Salta winery making typical aromatic but dry Torrontes white (gold medal Bd'x, '87) and sound range of reds in Salta and Mendoza.

Flichman, Bodegas Old Mendoza firm now owned by a bank. Top "Caballero de la Cepa" white and red, plus SYRAH, MERLOT and sp.

Giol The enormous State cooperative of Maipu province. Mainly bulk wines. Premium range called "Canciller" is good.

Goyenechea, Bodegas Basque family firm in San Rafael making old-style wines, including Aberdeen Angus red.

La Rural, Bodegas ("San Filipe")
Family-run winery at Coquimbito (Mendoza) making some of Argentina's best RIESLING and GEWÜRZ whites and some good reds. Also a charming wine museum.

Lopez, Bodegas Family firm best known for their "Château Montchenot" red and white and "Château Vieux" CABERNET.

Luigi Bosca, Bodegas Small Mendoza winery with excellent MALBEC and SAUVIGNON BLANC.

Nacari, Bodegas Small La Rioja winery. Its Torrontés white won a gold medal and Oscar at Vinexpo, Bordeaux '87.

Norton, Bodegas Old firm, originally English. Reds (esp. Malbec) are best. "Perdriel" is their premium brand. Also good sparkling wines.

Orfila, José Long-established bodega at St Martin, Mendoza. Top wines: Cautivo CAB and white Extra Dry (P BLANC).

Peñaflor Argentina's biggest wine company, reputedly the world's third-largest. Bulk wines, but also some of Argentina's finest premium wines, incl. Trapiche (esp. "Medalla"), Andean Vineyards and Fond de Cave CHARDONNAY and CABERNET. A sherry, Tio Quinto, is exported.

H. Piper Sparkling wine made under licence from Piper-Heidsieck of Champagne. Challenges PROVIAR.

Proviar, Bodega Producers of "Baron B" and "M. Chandon" sparkling wine under MOËT & CHANDON supervision. Also still reds and whites including v.g. Castel Chandon, less exciting Kleinburg, Wunderwein (whites), smooth Comte de Valmont, Beltour and Clos du Moulin reds.

Santa Ana, Bodegas Small, old-established family firm at Guaymallen, Mendoza. Wide range of wines include good Syrah Val Semina.

San Telmo Modern winery with a Californian air and outstanding fresh, full-flavoured CHARD, MERLOT, CAB and esp. MALBEC.

Suter, Bodegas Swiss-founded firm owned by Seagram's making best-selling "Etiquetta Marron" white and good "Etiquetta Blanca" red.

Toso, Pascual Old Mendoza winery at San José, making one of Argentina's best reds, Cabernet Toso. Also RIES and sparkling wines.

Weinert, Bodegas Small winery. Tough old-fashioned reds led by good CAB/MERLOT/MALBEC "Cavas de Weinert" and promising SAUV BLANC.

Chile

Natural conditions are ideal for wine-growing in central Chile, just south of Santiago. But political conditions have been difficult for decades, and the country's full potential has only really started to be explored in the past four years. Chilean Cabernets lead the way with resounding flavours that will one day lead to worldwide renown. Other varieties now show equal promise. New oak barrels are starting to revolutionize standards. The principal bodegas ("Viñas") exporting wine from Chile are:

Canepa, José Chile's most modern big bodega, handling wine from several areas. Very good frank and fruity CABERNET from Lontué, Curico, 100 miles south; recently particularly good CHARD, RIESLING and SAUV BLANC. Also SEMILLON, sweet Moscatel.

Concha y Toro The biggest and most outward-looking wine firm, with several bodegas and 2,500 acres in the Maipo valley. Remarkable dark and deep CABERNET, MERLOT, Verdot. Brands are St Emiliana, Marques de Casa Concha, Casillero del Diablo. CHARDONNAY and SAUV BLANC are now becoming established.

Cousiño Macul Distinguished and beautiful old estate near Santiago. Very dry SEMILLON and CHARD. Don Luis light red, Don Matias dark and tannic, good CAB. Antiguas Reservas ('81) is top export CAB.

Errazuriz Panquehue Historic firm in Aconcagua valley, n. of Santiago, making very rich full-bodied wines, esp. CABERNET.

Los Vascos Family estate in Colchagua Prov. 400 acres making some of Chile's best CAB ('84 '85) influenced by Bd'x and Cálifornia. Also stylish SAUV/SEM. Made headlines in '88 by link with Lafite-Rothschild.

Santa Carolina Architecturally splendid old Santiago bodega with old-style "Reserva de Familia" and better "Ochagavia" wines.

San Pedro Long established at Lontué, Curico. The second-biggest exporter, with a range of good wines. Gatto Negro and Gatto Blanco are biggest sellers. Llave de Oro is good CAB and Castillo de Molina is top cab. Also aromatic "blush" Amigo. Santa Hellena is associated.

Santa Rita Long-established bodega in the Maipo valley s. of Santiago. "120" brand CABERNET ('84) has made a name in Europe and USA.

Torres, Miguel New enterprise of Catalan family firm (see Spain) at Lontué. Good SAUV BLANC ("Bellaterra" is oak-aged) and CHARD, v.g. RIESLING. CAB is made more "elegantly" than others in Chile: ages well. (SAm)

Undurraga Famous family business; one of the first to export to the USA. Wines in both old and modern styles: good clean SAUVIGNON BLANC and oaky yellow "Viejo Roble".

Viña Linderos Small family winery in the Maipo valley exports good full-bodied CABERNET which gains from bottle-age.

Brazil

International investments, esp. in the Rio Grande du Sud, are starting much talk. Exports are beginning.

Peru

Viña Tacama has exported some Sauvignon Blanc and sparkling wine of very promising quality.

Australia N.S.W.

CLARE/ WATERVALE
MURRAY VALLEY
MUDGEE
RIVERINA
BAROSSA
Adelaide
Canberr
SOUTHERN VALES
LANGHORNE CREEK
RUTHERGLEN
PADTHAWAY KEPPOCH
CENTRAL VICTORIA
NORTH EAST VICTORIA
COONAWARRA
GREAT WESTERN
Goulburn River
YARRA VALLEY
Melbourne
GEELONG

It is little more than 20 years since new technology revolutionized Australia's 150-year-old wine industry, ending the dominance of fortified wines and making table wines of top quality possible. Old-style Australian wines were thick-set and burly Shiraz reds or Sémillon or Riesling whites grown in warm to hot regions. A progressive shift to cooler areas, to new wood fermentation and maturation, to noble varieties (with Cabernet, Merlot, Pinot Noir, Chardonnay and Sauvignon Blanc at the forefront) has seen a radical change in style which has by no means run its course. Nonetheless, extract and alcohol levels continue to be high and the best wines still have great character and the ability to age splendidly.

Exports have suddenly assumed great importance for Australia, increasing from 8 million to over 40 million litres in five years. At last Australia's best wines are to be found in London and New York. But it is not easy to keep tabs on them. There are now almost 500 wineries in commercial production. Labels are becoming less garrulous (but less informative) as Australian consumers become more sophisticated. Such information as they give can be relied on, while prizes in shows (which are highly competitive) mean a great deal. In a country lacking any formal grades of quality the buyer needs all the help he can get.

Wine areas

The vintages here are those rated as good or excellent for the reds of the areas in question. Excellent recent vintages are marked with an accent.

Adelaide Hills (Sth Aust) 84′ 85′ 86′ 87′ 88
> Spearheaded by PETALUMA: numerous new v'yds at very cool 1500ft sites in Mt Lofty ranges coming into production.

Adelaide Plains (Sth Aust) 82 84′ 86′ 87′ 88′
> Small area immediately n. of Adelaide formerly known as Angle Vale. Wineries incl. Anglesey, Normans, PRIMO ESTATE.

Barossa (Sth Aust) 66 75 76 80 81 84' 85 86' 87' 88

Australia's most important winery (though not v'yd) area, processing grapes from diverse sources (local, to MURRAY VALLEY, through to high-quality cool regions from adjacent hills to far-distant COONAWARRA) to make equally diverse styles.

Bendigo/Ballarat (Vic.) 73 75 80' 82' 84 85 87 88

Widespread small v'yds, some of extreme quality, re-creating the glories of the last century. 14 wineries incl. CH LE AMON, BALGOWNIE, Heathcote Winery and Passing Clouds.

Canberra District (ACT) 15 wineries now sell cellar door to local and tourist trade. Quality is variable, as is style.

Clare Watervale (Sth Aust) 71' 75' 80' 82 84' 85 86' 87 88

Small high-quality area 90 miles n. of Adelaide best known for RIESLING; also planted with SHIRAZ and CABERNET. 17 wineries spill over into near adjacent sub-district of Polish Hill River.

Coonawarra (Sth Aust) 66 71 72 76' 77 79 80' 82' 84' 86 87 88

Southernmost and greatest v'yd of state, long famous for well-balanced reds, recently successful with RIESLING, CHARDONNAY. Numerous recent arrivals incl. Hollicks, Haselgrove, Koppamurra, Ladbroke Grove, Zema Estate.

Geelong (Vic.) 78 80' 82 84' 85 86 87 88

Once famous area destroyed by phylloxera, re-established mid-60s. Very cool, dry climate produces firm table wines from premium varieties. Names incl. IDYLL, HICKINBOTHAM.

Goulburn Valley (Vic.) 68 71' 76 80' 82 84 86 87 88

A mixture of old (e.g. CH TAHBILK) and new (e.g. MITCHELTON) wineries in temperate region; full flavoured table wines.

Granite Belt (Qld.) 85 87'

Rapidly developing high altitude and (relatively) cool region just n. of N.S.W. border with 13 wineries; spicy Shiraz and rich SEM/CHARD are district specialities.

Great Western/Avoca (Vic.) 78 80' 82' 84 85 86 87

Adjacent cool to temperate regions in central w. of state; Avoca also known as Pyrenees area. High quality table and sparkling wines. Now 8 wineries, 6 of recent origin.

Hunter Valley (N.S.W.) 66 67 73 75 79 80 82 83 85' 86' 87

The great name in N.S.W. Broad soft earthy SHIRAZ reds and SEMILLON whites with a style of their own. Now also CABERNET and CHARDONNAY. Many changes in identity.

Keppoch/Padthaway (Sth Aust) 76 79 80 82' 84' 85 86' 87 88

Large new v'yd area (no wineries) developed by big companies as an overspill of adjacent COONAWARRA. Cool climate; good commercial reds and whites and CHARD/PINOT NOIR sparkling wines.   **(Aus)**

N.E. Victoria 66 70' 71' 75' 80' 82' 86' 87 88

Historic area incl. Rutherglen, Corowa, Wangaratta. Heavy reds and magnificent sweet dessert wines.

Margaret River (W. Aust) 73' 75 76 79' 81 82' 83 85' 86' 88

New cool coastal area producing superbly elegant wines, 174 miles s. of Perth. 20 operating wineries; others planned.

Mornington Peninsula (Vic.) 84' 86' 87

Seventeen commercial wineries on dolls-house scale making exciting wines in new cool coastal area 25 miles s. of Melbourne. 45 growers with total plantings of 261 acres, wineries incl. ELGEE PARK, Merricks.

Mount Barker/Frankland River (W. Aust) 80 81' 82 83 85 86 88

Promising new far-flung cool area in extreme south of state.

Mudgee (N.S.W.) 74 75 78 79 83 84' 86 87

Small isolated area 168 miles n.w. of Sydney. Big red of colour and flavour and full coarse white, recently being refined.

Murray Valley (Sth Aust, Vic. & N.S.W.) NV
 Important irrigated v'yds near Swan Hill, Mildura (N.S.W. and Vic.),
 Renmark, Berri, Loxton, Waikerie and Morgan (S.A.). Principally
 "cask" table wines. 40% of total wine production.

Perth Hills (W.A.). Fledgling area 19 miles e. of Perth with 6 wineries and
 a larger number of growers on cool hillside sites.

Pyrenees (Vic.) 82 84 85' 86 87' 88
 Central Vic. region with seven wineries producing rich minty reds and
 one or two interesting whites, esp. FUME BLANC.

Riverina (N.S.W.) NV
 Large volume producer centred around Griffith; good-quality "cask"
 wines esp. whites.

Southern Vales (Sth Aust) 67' 71' 76' 77' 80' 82' 84' 85 86' 87 88
 Covers energetic McLaren Vale/Reynella regions on s. outskirts of
 Adelaide. Big styles now being rapidly improved; promising CHARD.

Swan Valley (W. Aust) 75' 78' 81' 82' 84' 85' 86 88
 The birthplace of wine in the west, on the n. outskirts of Perth. Hot
 climate makes strong low-acid table, good dessert wines. Declining in
 importance viticulturally.

Tasmania 82' 84' 85 86 87' 88'
 Thirteen vineyards now offer wine for commercial sale, producing
 over 200,000 litres. Great potential for CHARD and P NOIR.

Upper Hunter (N.S.W.) 75' 79' 80' 81' 83' 85' 86' 87
 Est. early 60s; with irrigated vines produce mainly white wines,
 lighter and quicker-developing than Hunter whites. Often good value.

Yarra Valley ("Lilydale") 76' 78' 80' 81' 82' 84' 85 86' 87 88'
 Historic wine area near Melbourne fallen into disuse, now being
 rapidly redeveloped by enthusiasts with small wineries. A superb
 viticultural area with noble varieties only, and over 1,000 acres.

Wineries

Allandale Hunter Valley. Table ★—→★★★
 Small winery without v'yds buying selected local grapes. Quality
 variable; can be outstanding; esp. CHARD.

Allanmere Hunter Valley. Table ★★—→★★★
 Small winery run by expatriate English doctor making excellent SEM,
 CHARD and smooth reds.

All Saints N.E. Vic. Full range ★
 Once famous old family winery with faltering quality; recent
 shareholding and management changes may herald a renaissance.

Angove's Riverland. Table and dessert ★—→★★
 Family business in Adelaide and Renmark in the Murray Valley.
 Notable value in CAB and esp. CHARD and other whites.

Arrowfield Upper Hunter. Table ★★—→★★★
 Substantial vineyard, on irrigated land. Light CABERNET, succulent
 "Show Reserve" CHARD; also "wooded" SEM.

Bailey's N.E. Vic. Table and dessert ★★—→★★★★
 Rich old-fashioned reds of great character, esp. Bundarra Hermitage,
 and magnificant dessert MUSCAT and TOKAY.

Balgownie Bendigo/Ballarat. Table ★★★
 Specialist in fine reds, particularly straight CAB and P NOIR. Also
 exceptional CHARD. Now owned by MILDARA.

Bannockburn Geelong Table ★★★
 Maker of v. intense and complex CHARD and P NOIR using Burgundian
 techniques.

Basedow Barossa Valley. Table ★★—→★★★
 Small to medium winery buying grapes for reliably good range of red
 and white; SEMILLON White Burgundy esp. good.

Berri-Renmano Coop Riverland. Full range ▰▰←→★★★
By far Aust's largest winery following recent merger with Renmano, selling mostly to other companies. Now developing own brands on local and export markets. (See Renmano.)

Best's Great Western. Full range ▰▰★★ →★★★
Conservative old family winery at Great Western with good mid-weight reds and original tasty whites, incl. sparkling.

Blass, Wolf (Bilyara) Barossa. Table and sp. ★★★
Wolf Blass is the ebullient German winemaker. Dazzling labels and extraordinary wine-show successes, with mastery of blending varieties, areas and lashings of new oak. Not to be missed.

Bowen Estate Coonawarra. Table ▰▰★★★
Small Coonawarra winery; intense but not heavy CAB, good RIESLING. Sparkling CHARD on the way.

Brand Coonawarra. Table ★★→★★★
Family estate. Fine, bold and stylish CAB and SHIRAZ under the Laira label. A few quality blemishes in late 70s/early 80s, now rectified.

Briar Ridge Vineyard Hunter Valley. Table ★★
Formerly owned by Murray Robson. Wide range of varietals: CHARD, CABERNET and Hermitage in highly polished style.

Brokenwood Hunter Valley. Table ▰▰★★★
Exciting quality of CAB and SHIRAZ since 1973; new winery 1983 added high quality CHARD and SEM.

Brown Brothers Milawa. Full range ▰▰←→★★★
Old family firm with new ideas, wide range of rather delicate varietal wines, many from cool mountain districts. CHARD and dry white MUSCAT outstanding in a reliable range.

Buring, Leo Barossa. Full range ★★→ ▰▰★★★
"Château Leonay", old white-wine specialists, now owned by LINDEMAN. Steady "Reserve Bin" Rhine Riesling.

Campbells of Rutherglen N.E. Vic. Full range ★★
Impressive lively whites, smooth reds plus good dessert wines.

Cape Clairault Margaret River, W.A. Table ★★
Progressive producer of SEM, SAUV BL and CAB in reasonable quantity and with promise of better things to come.

Cape Mentelle Margaret River. Table ★★→★★★★
Idiosyncratic robust CAB departs from district style and can be magnificent; also ZINFANDEL and v. popular SEM.

Capel Vale S.W. Western Aust. ★★★
Outstanding range of whites, incl. RIESLING and GEWÜRZ. New v.g. CAB.

Cassegrain Hastings Valley, N.S.W. Table ★★→★★★
New winery on N.S.W. coast taking grapes both from local plantings and from Hunter Valley. CHARD can be outstanding.

Chambers' Rosewood N.E. Vic. Full range ▰▰★★→★★★
Good cheap table and great dessert wines, esp. TOKAY.

Château Le Amon Bendigo. Table ★★★
Very stylish minty CAB and peppery SHIRAZ.

Château Hornsby Alice Springs, N. Territory. ★→★★
A charming aberration. Full-flavoured clean reds from the Bush.

Château Rémy Great Western/Avoca. Sp. and table ★★
Owned by Rémy Martin. Trebbiano/CHARD blend surprisingly successful. Also good "Blue Pyrenees" reds.

Château Tahbilk Goulburn Valley. Table ▰▰★★→★★★
Beautiful and historic family-owned estate making long-lived CAB, SHIRAZ, Rhine Riesling and Marsanne. "Private Bins" are outstanding.

Coldstream Hills Yarra Valley, Vic. Table ★★★→★★★★
New winery, Yarra's second largest, built 1987 by wine critic James Halliday. International acclaim for prize-winning P NOIR, and v.g. CHARD.

Conti, Paul, Wines Swan Valley. Table ★★
Elegant Hermitage, also fine CHARD and other estate whites.

Aus

Craigmoor Mudgee. Table and port ★★→★★★
  Oldest district winery now part of WYNDHAM group and making very
  good CHARD and SEM, the two blended, and CAB/SHIRAZ.

Cullens Willyabrup Margaret River. Table ★★★
  Butch but kindly CAB/MERLOT, pungent SAUV BLANC and bold "wooded"
  CHARD are all real characters.

d'Arenberg S. Vales. Table and dessert ★→★★
  Old-style family outfit with strapping rustic reds and RIESLING.

De Bortoli Griffith, N.S.W. ★→★★★
  Irrigation-area winery. Standard reds and whites but magnificent
  sweet "botrytized" Beerenausleses of SEM, GEWURZ, RIESLING.

Delatite Central Vic. Table ★★★
  Rosalind Ritchie makes appropriately willowy and feminine RIESLING,
  GEWURZ, P NOIR and CAB from this very cool mountainside v'yd.

Diamond Valley Yarra Valley, Vic. Table ★★→ ★★★
  Producer of outstanding P NOIR in significant quantities; other wines
  good rather than great.

Domaine Chandon Yarra Valley, Vic. Sp.
  The showpiece of the Yarra Valley. Substantial production from
  grapes grown in all the cooler parts of Australia, with strong direction
  from owner Moët & Chandon. Early indications of exciting, perhaps
  exceptional, quality; first commercial release April 1989.

Drayton's Bellevue Hunter Valley, N.S.W. Table ★★
  Traditional Hermitage and SEM; occasionally good CHARD; recent
  quality improving after lapse.

Dromana Estate Mornington Peninsular. Table ★★★
  Largest and best producer in district. Great skill in making glorious
  CAB, P NOIR and CHARD.

Elgee Park Mornington Pensinular. Table ★★
  Substantial modern winery on longest-established v'yd producing
  very good CAB/MERLOT, CHARD, RIESLING and a hatful of VIOGNIER.

Enterprise Wines Clare Valley. Table ★★★
  Tim Knappstein, an exceptionally gifted winemaker, produces Rhine
  Riesling. FUME BLANC, GEWURZ and CABERNET. Now part of Wolf Blass.

Evans and Tate Swan Valley. Table ★★→★★★
  Fine elegant reds from the Margaret River Redbrook and Swan Valley
  Gnangara v'yds. Good SEM too.

Evans Family Hunter Valley, N.S.W. ★★★
  Excellent CHARD, fermented in new oak, from small v'yd owned by
  family of Len Evans.

Forest Hills Mount Barker, W.A. Table ★★→★★★
  Pioneer vineyard in region, with wines made under contract at
  PLANTAGENET. RIESLING, CHARD and CAB can all be and usually are
  excellent.

Giaconda Central Vic. Table. ★★★
  Very small but ultra-fashionable winery near Beechworth producing
  eagerly sought CHARD and P NOIR.

Hardy's S. Vales, Barossa, Keppoch, etc. Full range ★→★★★
  Famous family-run company using and blending wines from several
  areas. St Thomas Burgundy, Old Castle Riesling are standards. Top
  wines are "Collection" series and Australia's greatest vintage ports.
  Hardy's bought HOUGHTON and REYNELLA and, most recently, STANLEY.
  Reynella's beautifully restored buildings now group headquarters.

Heathcote Bendigo. Table ★★→★★★
  Stylish producer of eclectic range of white and red varietals, showing
  abundant flavour and technical perfection.

Heemskerk Tasmania. Table ★★★
  Most successful commercial operation in Tasmania. Herby CAB;
  promising CHARD. Also P NOIR and RIESLING. Recent partnership with
  Louis Roederer plans high class sparkling wine in years to come.

Henschke Barossa. Table ★★★
Family business known for sterling SHIRAZ and v.g. CAB. New high-country v'yds on Adelaide Hills add excitement.

Hickinbotham Winemakers Mornington Peninsula. Table ★★→★★★
Innovative winemaking by Hickinbotham family (since 1980) has produced fascinating styles from grapes grown in many regions.

Hollick Coonawarra. Table ★★★
Ian and Wendy Hollick won instant stardom with trophy-winning '84 CAB; also v.g. CHARD and RIES from small winery.

Houghton Swan Valley, W.A. Full range ★→★★★★
The most famous old winery of W.A. Soft, ripe White Burgundy is top wine; also excellent CAB, VERDELHO, etc. See Hardy's.

Hungerford Hill Hunter Valley and Coonawarra. Table ★→★★★
Medium-sized winery producing high-class varietals esp. RIESLING and CABERNET from COONAWARRA.

Huntington Estate Mudgee. Table ★★→★★★
Small winery; the best in Mudgee. Fine CABERNETs and clean SEMILLON and CHARDONNAY. Invariably under-priced.

Idyll Geelong. Vic. ★★★
Small winery with CAB and GEWÜRZ of highest quality.

Jeffrey Grosset Clare. Table ★★→★★★
Exceedingly elegant RIESLING, CHARD and CABERNET made in consistent style by fastidious young winemaker.

Kaiser Stuhl Barossa. Full range ★→★★★
Now part of PENFOLDS; a huge winery processes fruit from diverse sources. "Individual v'yd" RIESLINGS can be excellent. So can Red Ribbon reds.

Katnook Estate Coonawarra. Table ★★★
Excellent pricey CAB and CHARD; also SAUV BL, P NOIR, RIES.

Krondorf Wines Barossa Valley. Table ★★→ ★★★
Acquired by MILDARA in 1986, but quality and brand image will be preserved. "Burge and Wilson" wines are best.

Lake's Folly Hunter Valley. Table ★★★★
The work of an inspired surgeon from Sydney. CABERNET and new barrels make fine complex reds. Also exciting CHARD.

Lark Hill Canberra District ★★
Best and most consistent producer with RIESLING esp. attractive.

Leeuwin Estate Margaret River. Table ★★→★★★★
Lavishly equipped estate leading W. Australia with superb (and very expensive) CHARD; developing fine P NOIR, RIES, AND CAB.

Lilydale Vineyards Yarra Valley. Table ★★★
Foremost producer of CHARD using sophisticated techniques; also scented GEWÜRZ and crisp RIESLING. CAB and P NOIR recent additions.

Lehmann Wines, Peter Barossa. Table ★★→ ★★★
Defender of the Barossa faith, Lehmann makes vast quantities of wine, mostly sold in bulk, and v.g. special cuvées under his own label.

Leconfield Coonawarra. Table ★→★★★
Coonawarra CABERNET of great style. RIESLING improving.

Lindeman Orig. Hunter, now everywhere. Full range ★→★★★★
One of the oldest firms, now a giant owned by Phillip Morris. Its Ben Ean "Moselle" is market leader. Owns BURINGS in Barossa and Rouge Homme in COONAWARRA, and important v'yds at Padthaway: outstanding CHARD. Many inter-state blends. Pioneered new styles, yet still make fat old-style "Hunters". Bin-number "classics" can be v.good.

McWilliams Hunter Valley and Riverina. Full range ★→★★★
Famous family of Hunter winemakers at Mount Pleasant (HERMITAGE and SEMILLON). Pioneers in RIVERINA with noble varieties, incl. CABERNET and sweet white "Lexia". Quality showing marked improvement.

Marsh Estate Hunter Valley. Table ★★→★★★
Substantial producer of good SEM, SHIRAZ and CAB of growing quality.

186

Mildara Coonawarra. Murray Valley. Full range ★→★★★
Sherry and brandy specialists at Mildura on the Murray River also making fine CABERNET and RIESLING at COONAWARRA. Now own BALGOWNIE, KRONDORF and YELLOWGLEN.

Mitchells Clare Valley. Table ★★★
Small family winery, excellent RIESLING and CABERNET.

Mitchelton Goulbourn Valley, Vic. Table ★★★
Big modern winery. A wide range incl. v.g. wood-matured Marsanne, CAB and second label Thomas Mitchell offering esp. good value.

Montrose Mudgee, N.S.W. Table ★★ →★★★
Recent winemaking and marketing initiatives have had much success; superb CHARD, interesting BARBERA and NEBBIOLO; acquired by WYNDHAM in 1988.

Moorilla Estate Tasmania. Table ★★★
Senior winery on outskirts of Hobart on Derwent River producing superb P NOIR, v.g. CHARD and CAB in tiny quantities.

Morris N.E. Vic. Table and dessert ★★ →★★★★
Old winery at Rutherglen making Australia's greatest dessert muscats and tokays; recently v.g. cheap table wines.

Moss Wood Margaret River. Table ★★★★
Best Margaret River winery (with only 29 acres). CABERNET SAUVIGNON, P NOIR, CHARD all with rich fruit flavours not unlike best Californians.

Mount Langi Ghiran Great Western, Vic. Table ★★→ ★★★
Producer of superb rich peppery Rhône-like SHIRAZ, v.g. CAB and less exhilarating RIESLING.

Mount Mary Yarra Valley, Vic. Table ★★★
Dr. John Middleton is a perfectionist with tiny amounts of CHARD, P NOIR and (best of all) CAB SAUV/CAB FRANC/MERLOT.

Murray Robson Wines Hunter Valley. Table ★★
The reincarnation of Murray Robson with a deliberately similar label; the wines are made at Richmond Grove under Robson's direction.

Oakridge Yarra Valley. Red Table ★★★
Cabernet specialist making Yarra's finest, albeit in small quantities.

Orlando (Gramp's) Barossa Valley. Full range ★★→ ★★★
Great pioneering company, bought by management 1988. Full range from good standard Jacob's Creek Claret to excellent COONAWARRA CAB; CHARD and great Steingarten RIES. William Jacob is low-price line.

Penfold's Orig. Adelaide, now everywhere. Full range ★→★★★★
Ubiquitous and excellent company: in BAROSSA, RIVERINA, COONAWARRA, CLARE VALLEY, etc. Grange Hermitage (75', 76' 78, 80, 82') is ★★★★, St Henri Claret some way behind. Bin-numbered wines are usually outstanding. "Grandfather Port" is sensational. New: "Magill Estate" (84 85) from old Grange v'yd and "Clare Estate" from Clare v'yd.

Petaluma Adelaide Hills. ★★★★
A recent rocket-like success with CAB, CHARD and RIESLING, now centred around new winery in ADELAIDE HILLS using COONAWARRA and CLARE grapes. Bollinger now part owner, with ambitious sparkling wine v'yds and facilities in ADELAIDE HILLS. Sp. wine, called "Croser" (after the boss, Brian C.), from '85.

Petersons Hunter Valley. Table ★★★
On show results, most accomplished small Hunter winery, with exceptional CHARD and v.g. SEM.

Piper's Brook Tasmania. Table ★★★
Cool-area pioneer with very good RIESLING, P NOIR, superb CHARD from Tamar Valley near Launceston. Lovely labels.

Pirramimma S. Vales, S.A. Full range. ★→★★
Big supply of good standard; reds best.

Plantaganet Mount Barker. Full range ★★→★★★
The region's largest producer with a wide range of varieties, esp. rich CHARD, SHIRAZ and vibrant, potent CAB.

Quelltaler Clare Watervale. Full range. ★→★★
Old winery known for good "Granfiesta" sherry. Recently good Rhine Riesling and SEMILLON. Bought by Wolf Blass 1987.

Redman Coonawarra. Red Table ★→★★
The most famous old name in COONAWARRA make two wines (Claret, CABERNET). Recent quality disappointing.

Renmano Murray Valley, S.A. Full range. ★→ ★★
Huge coop (see Berri-Renmano). "Chairman's Selections" v.g. value.

Reynella S. Vales, S.A. Full range ★★→★★★
Historic red wine specialists s. of Adelaide. Rich CAB (partly COONAWARRA), Claret and excellent "port". See Hardy's.

Rockford Barossa Valley, S.A. Table ★★
Small producer, but a wide range of thoroughly individual styles often made from grapes grown on very old low-yielding v'yds.

Rosemount Upper Hunter and Coonawarra. Table ★→★★★
Rich, unctuous HUNTER "Show" CHARD is an international smash. This and COONAWARRA CAB lead the wide range.

Rothbury Estate Hunter Valley. Table ★★→ ★★★
Important syndicate-owned estate. Traditional HUNTER: "Hermitage" and long-lived SEMILLON: "Black Label" best. New CHARDONNAY (from Cowra) and PINOT NOIR are promising.

S. Smith & Sons Barossa. Full range ★→ ★★★
Big old family firm with considerable verve, using computers, juice evaluation, etc., to produce full spectrum of high-quality wines, incl. "Hill-Smith Estate". "Heggies Vineyard" is best.

St Huberts Yarra Valley. Vic. Table ★★→★★★
Erratic, much sought-after CABERNET; recent change in ownership should improve consistency for this largest YARRA winery.

St Leonards N.E. Vic. Full range ★★
Excellent varieties sold only at cellar door and mailing list, incl. exotics e.g. Fetyaska and Orange Muscat.

St Matthias Tamar Valley, Tas. Table ★★
Has joined the "big three" Tasmania wineries almost overnight; superbly situated v'yd and cellar-door sales on banks of Tamar estuary. Wines made under contract at HEEMSKERK.

Saltram Barossa. Full range ★→★★★
Seagram-owned winery making wines of variable quality. "Pinnacle Selection" best wines; also Mamre Brook.

Sandalford Swan Valley. Table ★
Fine old winery with contrasting styles of red and white varietals from Swan and Margaret rivers. Wonderful old Verdelho.

Saxonvale Hunter Valley. Table ★★
Medium-sized operation now making good early-maturing SEMILLON and CHARDONNAY. Also good soft CABERNET, SHIRAZ. Acquired by WYNDHAM ESTATE in 1986.

Seaview S. Vales, S.A. ★★
Brand name owned by PENFOLD's used for good value CAB, CHARD.

Seppelt Barossa, Great Western, Keppoch, etc. Full range ★→★★★
Far-flung producers of Australia's most popular "champagne" (Gt. Western Brut), good dessert wines, the reliable Moyston claret and some very good private bin wines, incl. CHARD, from Gt. Western and Drumborg in Victoria, and Keppoch and Barossa in South Australia. Top sp. is called "Salinger".

Seville Estate Yarra Valley. Table ★★→★★★
Tiny winery with CHARD, very late-picked RIES, SHIRAZ, P NOIR and v.g. CAB.

Stanley Clare Valley. Full range ★→ ★★★
Important medium-size quality winery purchased by HARDY late 1987. Good RHINE RIESLING, CHARD and CABERNET and complex Cabernet/Shiraz/Malbec blends under Leasingham label.

Stanton & Killeen N.E. Vic. Table and dessert ★★
Small old family firm. Rich muscats, also strong Moodemere reds.

Aus

Taltarni Great Western/Avoca. Table ★★★
Dominique Portet, brother of Bernard (Clos du Val, Napa), son of André (Ch Lafite), produces huge but balanced reds, good SAUV BLANC and fine sparkling wines.

Tarrawarra Yarra Valley. Table ★★
Multi-million dollar investment making limited quantities of idiosyncratic and expensive CHARD, with P NOIR planned for the future.

Taylors Wines Clare Valley. Table ★→★★
Large wine-producing unit making range of inexpensive table wines.

Tisdall Wines Goulburn Valley. Table ★★→★★★
Exciting young winery in the Echuca River area, making local ("Rosbercon") wines plus finer material from central ranges (Mount Helen CABERNET, CHARDONNAY, RHINE RIESLING).

Tollana Barossa, S.A. Full Range ★★→★★★
Old company once famous for brandy, has latterly made some quite fine CABERNET and RHINE RIESLING. Acquired by PENFOLD'S 1987.

Tulloch Hunter Valley, N.S.W. Table ★→★★★
An old name at Pokolbin, with good dry reds, RIESLING and VERDELHO, now part of PENFOLD'S group.

Tyrrell Hunter Valley, N.S.W. Table ★★→ ★★★
Some of the best traditional Hunter wines, Hermitage and SEMILLON, are "Vat 47". Also big rich CHARDONNAY, delicate P NOIR and v.g. sp.

Vasse Felix Margaret River. Table ★★→★★★
The pioneer of the Margaret River. Elegant CABERNETS notable for mid-weight balance, bought by Robert Holmes à Court 1987.

Virgin Hills Bendigo/Ballarat. Table ★★★★
Tiny supplies of one blended (CAB/SHIRAZ/MALBEC) red of legendary style and balance.

Westfield Swan Valley. Table ★→ ★★
John Kosovich's CABERNETS, CHARDONNAYS and VERDELHOS show particular finesse in a hot climate. Also good "port".

Wirra Wirra S. Vales, S.A. Table ★★→★★★
Under PETALUMA influence high quality, beautifully packaged whites and reds have made a big impact recently.

Woodleys Barossa, S.A. Table ★★
Well-known for low-price Queen Adelaide label. "Reference" CAB is best wine. Acquired by SEPPELT in late 1985.

Wyndham Estate Branxton, N.S.W. Full range ★ →★★
Aggressive large new Hunter and Mudgee group with Richmond Grove, Hunter Estate, Hollydene, Saxonvale, Montrose and Craigmoor as its brands.

Wynn Coonawarra, S. Vales. Table ★ →★★★
Larger inter-state company, originators of flagon wines, with largest winery and vineyards at COONAWARRA, making good CAB (esp. "John Riddoch"). Acquired by PENFOLD'S in 1985.

Yalumba See S. Smith & Sons.

Yarra Burn Yarra Valley. Table ★→★★★
Substantial boutique producing wines of variable quality and style, but usually excellent P NOIR and CAB.

Yarra Yering Yarra Valley. Table ★★★
One of the best Lilydale boutique wineries. Esp. racy powerful P NOIR and deep CABERNET.

Yarrinya Estate Yarra Valley. Table ★★→★★★
Purchased by de Bortoli in 1987 and being aggressively expanded; now has largest plantings (tho' not all in bearing) in the Yarra Valley.

Yellowglen Bendigo/Ballarat. Sparkling ★→★★
High-flying sparkling winemaker acquired by MILDARA. Sales are more impressive than quality.

Yeringberg Yarra Valley. Table ★★★
Historic estate now again producing v. high-quality CHARD, CAB, P NOIR, in minute quantities.

New Zealand

Over the last decade New Zealand has made an international impact with table wines of startling quality, particularly whites, well able to compete with those of Australia or California. It is now regarded as the foremost cool-climate viticultural region among the world's newer wine countries. Exports (to UK, USA, Europe and Japan) almost tripled in 1988.

Progress has accelerated since new vineyard areas were planted in the early 1970s in both North and South Islands. There are now well over 12,000 acres remaining after a Government subsidized removal of 3,750 acres in 1986 of lesser varieties which had created a surplus of wine on the domestic market. White grapes predominate. Müller-Thurgau is the most planted variety, but is being overtaken by varieties in demand overseas, Sauvignon Blanc, Chardonnay and Riesling in whites, Cabernet Sauvignon and Merlot for reds.

New vineyard areas opening up in Martinborough (North Island, north of the capital city, Wellington), and Canterbury and Central Otago, in South Island. NZ now boasts the world's southernmost (Otago) and easternmost (East Cape) vineyards.

The general style of wine is relatively light, with intensity of fruit and varietal character, and crisp acidity. Barrel fermentation and/or ageing are adding to the complexity and interest of its wines. The principal areas and producers are:

Auckland Largest city in NZ, location of head offices of major wineries, plus largest number of medium and small wineries in outskirts.

Babich Henderson, nr. Auckland.
Old Dalmatian family firm of some size, highly respected in NZ for consistent quality and value. Also using grapes from GISBORNE and HAWKES BAY. Good CHARDS (esp. "Irongate"), SAUV BL, SEMILLON/CHARD, GEWÜRZ, CAB SAUV and CAB/MERLOT.

Brookfields Meeanee, Hawkes Bay.
Small volume winery, newcomer to export. Noted for SAUV BL, CHARD and CAB.

Cape Mentelle Renwick, Marlborough.
Offshoot of W. Australia winery, better known by its NZ brand name, "Cloudy Bay" after nearby coastal feature. Excellent initial SAUV BL now joined by outstanding CHARD.

Cellier Le Brun Renwick, nr. Blenheim.
Small winery established by son of Champagne family, producing méthode champenoise, with v.g. Blancs de Blancs.

Collard Henderson, nr. Auckland.
Small family winery using grapes from several areas, CHARD, SAUV BL, dry CHENIN BL and CAB/MERLOT.

Cooks Wineries at Te Kauwhata, s. of Auckland and in Hawkes Bay. Large company now merged with Corbans and former McWilliams, using grapes from GISBORNE and HAWKES BAY. Steadily good record with CHARD, GEWÜRZ, CHENIN BL and CAB SAUV, now producing matching SAUV BL, also late picked MÜLLER-THURGAU.

Cooper's Creek Huapai Valley, n.w. of Auckland.
Small winery augmenting own grapes from GISBORNE and HAWKES BAY fruit. Exporting good CHARD, SAUV BL, RIES, GEWÜRZ and popular blends Coopers Dry (White) and Coopers Red.

Corbans   Henderson, nr. Auckland.

Old-established firm with wineries at GISBORNE and HAWKES BAY. Now incorporating Cooks and McWilliams, and second largest in NZ. New premium brand, "Stoneleigh", from vineyards in Marlborough producing v.g SAUV BL, CHARD, RIES and CAB SAUV. Wide range of sound wines under Corban label. Additional premium wines under affiliate label Robard & Butler.

De Redcliffe   Mangatawhiri, s.e. of Auckland.

Small progressive winery with associated resort "Hotel du Vin"; producing good CHARD, SEMILLON and CAB/MERLOT.

Delegat's   Henderson, nr. Auckland.

Medium-sized family winery, using grapes from GISBORNE and HAWKES BAY for good CHARD, SAUV BL and CAB SAUV, plus impressive Auslese style now from RIESLING.

Esk Valley   Bayview, Hawkes Bay.

Former large family concern, now merged with VILLA MARIA/VIDAL group, concentrating on small range of premium whites and reds.

Giesen   Burnham, s. of Christchurch, Canterbury, South Island.

Small winery established by immigrant German family, using own v'yd and MARLBOROUGH grapes. Good CHARD, SAUV BL, RIES and reds.

Gisborne   Site of three large wineries, MONTANA, CORBANS and PENFOLD'S, and centre of large viticultural area incl. MATAWHERO and TOLAGA BAY. Some 10% of vineyards were destroyed by a tropical cyclone in March 1988. Good area for MÜLLER-THURGAU, CHARD, SEMILLON and GEWÜRZ.

Goldwater   Waiheke Island in Hauraki Gulf, nr. Auckland.

Small vineyard at sea edge, known best for CAB/MERLOT and SAUV BL.

Hawkes Bay   Large viticultural region on e. coast of North Island, s. of GISBORNE, known for high-quality grapes, esp. CHARD and CAB SAUV.

Hunters   Marlborough.

Small, progressive winery using only MARLBOROUGH grapes. Highly reputed for outstanding SAUV BL (and oaky "Fumé" style), and CHARD.

Kumeu River   Kumeu, n.w. of Auckland.

Premium label of small San Marino family winery, establishing reputation for SAUV FUME, CHARD, CAB/MERLOT and light fruity CAB FRANC under Brajkovich family crest label.

Lincoln Vineyards   Henderson, nr. Auckland.

Medium-sized family winery now producing varietals esp. CHARD, CHENIN BLANC and MERLOT.

Marlborough   Leading export wine region, at north end of South Island, on stony plain formed by Wairau River. Well suited to white varieties CHARD, SAUV BL and RIESLING, but also good CAB SAUV and promising PINOT NOIR. Potential here for v.g. sparkling.

Martinborough   New smallish viticultural area in s. Wairarapa, North Island (n. of Wellington). Stony soils, similar to MARLBOROUGH. Own appellation.

Martinborough Vineyards   Martinborough.

Largest of the small operations in the area. Awards already for CHARD, "Fumé" SAUV BL and PINOT NOIR.

Matawhero   nr. Gisborne.

Small winery with longstanding reputation for GEWÜRZ, CHARD and SAUV BL.

Matua Valley   n.w. of Auckland.

Medium-sized family winery, pioneer with new varieties. Own grapes supplemented by HAWKES BAY and GISBORNE. Well known for Judd Chard (Gisborne), unwooded SAUV BL labelled "Fumé", unique PINOT NOIR/BLANC and excellent CAB SAUV and late-harvest Muscat.

Millton   nr. Gisborne.

Small new producer using organic cultivation methods. Good SAUV BL/ SEMILLON blend, CHARD and RIESLING (both dry and late harvest).

Mission Greenmeadows, Hawkes Bay.

The oldest continuing winemaking establishment in NZ, founded by French missionaries and still operated by Society of Mary. Good SEMILLON/SAUV BL blend and CAB/MERLOT.

Montana Auckland.

Largest winemaking enterprise in NZ, with wineries in GISBORNE and MARLBOROUGH and now incorporating PENFOLDS NZ operations. Pioneered viticulture in MARLBOROUGH, but draws grapes also from GISBORNE and HAWKES BAY. Marlborough labels incl. SAUV BL, CHARD, RIESLING, CAB SAUV and PINOT NOIR. Gisborne CHARD also sound wine and big seller. Success with "Lindauer" méthode champenoise has led to licensing agreement with Champagne DEUTZ.

Morton Estate Katikati, nr. Tauranga, e. coast North Island.

Expanding new winery with high reputation for CHARD from HAWKES BAY (esp. premium black label), SAUV BL, and CAB SAUV. Recently released its first (v.g.) méthode champenoise.

Ngatarawa nr. Hastings, Hawkes Bay.

Boutique winery in old stables of established HAWKES BAY family. Good CHARD, SAUV BL and CAB/MERLOT under "Glazebrook" family name label.

Nobilo Huapai Valley, n.w. of Auckland.

NZ's largest family-owned winery, with own grapes plus fruit from GISBORNE, HAWKES BAY, MARTINBOROUGH and MARLBOROUGH. Good CHARD (esp. from Gisborne), SAUV BL, SEMILLON, and long established reputation for age-worthy reds, CAB SAUV and PINOT NOIR. Associate label, "Classic Hills".

Penfolds See Montana.

Robard & Butler See Corbans.

St Nesbit Karaka, nr. Papakura, s. of Auckland.

Expanding boutique winery, specializing in single red wine blended from CAB SAUV, CAB FRANC and MERLOT, well made and matured in barriques.

Selak's Kumeu, n.w. of Auckland.

Small family firm with good export reputation for SAUV BL, SAUV BL/ SEMILLON blend (in "Fumé" style), CHARD and CAB SAUV. ("Founders" label for top wines of two last named).

Stoneleigh See Corbans.

Stonyridge Waiheke Island, nr. Auckland.

Boutique winery concentrating on two reds in Bordeaux style; LAROSE exceptional, AIRFIELD v.g.

Te Mata Havelock North, Hawkes Bay.

Oldest winery premises in continuous operation, now restored and producing good CHARD and SAUV BL from nearby vineyards, plus excellent "Coleraine" CAB/MERLOT from proprietor's home vineyard.

Vidal Hastings, Hawkes Bay.

Atmospheric old winery now merged with Villa Maria (see below). Good HAWKES BAY CHARD, SAUV BL, CAB SAUV and PINOT NOIR.

Villa Maria Mangere, outskirts s. Auckland.

Large company, now incorporating VIDAL and ESK VALLEY. Uses grapes from Ihumatao (nr. Auckland airport), GISBORNE and HAWKES BAY. Full range of wines, with emphasis on barrel-fermented CHARD, SAUV BL (and wooded "Fumé" variation), GEWÜRZ, CAB SAUV and CAB/MERLOT.

Weingut Seifried Upper Moutere, nr. Nelson, South Island.

Small winery started by Austrian immigrant. Good CHARD, SAUV BL, RIESLING (in dry and late-harvest styles) and PINOT NOIR.

NZ

South Africa

Quality in S. Africa's table wines began around 1970 when vineyard owners began to plant Cabernet Sauvignon, followed by better white varieties. The success of small new wineries in the 1980s has encouraged others to buy oak barrels from France. Cellarmasters are now showing more care in harvesting and cellar treatment and standards are rising steadily, though still not at (e.g.) New Zealand's pace.

Allesverloren ★★
> Estate in MALMESBURY with 395 acres of v'yds, well known for "port", and now also specializing in powerful, almost roasted, reds, incl. ripe, soft CABERNET, and Tinta Barocca.

Alphen ★
> Name is used as a brand by Gilbeys.

Alto ★★
> STELLENBOSCH estate of 247 acres high on a hill, best known for massive-bodied CAB and a good SHIRAZ/CAB blend: Alto Rouge.

Backsberg ★★ →★★★
> A prize-winning 395-acre estate at PAARL with notably good white wines (incl. CHARD) and medium bodied CABERNET and SHIRAZ.

Bellingham ★★→★★★
> Top brand name of Union Wine Co. Reliable reds and whites, esp. CABERNET. Johannisberger is top-selling blend.

Bergkelder Big wine concern at STELLENBOSCH, member of the UDE MEESTER group, making and distributing many brands (FLEUR DU CAP, GRÜNBERGER) and estate wines.

Bertrams ★★
> Gilbey's brand of reds, good CAB and SHIRAZ.

Blaauwklippen ★★→★★★
> Estate S. of STELLENBOSCH producing some of S. Africa's very best reds, CAB, P NOIR and ZIN, and good RHINE RIES, and SAUV BLANC.

Boberg Controlled region of origin for fortified wines consisting of the districts of PAARL and TULBAGH.

Le Bonheur ★★★
> STELLENBOSCH estate producing one of the Cape's best whites, Blanc Fumé, a non-wooded SAUV BLANC. Also Médoc-style CAB.

Boschendal ★★★
> Vast (617-acre) estate in PAARL area on an old fruit farm. Emphasis on white wines and sparkling "Brut". Blended Cabernet called "Grand Vin" launched with '85. Look out for '86. Also a charming restaurant.

Breede River Valley Fortified wine region east of Drakenstein Mtns.

La Bri ★★
> Interesting whites made in coop cellar from SAUV BL, RHINE RIES and SEMILLON. Blanc de la Bri best.

Buitenverwachting ★★★
> Exceptional v'yds plus bought grapes produce notable SAUVIGNON BLANC and Blanc Fumé. Good RHINE RIESLING.

Bukettraube White-wine grape with high acidity and muscat aroma, most popular as a blend component.

Cabernet The great Bordeaux grape, particularly successful in the COASTAL REGION. Sturdy, long-ageing wines. Use of new oak from about '82 has made great improvement.

Cavendish Cape ★★
> Range of remarkably good sherries from the K.W.V.

Chardonnay Classic white variety, fairly new in S. Africa due to official restrictions. Recent release of good vines has resulted in leap in quality and number: now 25 on the market. Great expectations.

Chenin Blanc Work-horse grape of the Cape; one vine in three. Adaptable and sometimes very good. Alias STEEN. K.W.V. makes a very good example at a bargain price.

Cinsaut The principal bulk-producing French red grape in S. Africa; formerly known as Hermitage. Very seldom seen with varietal label.

Coastal Region Demarcated wine region, includes PAARL, STELLENBOSCH, Durbanville, SWARTLAND, TULBAGH.

Colombard The "French Colombard" of California. High acidity and fruity flavour add interest to blended whites.

Constantia Once the world's most famous Muscat wine, from the Cape. Now the southernmost district of origin.

Delheim (★★★)
Winery at Driesprong in one of the highest areas of STELLENBOSCH, known for delicate STEEN and GEWÜRZ whites and impressive reds: CABERNET, PINOTAGE, SHIRAZ. Grande Reserve (CAB SAUV, CAB FRANC, MERLOT) is top class.

Drostdy ★★
Quality range of sherries from BERGKELDER.

Edelkeur ★★★★
Excellent intensely sweet white made with nobly rotten (p. 49) grapes by NEDERBURG.

Estate wine Strictly controlled term applying only to registered estates making wines from grapes grown on the same property.

Fleur du Cap ★★
Popular and well-made range of wines from the BERGKELDER. Good CAB; interesting SAUV BL.

Gewürztraminer The famous spicy grape of Alsace, best at NEDERBURG, SIMONSIG and (for drier style) STELLENRYCK. Naturally low acidity makes this variety difficult to handle at the Cape.

Grand Cru (or Premier Grand Cru) Term for a totally dry white, with no quality implications. Generally to be avoided.

Groot Constantia (★★★)
Historic estate, now government owned, near Cape Town. Source of superlative muscat wine in the early 19th century. Now making wide range of wines, esp. good RHINE RIESLING, GEWÜRZ.

Grünberger ★
BERGKELDER brand using STEEN to make range of dry and semi-sweet white wines.

Hamilton-Russell ★★★
Young estate in cool coastal valley. Among leaders with P NOIR, CHARDONNAY and SAUV BLANC.

Hanepoot Local name for the sweet Muscat of Alexandria grape.

Hartenberg ★★
Previously known as Montagne, this Stellenbosch estate producing fine CABERNET and SHIRAZ.

Hazendal ★★
Family estate in W. STELLENBOSCH specializing in semi-sweet STEEN, marketed by the BERGKELDER.

Kanonkop ★★★
Outstanding estate in N. STELLENBOSCH. Stylish full-bodied CAB and PINOTAGE. Paul Sauer Fleur is a Bordeaux-style blend.

Klein Constantia ★★★→★★★★
S. Africa's new star. No expense spared in vineyard or cellar. First Chardonnay in '88 extremely fine; '88 Cabernet will be when released in '92. Top class SAUV BLANC and RIESLING.

Koopmanskloof ★★
STELLENBOSCH estate making good dry Chenin Blanc-based blend "Blanc de Marbonne".

K.W.V. The Kooperatieve Wijnbouwers Vereniging, S. Africa's national wine cooperative created 60 years ago by the State to absorb surpluses. Vast premises in PAARL making a range of good wines, particularly sherries.

Laborie (★★)
k.w.v.-owned showpiece estate on Paarl Mtn. Blended white and red.

Landgoed South African for estate; a word which appears on estate-wine labels and official seals.

Landskroon ★★
Family estate owned by Paul and Hugo de Villiers. Good dry reds – PINOT NOIR, TINTA BAROCCA and CABERNETS SAUV and FRANC.

Late Harvest Term for a mildly sweet wine. "Special Late Harvest" must be naturally sweet (no added concentrate). "Noble Late Harvest" is the highest quality level of all.

Lemberg (★★)
Tiny estate in Paarl, making full-bodied, wood-aged Harsleveld and SAUV BLANC. Growing reputation.

Lievland (★★→★★★)
Little-known winery with modest packaging. Beginning to develop a reputation. RHINE RIESLING placed highly at 1988 Gault et Millau Paris Olympiad.

J.C. Le Roux ★★
Old brand revived as BERGKELDER's sparkling wine house. SAUV BLANC (Charmat) and P NOIR (méthode champenoise). Also CHARDONNAY.

Malmesbury Centre of the SWARTLAND wine district, on the w. coast n. of Cape Town, specializing in dry whites and distilling wine.

Meerendal
Estate near Durbanville producing traditional robust reds (esp. SHIRAZ and PINOTAGE) marketed by the BERGKELDER.

Meerlust ★★★
Beautiful old family estate s. of STELLENBOSCH making outstanding CABERNET, Rubicon (Médoc-style blend), MERLOT and P NOIR.

Monis ★→★★
Well-known wine concern of PAARL, with fine "Vintage Port".

Muratie
Ancient estate in STELLENBOSCH, best known for its port. Recently sold; bright future expected.

Nederburg ★★★→★★★★
The most famous wine farm in modern S. Africa, operated by the STELLENBOSCH FARMERS' WINERY. Its annual auction is a major event. Pioneer in modern cellar practice and with fine CABERNET, "Private Bin" blends, EDELKEUR and GEWÜRZ. Also good sparkling wines and Paarl RIESLINGS.

Neethlingshof (★★)
Being replanted. Full-bodied Colombard and CAB best. Also GEWÜRZ. To watch.

Neil Ellis Vineyards ★★→★★★
Wines made in central cellar from grapes grown in widely differing areas. Very fine SAUV BLANC, CAB.

Overberg Demarcated wine district in the Caledon area, COASTAL REGION, with some of the coolest Cape vineyards. (No labels from this area yet.)

Overgaauw ★→★★★
Estate w. of STELLENBOSCH making good STEEN, very good CABERNET, and Tria Corda, a CABERNET/MERLOT blend.

Paarl South Africa's wine capital, 30 miles n.e. of Cape Town, and the surrounding demarcated district, among the best in the country, particularly for white wine and sherry.

Paarlsack ★
Well-known range of sherries made at PAARL by the K.W.V.

Pierre Jourdan (★★★)
    Impressive méthode champenoise bubbly made from CHARD and P NOIR.

Pinot Noir Like counterparts in California and Australia, Cape producers struggle to get complexity of flavour. Best are HAMILTON RUSSELL, BLAAUWKLIPPEN, MEERLUST, RUSTENBERG.

Pinotage South African red grape, a cross between P NOIR and CINSAUT, useful for high yields and hardiness. Its wine is lush and fruity but never first-class.

Premier Grand Cru See Grand Cru.

Rhine Riesling Produces full-flavoured dry and off-dry wines. Generally needs two years or more of bottle age. See Weisser Riesling.

Riesling South African Riesling (actually Crouchen Blanc) is very different from RHINE RIESLING, providing neutral, fresh, easy drinking wines.

Rietvallei ★★
    ROBERTSON estate producing excellent fortified Muscadel.

Robertson Small demarcated district e. of the Cape and inland. Mainly dessert wines (notably Muscat), but red and white table wines are on the increase. Includes Bonnievale. Irrigated vineyards.

Roodeberg ★★
    Good-value brand of blended red from the K.W.V.

Rustenberg ★★★
    Effectively, if not officially, an estate red wine from just n.e. of STELLENBOSCH. Rustenberg Dry Red is a good CAB/CINSAUT blend. The straight CAB is outstanding. P NOIR is good.

Sauvignon Blanc Adapting well to warm conditions. Widely grown and marketed in both "wooded" and "unwooded" styles.

Schoongezicht ★★★
    Partner of RUSTENBERG, one of S. Africa's most beautiful old farms and producer of agreeable white wine from STEEN, RIESLING and Clairette Blanche. CHARD and RHINE RIES are good.

Shiraz Provides the base in many top red blends. Rich deep-coloured wine.

Simonsig ★★★
    Estate owned by F.J. Malan, pioneering estate producer. Produces a wide range, incl. GEWÜRZ, Vin Fumé (wood-matured dry white) and a méthode champenoise. Quality improving.

Simonsvlei One of S. Africa's best-known cooperative cellars, just outside PAARL. A prize-winner with PINOTAGE.

Spier ★★
    Estate of five farms w. of STELLENBOSCH producing reds and whites. COLOMBARD and PINOTAGE are best.

Steen South Africa's commonest white grape, said to be a clone of the CHENIN BLANC. It gives strong, tasty and lively wine, sweet or dry, normally better than S. African RIESLING.

Stein Name often used for commercial blends of semi-sweet white wine. Not necessarily to be despised.

Stellenbosch Town and demarcated district 30 miles e. of Cape Town, extending to the ocean at False Bay. The heart of the wine industry, with all three of the largest companies. Most of the best estates, esp. for red wine, are in the mountain foothills of the region.

Stellenbosch Farmers' Winery (S.F.W.) South Africa's biggest winery (after the K.W.V.) with several ranges of wines, incl. NEDERBURG and ZONNEBLOEM. Wide range of mid-and low-priced wines.

Stellenryck
    Top-quality BERGKELDER range, RHINE RIESLING, Fumé Blanc, CABERNET and GEWÜRZ.

Superior An official designation of quality for WINES OF ORIGIN. The wine must meet standards set by the Wine & Spirit Board.

SA

Swartland Demarcated district around MALMESBURY. ALLESVERLOREN is the best estate.

Tassenberg ★
Popular and good-value red known to thousands as Tassie.

Theuniskraal ★★
Well-known TULBAGH estate specializing in white wines, esp. RIESLING, GEWÜRZTRAMINER and Sémillon. No longer a leader.

Tulbagh Demarcated district n. of PAARL best known for the white wines of THEUNISKRAAL and TWEE JONGEGEZELLEN, and the dessert wines from Drostdy. See also Boberg.

Twee Jongegezellen ★★
Estate at TULBAGH. One of the great pioneers which revolutionized S. African wine in the 1950s, still in the family of its 18th-century founder. Mainly white wines, incl. "Schanderl" and "T.J. 39". New sparkling wine may herald revival.

Uiterwyk ★★
Old estate w. of STELLENBOSCH. Good CAB SAUV and pleasant whites.

Uitkyk (★★★)
Old estate (400 acres) at STELLENBOSCH famous for Carlonet (big gutsy CAB) and Carlsheim (chiefly SAUV BLANC) white.

Vergenoegd (★★★)
Old family estate in S. STELLENBOSCH supplying high-quality sherry to the K.W.V. and offering deeply flavoured CABERNET and excellent SHIRAZ under the estate label. Not as good as before.

Villiera (★★★)
Paarl estate with Tradition top class méthode champenoise. Winner of 1988 Gault et Millau Paris Olympiad with RHINE RIESLING. Fine CAB and CAB/MERLOT blend.

Vriesenhof ★★★
Small-scale winery with vines high on Stellenbosch mountain slope. Highly rated CAB and CHARD and CAB/MERLOT blend.

Weisser Riesling Alias Rhine Riesling. Producing good wines in S. Africa. They need time to mature and are not really appreciated.

Welgemeend ★★★
Boutique PAARL estate producing Médoc-style blends, delicate CABERNET and Amadé, a Grenache, SHIRAZ and PINOTAGE blend.

Weltevrede ★→★★
Progressive ROBERTSON estate. Blended white and fortified wines.

De Wetshof ★★★
Pioneering estate in ROBERTSON district. CHARDONNAY, SAUVIGNON BLANC, RHINE RIESLING and a sweet noble-rot white, Edeloes. Won best wine of show trophy at '87 Bordeaux Vinexpo with CHARD.

Wine of Origin The S. African equivalent of appellation contrôlée. Demarcated regions are described on these pages.

Worcester Demarcated wine district round the Breede and Hex river valleys, e. of PAARL. Many cooperative cellars make mainly dessert wines, brandy and dry whites.

Zandvliet ★★
Estate in the ROBERTSON area making a fine light SHIRAZ.

Zevenwacht ★★★
Large Stellenbosch Estate with wines only available through shareholders and restaurants. CAB SAUV is impressive.

Zonnebloem ★★
Good-quality brand of CABERNET, RIESLING, PINOTAGE, SAUV BLANC and SHIRAZ from the STELLENBOSCH FARMERS' WINERY. Much improved quality recently.

A few words about words

In the shorthand essential for this little book (and sometimes in bigger books as well) wines are often described by adjectives that can seem irrelevant, inane — or just silly. What do "fat", "round", "full", "lean" and so on mean, when used about wine? Some of the more irritatingly vague are expanded in this list:

Attack	The first impression of the wine in your mouth. It should "strike" positively, if not necessarily with force. Without attack it is feeble or too bland.
Attractive	Means "I like it, anyway". A slight put-down for expensive wines; encouragement for juniors. At least refreshing.
Big	Concerns the whole flavour, including the alcohol content. Sometimes implies clumsiness, the opposite of elegance. Generally positive, but big is easy in California and less usual in, say, Bordeaux. So the context matters.
Charming	Rather patronizing when said of wines that should have more impressive qualities. Implies lightness, possibly slight sweetness. A standard comment on Loire wines.
Crisp	With pronounced but pleasing acidity; fresh and eager.
Deep/depth	This wine is worth tasting with attention. There is more to it than the first impression; it fills your mouth with developing flavours as though it had an extra dimension. (Deep colour simply means hard to see through.) All really fine wines have depth.
Easy	Used in the sense of "easy come, easy go". An easy wine makes no demand on your palate (or intellect). The implication is that it drinks smoothly, doesn't need maturing, and all you remember is a pleasant drink.
Elegant	A professional taster's favourite term when he is stuck to describe a wine whose proportions (of strength, flavour, aroma), whose attack, middle and finish, whose texture and all its qualities call for comparison with other forms of natural beauty, as in the movement of horses, the forms and attitudes of women . . . .
Fat	With flavour and texture that fills your mouth, but without aggression. Obviously inappropriate in e.g. a light Moselle, but what you pay your money for in Sauternes.
Finish	See Length.
Firm	Flavour that strikes the palate fairly hard, with fairly high acidity or tannic astringency giving the impression that the wine is in youthful vigour and will age to gentler things. An excellent quality with high-flavoured foods, and almost always positive.
Flesh	Refers to both substance and texture. A fleshy wine is fatter than a "meaty" wine, more unctuous if less vigorous. The term is often used of good Pomerols, whose texture is notably smooth.
Flowery	Often used as though synonymous with fruity, but really means floral, like the fragrance of flowers. Roses, violets, etc., are sometimes specified.
Fresh	Implies a good degree of fruity acidity, even a little nip of sharpness, as well as the zip and joy of youth. All young whites should be fresh: the alternative is flatness, staleness . . . ugh.
Fruity	Used for almost any quality, but really refers to the body and richness of wine made from good ripe grapes. A fruity aroma is not the same as a flavoury one. Fruitiness usually implies at least a slight degree of sweetness. Attempts at specifying *which* fruit the wine resembles can be helpful. E.g. grapefruit, lemon, plum, lychee.

198

Full	Interchangeable with full-bodied. Lots of "vinosity" or wineyness: the mouth-filling flavours of alcohol and "extract" (all the flavouring components) combined.
Hollow	Lacking a satisfying middle flavour. Something seems to be missing between first flavour and last. A characteristic of wines from greedy proprietors who let their vines produce too many grapes. A v. hollow wine is "empty".
Lean	A bit more flesh would be an improvement. Lack of mouth-filling flavours: often astringent as well. But occasionally a term of appreciation of a distinct and enjoyable style.
Length	The flavours and aromas that linger after swallowing. In principle the greater the length the better the wine. One second of flavour after swallowing = one "caudalie". Ten caudalies is good; 20 terrific.
Light	With relatively little alcohol and body, as in most German wines. A very desirable quality in the right wines.
Meaty	Savoury in effect with enough substance to chew. The inference is lean meat; leaner than in "fleshy".
Oaky	Smelling or tasting of fresh-sawn oak; e.g. a new barrel.
Plump	The diminutive of fat, implying a degree of charm as well.
Rich	Not necessarily sweet, but giving an opulent impression.
Robust	In good heart, vigorous, and on a fairly big scale.
Rough	Flavour and texture give no pleasure. Acidity and/or tannin are dominant and coarse.
Round	Almost the same as fat, but with more approval.
Structure	The "plan" of the flavour, as it were. The French word "carpentry" relates it to the architecture of a roof, where the forces at work are expressed in beams. By analogy a wine needs a beam for breadth, another for length, a firm "backbone" or king-post, etc. Without structure wine is bland, dull, and won't last.
Stylish	Style is bold and definite; wears its cap on its ear.
Supple	Often used of young red wines which might be expected to be more aggressive. More lively than an "easy" wine, with implications of good quality.
Well-balanced	Contains all the desirable elements (acid, alcohol, flavours, etc) in appropriate and pleasing proportions.

A few words about health

"Contains sulfites". This message, meaningless to most people but carrying a vague air of menace, was the first in a series of "health warnings" now required by American law to be put on wine-labels.

The true warning it carries is that lobbyists have seized extraordinary power in America, enabling them to use scare-tactics to deter citizens from freedom of choice about wine. Every normal healthy wine-drinker takes into account the effects of imbibing alcohol and avoids excess. He or she knows perfectly well that under certain circumstances it is prudent not to drink alcohol at all. To present wines as a "health hazard" is a gross distortion of the truth and threatens to become a violation of individual rights. It denies the concept of individual responsibility. There is pressure on the US government to return to the era of Prohibition. All wine-lovers believe in moderation as a way of life and expect it from their governments.

What to drink in an ideal world

Wines at their peak in 1990

Red Bordeaux:
Top growths of 1981, 1980, 1979, 1976, 1975, 1970, 1966, 1962, 1961
Other Crus Classés of 1984, 1981, 1980, 1979, 1978, 1976, 1975, 1970, 1966, 1961
Petits châteaux of 1986, 1985, 1983, 1982, 1981, 1979, 1978

Red Burgundy
Top growths of 1984, 1982, 1980, 1979, 1978, 1976, 1973, 1971, 1969, 1966, 1964
Premiers Crus of 1984, 1983, 1982, 1980, 1979, 1978, 1976, 1971 . . .
Village wines of 1986, 1985, 1983

White Burgundy
Top growths of 1984, 1983, 1982, 1981, 1979, 1978 . . .
Premiers Crus of 1986, 1985, 1984, 1983, 1982, 1981, 1978 . . .
Village wines of 1988, 1987, 1986, 1985

Sauternes
Top growths of 1982, 1981, 1980, 1979, 1978, 1976, 1975, 1971, 1970, 1967 . . .
Other wines of 1985, 1983, 1982, 1981, 1980, 1979, 1978, 1976, 1975 . . .

Sweet Loire wines
Top growths of (Anjou/Vouvray) 1985, 1983, 1982, 1981, 1980, 1979, 1978, 1976, 1975, 1973, 1971, 1969, 1964 . . .

Alsace
Grands Crus and late-harvest wines of 1986, 1985, 1984, 1983, 1981, 1979, 1978, 1976 . . .
Standard wines of 1988, 1987, 1986, 1985, 1983 . . .

Rhône
Hermitage/top Northern Rhône reds of 1982, 1980, 1979, 1978, 1973, 1971, 1969
Châteauneuf-du-Pape of 1984, 1983, 1982, 1981, 1980, 1979, 1978 . . .

German wines
Great sweet wines of 1983, 1976, 1975, 1971 . . .
Ausleses of 1985, 1983, 1981, 1979, 1976 . . .
Spätleses of 1986, 1985, 1983, 1979, 1976 . . .
Kabinett and QbA wines of 1986, 1985, 1984, 1983 . . .

Californian
Top Cabernets, Pinot Noirs, Zinfandels of 1984, 1983, 1981, 1980, 1979, 1978, 1976, 1974
Most Cabernets etc. of 1985, 1984, 1983, 1982, 1981, 1980 . . .
Top Chardonnays of 1986, 1985, 1984, 1983 . . .
Most Chardonnays of 1987, 1986, 1985, 1984 . . .

Vintage Port
. . . , 1970, 1967, 1966, 1963, 1960 . . .

Quick reference vintage charts for France and Germany

These charts give a picture of the range of qualities made in the principal areas (every year has its relative successes and failures) and a guide to whether the wine is ready to drink or should be kept.

| drink now	**—** needs keeping	**✓** can be drunk with pleasure now, but the better wines will continue to improve
0 no good	**10** the best	

Combinations of symbols mean that there are wines in more than one category.

FRANCE	RED BORDEAUX		WHITE BORDEAUX	
	MÉDOC/GRAVES	POM ST-EM	SAUTERNES & SW.	GRAVES & DRY
88	6-9 —	6-9 —	6-10 —	7-9 ✓
87	3-6 ✓	3-6 ✓	2-5 —	7-10 ✓
86	6-9 —	6-8 —	7-10 —	7-9 ✓
85	6-8 ✓	7-9 ✓	6-8 ✓	5-8 ✓
84	4-7 ✓	2-5 ✓	4-7 ✓	5-7 ✓
83	6-9 ✓	6-9 ✓	6-10 ✓	7-9 ✓
82	8-10 ✓	7-9 ✓	3-7 ✓	7-8	
81	5-8 ✓	6-9 ✓	5-8 ✓	7-8 ✓
80	4-7		3-5		5-9 ✓	5-7	
79	5-8 ✓	5-7 ✓	6-8 ✓	4-6	
78	6-9 ✓	6-8 ✓	4-6		7-9	
77	3-5		2-5		2-4		6-7	
76	6-8		7-8 ✓	7-9 ✓	4-8	
75	7-9 ✓	8-9 ✓	8-10 ✓	8-10	
74	4-6		3-5		0	4-6	
73	5-7		5-7		0-4		7-8	
72	2-5		2-4		2-4		4-5	
71	5-8		6-8		8-9		8-9	
70	9-10 ✓	9-10 ✓	9-10		9-10	

FRANCE	RED BURGUNDY		WHITE BURGUNDY	
	CÔTE D'OR	CÔTE D'OR	CHABLIS	ALSACE
88	7-10 —	7-9 —	7-9 ✓	6-9 ✓
87	6-8 —	4-7 ✓	5-7 ✓	7-8 ✓
86	5-8 ✓	7-10 ✓	7-9 ✓	7-8 ✓
85	7-10 ✓	5-8 ✓	6-9 ✓	7-10 ✓
84	3-6		4-7		4-7		4-6	
83	5-9 ✓	6-9 ✓	7-9 ✓	8-10 ✓
82	4-7		6-8		6-7		6-8	
81	3-6		4-8		6-9 ✓	7-8	
80	4-7		4-6		5-7		3-5	
79	5-6		6-8		6-8		7-8	
78	8-10 ✓	7-9		7-10		6-8	
77	2-4		4-6		5		3-5	
76	7-10 ✓	7-8		8		10	

Beaujolais: 88 was good, 87 rather better, 85 v.g. Mâcon-Villages (white) 87, 86, 85, are good now. **Loire:** Sweet Anjou and Touraine. Best recent vintages: 88, 85, 84, 83, 82, 79, 78, 76. **Upper Loire:** Sancerre and Pouilly-Fumé 88, 86 are good now. **Muscadet:** D.Y.A.

FRANCE	RHÔNE	GERMANY	RHINE	MOSELLE
88	7-9 ✓	88	6-8 —	7-9 —
87	3-6 ✓	87	4-7 ✓	5-7 ✓
86	5-8 ✓	86	4-8 ✓	5-8 ✓
85	6-8 ✓	85	6-8 ✓	6-9 ✓
84	5-7 ✓	84	4-6 ✓	4-6 ✓
83	6-9 ✓	83	6-9 ✓	7-10 ✓
82	5-8 ✓	82	4-6		4-7	
81	5-7 ✓	81	5-8 ✓	4-8 ✓
80	6-8 ✓	80	4-7		3-7	
79	6-7 ✓	79	6-8		6-8	
78	8-10 ✓	78	5-7		4-7	
77	4-6		77	5-7		4-6	
76	6-9		76	9-10 ✓	9-10 ✓
75	0-5		75	7-9		8-10	